CUNARD

Library

Out of respect for your fellow guests, please return all books as soon as possible. We would also request that books are not taken off the ship as they can easily be damaged by the sun, sea and sand.

Please ensure that books are returned the day before you disembark, failure to do so will incur a charge to your on board account, the same will happen to any damaged books.

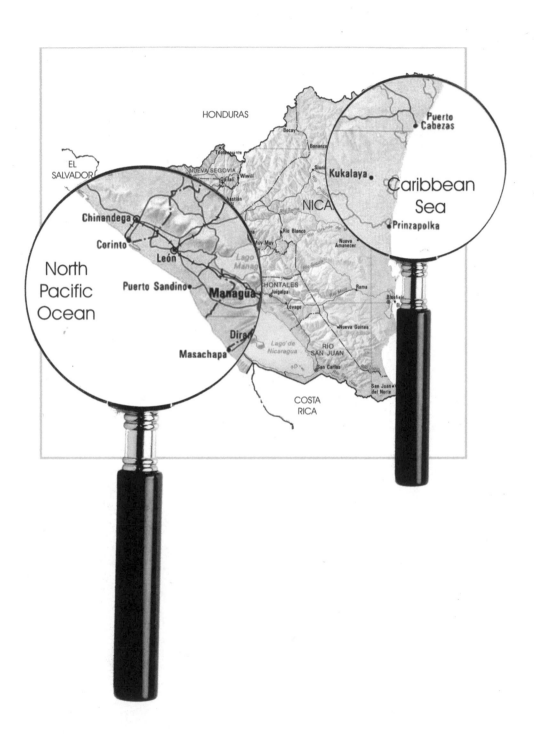

ALSO BY JOSEPH AGRIS, M.D.

Tears On The Sand: Horror, Hope & Healing in Pakistan & Afghanistan
White Knight in Blue Shades: The Authorized Biography of Marvin Zindler

MIRACLES IN
BEDLAM

A Doctor's Adventures
In A War Zone

Joseph Agris, M.D.

A-TO-Z PUBLISHING • HOUSTON, TEXAS

Miracles in Bedlam
A Doctor's Adventures In A War Zone

First Edition
ISBN: 978-0-9712348-2-6 (paper)
ISBN: 978-0-9712348-3-3 (cloth)
ISBN: 978-0-9712348-6-4 (e-book)

Literary collaboration and book & cover design provided by
Schmidt Kaye & Company Professional Literary Services
Ron Kaye & Connie L. Schmidt
schmidtkaye.com

Dedication

To my loving wife Terry
For all relationships, it's actually the shared journey that brings out the potential of both
parties, plus a lifetime of commitment so essential to developing that potential together.
Always together with hearts hungry for each other.
Every moment brings new things along this shared journey that we call Life.
I am so lucky to spend it with you as our future continues to unfold.

To Robert Jacob Agris
A very loving and gentle man

To Evelyn Pearson Agris Rokaw
You did a great job with your "Three Musketeers," Joseph, Robert, and Paul

I love you all. You are an important part of my life.

And…
To Maggie, Trucker, Hero, The Black Panther
Dolly, Romeo, Juliet, and P.T. Cruiser…
And all creatures large and small

Acknowledgments

I owe a debt of gratitude to…

The people of Nicaragua – not just my patients and former patients, but everyone I've met and befriended there as well – for continually inspiring me with their remarkable power to rise above adversity. Through wars, insurgencies, political upheaval, interference by foreign governments, exploitation, and devastating natural disasters, their spirit always manages to shine through.

The Children's Foundation, for being the reason this "crazy Texan" keeps on doing what he's doing, long past the age when a sane Texan might think of hanging up his hat for good.

My intrepid team members, who have tirelessly assisted me for many years both at home and abroad, including but not limited to JoAnne, Elia, Kimberly, Carolyn, Jeannie, and of course Barrett and Jose.

The medical community in Houston, especially The Texas Medical Center; The Houston Methodist Hospital and its wonderful staff; Texas Children's Hospital; Memorial Hermann Hospital; and last but not least Medical Bridges, whose mission is "Bridging the healthcare gap worldwide."

Journalists such as Lori Reingold, the late Bob Dows, and the late Marvin Zindler, for their integrity, sense of adventure, and fearless determination to tell stories that needed telling.

My patient and capable assistant and transcriptionist, Bev Winter, for transcribing hundreds of hours of tapes and acting as liaison with my literary collaborators; for keeping my publishing and promotional efforts on track; and for providing invaluable support on recent missions to Nicaragua.

My long-time literary collaborators Ron Kaye and Connie Schmidt of Schmidt Kaye & Company, who have repeatedly gone above and beyond to help bring my books to life.

Contents

Introduction

This book is the view of one doctor who has worked throughout Nicaragua – not only at the end of the Contra-Sandinista conflict but up through the present day as well. As a doctor, I had the dual advantage of working closely with the civilians and observing the conflict at its end and throughout its aftermath.

In an era when hybrids have come into their own, with everything from automobiles to music to food being marketed as "hybrid" or "fusion," this book is somewhat of a hybrid as well. It is part memoir and part novelized compilation of some of the many diaries I kept, and random notes that I made, during my annual visits to Nicaragua over the course of the past several decades. Though I have taken minor literary license – some details have been modified and some timelines slightly altered for the sake of narrative flow, as well as a couple of names changed to protect individuals' privacy – I am satisfied with the basic integrity of the narrative. I feel that I have presented an accurate portrayal of what it was like to be in the middle of the action, during crucial times in the history of a Central American country with which too few U.S. residents are familiar. And, of course, the accounts of the patients and the surgical procedures are as real as it gets, and I've included some photos to provide a better idea of some of the cases we've handled.

Although this narrative focuses on our medical missions, it also touches upon the social, cultural, and, yes, political issues that my teams and I encountered. One task I hoped to accomplish by writing this book was to clearly share the feelings of the Nicaraguan public, as well as those of the fighters in the Contra-Sandinista conflict. If you thought this was ancient history and no longer relevant, I'm here to tell you that that's not the case at all. The issues around the conflict linger even today, and there are many misconceptions about what the United States did and did not do in the region, and about the promises that America did not fulfill. That's why I felt it important to weave some of these issues into my story.

As my medical team and I traveled from north to south and east to west in Nicaragua at that time, we had a chance to see many things, but we don't pretend to have seen it all. Our first visits took place towards the end of the Nicaraguan Contra-Sandinista insurgency. But we were able to acquire a basic understanding of the effects and after-effects of that war, and we've gained a deeper understanding of the long-term effects through our yearly trips to Nicaragua, which, as noted above, have continued through the present day.

My team and I had the opportunity to meet with four different Nicaraguan presidents over the course of several decades, so we were able to observe (and even, to a small degree, to influence) some of the decisions made in the seats of power. At the same time, we also got an intimate look at the lives of the people for whom power was beyond their imaginings, much less their grasp. I quickly learned that the Nicaraguan people experience a very different culture and a very different world from the relatively privileged existence enjoyed by most people in the U.S. The medical team had to come to terms with this social and economic disparity, while at the same time acknowledging that there was little we could do to change it. With that said, we were conscious of the need to view ourselves through the eyes of our patients, and to model our behavior in such a way as to better gain their trust. In addition to bringing much-needed medical care to the region, we also strove to act as peace envoys, doing our small part to help finally bring Nicaragua's decade-old civil war to an end.

Nicaragua is bisected east from west by a nearly impenetrable mountain range. The Spanish, Catholic community that controls the country occupies the Pacific side, including some of the oldest cities in Central America, such as Granada, León, Chinandega, Corinto, and Managua. The other half of the country on the Atlantic or Caribbean side was settled by the English, and is occupied by the Miskito Indians. Their lives are simple, most being fishermen or small farmers. They have their own language and religion, but over the course of the centuries since the English landed on this coast, they have been indoctrinated in the English language and the Moravian Church. Understanding these cultural differences became the key feature in working with both groups as a physician as well as a peace envoy. The differences are as great as the volcanic mountain range that divides the country, and they cannot be overlooked. The understanding of these cultural differences was essential not only to our personal safety, but also to the success of our medical and surgical activities in each area.

For too many people in too many parts of the world, the "ugly American" stereotype still prevails, largely because so many Americans have difficulty comprehending, much less accepting, that other people don't think like we do. Our worldview is all most of us in the U.S. know, and we tend to mistakenly assume that everyone else shares that worldview. I was determined that my medical team and I were not going to make that mistake in Nicaragua.

In order to deal effectively with the medical problems as well as the ongoing insurgencies, I thought language skills were absolutely essential. Most of the members of our medical team spoke Spanish, which allowed us to develop a deeper cultural interaction with our patients and many other people in Nicaragua, including the Contras. While my own Spanish leaves something to be desired, as I'll be the first to admit, my team possessed a level of overall fluency that allowed us to sit by a campfire eating tamales, rice, and beans, joining in with the locals as they told jokes, and participating in sing-a-longs. It was this type of interaction that fostered trust, not only with the locals, but also with the guerilla fighters we encountered.

We lived and ate with the locals and experienced their lives close-up. And we learned so much. For example, once we were directly involved with them, we were all struck by the nature of communism under the Sandinistas. It was not just some vague or abstract philosophy; it was truly a way of life. And before I go any further I want to acknowledge that the saga of the Contras and Sandinistas is not a simple, black-and-white tale of good versus evil, with the Sandinistas as the bad guys and the Contras as the good guys. The history of their struggle is long and complex, and violence and atrocities were committed on both sides. But my team and I were dealing with people who, for many good reasons, did view the Sandinistas as the enemy, and I have no doubt that the Sandinistas viewed us Americans as adversaries, even threats.

Indeed, the appearance of the American medical team with the ABC-TV camera crew was unexpected, and surprised all those whom we encountered. Although not everyone was pleased about our presence, our linguistic skills quickly won the trust and support of the locals wherever we traveled. Honesty was paramount, and we had no hesitation in discussing America's deficiencies, as well as the issues that the Nicaraguans' own government needed to resolve.

* * * * *

In addition to chronicling social and political issues and recounting our various adventures – some of which were pretty harrowing – I have attempted in this book to paint as nuanced and revealing a picture as possible of my experience as part of the medical team working in a difficult place during difficult times. It was Bedlam on many levels, and we were able to accomplish some amazing things – some might say miraculous things – against formidable odds.

My team and I worked closely with the local doctors and nurses. In the university city of León, we incorporated the residents and students into our teaching program. They trusted me, and they trusted the members of my team, and regardless of what happened I have always been committed to never violating that trust. During those early visits, as I've mentioned, the war was not yet completely over, and I naturally didn't want to put any of my team members in danger. We were all aware that the support of the locals was important to the safety of all of us.

Most of the towns and villages we visited had not seen a physician for a decade. We typically worked fourteen- to sixteen-hour days and cared for hundreds of children and some adults as well. In a few days we had filled every bed in the hospital and we had others sleeping on the floor. Infants and young children were placed into locally made hammocks that dangled above the beds.

We treated children and adults with cleft lip, cleft palate, burns and burn contractures, tumors, farm injuries, and war-related wounds, and we also encountered some victims of human rights abuses. We got a first-hand look at the frequently devastating results of the Iran-Contra debacle. We were able to see and understand the locals' animosity when the United States wanted to call an end to their support while the Contras, whom many considered to be our Nicaraguan partners, wanted to fight on.

Joseph Agris, M.D.

How should our personal national values affect our medical team's interaction with our guerilla allies? That was a very serious topic for my team members and me. I had some concerns before embarking on these earlier trips, because for many in my medical-surgical team of nearly two dozen persons, this would be their first trip outside the United States. In those early days, the team members had only a vague notion of where they were going and what they would be doing, and most had no idea as to the conditions under which they would be working. All were volunteers, and I doubted that they fully understood that we were going to be in a war zone. There would be no pay, and while the Nicaraguans had guaranteed us food and lodging, they had made no other commitments to us.

But my team members were troopers, and professional to a fault, as they have been on all subsequent trips, with only a few notable missteps. On one trip, a passionate love affair threatened to destabilize the team. One element that I have always felt to be essential to the effectiveness of a medical mission team is professionalism in personal conduct as well as in execution of duties. Accordingly I have always imposed strict guidelines forbidding dating or romantic involvement, not only among my team members but also between those members and the locals. Socializing is fine and in fact is strongly encouraged, but I have to draw the line at dating. My own team has referred to these guidelines as "the rules" – sometimes uttered in a mock-stern voice when spoken. Teams are briefed on these rules ahead of every mission.

There's a sound reason for the guidelines, of course, and despite occasional protests from a team member, they all understand that romantic involvement on the job makes it all too easy for personal feelings to get in the way of work. Emotional entanglement doesn't affect only the lovers; it can also compromise our patients, our medical team, the local medical team, and the mission as a whole. Our level of professionalism determines whether or not we'll be invited back to a country. It can also influence the country's opinion of America and Americans. Like it or not, all of the team members are ambassadors in addition to their normal duties; it's just part of the job. So I've always been pretty strict about "the rules." When one of my male nurses and a local nurse who was working with our team violated those rules, I reacted as you might expect, and it created quite a stir throughout the entire team. But we'll get to that in a little while.

* * * * *

I arrived in Managua the first time wearing my standard attire: Texas boots, a white Stetson hat, a white shirt, and jeans. Doubts about the entire endeavor intensified as the plane landed and I departed for a building that was purported to be the terminal. At the time, I did not know that this trip would be the start of more than three decades of almost continuous involvement in Nicaragua and the adjacent countries. I was befriended by a charming group of high-spirited nuns and a priest named Father Marcus, who deserve tremendous credit for making the impossible possible.

Although the world has changed quite a bit since my early trips to Nicaragua with the medical team, some things have not changed. For one thing, outside of the operating theater I have for the most part stuck to my standard cowboy attire, which explains the "Texan" part of my nickname "The Crazy Texan." I'll leave it to you to figure out the "Crazy" part. On a more serious note, many of the problems we encountered on those early missions to Nicaragua linger on very tenaciously, and some have actually intensified. As tensions and issues around immigration mount, so too do environmental issues that have affected Nicaragua and other parts of Central America and, ultimately, all of the Americas and the entire planet. I hope that reading this book will make more people care about these issues and about the need to address them in humane and sensible ways.

I also hope that as you read this book, you can get some idea of the trials, tribulations and extraordinary adventures my medical teams have faced. One of the noteworthy adventures was our visit to the Atlantic and Caribbean coast of Nicaragua in the early 1990s. At the time, Cubans and their Russian masters had occupied the Atlantic coast for several years, supporting the Sandinistas. We had been warned about the risks involved in visiting this region, but were not entirely prepared for what happened. Among the hazards we encountered were groups of rowdy locals who were theoretically on our side, but we had no way of knowing whether some of them might suddenly turn on us with little or no warning. And even though we had heard that most of the Cubans and Russians had left Puerto Cabezas when they got wind of an American medical team and TV crew coming, it was still rumored that some of the Cubans remained behind, in hiding.

We simply had no way of knowing. The stakes seemed to grow higher as these locals marched down the main street in Puerto Cabezas, shouting, "Americans stay, Cubans go home!" Their behavior was that of vigilantes, their courage heightened by alcohol consumption. The ensuing unrest exploded across the city of Puerto Cabezas, and my medical team and I found ourselves caught in the middle of it.

But I suppose I'm getting ahead of myself. Let's begin at the beginning.

Principals

(This is only a partial list, and in no particular order of significance or appearance in this book)

Dr. Joe Agris, aka "Dr. Angel" and "The Crazy Texan" – Team leader

Elia – Dr. Agris' personal nurse

Kimberly – Dr. Agris' secretary, record keeper, and nursing assistant

JoAnne – Circulating nurse

Mr. Barrett Phillips – scrub nurse (and bodyguard when necessary)

Jose Dixon – Operating room nurse and interpreter

Mr. Marvin Zindler – ABC-TV reporter, consumer advocate, altruist, and voice for the voiceless all over the world

Lori Reingold – ABC-TV director and writer, who worked closely with Marvin Zindler

Bob Dows – ABC-TV cameraman, who worked closely with Marvin Zindler

Michael – Nurse on Doc Agris' team (not his real name)

Marta – Local nurse in Chinandega (not her real name)

Dr. Baladares – Local surgeon

Dr. Canteras – Local surgeon

The Callejas Family – Chinandega hosts on all of our medical missions, and the closest of family friends

Violeta Chamorro – President of Nicaragua (April 1990-January 1997)

Maria Torres – Niece of Violeta Chamorro

Arnoldo Alemán – President of Nicaragua (January 1997-January 2002)

Enrique Bolaños – President of Nicaragua (January 2002-January 2007)

Daniel Ortega – Sandinista leader (July 1979-January 1985); and President of Nicaragua (January 1985-April 1990; January 2007-Present)

PROLOGUE
Roads Less Traveled

Getting off the plane in Managua, Nicaragua, it becomes immediately obvious to a first-time visitor from an affluent country that one is in another world altogether. While the phrase "Third World" rolls as easily off the tongue as does "culture shock" in casual conversation, the profound impact of the experience loses more than is imaginable in the telling. Those were my thoughts on my first trip to Nicaragua back in the 1980s, and even though I have been back numerous times since then, I never fail to be struck by the many differences between this beautiful but troubled country and the world I inhabit every day. It is never difficult for me to view Nicaragua through the eyes of someone visiting for the first time. And yet every time I return, it also feels, in an oddly comforting way, as if I am coming home.

* * * * *

Nicaragua is bordered on the south by Costa Rica and on the north by Honduras. On its eastern side is the Atlantic coast, and on the west is the Pacific Ocean. Both boast some of the most beautiful beaches in the world. The country is literally bisected by a chain of volcanic mountains with poor gravel roads, rendering the days-long journey to cross Nicaragua quite hazardous. The journey was made even less pleasant on some of our trips in the 1980s and early 1990s by the constant fear of being attacked by Sandinista military units (FSLN) or the many bandits that roamed free throughout the countryside.

The Spanish originally landed on the Pacific coast, and as a result the population in that area is predominantly Spanish-speaking and Catholic. The British had landed on the country's east coast – often referred to as the Caribbean side – where they encountered the Miskito tribes, who lived the simple lives of fishermen and farmers. The British indoctrinated the Miskito in the English language, and the Moravian Church became the predominant religion in the area, which is known as La Región Autónoma de la sur, or Region of Guaranteed Autonomy. There was little if any communication or social or political interaction between the Spanish controlled west and its capital – originally named Leal Villa de Santiago de Managua, but eventually shortened to Managua – and the autonomous Miskito region on the Atlantic side. Because of this the country suffered through repeated theological, economic, and political conflicts, many of which continue to this day. As a result, this small, very poor country is still struggling to become a modern democracy.

Beginning about 1980 and continuing into the early 1990s there was a Russian and Cuban presence in the major Caribbean Coast city of Puerto Cabezas. Russians had established medical clinics and other facilities, using the Cubans as a front, and the Cubans, with Russian support, worked closely with the Sandinistas against the U.S.-supported Contra forces. This matter never received much coverage in the U.S. press, and many people remained unaware of the extent of the problem. But my team and I got to experience some of the disturbing results of the Cuban and Russian presence first-hand.

Despite the fact that the United States has involved itself in the politics of Nicaragua (as well as other Central American countries), Nicaragua remains a little known and widely misunderstood nation. Certainly very few people in the U.S. knew or cared about the country prior to public revelations regarding the so-called Reagan Doctrine, under which the administration's CIA involved itself in the Contra-Sandinista war during President Reagan's second term in the mid-1980s. At that time, Marine Colonel Oliver North, Assistant Secretary of State for Human Rights and Humanitarian Affairs Elliot Abrams, and National Security Adviser Admiral John Poindexter secretly formed an operation they called "The Enterprise." This was actually a secret arm of the United States government, with its own funding source that was covertly providing weapons and assistance to the Contra rebels in violation of the Boland Amendment.

The sole purpose of The Enterprise was for this group of men to have their own secret military personnel, to be administered by Admiral Poindexter and Colonel North, and accountable to no one. The Enterprise was funded by the United States CIA through the illegal, clandestine sale of weapons to Iran, which was under an arms embargo, in what came to be known as the Iran-Contra Agreements. The operation was intended to be hidden from both the American Congress and the public, but of course it did not remain hidden long, and the Iran-Contra Agreements soon became the Iran-Contra scandal.

It was into this conflict that our Houston, Texas medical team ventured more than once on several mission trips throughout the mid-1980s to early 1990s. With our military armed guards, we traveled along dangerous, dusty roads through small country towns and villages, to provide needed medical and surgical care to the poorest of the poor children – and adults – who had been neglected for more than a decade because of the war.

At the time of our earlier visits to Nicaragua, medical care in the country had been virtually unavailable for many years due to the civil war and ever-present sporadic fighting. Although the Somoza regime was overthrown in 1978-1979, ending a bloody dynasty that had been in power almost nonstop since 1936, and democratic elections were planned, elements of the Contra-Sandinista forces still remained active over a decade later.

When the Agris-Zindler Children's Foundation received its first request from the president of Nicaragua for medical equipment, medications, medical supplies, and of course, doctors, I couldn't say no. In response, I organized a volunteer medical team from the Texas Medical Center in Houston.

In preparation for that first trip, the doctors, nurses, and ancillary medical personnel spent almost three months gathering the needed medical supplies and equipment and making other arrangements for this dangerous upcoming trip. We have taken the same level of care when preparing for all of our medical missions; I've learned that it's almost impossible to over-prepare.

The early teams operated under the flag of the Agris-Zindler Children's Foundation and, in more recent years, they were also sponsored by an organization called People Helping People, in conjunction with a team from Smiles Gone Wild. Smiles Gone Wild specializes in the treatment of children born with congenital defects such as cleft lip and palate. Before our first trip to Nicaragua, we had been told that thousands of children suffering with these defects had gone untreated for the past decade due to the civil war. And sadly, we found that to be the case.

* * * * *

Every trip to Nicaragua is extraordinary for me, but some of my most memorable ones took place in the early 1990s. The country was still reeling from the civil war, and while things were marginally less unsettled than they had been in the 1980s, Nicaragua was far from a peaceful haven.

On one particularly memorable trip the bulk of our mission took place at hospitals in Chinandega and León. We were told that the hospital in Chinandega lacked everything, but fortunately we were well prepared. Prior to leaving the U.S., the team members collected the necessary instruments and supplies and packed them for shipment at the Houston Methodist Hospital at the Texas Medical Center. In addition, I donated a portion of my own personal library and obtained duplicate copies of medical books from other physicians at the Texas Medical Center and from the Medical Center's library, some 600 volumes in all. These medical texts were for the university library in León, which had been destroyed during the war.

In preparation for the trip, I contacted the Continental Airlines home office in Houston, and spoke with Mr. Gordon Bethune, who was the CEO at the time. (Continental merged with United Airlines in 2010.) Mr. Bethune was gracious enough to say that Continental Airlines would participate in this humanitarian effort and ship the medical supplies, equipment, and books on behalf of the Agris-Zindler Children's Foundation, free of charge.

Nurse Jose Dixon and I rented a truck to transport all the medical equipment and books to the airport, and we were granted security clearance to allow the truck to drive directly onto the tarmac and up to the under-belly of the aircraft for easy loading.

When we arrived with the truck of supplies, I had noticed that there were only two Continental employees there to load the material. It would take hours to move the roughly 460 boxes from the truck into the aircraft. Knowing that this wasn't going to work, I had six members of my medical team form a line from the truck to the conveyor belt. We moved the boxes from person to person, and onto the conveyor belt, which carried the crates, boxes and luggage up into the aircraft. The two Continental employees remained inside the cargo well of the aircraft, stowing the gear. With everybody participating, the task was accomplished in less than thirty minutes. Can you imagine such an effort happening today, with everything having to pass through x-ray units and metal detectors, among the ever-growing list of overwhelming TSA and Homeland Security requirements? Obviously, the trip took place pre 9/11, in an era that will never be seen again.

My team members and I then crossed the tarmac under the belly of the aircraft, climbed the stairs, and buckled ourselves in. The flight attendant swung the heavy door closed and sealed it. The aircraft immediately taxied to the runway, and then we were on our way to Nicaragua.

Apart from our medical team, the aircraft was almost empty of passengers except for a few businessmen who were seated toward the rear. This allowed the team to spread out into adjacent seats and get more comfortable. The low passenger count on this flight had not been unexpected. After all, who would want to be going to a country that was still damaged from a civil war and lacked all of the amenities that most travelers would want and expect – not to mention the prevalence of such travelers' nightmares as dysentery, jaundice-inducing diseases, and malaria? Perhaps this gives a clue about the reason for the "Crazy" part of my "Crazy Texan" moniker.

In those days, simply landing in Managua was sufficient to make many people question their own sanity. Even before the landing gear was lowered, you couldn't help but notice that the public airport more closely resembled a military forward control base than a civilian facility. Armored vehicles and personnel carriers scurried to and fro, keeping a constant vigil against revolutionary forces that were continually seeking points of weakness to attack. Squads of foot soldiers could be seen patrolling as well, reconnoitering any possible hiding places that the mobile forces might overlook.

But our group was in high spirits as we landed, with jovial faces pressed against the windows as the plane ambled down the tarmac and stopped about thirty yards away from the small enclosure that was the airport terminal building. The jet taxied toward what could only loosely be called a terminal, whereupon a large squad of military personnel quickly swarmed toward us. As the plane rolled to a stop and cut its engines, two men pushed a battered and rusting portable staircase to the side of the aircraft, then the passenger door was opened, and the passengers began to disembark.

I stepped through the cabin door and onto the stairway, and beheld a surreal scene. The first thing that hit me was, as always, the oppressive heat. Now that I've lived for many years in Houston, Texas, I consider myself well-acclimated to scorching summer temperatures, although at the time of my initial visit to Managua I hadn't been in Houston all that long. I remember thinking that this was a whole new level for a boy from back east, like stepping from an alpine vacation spot directly into Dante's inferno. I had learned all too quickly that the combination of heat and humidity is omnipresent here, and refuses to be warded off by anything short of high-capacity air conditioners, of which there were few at the time. Even taking a shower seems futile, as no sooner than you dry off, sweat replaces the cooling water from the shower. Not perspiration, mind you. No, this is real, toiling in Death Valley grade sweat, and it stakes its claim on you and refuses to share you with anything refreshing. You never really get used to it.

The second thing I noticed as I paused on the platform at the top of the stairs – and this was the surreal part – was that our path from tarmac to terminal was lined with soldiers carrying American M-16s, all facing outward, peering into the distance for any sign of an impending attack. There were so many of them that I mumbled to myself that it looked like a reverse gauntlet, and the officer who was standing guard on the platform outside the plane overheard my statement and informed me that that was exactly what it was: a dare to anyone to approach. Fortunately, nobody did this time. The officer scoffed at the notion that anyone would make such a brash attempt, but in his eyes, I remember seeing an uneasiness that told me such attempts had been made before, and likely quite often.

We were met at the base of the stairs by our friend Haydee Holmann, whose family was hosting some of the team during our stay, and Maria Torres, the niece of recently elected president Violeta Chamorro, who held the office from April 1990 to January 1997. We followed the yellow painted path lined by the grim-faced military men to the small terminal building, and were then led to a small room that we were told was the VIP lounge. There we were offered bottles of water and cans of cola. I thought it in our best diplomatic interests not to laugh at their description of the room as the VIP lounge, and wondered if they had traveled abroad, and if so, whether they could see the irony.

An immigration official appeared, saluted the group, and requested all of our passports. He had them stamped and returned to us in a few minutes, supposedly to allow us to avoid the usual immigration and customs lines. This was very considerate of him, but inasmuch as there was only a handful of people on the aircraft with us, I couldn't imagine there being any lines.

As we approached the terminal, I noticed that quite a few of the windows were either broken or missing. I asked our hosts what had happened, and they attempted to brush aside my question. "Just repairs delayed by slow shipments of glass." But their cavalier response was betrayed by the same look I had noted in the officer's eyes a few moments before.

Inside, the terminal looked even more decrepit, like the aftermath of a protracted battle. Our hosts obviously heard our unspoken questions, and attempted to make light of the appearance, stating unconvincingly that the facility was being remodeled. And I found myself wondering, as I had the first time I visited Nicaragua and just about every time since then, "What the hell have we gotten ourselves into?"

With my cold cola in hand, I walked over to a small window that faced the tarmac and parted the curtains, where rather than the customary baggage trucks, I saw several men pulling hand drawn wooden carts with large wheels under the belly of the aircraft. There was no mechanized equipment. They began unloading the luggage, boxes of medical supplies and crates of books one item at a time, placing them in the wagons. It took them almost an hour to complete the task and haul the wooden wagons stacked high with our luggage and supplies to the small terminal building.

The customs officer returned with our passports and said we could take our personal luggage and go, but that he would first need to select several of the boxes to be opened so he could look inside. I joined him in the short walk to the cargo, and attempted in my limited Spanish to describe the contents of the boxes. The customs officer seemed to enjoy giving me a Spanish lesson, good-naturedly correcting my pronunciation and sentence structure. We both laughed, equally amused by the exchange.

The baggage handlers then pushed and pulled the high wooden carts laden with our equipment through the small terminal to the front doors. Two canvas-covered five-ton military trucks were already parked and waiting to receive our equipment. A crowd of onlookers had begun to gather, and despite the fact that they appeared more curious than threatening, the local police moved them back away from the loading area.

The officer who had first greeted us was standing at the rear of the vehicle, holding the canvas flap open, looking inside. He came to attention and saluted as I approached. I returned the salute, introduced myself, and shook his hand. He then took charge, barking orders to the baggage handlers, and the loading began. The second truck was loaded with our personal luggage. Between the two trucks was what appeared to be a school bus, except that it was painted with camouflage colors and there were bars on all the windows. I climbed the three steps into the bus and addressed the driver, "*Buenas tardes.*" ("Good afternoon.")

The front portion of the bus with the driver's seat was enclosed by a steel cage that separated it from the seats in the rear. Then it struck me: this was not a school bus. It was a bus utilized for transporting prisoners. The implication was unsettling, to say the least. I turned to the driver and asked him if this was the vehicle sent to transport the members of the medical team and the ABC-TV camera crew that had accompanied us, and he nodded his head enthusiastically, proclaiming, "*Si, si!* It is for your protection and safety. We will be traveling on back roads through the city of León, and then on to the hospital in Chinandega. Since most of the trip will be taking place after dark, we should be pretty safe. Military convoys are not usually a target like lone cars are."

My anxiety immediately went up another notch.

I stepped back off the bus to supervise the loading, and just as I approached the last truck in the convoy, a Jeep with a .50-caliber machine gun and several men sitting on wooden benches on either side pulled out. Another similarly equipped and manned Jeep moved to the front of the convoy, taking the point position. Seeing this, my anxiety didn't just move up, it spiked.

I waved to Mr. Barrett Phillips, who was one of my scrub nurses and also my part-time bodyguard; his powerful six-foot-two frame and formidable appearance made him a natural for the latter role. Together we re-entered the terminal building to ensure that all of the luggage and our supplies had been removed. I asked Maria Torres where I could exchange some dollars for Nicaraguan córdobas so I could tip the baggage handlers. She waved me off and informed me that she had already taken care of that.

I thanked her and boarded the bus. I made a head count of the twenty-two team members, as well as TV personality Marvin Zindler, cameraman Bob Dows, and ABC-TV writer and producer Lori Reingold. Marvin, Bob, and Lori had been covering international politics, war, corruption and abuses at home and abroad for many years.

Marvin is gone now – he passed away in 2007 – but he and I were close friends for the last three decades of his long life, and I wrote his authorized biography, *White Knight in Blue Shades* (A-to-Z Publishing, 2002). Marvin's and my relationship got off to a rocky start back in 1977 when we butted heads over the logistics of a delicate and complicated surgical procedure for a little girl whom we were both trying to help. I had gone to great trouble to make arrangements for the surgery to take place at The Methodist Hospital in Houston, and Marvin, unbeknownst to me, had made arrangements of his own with a Dallas hospital. I only found out about it when I saw a TV report of the little girl being boarded on a plane bound for Dallas. But we got past that and I soon became Marvin's plastic surgeon and then his friend, and we were partners on many missions of mercy all over the world. He and I founded a charity, the aforementioned Agris-Zindler Children's Foundation, which is similar to Doctors Without Borders and has sponsored or co-sponsored hundreds of medical missions over the decades.

Marvin was truly a Texas eccentric, a man with a big ego but an even bigger heart. Though he had had numerous careers in his life, he became most known and loved for being an ombudsman and philanthropist. He was an incorrigible publicity hound too, having made his mark across the spectrum of media from print to radio to television, and at the time I met him he was already a TV icon.

Marvin had gained a special brand of notoriety in 1973 when he released a series of news stories that led to the closure of the Chicken Ranch, a boarding house outside of Houston that had been an active brothel for more than 100 years. The Chicken Ranch's lesser-known sister house, the Wagon Wheel, also closed down. The closures resulted in a brouhaha that was written about by the late Texas journalist Larry L. King (not to be confused with the retired talk show host, Larry King). King's writings eventually became a hit Broadway play, *The Best Little Whorehouse in Texas*, and then a movie by the same name, starring Dom DeLuise, Burt Reynolds, and Dolly Parton. Marvin was a guest at some 100 openings of the play and the movie.

Wherever he went, Marvin Zindler continued to make news as an advocate for the most vulnerable people – the poor, the sick, the elderly, and the very young – not just in the United States but in many countries all over the world as well. He could seemingly move mountains; if something needed doing, he could make it happen. He had a fierce need to do everything better than the average person, but he also insisted that that every action be absolutely honest and above-board.

Marvin and his team had guts, no doubt about it. And I know that he wondered more than once, as I did, if getting involved in a Third World country such as Nicaragua helped or hurt. But I am reasonably satisfied that Marvin came to the same conclusion that I did: despite the difficulties and doubts, we were doing something good for people who truly needed help. My contribution lay not only in delivering medical services and supplies, but also instructing the local medical teams in surgical procedures. Marvin did his part by helping to make arrangements for countless procedures and missions over the decades. And Marvin, Bob, and Lori contributed to the greater good by making the world aware, through their resolute reporting, of the struggles of millions of people in poor or war-torn countries.

Sadly, Bob Dows has also left us; he died peacefully in 2013 after a lengthy illness. He had been with ABC-13 for more than three decades, and is sorely missed by his colleagues there and by those of us who had the privilege to travel with him on his pursuit of stories around the globe.

* * * * *

Now as we set off on our mission, Bob wanted the front seat next to the bus driver so he could photograph through the front window as we traveled from Managua to Chinandega. Within minutes our caravan of military trucks and prison bus moved out, the diesel engines on the vehicles rattling, and the tailpipes belching a thick dark cloud of smoke.

I was thinking ahead to our arrival in Chinandega. Although several of the team members had accompanied me to Nicaragua on previous trips, for others this would be a brand new experience. They would be "roughing it," relatively speaking. There were no hotels or other basic comforts in these remote parts of Nicaragua back then, and some of the medical team members would be sleeping on cots in the hospitals where they were working. Others – the lucky ones – would sleep in the homes of locals who offered to house them within walking distance of the hospital. As always, meals were to be provided by local families and a wonderful volunteer group, the Ladies of the Hospital, and would consist of red beans, toasted corn, tamales, and tortillas – all homemade and cooked over outdoor wooden fires. Food was usually served outside on the verandas, where it was cooler and graced with the beautiful view of the silhouettes of San Cristóbal and the Maribio volcanoes.

León and Chinandega are in the volcanic lowlands of northern Nicaragua, with high humidity and temperatures frequently reaching over 100 degrees, sporadically interrupted by short-lived afternoon rainstorms common during the summer months. The town of Chinandega is a very old colonial city situated at the foot of the Maribio volcanoes. In the past, Chinandega was an important political and economic center in the northwest corner of the country, where large plantations of sugarcane, peanuts, and at one time cotton flourished. Along the coast of the Coseguina Peninsula are located numerous small fishing villages and beautiful but empty beaches.

During our earlier visits to Nicaragua, even into the early 1990s, gunfire could still be heard at night as the small remaining groups of both the Contra and Sandinista armies engaged each other. Periodically, the Sandinistas would blow up electrical power stations and coastal facilities in the area. As you can imagine, this war-torn region wasn't a vacation destination, and I err on the side of understatement to say that it certainly wasn't a top choice of locations to set up a medical practice. Medical care was sparse or nonexistent during the most tumultuous years, and the Agris-Zindler Children's Foundation doctors were the first medical team to visit Chinandega since the beginning of the country's civil war.

All things considered, it probably *was* a little crazy to repeatedly put ourselves in harm's way. But, crazy or not, here we all were now, on our way through Managua with our armed escorts, headed out for the wild world beyond.

Joseph Agris, M.D.

PART 1

Mayhem and Marvels

Joseph Agris, M.D.

CHAPTER 1
The Road To Chinandega

It had been a clear day, though the day was dying in a lovely and spectacular way as our convoy progressed through Managua. The volcanic mountains were visible in the distance, with the sun beginning to set behind them. We were all struck by the beauty of the Cordillera Los Maribios and adjacent mountain ranges, which consist of active and dormant volcanoes. Each volcanic mountain is unique, with its particular environment the result of rainfall and other factors in the area where it is situated. ABC cameraman Bob Dows wasn't the only one who was busy shooting pictures as we drove. Several members of the team – myself included – had grabbed their cameras too, and we were all taking pictures of the breathtaking sunset and volcanoes in the distance.

The city of Managua is the capital of Nicaragua, home to the sitting government, and it sets the political and economic tone that has long shaped the country's destiny. But other factors quite beyond the control of governments have also shaped Nicaragua, and have been particularly cruel to its capital city. It isn't only volcanoes that pose a constant threat, nor floods and the resulting mudslides, though these have surely wreaked their havoc on Nicaragua. The unsettled earth has done its damage in other ways as well.

Joseph Agris, M.D.

On December 3, 1972 an earthquake registering 6.2 on the Richter scale laid waste to Managua. The capital was suddenly shattered by an ominous raging roar that came from the depths of the earth and moved quickly across Managua. This first shock radiated throughout the surrounding smaller towns and the countryside as well, sweeping away all in its path. It was all but inevitable: the walls of the fault lines had been grinding against each other for millions of years, and suddenly and abruptly had split apart under Managua and the outlying areas, creating the massive quake. This unimaginable force rampaged through the area at more than 5,000 miles per hour, leaving monumental destruction and death in its wake.

Many in the downtown area ran to the main cathedral to seek safety and to pray. Unfortunately the entire massive roof caved in, and all that remained were some of the stone pillars on the outer walls. The one building that withstood the quake fairly well, though it did sustain some damage, was the Intercontinental Hotel overlooking Lake Managua, where reclusive billionaire Howard Hughes had his penthouse apartment for many years. The hotel has since been refurbished, and it stands as a four-star hotel (currently called the Crowne Plaza Managua) in the downtown area.

After the initial shock wave, multiple undulating secondary waves followed with relentless swiftness, compounding the destruction. The pavement of the streets began to rise and then fall into troughs, and block upon block of buildings crashed to the ground, while others swayed off their foundations like palm trees in a hurricane.

Few cities in the history of human records had suffered as much devastation and destruction in such a short time by a natural disaster. Mud-brick and wooden one- and two-story homes tilted and angled bizarrely in all directions, having been flung from their foundations. Mud bricks, mortar. and tin roofs were never meant to withstand such a force. As the secondary shock waves moved across the city, homes and businesses crumbled and clouds of dust and debris rose from the streets. Jagged shards of glass burst from every window onto the adjacent streets, slaughtering pedestrians and animals alike as if a bomb had gone off. As chasms opened along the streets, sewer and water pipes ruptured, filling the openings with rushing water and foul-smelling debris. The damage was done by these first violent shocks in mere minutes, though the effects lasted for decades, and in fact the events following this disaster contributed significantly to the Sandinista Revolution a few years later. Smaller after shocks continued throughout the day.

When the sun rose the next day, virtually all that was left of the city center was the Intercontinental Hotel. Homes, schools, theaters, offices, banks, restaurants, stores, and the market area were gone. In their place were stacks of shattered wood, twisted metal, and broken masonry. Most of the structures were more than a hundred years old. None had been reinforced in any way, so most were destroyed with the first shock waves. The recurring shock waves only amplified the damage. The presidential palace,

Nicaragua's equivalent of the White House, remained only a skeleton of its former self.

Thousands of people had died in just minutes as heavy roofs caved in upon them or walls collapsed. Those who had survived the earthquake, and in particular those who were injured, were in shock from the experience and from their injuries. The civil authorities were non-existent. Police, fire, and rescue squads were themselves devastated or could not get to victims because the roads were impassable – filled with water from the ruptured pipelines and clogged with debris from fallen buildings. Anastasio Somoza, who was president at the time, ordered the entire city of Managua evacuated, but the order was ignored in many places. The government had made no provisions for the distribution of food, so there was much looting, but police were ordered to shoot looters on the spot. And because four of the major hospitals in the city had been destroyed in the quake, many thousands of injured victims received no medical care.

To add to the chaos, hundreds of wooden poles that supported electrical lines had toppled. The highly charged electrical wires snapped apart and ripped back and forth, shooting sparks across the streets. The powered ends of the overhead electrical wires danced and sparked until they found dry wood or fuel oil from adjacent destroyed homes and businesses, causing these to ignite and burst into flame, adding to the overwhelming destruction. The only place that was now safe, if you could get there, were the hills surrounding the city of Managua, away from the devastation below. What remained of the city was going to require police, firemen, medical personnel, and the military to control the chaos that was yet to come.

Clouds of dust remained over the city for several days, making it difficult to breathe. But the secondary tremors gradually ceased, and with that an eerie silence settled over what was once the city of Managua. The once-great capital city was a vast no-man's land of doom and death and devastation. In the following weeks, some sugarcane storage warehouses were turned into temporary morgues, and bodies of the dead that were retrieved were taken there, many yet to be identified.

Managua was scarcely recognizable as a city. It looked more like a war zone. The roads and sidewalks were barely discernible, as they were now filled with the crumpled pieces of buildings and timber from rooflines, which extended across the streets. Metal awnings that once shaded fruits and vegetables from the sun were crumbled, their twisted fragments scattered about. The destruction was similar from block to block throughout the city.

Every family in the city had lost at least one person, and many had lost several members from this massive earthquake. When it was all over and the dead were counted, the official toll was more than 10,000 – and they had all been killed in just minutes. Another three to four hundred thousand were now homeless.

The international community, including the United States, responded to Nicaragua's desperate need. The U.S. sent $32 million in aid, but only about half of that was ever accounted for. President Somoza is believed to have profited enormously by buying land cheaply and reselling it to developers. Meanwhile the homeless poor were left in the lurch, as is so often the case in too many places all over the world.

Twenty years after that quake, due largely to decades of unrest, civil war, and the corruption of former regimes, many buildings still lay reduced to rubble throughout the city. When my team and I saw the damage close-up, it was clear to us that even under good conditions, it would be many years before the cleanup and reconstruction were completed. And the conditions in Nicaragua – including Managua – were still anything but good at the time. Beyond the problems caused by the ongoing conflict, the funds for rebuilding were lacking in this very poor country, and even being the optimist that I like to believe I am, the future I saw for the country then was bleak, and remains so even to this day.

When our medical team entered the city, many buildings were still only shells of what they once were. Public works, including water and electric, had been restored, but only partially so, and even in the 1990s, brownouts were common. The hospitals were still not fully functional.

The electrical equipment came to a standstill in our hospitals almost daily – not just in Managua but also in Chinandega and other cites where we worked. Not only was the medical team threatened by the ongoing civil war between the Contras and the Sandinistas during those early visits, but the lingering effects of the devastating earthquake of 1972 – not to mention subsequent quakes and other natural disasters – only exacerbated our difficulties.

But we were there to do what we could to make things better. I suppose we could be forgiven for sometimes wondering if we would be up to the challenge.

* * * * *

Leaving Managua, we began traveling north by northwest on what is laughingly referred to as the Pan-American "Highway" (which, in this area, was not a highway by any measure), and before long we were passing along the base of the Maribio Volcanoes. To our left, I could see the village of Posoltega and hundreds of acres of sugarcane farms. In the rapidly waning light, the more determined members of the team were still staring out the windows, peering intently for anything resembling a landmark to break the seemingly endless fields of cane that stretched to the horizon on either side of the road. Our driver, Juan, told us that a few miles to the south of us was the town of Chichigalpa, home to Nicaragua's largest sugar refinery, Ingenio San Antonio, owned by the wealthy and powerful Pellas family. "It is also an alcohol production monopoly that produces Toña, Victoria, and our very famous Flor de Caña rum, which is exported worldwide," he said.

During the Sandinista insurgency, the Sandinista communists had appropriated

Ingenio San Antonio. The refinery, alcohol production plant, and surrounding sugarcane fields were returned to the Pellas family under the democratic government of President Violeta Chamorro. These sugar refineries and alcohol distilleries remain an important part of Nicaragua's economy and a mainstay of the local culture.

Time passed, and the team members, apparently weary from the fruitless search for a break in the scenery, were all dozing contentedly – or as contentedly as possible while traversing a war-ravaged country in a bus designed for prisoners rather than comfort. Its lack of air conditioning would have been bad enough, but the fact that the windows were welded shut undoubtedly contributed to the team's drowsiness. For my part, the anxiety that I had begun to feel as we had arrived in Managua hadn't fully abated, and pretty well ruled out the possibility of napping. At last Juan turned to me and informed me that we would be entering the town of Chinandega in twenty minutes.

Chinandega is a local traditional capital in the north. It is the last major town before reaching the Honduras border, which is why, from 1980 to 1992, many rebels would cross over the unguarded border to a place of safety on the Honduran side. Chinandega sits below the threatening crater of Volcán Cosegüina, which has erupted multiple times over the millennia, and is responsible for the rich fertility of the local soil that makes possible the massive sugarcane and peanut plantations, as well as the plentiful crops of bananas, plantains, sesame, and soybeans.

In addition, the town sits a short distance inland from an inlet off the Pacific Ocean where the Port of Corinto – the major export destination for the agricultural products of Chinandega as well as for imports – is located. Unfortunately, there were few imports or exports at the time due to the lingering effects of the war.

Temperature-wise, Chinandega is indisputably the hottest corner of the small nation. Granted, since our team was from Houston, we had grown pretty well accustomed to high humidity and temperatures. The big difference was that in Houston, we would go from our air-conditioned homes to our air-conditioned cars, and then to our modern air-conditioned hospital. In Chinandega, there was no air conditioning. In fact, it was often hotter inside the typical thick adobe-walled buildings than it was outside. That is why the town is known for its wide porches and verandas and beautifully handmade rocking chairs. People can be seen sitting outside every evening in the rockers, in anticipation of an occasional cool breeze to ease the inferno-like summer air.

This was a poverty-stricken area with most people earning less than five dollars a day, a situation made even worse by the Contra-Sandinista conflict. However, the area was also home to several older families whose money was based primarily on sugarcane, peanuts, and bananas. In addition there was the coastal shrimp industry nearby, which also had fallen on hard times during the civil war, but which was now being redeveloped. If you were one of the lucky ones, you would get a job on one of the plantations guaranteeing you a few córdobas and a meal every day. Fortunately, the town's agribusiness has grown prosperous in recent years, thanks in great part to the rich volcanic soil, plus the fact that Chinandega is located only twenty kilometers away from the Port of Corinto.

The town of Corinto is Nicaragua's primary port complex, linking the country with the Pacific Ocean shipping lanes. This port southwest of the city of Chinandega is kept busy, primarily thanks to its proximity to the agricultural center. During the civil war, the Sandinistas had taken control of the shipping facility and the port as a profit base, but also used it as a safe harbor for oil tankers and cargo ships to bring them needed war materials.

At one point during the war, American CIA operatives had entered the Corinto Harbor under the cover of darkness, where they blew up several oil tankers that were docked there, then proceeded to mine the harbor. When this action was later disclosed to the public, the Nicaraguan government, along with the international community, loudly condemned the United States. Under international pressure, the U.S. ultimately removed the mines, paving the way for the port to be rebuilt and a vibrant coastal community re-established.

The city of León was the next major town on the road to Chinandega, and as our bus approached the roundabout on the outskirts of the city, we passed an old Texaco gas station on our right, a solitary figure in the otherwise dark and empty roads. Not only was there no traffic, there were not even any automobiles parked on the street. The shops that lined the streets were not merely closed, they appeared fortified, with heavy iron gates that had been pulled across their fronts and chained closed. The homes I saw were all surrounded by high walls, most with sharp fragments of glass embedded or tangles of razor wire strung along the tops. A few others were surrounded by strands of barbed wire. This was obviously a country where daily upheavals were still a fact of life. These sights did not exactly instill confidence.

As we passed the church, Iglesia Guadalupe, the driver turned right and continued along five very dark streets, north and into the heart of Chinandega. We reached a wider boulevard – the Calle Central – and made a left turn. Even in the center of the town, all the shops were closed and gated up, and neither a soul nor a single automobile could be seen on the street. There were the occasional push carts, but even those were securely chained to electric poles or to the trees that lined the sidewalks. I thought to myself, *There have to be cars, motorcycles, and other forms of transportation here. Where are they?*

Across from Chinandega's central plaza or park, and next to the police station, was a large concrete building, completely surrounded by high black iron fencing. The police station occupied the remainder of this block along the west side of Chinandega's central plaza, and the hospital was directly across the street.

Other than the clatter of the diesel engines in our Jeeps, military trucks, and prison bus, there was not a sound. The pervading silence, combined with the heat and the humidity and the smell of the open sewage portals along the side of the road, filled the air with a sense of general decay, of death.

Our small convoy pulled up to the Children's Hospital, filling the entire street. Juan leaned on the horn, shattering the silence and echoing through the narrow streets. I felt certain that the harsh sound woke everybody within several blocks. Two armed men appeared from behind the hospital walls and unlocked the heavy iron gates. Then they slid a big iron bar from its moorings inside the gates, whereupon they were able to fling open the massive gates to their fullest.

The driver had exited the bus and was conversing with the guards, as the members of the medical team, many no doubt awakened by the noise, were groggily making their way from the bus to the sidewalk. Everyone was utterly exhausted, and ready to get some sleep.

Fortunately the local personnel were well prepared for our arrival, and after greeting us and exchanging pleasantries, they proceeded escorting team members, in groups of two or three, to their accommodations. Most of the team members would be staying in private homes for the next several weeks, there being no hotels in Chinandega at the time. I monitored the proceedings for a while and then, satisfying myself that everyone was being taken care of, I returned to the bus to retrieve my camera and my few other personal belongings.

Seeing our driver, Juan, I thanked him, and he said he would stay in Chinandega and would be available for trips in and around the city. "Thank you, that's good to know," I said. After retrieving my belongings, I walked to the back of the bus to make sure none of the team members had left any of their things on the seats or in the overhead racks.

To my surprise I found one of my scrub nurses, Michael, fast asleep on the large bench seat in the back of the bus. His shoes were off and his legs were stretched out. Michael was young and good-looking, a competent enough nurse but just this side of arrogant. I knew he had a lot to learn about working as part of a team in a challenging environment where there were limited resources. Yet he had eagerly volunteered for the mission, and since we really needed personnel, I decided, somewhat against my better judgment, to give him a chance. At this moment I was thinking that perhaps I should have heeded my initial gut instinct.

I cleared my throat, startling Michael awake. He jumped up, striking his head against the roof rack. Then he sat back down and without saying a word began to put his shoes on. He was glassy-eyed and still half-asleep, looking as if he didn't quite know where he was. I shook his shoulder and said, "Michael, we're in Chinandega. Get your things and get off the bus now!"

He scrambled up and was halfway down the aisle when I called to him. I picked up his backpack, which he had left behind, and threw it at him. It startled him, but he caught it with ease and continued out of the bus.

I thought to myself, *Nurse Michael is going to need an attitude change if he has any hope of making it through the next several weeks.*

Exiting the bus, I walked over and stood next to Sister Esperanza, a nun who played an invaluable role on numerous missions over the years. She handed me the list of hospital volunteers, which I started to peruse, while still keeping some of my attention on Michael. I signaled to one of the local police officers to usher Michael away and direct him to the home where he would be a guest for the next several weeks.

But before Michael could be whisked away, a stunning young woman walked up to me and introduced herself as Nurse Marta. Marta explained that she would be at the medical clinic in the morning to help interpret as well as to work with the patients. "I'll help out wherever I am needed," she said. Although she was talking to me, I couldn't help but notice that she did not take her eyes off of Michael the entire time. This fact did not go unnoticed by Michael either, and he had a big broad grin on his face as he turned to leave with the police officer.

I thought to myself, *Trouble in the making.* But I thanked Nurse Marta and told her that I looked forward to seeing her at the clinic in the morning. She nodded, but her eyes were still on Michael as he walked away. He looked back at her once, very quickly, and I could almost see her melt before my eyes. When I bade her a perfunctory "Good night," Marta nodded again, absentmindedly, but didn't reply.

As Marta wandered away towards some of the other folks who were still milling around, I thought to myself that it might not be a bad idea to hold a meeting for my team and the local medical personnel. I would go over some of the ground rules, particularly those involving fraternization. My own team was well versed in "the rules," but perhaps they could benefit from a reminder, and it wouldn't hurt to put the local teams on notice regarding our necessary commitment to utmost professionalism. That way there could be no question about boundaries.

When I turned my attention again to the list of volunteers that Sister Esperanza had handed me, the sister said, "Let me know if you have any questions, Doctor. And by the way, you, Barrett Phillips, and Jose Dixon will be staying again at the home of Roberto Callejas." I was glad to hear this, because I had become quite fond of Roberto and his family after having stayed at their home on previous trips. The first time I was a guest at his house, I realized that this was the beginning of a decades-long friendship, which only deepened every time my team and I returned to care for the children of Nicaragua. Roberto was a sugarcane plantation owner and a well-known artist. He had painted portraits of saints, and some of his work hung in the Vatican. He also created gorgeous colorful still-life paintings of the local flora. And to top it off, he was known as "the Godfather of Chinandega," but that's another story.

Our group continued to disperse, and soon only Barrett, Jose, and I remained. Sister Esperanza insisted upon walking us personally to the Callejas home, which was located off of Calle Central, only a few blocks from the Children's Hospital, as well as from the central market. We were the only pedestrians on this dark, unlit street, and there were no sounds except those of our heels on the cobblestones, and the occasional barking of a dog.

I was profoundly weary by now, and even though the interchanges with Michael and Marta had left me with yet another reason to be uneasy, I knew I had to keep my focus on the job ahead. What I needed more than anything right now was a good night's rest. I would deal with tomorrow's problems tomorrow.

CHAPTER 2
Jumping In With Both Feet

When we arrived at the Callejas house, Barrett rang the bell, and the house-boy opened the door for us. Sister Esperanza introduced us to some of the new members of the household staff who were still up, and then bid us good night and left. Because it was so late, we were shown directly to our rooms. I needed a shower, but I was so exhausted I just dropped into the bed and closed my eyes. I don't remember anything after that until I was awakened by the sound of a rooster crowing. I couldn't believe that the whole night had passed so quickly. It seemed as though I had just walked into my bedroom and lay down, and now the sun was coming up.

After showering and putting on some clean clothes, I headed toward the dining area off the veranda. Circling the veranda at the Callejas house now that the sun was up, I could better appreciate its beautiful garden and the flowers. Several gardeners were already at work. Jose Dixon and Barrett joined me, and the three of us were awe-struck by what we were seeing inside this gorgeous villa, especially compared to what we had seen in the streets entering Chinandega at night. Though we had been to this home on previous trips, we never failed to be struck anew by the beauty.

Connie, one of the house staff, appeared in a starched, crisp, white uniform and directed us to the dining room. In the center of the room was a large table with sixteen chairs around it, and she asked us to please sit.

Another lady, whom I assumed to be one of the cooks, walked in dressed in a similar uniform and asked us how we would like to have our eggs cooked. Yet another member of the household staff approached the table carrying a silver tray, on which there was a pitcher of fresh orange juice and a pot of coffee. After all these years, I can still remember the wonderful aroma of that pot of coffee, the likes of which I've yet to experience here in the U.S.

As we were seated, our host, Roberto Callejas, walked in and welcomed us to his home, apologizing for not being there to greet us upon our arrival the night before. After breakfast, Roberto walked us to the hospital. Because of the war, he explained, it was still more or less a guarded fortress. But he really didn't need to explain this, because we had been expecting it. The first time we'd been there a few years ago was quite a shock, though.

Once at the hospital we made perfunctory rounds of the facility, which was still pretty dark, and noticeably damp and musty inside. There were no elevators; instead, ramps were used to bring the patients to the different levels. After the rounds were completed, I gathered all of the medical teams together for a review of the goals of our mission, including a briefing about "the rules." When discussing the rules, I made it a point not to look directly at either Michael or Marta, but I thought I detected a quick exchange of glances between the two of them. Or maybe it was just my imagination.

Then it was time to make assignments. Each of the doctors and two of the nurses would begin with examinations, then the nurses would start preparing the surgical schedule. Nurses Carolyn and JoAnne would begin unpacking the equipment and setting up the operating rooms in conjunction with the local staff nurses.

There were only two examining rooms in the hospital, but we were told that there were two outbuildings near the road that the hospital used as storage facilities, though they were mostly empty. We moved chairs and an old desk into each of the buildings so that we could have four examining rooms working at the same time.

We already had 250 little patients, and more were arriving all the time. I located some sheets of paper and cut them into squares, then numbered them from 1-200. A group of women known as the Ladies of the Hospital – a volunteer organization – joined us, and I asked them to pass these numbers out in an orderly fashion. These volunteers had been providing water and food to the families that had been waiting for several days. They also spoke Spanish a lot more fluently than my team members, and helped with the translations. I thought this would prove quite helpful, and I was right.

My first patient was a young man with a burn to his hand and arm that had gone untreated, resulting in contraction that severely limited its use. Almost half the patients we examined that day had either burns or farm injuries. The farm injuries I could understand, but the burns I had been hard-pressed to figure out when I first began treating patients in Nicaragua. I had soon learned that most of these people lived in small, thatched roof houses, where the cooking is done just outside the house, over open fires. As a result, burns are a common occurrence, and most of the time they are not treated by a physician. A common practice was to wash the burn and apply honey, which is soothing and actually antibacterial. Then the burn is wrapped, and it's the wrapping that causes the scarring and contractures. This eight-year-old would need a release of the contractures by cutting through the scar tissue, while avoiding nerves and arteries. Then would come the application of skin grafts, after which he would have 95-98% function of his hand.

The next family presented with two children, each with a cleft lip and cleft palate. Nicaragua had a nationalized health program, and there were also private doctors. However, some burns, cleft lip, cleft palates, and other congenital defects were not considered life threatening, and were therefore not treated unless the family could pay for the doctor and hospital stay. Situations such as this are why I am convinced that nationalized health care systems do not work.

In addition, after ten years of civil war, the medical community had been stretched thin, and what little equipment and supplies remained had been utilized for soldiers who had been injured. The public had therefore been denied medical care for the past decade, even though the government claimed to have a national medical program that was available to everyone. Even when the program was working, prior to the Contra-Sandanista conflict, the only way you could get treated for medical problems that were considered non-life threatening was to pay for treatment by a private physician or go to the national-run hospital facilities where you would have to "tip" the doctor. If you could not pay the "tip," you would not be treated.

The children were examined, had their photographs taken, and were then sent to the laboratory to have a blood test. If they were otherwise healthy and had no other medical problems, they would be safe candidates for the anesthesia and surgery.

A child with a burn or a deformity such as a cleft lip or a cleft palate is often ostracized by friends and family. Regardless of how much the parents say they love them, these children are often hidden in a back room or sent out in the fields to take care of the goats or sheep. They do not attend school. They don't have a good relationship with their brothers and sisters. They have no relationship with the community, and are shunned when it comes to participating in sports or even going to church on Sunday. The parents are also embarrassed because they have a child with a deformity, as if it was their fault. I find it profoundly sad that these children, who suffer greatly anyway, must also carry the burden of shame, even from their families. The problem is not limited to Nicaragua, of course. I have seen it many times, in countries all over the world.

The benefits of surgical repair of a burn and the return to normal function, or the surgical repair of a cleft lip and palate, go well beyond the surgery itself. All of a sudden the parents, brothers, and sisters open their hearts again to this child. He or she is again part of the family. The distant family, aunts, uncles, and cousins now accept the child.

And finally, the community will then accept and integrate the child into the social activities of the school and the church. Treated children as they grow up are less likely to end up on the street as beggars, or so humiliated and psychologically damaged that they pick up a weapon. With treatment they go to school, get educated, and interact with their family and community. Even a relatively minor surgical procedure can make the difference between a life of solitary suffering and a fulfilling, happy life.

* * * * *

Several hours had passed and we had seen eighteen patients. The next patient that came into the clinic presented his numbered square piece of paper. The number was eight. I could swear we had seen a child several hours ago who presented with number eight, but given the onslaught of patients, I realized that I could have been mistaken. We examined this child and continued on, not giving it another thought. About an hour later, another patient presented with a slip of paper that had the number eight written on it. I excused myself and went to the small bungalow across the street where Barrett was assisting a local doctor who was examining the children. I asked if they had noticed the same thing. They thought about it for a minute and Barrett said, "Yes, now that I think about it, it seems like the number eight keeps reappearing on the admission slips."

I returned to the building in which I was working. I had a suspicion about what was going on, but I couldn't prove it. I was hoping for another number eight to show up so I could test my theory. Sure enough, within the hour, a family presented themselves with a slip of paper on which there was the number eight. I opened the desk drawer where I had saved previous admission slips and compared them. The writing was the same, and it was not mine.

I got up from the desk and went outside to where one of the hospital volunteers was escorting the children to the different clinics. Showing her the suspicious admission slip, I explained my theory to her. We casually walked down the street along the line of patients who were still waiting to be seen, past the police station and into the park where many more patients had gathered. There was a young man in his late teens going from one family to another. We stood back and watched as he tore off a piece of paper and wrote the number eight on it. He sold it to the family for a few córdobas, and then guided them up toward the front of the line.

I returned to the hospital, where I asked Jose Dixon and Barrett to join me in the park. I figured that Barrett's intimidating appearance would work in our favor. We quickly located the young entrepreneur and cornered him. At first he denied that he was selling admission slips with low numbers on them to the families and guaranteeing them he would get them in to see the doctor today. But he could see that we weren't buying it.

Miracles in Bedlam

In effect he was telling these poor people that the American medical team couldn't possibly care for everyone who arrived here, and that their only hope for getting treatment was to buy a low-number admission slip from him so they could move up to the front of the line. He was quite the clever entrepreneur. We offered to escort him to the police station and let him explain it there, or he could simply leave the area and if we saw him again, he would be taken to the police station. Then we walked him to a spot out of the park where he had a bicycle chained to a tree, and waited until he had pedaled several blocks away from the hospital facility.

I have to admire this young man's ingenuity, but he was stealing from poor people who really couldn't afford to pay for a ticket to move them to the front of the line. Since hospitals in Nicaragua do not provide meals, whatever little money these poor farmers had was needed for food and water, making the young scam artist's deeds particularly egregious. We told all the team members what had happened, and told them to keep their eyes open for duplicate admission numbers. With that problem quickly resolved, we returned to our clinic and patient examinations.

Every few hours I needed to get up and stretch my legs, at which time I accompanied several of the Ladies of the Hospital up and down the lines extending from the hospital to the park. We reassured everybody that they would be seen and treated or scheduled for surgery, no matter how long it took. There were a lot of people here, and we let them know that they simply needed to be patient.

I realized we had already seen more than 100 children, and the line was at least as long, if not longer, than it was earlier that morning. I also noticed something else about the people we were talking to now. The style and colors of their clothing, their facial structure, and way the women wore their hair were all quite different than the people I had seen earlier in the day.

I mentioned this to one of the volunteer ladies, and she explained to me that the new arrivals were not from Chinandega, but from the various Indian tribes in the area. They were of Inca or Aztec origin, rather than Spanish. These were the new arrivals.

Few of these people had telephones at home, and there were no cell phones. The radio and the church pulpit were the main sources of information. The priests would make announcements about the arrival of our medical team, where we were located, and what medical services we were there to provide. One of the ladies who was very active and helpful was Haydee Holmann, who had met us at the airport when we first arrived in Managua. She was married to Hugo Holmann, the CEO and owner of *La Prensa*, which at the time was the largest newspaper not only in Nicaragua, but all of Central America. Hugo had begun running stories about the team, and later on in the week, he sent a reporter to take before and after photos of the work we were doing, and he published a full-page story in the newspaper. Many could not read, but the photos said it all.

There were also trucks with megaphones mounted on their roofs that went up and down the streets in Chinandega and the surrounding villages, announcing the arrival of our medical team. They let the people know where we would be working, and announced that preference was being given to children with cleft lips and palates, burns, farm injuries, and tumors. It was amazing to me just how fast the word of mouth carried to the small villages and the farms.

We definitely had our work cut out for us.

CHAPTER 3
The Miracle Baby
Of Chinandega

To truly appreciate the story of the "miracle baby," you have to understand the conditions under which we were working in Chinandega. Not only were the hospital and its equipment very turn-of-the-century, and the local doctors and nurses tremendously overworked, but it was also quite common for the electrical power to cease without warning. While in some areas of Nicaragua the locals could almost predict when they would be without electrical power, occasionally there was a sudden, unexpected, and prolonged loss of power, which extended well into the evening. Part of this was a carryover from the Contra-Sandinista war. During the war years and even afterwards, the cause of a power outage could be some rebel force blowing up a transmission tower or a transformer. But sometimes the culprit was a force of nature, particularly during the rainy season, which often brought severe, prolonged rainstorms. As the civil war abated, electric power was usually uninterrupted throughout the day, but we were still often at the mercy of the weather.

Regardless of the cause, the loss of power would render further surgery all but impossible. Unlike the modern medical facilities in which my team was accustomed to working, most of the hospitals in Third-World countries did not have the luxury of backup generators, and the few that did have them often lacked the diesel fuel to run them. In some cases the generators were so badly in need of repair that they did not work, anyway. Things are marginally better today, particularly in the larger cities, but in the 1980s and early 1990s it was still a big problem.

Nevertheless we always tried to be as prepared as possible. On our earliest trips, we had brought large battery-powered lights, but as the military situation stabilized somewhat, we had begun carrying only small portable flashlights in our belts. I insisted that all team members carry their mini-flashlights in their belt packs or tied to the drawstrings of their operating scrub suits.

And indeed, it was not uncommon that the electric power would fail while we were in the middle of an operation. Because the operating rooms had no windows, when the lights went out we were left in pitch-blackness. All equipment would stop as well, including the respirator. We had to maintain the patient's breathing by hand. The suction pumps were also electrically driven, so without power there was no suction available to remove blood or secretions. And the electric cautery unit was rendered useless as well, so the surgeon would also have more difficulty stopping bleeding.

In the early evening of one particularly long day – a day punctuated not only by a massive thunderstorm but also by sporadic gunfire that sounded a little too close for comfort – I was in the O.R., finishing a surgical procedure. I was just placing the last of the skin sutures when the electricity went out. Although in retrospect it seems clear that the cause was weather-related rather than Sandinista-related, at the time it happened, I wasn't at all certain. That was cause enough for worry, but I knew that we had a more immediate problem: the operating room was blacker than black, and you couldn't see your hand in front of your face. I took a deep breath, my mind racing.

I was grateful that the operation had been completed. We had already begun to wake the patient up, and we were able to set the monitoring equipment on battery power. We knew we could maintain the oxygen level manually, and even though the anesthesiologist did not have a suction machine available, I was confident that he could deal with this. I was relieved, because even with all of our small flashlights on, visibility was almost nil; my nurse assistant standing in the back of the room was nearly invisible in the darkness.

Then we heard a loud commotion in the hallway between the operating rooms. Satisfied that our patient was doing well, I cautiously opened the door of the operating room. The hallway, as expected, was black, but I detected two shadowy silhouettes frantically groping the walls and working their way to the adjacent operating room. I couldn't understand all they were saying, but their conversation was anxious and rapid, and was focused not on the power outage, but on their concern for a patient.

I quickly learned that immediately before the electrical failure, a pregnant woman had been rushed into the adjacent operating room for an emergency Caesarian section. Unfortunately, just as the surgeon made his first incision into the woman's abdomen, the lights went out, and the surgeon could not control the bleeding, because he could not see anything. Naturally, the electric cautery equipment wasn't working because of the power failure, but in the profound darkness of the operating room, the surgeon couldn't find it anyway. The infant had not been delivered and was clearly still in trouble. Without sufficient light, both mother and child could die.

I knew I had to help.

I worked my way down the hall and entered the operating room, which was dimly illuminated by a single kerosene lantern that was spewing acrid smoke into the air; it burned my throat and made me cough uncontrollably. In the shadows, I could see several nurses and the anesthesiologist. I asked her if everything was good from an anesthesia standpoint, and she gave me a thumbs-up.

She was calm and experienced, and immediately after the power went out she had switched the machine to manual and was hand-breathing the patient without any problems. I looked up and saw a full, fresh bag of IV fluid, running wide open to replace the blood the mother was losing. Turning toward the surgeon, I noticed that the gauze sponges he had placed in the woman's abdomen were already saturated in blood, and that it was beginning to trickle over the side of the wound and onto the surgical drapes. At that point, the gynecologist who was performing the C-section hollered out, "We need to see where this bleeding is coming from! We need light! *Now!*"

I knew that if we didn't stop the bleeding quickly, we were going to lose the mother and most likely the child as well. For a second, I just stood there, transfixed. Then it struck me like a message from God. The ABC television team from Houston had come to the hospital early today to interview the patients for a series they were putting together, featuring before-and-after photographs of the children we treated. Cameraman Bob Dows had spent the whole day lugging around a massive forty-pound professional camera with a battery pack and a very large floodlight, in addition to a battery belt that weighed another thirty-five pounds. By the time they had finished for the day, it was late, and he and the rest of his team were exhausted and hungry. A few hours earlier, Bob had come to me and asked if there was a safe place where he could leave the camera and the heavy batteries for the night. He said they would return in the morning to complete the filming and join the medical team when we made rounds in the ward, and perhaps do some filming in the O.R.

I told Bob to put the equipment under the instrument table at the back of my operating room, and we would cover it with a sheet. It would be securely locked in the room overnight, and he could retrieve it in the morning. That way he wouldn't have to carry seventy-five pounds of camera and batteries around, and could just leave and go to dinner.

I had a much smaller version of the same camera, and knowing that I was interested in photography, Bob had given me some lessons on the use of the larger professional unit. That is probably why it came to me that the big camera in the adjacent operating room could provide more than enough light for us to see what we needed to do to stop the bleeding, and more than enough reserve battery power to run the powerful light through the entire surgical procedure.

The gynecologist and O.R. team must have thought I was loco, or just couldn't deal with our current crisis, as I turned and quickly strode across the operating room toward the door. I tore off my gloves, pushed against the big door with one hand, and was out of the room and into the pitch-black hallway in a flash. Running my hands along the crumbling plaster of the wall to orient myself, I worked my way to the adjacent operating room. I reached that room and opened the door slightly, in case there was someone on the other side. The last thing we needed was to injure one of the staff or add to the injuries of a patient who might be inside. The room, however, was unoccupied.

Once inside the completely dark O.R., I crawled on my hands and knees, guided by my hands, to the back of the room, until I felt the base of the operating table. I knew the instrument table would be directly behind it, so I continued crawling along the side wall and found the instrument table I was looking for. I reached underneath and pulled the cloth from the camera. I ran my hands along the camera to the power switch and flipped it on, whereupon the powerful strobe filled the room with a near-blinding light. As I raised my head, my scalp banged against the sharp corner of the steel table. I felt a searing pain, but it didn't seem to be bleeding. Nevertheless I raised my surgical mask from around my neck, placed it over my forehead, and tied it snugly to the back of my head just in case. I ducked back under the table to search for the battery packs, and found them still attached to the big forty-pound camera. I grabbed the camera, stood up, and ran from the room.

A few feet down the hallway, I turned right and entered the operating room, now completely illuminated by the powerful light I was carrying. I could see the worried look on the gynecologist's face, still standing there, applying pressure to the woman's abdominal wound. Barrett came into the room and asked if he could help. I gladly transferred the camera to his shoulder and told him to aim the light into the wound, then I quickly re-scrubbed, put on a fresh surgical mask, pulled on a pair of gloves, and proceeded to pull the blood-soaked sponges from the wound. The gynecologist and I began clamping the bleeding vessels that we could now see as fast as we could do it. In about a minute the bleeding was stopped.

Still working without suction, we had the nurse bring in more sponges to soak up the remaining blood, as well as a bottle of sterile water to irrigate the still-open wound. The gynecologist carefully completed the incision as I applied clamps to the wound edge to prevent any further bleeding. I asked the anesthesiologist if everything was going well. She said the patient was stable, and added that she was hanging another bag of IV fluid, since there was no replacement blood available. At this point, the gynecologist removed the baby – a healthy little boy – and I clamped the umbilical cord and cut it.

The gynecologist then passed the roughly six-pound infant to the nurse, who began cleaning him up. Since we still couldn't use the suction machine, another nurse came into the room with an old fashioned hand-held suction bulb and used it to clear the infant's mouth and throat. Almost immediately, we were graced with the most beautiful music imaginable: the baby's first cry. And we knew that everything was going to be okay. God was looking after us this day.

We moved rapidly as a team, and I assisted the gynecologist in closing the inner wound. The nurses had cleaned the baby and were putting drops in his eyes to clear them. I called out for a baby bassinet, and one of the nurses rushed from the room to get one. I asked Barrett how he was doing with that heavy camera on his shoulder, and he said he was okay. The bleeding was stopped, and in a few more minutes we would have everything closed.

The nurse arrived with what she called the bassinet. At first I was I confused, and then I just laughed. It was a wooden box, similar to those that I would see at the market, filled with apples or peaches. She placed one of the sterile operating towels in the base of the box and laid the baby in it. They had two kerosene lanterns on either side to keep the child warm. I was afraid that if the lanterns tipped over, the baby would be burned. In addition, the smoke from the lanterns was starting to fill the room and make it very uncomfortable to breathe. I asked the nurses to turn the lanterns off and to get a blanket from one of the beds in the ward, wrap the baby in it, then put him back in the "bassinet." The gynecologist was completing the final closure, and said he and the nurse could finish it. I stepped back from the table, pulled my gloves off, and went across the room to check the beautiful baby boy. He was doing just fine.

I was sweating profusely, partly from the lack of air conditioning in the operating room, and partly from my adrenaline rush. Then I walked to the front of the hospital and stepped outside on the veranda, which was also the waiting room for family members.

There were at least twenty people there, all on their knees, hands together and praying. I kept hearing, "*Muerto, muerto.*" ("Dead, dead.") The rain had stopped and the night was clear, and the moon and stars above gave off the only light. Gunfire could still be heard in the distance. It sounded to me like automatic weapons, but nobody seemed concerned, since gunfire was still an everyday occurrence here.

I had put my white coat on, and the waiting family could all see me in the moonlight. The expressions on their upturned faces made it clear that they were all expecting the worst. I could hear someone whisper, "*Muerto?*" Just then, the nurse came out from behind me carrying the wooden crate with the baby in it. As if on cue, the baby cried and then smiled up at me, his little arms pulling up and back as if to say, *I'm here! I have arrived, and I am well!*

Some of the family members came over and gathered around, while the others stood, hands clasped together, faces turned up toward the heavens. They were now praying out loud. I could understand some of the words they were saying: "This is not possible, there was no electricity and no lights." Someone was saying it was a miracle, and that the baby was a Saint, or that God was sending a message. I was reminded that this was a very religious Catholic community of farm workers and shopkeepers. We had all needed a miracle, and the battery-powered light on that TV camera had provided it. Suddenly shouts of "miracle baby" began to ring out through the group, and I was not inclined to argue.

I re-entered the hospital and returned to the operating room. The nurses were moving the mother out; she had been extubated and transferred to the gurney that would take her to the women's ward. I looked at the glowing dial on my watch and saw that it was almost midnight. The adrenaline rush had dissipated, and now all I felt was pure exhaustion. I knew the entire team was exhausted as well, but really feeling good about the "miracle baby." It occurred to me that Barrett must be exhausted from carrying the camera, batteries, and light on his shoulder for the past hour. I found him standing in the hallway, holding the light so they could move the patient on the gurney across the hall to the ward. I followed behind, feet dragging, my arms limp at my sides. I remember wondering, *Why did Bob Dows decide to leave his camera at the hospital tonight, of all nights? Was this really a "miracle baby?"*

Barrett, with the camera still on his shoulder, walked across to the children's ward, where we joined the other team members and visited the post-op patients from earlier in the day. Some were sleeping, others were being tended to by their families at their bedside. Everyone was doing fine, and nobody was complaining of any unusual pain or discomfort.

Barrett stopped, still holding the light, while Carolyn changed a dressing, then moved further up the row of beds where JoAnne was struggling to restart an IV in the light of an old gas lantern a local nurse was holding. Barrett stood there for a few minutes with the powerful television camera light, allowing JoAnne to quickly restart the I.V. I asked if there was anything else we needed to do before we left, and the team reassured me that everything had been taken care of.

Barrett was then finally able to remove the camera from his shoulder and sling it on his side. Jose Dixon was speaking rapidly to the night staff nurse in Spanish, giving instructions and answering last-minute questions. By 1:00 a.m. the medical team members were departing to the homes in the surrounding area that our hosts were providing for us. We couldn't be happier, but we were all completely exhausted. I told Barrett to bring the camera and battery pack; I would store it under our bed and bring it back to the operating room in the morning. We always got there much earlier than the TV crew anyway.

At that time, I had no idea how much of a public relations coup that "miracle baby" would prove to be. Was it really a miracle? Your guess is as good as mine, and I suppose it depends upon your definition of "miracle." But I'll tell you one thing: I am more than willing to accept that a higher power could have been guiding all of us as we brought that child into the world.

CHAPTER 4
Trouble Brewing

The medical teams had settled into a routine – or at least as much of a routine as can be established in Bedlam – and my team members were working well with the local doctors and nurses to provide the care that the people of Chinandega so desperately needed. Our work days (and nights) were impossibly long, but that was of little concern to either the American or Nicaraguan teams. We had all expected long days and hard work. What bothered the Americans was the uneasiness surrounding the lingering war: the sporadic gunfire, the occasional unexplained explosion, the constant rumors of potentially hostile forces bent on sabotaging our mission. The Nicaraguan doctors and nurses were accustomed to instability and upheaval – not unconcerned, of course, but they had adapted to the uncertainties.

Our days were marked by blessings and celebrations as well as by uneasiness. The tale of the "miracle baby" had spread far and wide, and as a result we had many visitors who were not in need of medical care, but had simply traveled to the hospital to visit the site of the miracle and perhaps to catch a glimpse of the magical child. While I was glad that these people had found something to bolster their faith, and was relieved that they weren't all in dire need of medical care, their presence added to the confusion and made it more difficult at times to carry out our duties with utmost efficiency. But we managed.

Besides the normal concerns related to the medical mission, and my hyper-alertness regarding the Sandinista situation, I still had concerns about Michael and Marta. There were rumors and whispers about the two of them, and even though both were managing to live up to their professional commitments thus far, their flouting of the rules was almost bound to result in trouble, sooner or later. Even so, I had too many other things on my mind to bird-dog Michael. He had been warned, more than once, and he was an adult. I think that at this point I was still hoping things would simply work out for the best.

One afternoon the hospital was rocked by a particularly loud explosion, seeming to validate the worst of the war-related rumors. I ran to the nearest window and beheld a chaotic scene: clouds of smoke in the distance, and crowds of people rushing every which way.

We knew that there was a good chance that injured people would soon be filling our emergency room and operating rooms. There was no time to waste, so my team members and I ran past the stunned administrators. We headed up the ramps to the top level, where we could look out over the park and the surrounding areas and better survey the scene.

We found to our relief that the crowd was quickly dissipating. Those closest to the hospital pushed through the gates and were filling the central courtyard, and those who were nearest to the park disappeared into adjacent buildings. We heard police sirens in the distance, but from our observation point we could not see any injured. It seemed that God was again watching over these people.

I knew very well that things could have easily gone the other way, and I would have felt at least partially responsible. After all, many had come to the hospital to see and touch the miracle baby, and many others were bringing ill members of their family specifically to see me.

Michael appeared at my side just then and told me, "The operating rooms are ready for us to proceed. Patients are asleep on the table. We need to get back down to the second level."

As I turned, I could see lovely Marta standing nearby, her attention fixed on Michael. I turned to him and said in a low voice so no one else could hear, "You look a little tired. Something keep you up last night?"

Michael was caught by surprise; he had no time to gather his thoughts, but it was clear that he knew denial wasn't an option. I think he knew perfectly well that I was aware of what was going on. He smiled a little sheepishly and said nothing. But as he walked away from me down the hall, his eyes locked with Marta's in the type of I-can't-look-away manner that was clearly intended as a private communication between the two of them, but was painfully obvious to all of us who were watching. They didn't even try to look away from each other as Michael walked past Marta.

After he had passed, Marta just stood there, nervously wringing her hands. She said nothing but her large green eyes spoke volumes. Abruptly our senior nurse Carolyn crossed over to her, putting her arm around her and saying, "You need to get to Operating Room 3...Now!" Startled out of her trance, Marta nodded and began making her way to the O.R. with the rest of us.

As we walked down the ramp that led to the second level, I looked ahead and noticed that Michael was limping. I caught up to him and put an arm on his shoulder, whispering, "What gives with the limp?" I knew he hadn't had it 24 hours ago. I hadn't even noticed it earlier today.

Michael cleared his throat and replied with a forced casualness, "I bumped my leg yesterday rushing in and out of the operating rooms. It's nothing. It will be fine tomorrow."

I said, "Michael, if you want me to look at it now, I'll be happy to do so."

"No, let's give it another day," said Michael, making it clear that the subject was closed for now.

Frankly, I was too tired to push it, and there was too much work ahead. I figured that if Michael said it wasn't bothering him, I could always look at it tomorrow after things had settled down somewhat.

* * * * *

The hospital administrator had allowed the press to enter the hospital on the first level. It seemed that he and his assistant administrator were enjoying the attention and publicity they were now getting due to the birth of the "miracle baby" and the presence of the American surgical team in their sleepy little town. But I wished to avoid the fuss, so I had quickly learned not to use the ramp in the main area. Now as the others proceeded to the operating rooms, I retreated quietly to the back of the hospital, where there was a stairwell. It was damp and dark and musty, but it kept me out of the glare of publicity, and I welcomed it. I climbed the almost vertical concrete steps to the second level, emerging into an area located behind the operating rooms.

Once there, I quickly went from room to room, checking to make sure everything was progressing well and that there were no problems. I entered surgical suite number 1, where there were two tables, a mere three feet apart, each one bearing a child who was asleep and ready for surgery to proceed.

I stopped at one table and quickly reviewed the planned procedure with the local surgeon and a couple of residents and student nurses from the National Autonomous University of Nicaragua in León, who would be assisting. León is the hub of education in this part of the country, located less than an hour from Chinandega, and the university there is the oldest institution of higher education in Nicaragua. The students I'd met seemed very appreciative of the more than 1,000 books and journals that we had brought with us and placed in the León Medical Center library, which like so many other things had been destroyed by the Contra-Sandinista conflict.

I glanced over to the corner where two of my nurses, Carolyn and JoAnne, were giving some instructions to the local nurses, who were already scrubbed in. I was pleasantly surprised to see there were several other young nurses in their blue training uniforms; they were also going to be participating and learning.

In my medical missions all over the world, the surgical procedures are only one part of what we do. The teaching, which allows the continuation of our work, is just as important, if not more so. I guess you could say that it's much the same principle as that expressed in the old saying about giving a man a fish versus teaching him to fish. When my team and I pass our surgical skills and knowledge on to the doctors and nurses in the countries we visit, they are able to continue helping, healing, and teaching long after we are gone. Of course it works both ways: we always learn from them as well.

I stood watching and adding some comments while the resident doctor made the surgical markings with the blue medical ink. Then I went out to scrub so I could assist if needed with the other child, who was being operated on for a moderate-sized cleft lip.

The local plastic surgeon had already begun the procedure, assisted by the resident doctor and one of the student nurses. As we worked, we had a discussion about some of the other surgical procedures that were available for correcting these defects. I quizzed the resident and students as to their knowledge of the procedure and the aftercare that would follow the surgery.

The conversation then drifted inevitably to the birth of the miracle baby. Everyone was curious about how I was feeling, since the spot on my forehead where I'd hit it was still bandaged, as it had bled some after all. I assured them that I would be fine, and urged them to turn their attention back to the procedures at hand. I continued my instructions and questioning of the students and nurses. The procedures went well, and the children were in the recovery room within the hour.

It was turning out to be another very long day, and the medical team and I worked straight through. We didn't even take a lunch break; between cases we would refresh ourselves with a few sips of papaya juice or coconut milk, and then it was on to the next case.

But I was in my element. I love the operating room and the things that we can accomplish there. And in this case, I was quite happy to stay away from the masses and the visiting press, who were all abuzz over the "miracle baby." No doubt about it, the case had brought favorable publicity to the hospital and the city of Chinandega, and several of the hospital staff were delighted. But I was more than happy to stay in the O.R. with my staff and patients.

Miracles in Bedlam

* * * * *

The Marta and Michael problem reared its head again later that afternoon. The nurses and students were allowed to rotate so that they could take bathroom breaks or grab something to eat or drink, and on this day the love-struck Marta was doing the relief, filling in while others had a chance to take a break.

In the early afternoon, as I was completing a surgical procedure, she entered my operating room and spoke to a couple of the nurses, who promptly left on a break. As she was preparing the adjacent O.R. table for the next patient, I glanced up and our eyes met. Marta immediately turned away, and I returned to putting in the last couple of sutures.

That brief, wordless exchange got me worrying about Michael again. I wasn't just concerned because of Michael's violation of the rules. I was almost certain that Michael had broken them and had gone far beyond mere fraternization; he looked to be the very definition of a "lovesick puppy." That was bad enough, and sooner or later I was going to have to confront him with the issue. But as a doctor, I was even more worried about his limp, which seemed to be growing steadily worse. When I had passed him in the hallway in between procedures a little earlier, the limp had seemed even more pronounced.

My case completed, I decided to take a break. I went to the doctor's lounge, where they had some small sandwiches, papaya juice, coconut juice, and orange juice. Hoping that my face and demeanor did not betray my worries, I grabbed a drink and sat down with a small group of residents and students, who were discussing the next two procedures.

One of the residents looked at me closely and said, "Hey, Doc, you look like you have the weight of the world on your shoulders."

"I'm fine," I replied, with a casual wave of my hand. "It's been a long day, and we still have a lot of work to do."

The resident suggested that we should all get some *chicha*. Winking, he said to me, "You just mix a little with your juice and it will help you get through even the longest day." Everyone laughed.

And that's how *chicha* became the newest word in my limited but ever growing Spanish vocabulary. I had an idea what they were talking and laughing about but wasn't sure, so I said, "*No comprendo.*"

The group began to laugh harder.

Another resident volunteered an explanation. "You know how when you are walking or driving down the road in the country area, you pass some small farms and villages and there is a long pole and a white flag on the end?"

I nodded and said, "Well, yes. But I thought it was a political flag. They seem to be everywhere." That was true; there was the black and red flag of the FSLN, or the Sandinistas, and the white flag of one of the conservative groups, and a host of others.

By now everyone in the room was laughing. I was killing them today. Clearly I was way off track about the flags.

Finally the senior resident, Carlos, who had studied at the English school and spoke excellent English, stopped laughing and said, "When you see the white flag in front of a farm or country home, it means they have *chicha* for sale."

"Okay, I'll bite, what is *chicha?*"

"It is homemade corn alcohol – pure alcohol. When you drink it, you will feel it go from your mouth all the way down."

"Ah, yes," I said. I told him that I had traveled to Kentucky and the mountains of Virginia, and at a restaurant in one of the little towns I visited, there was a drink on the menu called "white lightning," a term often used to describe illegal moonshine. But that white lightning, though homemade, was legal and properly licensed; it was distilled on the property and sold in the restaurant. The best I can say about it is that a little goes a very long way.

When I tried to describe the concoction to Carlos he nodded and said, "Then you have a good idea of what *chicha* is. It's a clear liquid, pure alcohol, inexpensive and readily available." It was, he explained, the alcoholic drink of choice on the farms and in the fields. "It's a poor man's alcohol," he said, "but it is the strongest of all alcohols that you can purchase, and certainly a lot stronger than the commercial ones that you would get at a bar. But it is also a lot cheaper."

I looked at Carlos and said, "Now you are my teacher, and I'm learning something new every day. Tell me, is there anything else I need to know?"

Carlos laughed and said, "Now you know where to get the *chicha*, so all you need is a *señorita*, and the evening will progress quickly and much more favorably."

As the laughter continued my face felt a little warm, and I knew that I must be turning red. I looked at Carlos with a stern face but found it difficult to keep from laughing myself. So I simply said, "I think they are ready for you now, so please check on the next two patients."

Carlos got up and as a parting shot before leaving the doctors' lounge, he said, "You are working very hard. I will get you some *chicha* tomorrow."

And that of course caused another round of laughter. This was actually very good, I thought. It was indicative of the great rapport our team was building with the locals, especially the students and residents. This type of bond lends itself to more effective teaching and greater respect for each other. That's what I call appropriate fraternization.

I stood up, preparing to leave the lounge and go back on duty. As I did, everyone else in the lounge area quickly took a last sip of their juice or a bite of their sandwich, and they rose as well, and we all made our way towards our respective operating theaters.

It was almost midnight when Kimberly, my personal office secretary and part-time O.R. assistant, told me that the last patients were on the table, and that when we were finished with them, we would have completed 42 surgical procedures for the day. I smiled. We were well on our way to the 350-400 surgical cases planned for this medical mission trip.

Don Roberto had invited the entire surgical team to his home for a midnight dinner. We were all looking forward to that, as we were tired and hungry, having worked straight through for nearly fourteen hours. I sent the resident doctors and nurses home. The American medical team would finish the last two cases while Kimberly completed the charts, labeling and placing them with the Polaroid shots that we used for before-and-after photos. She also sorted the duplicate copies of the before-and-after pictures, which we gave to the parents after the surgery. Back then, most of these people had never seen a photograph, much less a Polaroid that would develop right in their own hands. Giving out those Polaroid pictures was one of the best public relations ideas I had ever come up with.

I was looking forward to an evening of relaxation, and hoped I could actually relax. Michael and Marta were still very much on my mind, and I feared that the trouble that was brewing would soon spill over, compromising the entire mission. On our first night in Chinandega, when Michael and Marta had initially discovered each other, I had told myself that I would deal with tomorrow's problems tomorrow. In the interim I thought I had done my best to nip any trouble in the bud. But now it seemed likely that "tomorrow" was upon us, and the problems were still there, larger than ever.

Joseph Agris, M.D.

CHAPTER 5
Masaya Interlude

*I*n my biography of my late and sorely missed friend Marvin Zindler, *White Knight in Blue Shades*, I wrote about the awesome power of photographs. Over the years I have witnessed this power many hundreds of times, with some of the most memorable experiences being in Nicaragua.

On a Sunday not long after the mysterious explosion near the hospital, my team and I were taken to Masaya, a heavily populated but picturesque area in southwest Nicaragua. We were taken through the region's capital city, which was also called Masaya, and we traveled through several other small villages and towns too, as well as the farmlands. In one village I took a Polaroid picture of an elderly gentleman, and I handed the picture to him as it slid out of the camera. He stood looking at it in a very quizzical manner, so I said in my halting Spanish, "Just wait, have patience. Hold it to the sun and then the picture will appear."

It was a routine I had been through many times before. Most folks, particularly the children, would break out into a big smile when they saw the image appear. But this old man stared without smiling, even after the picture had developed. For several moments he just stood there looking at it in utter amazement, saying nothing.

To break the silence I said, "*Es muy bonito.*" ("It's beautiful.")

He stood there shaking his head and finally said in Spanish, "Only a god can produce an image like this."

I smiled and assured him that I was not a god. "It is simply science and chemistry," I explained.

He kept shaking his head and finally he said that he wanted to go to his house. He held his hand out to me, inviting me to come along.

We walked together up the dirt path, a gentle incline leading to a one-room mud brick house with a thatched roof. Upon entering his home the first thing I noticed was a small alcove on the back wall of the room. Tacked to the wall in the center of the alcove was a simple but lovely hand-carved wooden cross, and below that were several small candles. Clearly it was a shrine, and this is where he placed the Polaroid. He then crossed himself and said a silent prayer, after which he turned to me with a big smile and said, "When my time comes, I will give them this. When I am gone, they will have something to remember me by. I have never had a photograph."

Although this man's response was unusually reverent, it wasn't far removed from other responses the team and I had seen, particularly from the families of our young patients, when we gifted them with the before-and-after photos of their children. Freely giving away photos might seem like a small thing to people who are used to abundance, but it was deeply appreciated by the poor people of Nicaragua, and I can't overstate the role these small offerings played in building rapport as we traveled in the countryside. When we visited the farms and plantations and presented photos along the way, many people refused to accept the photos until we would accept some fruits, vegetables, or eggs in return. Our guide told us that it was only proper for us to show our appreciation by accepting these gifts.

As a plastic and cosmetic surgeon, I have had to make photography a necessary part of my everyday medical practice. But long ago it also became a nearly obsessive hobby, as reflected in my equipment purchases. On this trip I had brought what at the time were state-of-the-art cameras and accessories: Nikon and Pentex cameras with various types of extended, wide-angle and telephoto lenses. I'd had precious little time to indulge in my hobby on this trip, so I was all too eager to take the cameras with me on a rare leisurely jaunt into the countryside. I kept busy photographing what must have seemed like mundane, everyday activities to the locals, but were rarely seen or appreciated by the average American. I particularly enjoyed photographing the very young, especially at play, as well as close-ups of the faces of the very old. Both ends of the age spectrum have their own very appealing and unique character, and set within the environs of the Nicaraguan countryside they made for some truly outstanding photographs, if I do say so myself.

No doubt about it: photography has come a long way in the years since I first visited Nicaragua. At that time the digital revolution was still years in the future. Everything was on film back then, and I carried more than 100 rolls, half of which were black and white. At that time, I was striving to master the techniques of black-and-white photography, which was no small challenge. Timing was everything: it was the location of the sun and the casting of shadows that made the difference between a mediocre black-and-white photo and a great one. With trial and error I learned that the best results could be obtained early in the morning, when the sun was just coming up, or later in the day, as it was about to set. But I found that I could not achieve the same results at midday, when the sun was directly overhead and the shadows that brought out the striking characteristics in the faces of the very old and the very young were absent.

Those who have grown up in the age of computers and digital photography may take a lot for granted, and more power to them, but I honed my skills back in the time when you had to plan your photo in natural lighting. There were no computers to make easy corrections, create highlights, or soften backgrounds. Professional photo retouching existed, of course, but it was laborious, expensive, and not normally accessible even to the most dedicated amateur. When you pushed the button you heard the click as the shutter opened and then closed ... and that was the picture you got. It was permanent and it was not correctable, and you could never carry enough rolls of film to allow you to just keep clicking away until you got it right. If you ended up discarding the photo, you had wasted not only time but money as well.

In those years, photography was an art. But today, with computers, I see it more as a science, though it may still take an artist's eye to achieve the most stunning results. In any case computers have completely changed the approach to photography. During my earlier visits to Nicaragua and other areas, I carried a special piece of luggage that I had designed myself; it had carefully hand-cut padding to fit all of my lenses and cameras. In addition, I had a lead-lined case in which I kept my film so it would not be inadvertently exposed, particularly at airport check-ins with their X-ray scans.

Today with digital cameras and a chip, all that has become passé. Lenses that we'd never thought possible thirty or forty years ago exist today, designed by computers, with the glass cut by lasers. One lens can provide close-up, intermediate, and telephoto capabilities. For most photographers, there is no longer a need to carry a special case weighing over forty pounds. It's true that there are "extreme" photo lenses used by sports and wildlife photographers, but most of us travel a lot lighter these days.

That said, I still enjoy taking black-and-white film photos. The biggest problem today is that even in a big city like Houston there are few places available that will develop both black-and-white and color prints. But these prints are developed by hand on heavy-duty Kodak paper that will last years longer than the average print produced on the glossy thin paper with inks from a computer, which may last 15-20 years at the most. They may even begin to fade in 10 years. It is a shame that the public is not more aware of this, that they don't know their photos will not be viewable in two or three decades. Of course many folks probably assume that they will always have a digital copy available and can print out another one whenever they want, but I think it is a mistake to take anything for granted. To me there's still nothing like the lasting power of a good quality printed photo.

* * * * *

Marbles seems to be one of the most popular games for youngsters in many parts of the world, particularly in some of the countries I've visited in the Middle East and Central America. I can remember playing marbles myself as a child, but you really don't see kids playing it in the U.S. today. Walking through one of the villages near Masaya that Sunday, we came across half a dozen children covered in dust and dirt, engaged in a game of marbles in front of a small house. They had no shoes; the boys only wore shorts, and the girls had tattered, torn, and dirty T-shirts over their shorts. They were probably six to eight years old.

There was a circle drawn in the sand in front of the house, and lines were drawn several feet outside of the circle. Several multi-colored marbles lay in the center of the circle, and I saw that each child had a larger marble called a shooter. Before I got out of the car I attached my telephoto lens to my camera, because I wanted to stay as far back as possible while still capturing the earnest expressions on the faces of the players, who clearly took their game very seriously. I didn't want to disturb them. It was late in the day, and the angle of the sun was perfect: the shadows were long and the serious little faces well defined. I couldn't have wished for more.

The kids looked up momentarily as I stepped out of the car, but then went back to their game. Perfect. I got down on the ground on my stomach and found a soft spot in the sandy soil to position my elbows. I then focused in on the group. I first watched the interplay between the older, more experienced boys and the younger children. There was one girl about seven or eight years old, and she was a real tomboy – she was feisty and seemed to be holding her ground against the six boys she was playing with. She had curly hair that was very light, almost blond, and was wearing a shirt that looked as if hadn't seen a good washing in many a month.

The game the children was playing was simple but took skill. You had to keep your shooter behind the designated line, and then you would place it between your thumb and index finger and fire it into the circle, hoping to knock one of the smaller marbles outside of the circle. If you achieved this, you got to keep the marble that you'd knocked out, and then you could go again. If that didn't happen, then the next person took his or her turn.

It was a child's game, I thought, but it was also gambling. If you were skilled you won many of the marbles, which you kept and took home. If you were a winner that meant the others were the losers. It was a good life lesson in skills and sportsmanship, as well as a way of teaching that not everyone can be a winner.

Miracles in Bedlam

These are the lessons that I think are lacking in our modern educational and social system in the U.S. I see examples of this lack whenever I watch a little league baseball game or other event in which children are participating. The winning team always gets a trophy or a medal, which is to be expected, but all too often it seems that the losers have to receive a trophy or medal as well, a consolation prize if you will. I don't think that this prepares kids for the future. They won't always have someone there, ready to bestow an award upon them to soothe their disappointment or their hurt feelings. The hard truth is that in real life there are winners and there are losers, and everyone does not get a medal simply for participation. Certainly children need to learn that there's no shame in losing if you gave it your best shot, and that just because you fail at one endeavor, it doesn't brand you as a loser in life. It isn't a judgment on your worth as a human being. But all of these profound truths are muted or lost when everyone receives a prize or award for each and every effort.

The children who get patted on the back for everything they do are developing a misplaced sense of entitlement at a very young age. This won't do them any good when they reach college age and are trying to get into a university with limited enrollment and strict academic standards. It will do them even less good when they have a job and are competing with others who are as skilled as, or more skilled than, they are. Being in an environment where they are judged on merit – on results rather than simply on effort or intention – can be a shocking experience, and it's a hard lesson for someone to have to learn in their twenties, when they should have learned it as a youngster.

I was mulling over these matters when I realized that a new marbles game was starting, and I returned my focus to the activity. I began shooting photos of the group as well as some of the individual players. Their facial expressions as they lined up their shooter to take their shots, and the unadulterated glee on their faces when they were successful, made for the some of the best black-and-white photos that I was able to capture on this trip.

After taking a series of black-and-white shots, I stood up and took out my favorite good-will ambassador, my Polaroid camera, and walked toward the circle of players. Even as I approached them they were so engrossed in the game that they were still paying little attention to me as I took some Polaroid photos. As I came closer, however, a few of them looked up. The first to speak was the little girl, who asked who I was and what I was doing there.

I sat down in the sand next to them, told them my name and then handed them each a Polaroid. The pictures had not yet developed and the little girl kept turning her photo over, front to back, with a puzzled expression. I took her hand and held it out so the sun could expedite the chemical process, and the others in the circle did the same. As the photos began to appear the children were all smiles and giggles, and eagerly showed each other their pictures. I got up and stepped back again from the circle, and began taking close-ups with my 35mm Nikon.

Suddenly the littlest child broke from the circle and ran toward a group of mud-brick, thatched-roof homes about twenty yards away. It was only seconds later that I heard the squeak of iron hinges as the heavy handmade wooden door of one of the homes flew open, and I heard approaching footsteps.

A large and well-endowed woman of medium height appeared. Her hair was graying at the roots, and she was dressed in a light blue faded blouse and a well-worn yellow skirt with smears of dirt on the pocket near the waist. Like most of the women in the area, she was wearing sandals. Her eyes quickly scanned to where the children were seated and had been playing marbles, and then she looked nervously toward me, but did not step any closer.

I could see in her eyes and her gaze that she was questioning what this stranger was doing here. Then after a few moments she grinned broadly, as if to say, *I'm about to get some answers*. Despite the grin, her eyes told me that she was still a little unsure and cautious. I'm sure she was wondering what this gringo was doing on a sugar plantation so far from the city.

I quickly introduced myself and explained I was one of the doctors with the medical team that was working in the Children's Hospital in Chinandega.

At once she handed the little girl the Polaroid photo and ran forward like a bull charging the cape of a matador. Before I knew it her arms were around me in a big bear hug, and she was kissing me on both cheeks, taking me completely by surprise. As she finally loosened her grip, we were standing inches apart and eye to eye.

The first thing she said was, "It's the miracle baby."

"*Si, si.*"

The hugging commenced again. As she backed off she shouted something to the children, and several of the boys came over to me, wanting to shake my hand. The little girl just stood there looking up at me, so I knelt down so she could kiss me on the cheek.

The oldest of the boys handed me his shooter and a leather pouch full of marbles. He took me by the hand to the circle and explained that in the game they were playing, I should take some of the marbles from the pouch in the center circle. Though I was familiar with the game, I let him talk me through it. I stood there patiently and listened, after which he reached up, took my hand and pulled me down to the ground.

I knew the rules of the game, but I wanted to see what would happen if I placed my hand at the edge of the circle and lined up a shot. The other children had gathered around me, and the woman stood a few feet away, laughing.

As I was preparing to take the shot, the little girl clasped her hands over mine, shaking her head and saying, "No! No!"

She pointed to the line drawn in the sand, from which I was suppose to take the shot, and then she pushed my hand backwards. I don't know if the boys were being polite in allowing me to take the shot from the edge of the circle, or if they were afraid to criticize me, but this little girl had no such reservations. She was insistent that I follow the rules.

I slid back and repositioned my hand along the line, and she said, "Si, si."

I took my shot, and as a multi-colored green and yellow marble popped outside the circle they all started to clap. The oldest boy picked the marble up, put it into my left hand, and said that I should put it in my pocket. It was a game of winners and losers, after all, and the rules stipulated that if you knocked the marble out of the circle, you got to keep it.

I moved around to the other side of the circle to get a better shot, and a beautiful red and gold speckled marble flew out of the circle, resulting in more clapping. The oldest boy retrieved this one too and pushed it into my pocket.

On the third shot I hit the marble but it didn't get completely outside the circle. There was a discussion in rapid-fire Spanish amongst the children. The best I could understand was that they were trying to determine who would have the next shot following me.

The little girl pushed her way through the circle and took up her position with shooter in hand; she was playing it smart. The marble that I had most recently struck was right at the edge of the circle, and even a light touch would bring it outside; it was a sure thing. She took the shot successfully, after which she picked up the marble and opened her little leather pouch, placing it inside with a big smile as she repositioned herself for the next shot.

She was actually pretty good. She took out three more marbles, and I could see the turned-down corners of the mouths on the boys who were standing around. They were losing, to a girl no less. Several others took their turns. I went to return the marbles that I'd won but they rejected my offer. Even in a simple game of marbles they fully understood the concept of winners and losers.

After a while the mother stepped forward again, saying that it was very hot, and asking me if I wanted some water. I said yes, and she turned to go back to her house, inviting me to follow. "Before we go," I said, "Could I take a picture of you?" I pointed to the Polaroid camera and then to her, and she shook her head no, pointing down at her soiled blouse, apron and skirt.

Clearly she felt that she was not appropriately dressed for a photograph, so I didn't push it. We walked to her house and she motioned for me to sit down on a wicker rocking chair on her little porch. She disappeared into the house, and a couple of minutes later came back out with a blue plastic cup. At the far corner of the house was a rainspout that emptied into a large wooden barrel held together at the top and bottom by hand-forged steel bands. It was probably more than 100 years old, I thought, watching her as she filled the cup from the water in the barrel. There was a layer of green algae growing in the water, but she pushed it aside before she dipped the cup into the rain barrel. When the cup was full she came to where I was sitting, and with a big smile, handed the cup to me. Surprisingly, even in this heat, the cup felt cold in my hand. I hesitated a moment and she smiled even more broadly, saying, "*Agua.*"

I was keenly aware that it was water, but couldn't help wondering, a little uneasily, what else might be growing in it. I was well aware that the locals had developed a resistance to most of the organisms in the water, but there was still a high infant mortality rate due to dysentery. No telling what the local microflora and fauna might do to my own system. My brain was working overtime as I thought of all the possible consequences of accepting this good woman's hospitality. I mentally reviewed the immunizations I had taken before making the trip, including the painful typhoid and paratyphoid shots. I was also thinking that I had a good stock of Cipro antibiotic should it come to that.

She was still standing there smiling down at me, but I needed a few more moments to think this out. I pulled a large bandana-like handkerchief from my pocket so I could wipe the beads of perspiration from my forehead and scalp as I mulled over my next step.

Finally I decided that I had a duty to accept her gesture of hospitality; I could not reject the glass of water. I returned the handkerchief to my back pocket, then took a sip, and decided that if a small amount might be harmful, the entire glass couldn't be any more harmful – and besides, I was thirsty. I drank all of it.

She reached out again to take the empty glass and asked if I wanted any more. I politely declined, telling her I'd had all I needed.

My driver Julio had been sitting some distance away on the right front fender of the Jeep, and she looked over at him and began to wave to him to come up to the house. He trotted past the children still playing marbles, and up the steps to the porch.

Julio introduced himself and she took the same blue cup, went to the rain barrel, and with her left hand parted the green algae growing on top of the water as she filled the glass. Julio did not hesitate; he drank a glass and then refilled it himself, thanking her.

Then she sat down in a rocking chair next to mine, while Julio positioned himself on the hand-carved wooden railing at the edge of the porch. She began asking him a series of questions in Spanish, and after a couple of minutes of this I interrupted, asking her to slow down a little so I could understand her better. She did so, and I could indeed better understand what she was saying, but even so I let Julio answer most of her questions. She asked if the "miracle baby" was doing well, and if the mother was okay, and if I was the physician that some of the people called "Dr. Angel." And the questions went on and on.

Suddenly I heard a distant sound that might have been gunfire, and immediately my adrenaline began to flow as my eyes scanned the sugarcane fields stretched out in front of us. I'm sure my facial expression must have betrayed my concern, because our hostess quickly explained, "We hear gunfire every few days; the sounds are soft and muffled because they are far away. The Sandinistas would not come out here anyway, because we are poor. There is nothing for them here. If they want sugarcane there are hundreds of miles of it but it is of no value to them."

I glanced over to where the children were playing marbles. They hadn't even seemed to notice the sound; they just went on with their game.

Julio shrugged his shoulders at me and continued his conversation with the woman. Then I noticed her pointing to the camera and telling Julio that she was now ready to have her photo taken. She looked at me with a mysterious grin, and the twinkle in her eye told me in no uncertain terms that I had made a new friend. And as much as I cherish the work we do on these medical missions, I cherish even more the friendships I make with local medical staff, with patients and their families, and with randomly encountered people like this woman. It is the friendships that will stay with me long after my days in these remote areas are behind me.

Joseph Agris, M.D.

CHAPTER 6
Love Stings

The following week was very hectic, marked by the controlled chaos that we had come to accept as normal, and when Sunday rolled around again, I felt that the team deserved a half-day off to recuperate. For myself, I decided to take a leisurely walk through the surrounding jungle, and perhaps visit one of the nearby villages. Cameras in hand as always, I began my stroll down a well-traveled dirt path that was almost a tunnel through the tangled undergrowth of the surrounding jungle. In most places, the sun had likely not touched the road in years, unable to pierce the seemingly impenetrable walls and rooftop of the trees.

While I explored on my own with my cameras, other members of the group had their own ways of spending their Sunday. After church services, some went to the beach at San Juan del Sur. Hugo and Haydee Holmann had a beautiful home overlooking the ocean, and they had graciously opened it to the medical team. Other members of the community with beachfront homes made similar offers to the group of doctors and nurses, so everyone had a chance to enjoy a peaceful day, either in the coolness of the jungle shade or on the pristine beach.

After I had walked for a while, I came upon a small village of modest homes, some built of locally-produced brick, and some obviously constructed of materials salvaged from other buildings that had been abandoned or severely damaged in one of the storms that frequently struck the region. As I reached what appeared to be the center of the village, I came upon a group of children at play.

Most of the dozen or so children were no more than six or seven years old. Their multicolored T-shirts were tattered and torn; some were in shorts, while others wore slacks that were badly in need of washing. All were hot and clearly exhausted, but they were talking excitedly amongst themselves, the presence of an elderly ice cream vendor most likely having something to do with that excitement. Unable to help myself, I took out my camera and began photographing them and the unfolding scene around me.

An older girl in her teens seemed to be watching over the group. She walked up and introduced herself, saying her name was Elizabeth, and asking me my name and what I was doing there. I found her obvious protectiveness of her charges so charming that I forgave her apparent suspiciousness, and I attempted to answer her in my admittedly halting butchery of the Spanish language. Apparently my answers satisfied her, for the querying look in her face melted into a warm smile, and she even occasionally laughed at my mispronunciations.

After we had properly introduced ourselves, I turned to the children, shook their hands, and asked each of them his or her name, telling them mine in return. Turning back to Elizabeth, I asked in my halting Spanish, "Would they like some ice cream?"

She responded, "I'm sure they would love it, but there are quite a few of them. Can you afford to buy ice cream for all of them?"

I smiled and nodded, saying," *Si, si.*"

The children rushed toward the older gentleman and his ice cream cart, almost running him down in their zeal. Hands were in the air in every direction, and excited little voices were yammering nonstop. The old man seemed frustrated by the commotion, so I turned to Elizabeth and told her we needed to get the children into an orderly line or there would be no ice cream. I asked her if she could please explain that to them.

Once the initial excitement subsided and the children fell into line, the vendor began to pass out the small ice cream cones. Most were vanilla, but we found several chocolate ice cream cones and handed those out as well. Then the fun really started. To my surprise, the kids took turns licking each other's ice cream, so that each got a good taste of both the chocolate and the vanilla. It was a sight to behold – the ice cream was on their lips, on the tips of their noses, and dripping down their chins in the heat of the day.

Suddenly and seemingly out of nowhere, a looming shadow emerged in my peripheral vision. I turned and saw that the shadow belonged to a massive woman who was now standing in the door, hands on her hips. In both her appearance and her demeanor, she could not have created a greater contrast to the children. She was tall, probably close to six feet, and must have weighed at least 300 pounds. Her huge pendulous breasts were tucked into a loose fitting blouse. A multi-striped apron, smudged with flour, protruded at her waist, and she wore a long skirt that came down almost to her blue plastic sandals. She had unkempt hair that cascaded around her broad shoulders; her skin was dark brown, and other than a few pockmarks on her face, there were no imperfections that I could see. She was really quite striking, if a little intimidating because of her size and the scowl on her face.

For a few tense moments she scrutinized us, looking at the children and at me in a very questioning and almost suspicious manner. Then suddenly her mouth turned up into an infectious smile.

I felt my own smile grow as I looked at her. I couldn't help it. She continued to stand there with feet planted and hands on her hips, and as she and I made eye contact, both of us began to laugh. At once the children ran up to her, proudly displaying their ice cream cones.

She gathered up the end of her floury apron and wiped their faces as I stepped back a few feet and began taking photos. It was a scene of pure joy; they were all having a good time, children and Mamma alike.

I approached the ice cream vendor and paid him. Then he lifted the stainless steel latch and popped the hood; there was only one more cone remaining, which he handed to me. I took out some money but he refused. As soon as the cool ice cream touched my lips, it provided a wonderful, sublime respite from the oppressively hot and humid day. Finally, and with some reluctance, I waved goodbye to the children. Some of them came up to me and gave me a hug. I knew it was time for me to begin my long trek on foot out of the jungle on my way back to Chinandega.

I knew that tomorrow would be a full day in the operating room, and the clinic would also be active. New patients were due to arrive, but hopefully not in the almost overwhelming numbers of the past week.

As I walked, I was taking a mental inventory of the children's ward, bed by bed. In my mind, I was reviewing each child and each procedure, and trying to figure out which of my young patients might be well enough to discharge tonight or in the morning. It was an important matter because I knew that we would need at least thirty to forty beds for tomorrow's new post-op patients.

I was moving along at a trot now on a dusty, gravel-strewn donkey path, passing under large beautiful banyan and other tropical trees. My reverie was shattered by a wild pig that dashed across the path in front of me. Some of these creatures can be quite aggressive and dangerous, but this poor pig was probably just as startled as I was, and he quickly disappeared into the underbrush.

As I continued on my way, I found myself thinking again about the situation with Michael and Marta. By now Michael had a bad limp, and he'd seemed to be in real pain when I saw him last. Despite his obvious and worsening discomfort, he still refused to allow any of us to examine his leg, saying that he'd just bumped it and that it was getting better. *Then why the limp?* I wondered.

At last I reached Chinandega and went to the home of Don Roberto, where I showered and changed, and then walked to the hospital. My nurses JoAnne and Elia were circulating on the wards with the local nurses, tending to the children – changing bandages, checking on IV's, and dispensing medications. I pulled the clipboard that was hanging on the wall by the door, and Elia and I began going from bed to bed, making a list of the children who would be healthy enough to leave in the morning. We carefully questioned the patients, their parents, and the local nurses about each child. It took several hours to visit all of them, answer their questions, and evaluate their medical status.

When we finished at last, I turned to Elia and asked how everyone else on the team was doing. She said most of them had gone to San Juan for the afternoon, while others went to the market. I asked if anyone had seen Michael. JoAnne responded that she had seen him earlier in the morning, and he was walking with even more difficulty than the day before. She said that not surprisingly, he had left with Marta.

Michael's leg continued to worry me. I made up my mind that when he came to the hospital the next morning, we would examine his leg regardless of his protests.

All things considered, apart from worrying about Michael and his leg – and, of course, the breaking of "the rules" – this had been a delightful day. I had enjoyed a much-needed rest, a quiet morning in the countryside with my camera, and most of all, the time I had spent with the children. And since all of the post-op patients were looking well, with no problems to speak of, I smiled to myself, thinking, *life is good.* But now that I had completed the tasks I had set out to perform, I decided to take another short walk and get a better feel for just how far the relationship between Michael and Marta had progressed. I really couldn't put off dealing with it any longer.

* * * * *

The walk to Marta's house took only about ten minutes, as she lived a short distance beyond a cheerfully bubbling creek outside of Chinandega, on the edge of a sugarcane plantation, in one of a cluster of a half-dozen mud-brick homes with tin roofs. The homes were situated around a water well, and some had small vegetable gardens, and the occasional fruit tree. Still unsure as to what I would say to the couple, I approached Marta's house and knocked on the door. I could hear Marta and Michael moving about and speaking in low tones inside, so I waited. After a couple of moments, Marta lifted the heavy iron latch, and pulled open the massive wood door, its rusty hinges grating loudly. She invited me in, and between her nervousness at my arrival and Michael's disheveled appearance, it was obvious to me that I had interrupted an intimate encounter.

Glancing around the room, I noticed that her home had a dirt floor, and that there was almost no furniture and few amenities. No pictures or photos hung on the interior walls, which were plastered but unpainted. On the floor in one corner of the room was a mattress with wrinkled bedcovers. There were no closets for clothes, but closets really weren't necessary because most people here had only two or three articles of clothing anyway. The few clothes that Marta owned hung from wooden pegs that lined one wall. On the wall opposite the door were several hand-cut wooden boards that had been formed into shelves, laden with cooking utensils and some personal items. The room was poignantly indicative of a simple life, shaped by the deprivations of war and by an almost complete lack of materialism.

After a few moments, sensing the uneasiness that hung in the room, I decided that it was best to deal first with my primary concern, Michael's leg, and to wait until a less stressful time to talk with them about their relationship. I began speaking in the blunt efficient manner that we doctors so often use, saying, "Michael, you seem to be favoring that leg even worse than you were yesterday. I know that you would prefer that I ignore it, but I can't do that any longer. My personal concern for your well-being aside, you are having a hard time keeping up with our admittedly hectic schedule at the hospital, and I need you and everyone else to be at your peak performance if we're going to give these children the care they need."

Michael said nothing, just stood there looking miserable, so I added, "Aside from the obvious pain you are feeling, you also seem to be soaked in sweat, and I'm worried that you might have an infection that could easily be passed on to our patients."

At this point, Marta spoke up. "He is wet because I dumped a pan of water on him. He was burning up. I've tried to get him to have his leg looked after, but he refuses. I'm angry not just at him, but at myself, too. I should have known better as a nurse, and made him see one of the doctors.

"All men are stubborn, particularly when it comes to needing a doctor. It must be the testosterone and the macho-ism. I always thought it was unique to Spanish males, but it seems to be characteristic of all men."

I turned to face Michael, and told him, in no uncertain terms, "We are going to the hospital now, and we're going to take care of that leg. I won't have one of my team lose a leg or be eaten up by an infection, just because he is stubborn."

The walk to the hospital, a distance that had taken me only ten minutes, would have been torture for Michael, so we enlisted the help of one of Marta's neighbors, a merchant named Felix. I offered him a few córdobas to give us a ride to the hospital in the horse-drawn cart he used to transfer his goods to the market in town. He refused the money, and we helped Michael into the cart and were on our way.

The road was bumpy, and I could see Michael wince every time we hit a rut. When we crossed over the small river, the rutted road was replaced by smoothly paved streets, which made the ride smoother and marginally more comfortable. But clearly Michael was still in pain.

As we continued south into the center of Chinandega toward the hospital, I knew that my team was already there making afternoon rounds in the wards, changing dressings, and tending to the other needs of our little patients. When we turned onto the street leading to the veranda outside the hospital, one of the nurses saw us from a distance and came running up the street toward us. Like the rest of us, she had noticed Michael's worsening condition, and assumed that we were here to finally take care of it. She thought it best that we take Michael to the far end of the building where the emergency room was located, rather than through the main entrance. I agreed with her, and they headed in that direction. At this point, I went ahead into the hospital to check again on my patients, satisfied that at least this part of Michael's problem was being taken care of.

Marta later told me that as they had approached the hospital, the nurse had directed Felix to the emergency entrance. He drove his cart through the curve and then helped Michael as he hopped toward the entrance gate. Marta was on a first-name basis with the armed guard at the gate. She had explained the problem, and the guard opened the gate immediately, but said he would not let Felix enter. Marta thanked Felix and offered him money once again, which he had emphatically rejected, saying, "The American doctors are doing so much for the children here and from my village, this is the least I can do for one of them."

The guard then slung his automatic weapon over his shoulder, pushed the gate closed, and dropped the heavy metal bolt. Placing an arm under Michael's shoulder, he helped Michael into the building. There were several other patients sitting on wooden benches outside the emergency room waiting for the doctors, and they gawked as the guard half-carried Michael into the emergency room, then helped him up onto the gurney.

Michael pulled up his trouser leg as the unshaven, burly guard leaned forward to peer at the angry looking wound on Michael's leg. He shook his hand and turned to Marta, proclaiming, "That's a scorpion sting."

Marta thanked him and he returned to his post at the gate. Then she turned to Michael and said, "We have a diagnosis from an experienced local. He says that this is a scorpion sting." What she did not say aloud was something she and Michael both knew: Michael had sustained the sting in her house, on one of the first nights he visited her. Scorpions, spiders, and a variety of nasty insects were always a hazard in this part of the world, but marginally less so in some of the more soundly built structures such as the hospital, or the fine homes in which most of my team members stayed at night. In any case, this sting, or bite, or whatever it was, had happened under her roof, and she felt responsible.

Michael, apparently reclaiming some of his previously indignant attitude, stated a bit more forcefully than appropriate, "I want to hear a diagnosis from a local doctor."

Shaking her head in frustration, Marta left the emergency room for the interior of the hospital, in search of a doctor. Michael's wound was steadily growing worse, not better, and there was no time to waste.

CHAPTER 7
The Fever And The Cure

W hen Marta left Michael in the emergency room she immediately came looking not for a local doctor but for me, finally finding me as I was completing the rounds of the children's ward with my team. I could tell that she was worried. She explained to us that she was sure that Michael had been stung by a scorpion, or perhaps bitten by a spider or insect, and that it now appeared that the wound had begun to abscess. She said that she didn't have a thermometer, but that his body felt extremely warm and feverish.

Kimberly, who was always outspoken, often to the point of being quite blunt, said, "You're right, honey. But the fever is between his legs, and you are the heater." A couple of the nurses' mouths dropped open with a gasp. They turned first toward Marta, then to me, gauging our reaction, as this was probably the first open acknowledgement of the affair of which apparently everybody was aware. Marta's face instantly flushed crimson, and I knew I had to derail the inevitable conversation if I hoped to handle the forbidden relationship in a professional manner.

I blurted out, "Let's examine Michael, deal with the medical problem, and get him healthy. Ladies, I want you to stay here and finish changing the dressings."

Grabbing Marta by the wrist, I said, "You are coming with me." As we started out of the children's ward, the others just stood there, frozen in place. I looked back over my shoulder, and seeing them still standing, I barked out, "Get to work. We have patients to take care of; that's what you came here for." They immediately scattered, almost running to their tasks. They knew me well enough to know that I was normally pretty easygoing, but they also knew that when my demeanor became gruffer, it was best to do exactly as they were told. For myself, I didn't like being a hard-ass, but knew that if I didn't handle this situation in a strictly professional way, it could turn into a nightmare among the staff.

When we arrived in the emergency room, Michael blinked a few times and pushed himself up straighter in the bed, grabbing the handrails on either side for support. Michael looked first at Marta, then focused his gaze on me, his furrowed brow revealing the worry and indecision in his mind. I was his boss, and the senior surgeon on this team. He knew that his relationship with Marta was forbidden, and I suppose he was as worried about the potential repercussions as he was about the obviously intense pain in his leg.

I sensed his discomfort and turned my gaze to meet his. Michael's voice was low and sounded strangely unfamiliar, as though someone was speaking through him when he addressed me. "Dr. Joe, I guess we need to talk..."

At that point, he told me in a rush of words what I suspected he had refuted numerous times: the truth about his "secret" affair. All of his arrogance had disappeared. He admitted that he knew that this level of fraternization with the Nicaraguan staff was specifically forbidden, but said he just couldn't hide, much less deny the feelings he had for Marta. After describing, in the kind of detail typical of an adolescent crush, how the two of them had come to this point, he looked me in the eye and finished with a nervous, "So, Dr. Joe, now what?" Marta just stood there silently, her eyes cast downward. When Michael had finished his speech she asked if she could be excused, and I nodded curtly.

As deeply as I felt for Michael's predicament, I also knew that I needed to deal with one thing at a time in a professional manner. Sometimes, being the man in charge is particularly difficult, especially where my trusted staff are concerned. So as soon as Marta left I put on my "boss" face, and addressed him more sternly than I ever had before, saying, "Michael, this is how it has to be. You can no longer be a scrub nurse on this mission team, and you already know why. From this point on, you are a patient. You have a serious problem beyond your leg, but for now, I have to deal with one thing at a time, and right now I will deal with your medical problem."

Michael wiped the tears from his eyes, seemingly unsure which emotions were foremost in his mind: nervousness or relief. I'm pretty certain that he was feeling both at once. He lay back in the bed and closed his eyes, probably adding resignation to the burgeoning list of competing feelings.

We both remained silent for a couple of minutes, each weighing what we had to do. Then his leg twitched, and he grimaced with pain. "I can see that you are in a lot of pain," I said. "It must hurt like hell. It will continue hurting, and will no doubt grow worse as the abscess grows, until we open it up and drain it. I'll have a nurse bring you some medicine – antibiotics and something to ease the pain. But remember that we are limited in supplies and medication, and that you are taking away from what we brought for the children."

Tears streamed down Michael's cheek. He later told me that all he could think of at that moment was that he needed some time to himself. He needed to think about what was happening, and how to deal with the conflict he was feeling. As much as he loved his work with the team, so too did he love Marta. He knew that he would have to give up one or the other, but it was a decision he was loath to make, as either choice would be profoundly painful.

I turned to exit the room and leave Michael to his thoughts, and as I did so I drew a deep breath, and managed to switch mental tracks. Walking through the doorway into the corridor, I was alert, awake, and completely focused upon the surgical procedures and tomorrow's schedule. I was also anxiously looking forward to meeting the new residents, students, and nurses who would be rotating through the wards and operating room as part of the teaching program.

All of a sudden I realized that I was famished, which always happened when I was anxious. It was time for me to call it a day. We had a packed schedule on Monday.

As I proceeded down the corridor, I suddenly felt a lump in my throat, then my eyes began tearing up, and my breathing quickened as if I'd been running sprints. I thought to myself, *I worked my ass off all my life to be a doctor.* No one had given me anything. I was only ten years old when my father passed, leaving my mother with my two younger brothers and me. My mother had minimal education, and no savings to speak of. The hurdles we all faced had been immense, especially for my mother, left alone to fend for herself and her three young boys.

My mother's guidance was often punctuated with the back of a long wooden spoon, and my brothers and I – the Three Musketeers – often felt its "wisdom" imparted to our backsides. *I didn't get this far in my trip, or this far in my profession, for someone like Michael to screw it all up with his stupidity,* I thought. Conjuring up my best resolute façade, I cleared my throat and said good night to the staff. I felt certain that they couldn't pick up on the turmoil I'd been feeling, but I also knew that tomorrow was going to be a long day, for many reasons.

* * * * *

The first case the next day was a small boy who had been born with a cleft lip and palate, which in itself would have been an easy problem to deal with. But there were other potentially life-threatening conditions as well, which would require delicate surgery and which I knew could not be taken care of properly here in Chinandega.

However, it could all be easily done at the Texas Medical Center in Houston.

I turned to Elia, who was our "fixer." I told her we needed a visa for humanitarian and medical problems, and since she was fluent in English and Spanish, we asked her to prepare a letter to go to the American Embassy. We told her that the letter should be marked "Life Threatening" and "Urgent." I told her to describe the boy's family and their situation, and to also include photos. Elia needed to either drive herself or get a driver to hand-deliver the letter to embassy personnel. I wanted her to stress the urgency of the child's condition, so we could have the visa before we left, knowing that if we couldn't take the little boy back with us, it was never going to happen. It was easily Elia's most crucial task for the day.

I finished scrubbing and entered the operating room, which was filled with students and several doctors who had never seen a patient with this set of conditions. They were all curious, but anxious to learn. The child was already asleep and the nurse was washing the boy's face. I nodded to the anesthesiologist and got a thumbs-up. He was on one side of the O.R. table, and my nurse JoAnne was on the opposite side.

But when I looked around I noticed that nobody else was scrubbed and gowned. That pissed me off. I pointed to one of the local doctors and a resident, and picked two of the local nurses, telling them, "You are not going to learn anything standing out there. Get back in here, scrub up, put gloves and gowns on, and get next to this table and help." In an instant, the crowd parted as they literally ran to the scrub sink.

Though it might be tempting to chalk up my brief display of temper to the cumulative effect of the tension regarding Michael and Marta's drama, that wasn't a factor. Rather, I was driven by the awareness that our time here was limited, and I was committed to getting in as much training as possible. You can't train surgeons by just having them watch, and I was determined to leave better-prepared medical personnel behind when our mission was over. As I've said elsewhere, on our mission trips we not only perform the surgeries, but we also teach, and this includes hands-on procedures as well as lectures. We also leave equipment and supplies behind when we depart, so that the locals can carry out these procedures during our absence, until we return with the team the following year.

Once the errant personnel were scrubbed up and properly attired, I began demonstrating the use of the blue marking pen directly on the little patient's skin to lay out the procedures, explaining the benefits of doing so to those who had gathered around the table. Then, midway through my demonstration, we felt the building literally shudder. The sound echoed through the operating room, and even the overhead operating light began to shake. All I could think of was that we were under a mortar attack.

The nurse standing to my left gently tapped me on the shoulder, smiled reassuringly, and said, *"Mas trueno."* ("More thunder.")

If it was a lightning strike, it had to have been close by. Almost immediately, the skies opened up, and I could hear a heavy rain beating down on the tile roof above us.

Miracles in Bedlam

The rain broke the grip of the oppressive heat, and the room suddenly got cooler. At least that felt good. The nurse reminded me that we were entering the rainy season, and could expect these heavy showers pretty much every day.

So far, however, the electric power was still on, and I began the procedure with JoAnne's assistance. There were questions from all sides. From a teaching perspective, I couldn't have hoped for a better response, despite – or perhaps because of – my earlier scolding. The conversation was divided between English and Spanish so all could understand. I asked JoAnne to step towards the foot of the table and I motioned for the local doctor to come forward.

I placed the small scalpel in his hands and told him to continue the incision along the marked lines. His eyes met mine for a few seconds and then he did as I asked. As he proceeded, I guided his hand as needed and spoke softly to him, as I took more questions from the group. He did a smooth job of releasing the skin from the underlying muscle, and JoAnne picked up a small hook to retract it.

I then explained how to repair the muscle so that the lip would be functional as well as being aesthetically pleasing. I completed my side, then asked the doctor to do the same on his. It went very well.

I then showed the doctor and the others how to align the muscle and place the corner sutures. After that, I traded places with the senior resident, who was standing next to me, and told him to complete the suturing. He was hesitant at first so I pushed the suture and forceps into his hand. As he placed the first suture, I noticed a slight tremor in his hand movements, and realized that he needed reassurance to boost his confidence. "I know you have applied sutures in the course of general surgery. These surgeries and the principles are the same. They are just much smaller. Go slowly, and you will do fine."

JoAnne stepped aside and gave the suture scissors to one of the nurses, showing her how to position her hands. The surgery was completed in about an hour, with the end result being both functional and beautiful.

I can't stress enough that I actually think that teaching the procedures to the local doctors, residents, and students so they can continue the work is even more important than our performing the actual procedures themselves. This is what we came here for, to help these children, but also to teach the next generation of doctors. If our team can do that, we can accomplish so much more than we can with our own hands, no matter how practiced and skilled we might be. It is a realization that is at once humbling and immensely gratifying.

I told everybody we should go out in the hall and discuss the child's case – in particular the eventual treatment and expectations. The nurses were going to move a second operating table into the room so we could perform two procedures at a time, a policy we had already implemented in other operating rooms here and in other countries.

All of a sudden the main operating doors burst open, and we all jumped back. I thought to myself, *Is this an emergency?* No, it was the administrator and his assistant, both dressed in street clothes. Always conscious of the potential for infection by anyone not properly scrubbed and attired in the operating room, I shouted at him, "Get out, out! No street clothes in my operating room, get out!"

Both of them had irritated expressions on their faces, but they immediately turned and walked into the public hallway. I stepped under the arch of the doorway and asked what they wanted.

The administrator spoke first. "I understand you have sent someone to the American Embassy to apply for a visa for one of these children."

"Yes, I did."

"You didn't consult me."

"I didn't feel that was necessary."

"I am the administrator of this hospital."

I thought to myself, *Typical hospital politics, rearing its head where it doesn't belong.* This wasn't the first time and certainly wouldn't be the last that I ended up butting heads with hospital administrators.

I said, "Obtaining an American visa for this child is between the mother, the father, and the American Embassy. It has nothing to do with hospital administration."

He gave me a hard look and started to turn away, with his lackey falling in behind. I reentered the operating room. As soon as the operating room doors closed, the small crowd started to giggle and everyone began to clap, pleased that the administration in this case had been outgunned and outmanned.

Stepping back out into the hallway, I looked through the window onto the veranda where waiting patients had gathered. The skies were still black, pierced frequently by lightning overhead. The thunder clattered repeatedly, and raindrops that seemed as big as robin's eggs were splattering down by the bucketful. This was a true tropical storm. We had enough problems with rotating brownouts and the occasional destruction of a power plant by the Sandinistas. I was hoping that lightning wouldn't strike and knock out the power we needed in the operating room again, but the miracle baby incident had given me renewed confidence in our ability to work under conditions more common to a M.A.S.H. unit than a hospital. We would overcome.

While the O.R. was being set up with two tables and the next little patients were being brought in, I visited the other rooms to see if everything was going well. I stopped tableside to make some suggestions, and noticed that water was dripping in the corner of several of the rooms – not an ideal situation by any means, but at present not posing a significant problem. By the time I returned to the operating room I was working in, two children were on the tables and asleep. One had a wide double cleft lip and palate, which required more detail and experience, so I decided to start on that one myself. The other was a simple one-sided cleft lip, and the local doctor said that with the residents' help, he could do that one.

I assigned JoAnne to the table with them since she was my most experienced nurse. Carolyn joined me at the other table. As we began, the other residents and students crowded around. The thunder and lightning persisted, but we were all okay. Better than okay, actually, because I knew that in this weather, the military units would be hunkered down, unable to traverse the muddy roads to wage an attack. And that meant that for the time being at least, the team would be safe.

The procedures were progressing well, and we were at the point of closure when I noticed a drip, drip, drip striking my patient's abdomen. Thank goodness it was away from the area on which we were operating. Standing with one of the residents and a student nurse, who was helping him complete the suturing, I kept looking from left to right, following what he was doing and at the same time observing the leak in the roof. I grabbed a towel and rubbed it over the child's abdomen to soak up the drips. At first, it didn't seem to be a particular problem, but then I noticed flakes of green paint and white chips of plaster appearing on the towel. I hollered, "Shit! The ceiling is going to give way."

At that instant, a piece of plaster the size of my hand dropped onto the patient's abdomen, and another smaller piece fell at the foot of the table. I yelled to the anesthesiologist that we needed to move. She looked up and saw what was happening. The resident and nurse stopped suturing, and I told them to place a sterile cloth over the child's face and the wound. I stepped to the end of the table, released the lock and brake, and we all pushed the table to the side of the room. Our action came not a second too quickly, as even larger pieces of plaster began to break loose from the ceiling and strike the floor. It was only then that the doctors working on the adjacent table became aware of what was happening. I told them to release the wheel locks on their table and move it with the anesthesia machine as close as possible to the wall on the opposite side. The local doctor said he only had a few more sutures to place and he would be finished. He felt comfortable completing the procedure and waking the child up. A couple of the nurses who had run from the room now came back with stainless steel surgical basins and placed them in the middle of the room to collect the dripping water and crumbling plaster.

The ceiling seemed compromised only in the center, but along the walls it appeared intact. It wasn't as if we didn't have enough to worry about, operating with minimal equipment and supplies. The prospect of the ceiling cascading down on our patients was the icing on an already unpleasant cake. I turned to the local doctor and asked how long we could expect this heavy thunderstorm. He said usually until three or four in the afternoon, after which it would clear. I thought to myself, *Great, just great.*

But it seemed that a crisis had been averted for now, so with everything under control in my operating room, I went to check on the other rooms. I noticed that water was dripping down the wall in the far corner of one. They had already placed some basins there, but the ceiling still appeared to be sound, the lights were on, and everybody was proceeding as if nothing unusual was happening. I thought to myself, *Just another day in the operating room in Chinandega, Nicaragua.*

CHAPTER 8
Kicked Off The Team

With the ceiling problem under control for now, I needed a breather, and so did everyone else. I went from room to room and told everyone to take a half-hour break and get something to eat or drink, and we would start again at eight and continue until midnight or 1 a.m. By that time, the rain would certainly have stopped and the water trapped on the roof would have ceased dripping into the rooms.

At that moment I saw Sister Esperanza coming down the hall arm-in-arm with a distinguished looking gentleman, a bear of a man with a neatly trimmed white beard and mustache and salt-and-pepper hair. He had a big smile on his face. Sister Esperanza introduced him to me as Dr. Canteras, telling me that he was a general surgeon in the area who visited Chinandega and León when his services were needed. He stuck out a large powerful hand and as we shook, I presented him with a quick summary of Michael's problem, and my tentative diagnosis of a scorpion sting or insect bite, with a resulting abscess and cellulitis. I told him that the patient hadn't had anything to eat or drink, and that he had an IV and had been administered antibiotics, so we could proceed immediately with surgery. He moved to my side, threw his massive arm over my shoulder, and said, "Let's go see this unfortunate young man."

I took him down a long dark hallway to the small private room to which Michael had been moved. I introduced Michael to Dr. Canteras, telling our patient that he was the local general surgeon. I could see the pain in Michael's face, but he managed a weak smile and stretched out his hand to the doctor. Doctor Canteras asked Michael a few questions about his general health and about allergies he might have. Finally, he asked Michael, "When do you think this occurred?"

Michael answered, "The week before last, I think. I thought it would get better on its own, but it hasn't. It's only gotten worse."

The doctor then asked where he was hiking, in the mountains or forests.

Michael's face changed. He looked up through the small window at his left where the rain was still beating down and showing no signs of letting up. Then he turned back towards Dr. Canteras, looking wildly uncertain about how he was going to answer the doctor's question. I thought it would be easier for Michael if I asked Carolyn and JoAnne to leave the room, which they did, although Carolyn's expression showed that she was clearly not happy at the request.

Michael then began to phrase his answer in a voice unlike his usual one. Dr. Canteras listened quietly, but I could see he was trying to keep from smiling as he heard the story. He explained to Michael that this was a jungle, and that there were many insects, spiders, scorpions, and other creatures that could inflict such a wound. The doctor told him that the specific creature was not particularly relevant at this point, but that Michael had a large abscess and cellulitis, and the abscess needed to be opened and drained. I joined in, suggesting that after draining and debriding the wound, it would be best to be packed open rather than sutured closed. Dr. Canteras nodded in agreement.

Michael asked if a scorpion could have caused the wound, and the doctor said, "Yes, it could have been a scorpion, or any one of several other creatures, some that live in the jungle, and others that choose to hide away in people's homes, usually in their beds." I wanted to laugh at what the doctor had left unstated, but out of respect for Michael's pain, I didn't.

The doctor continued, "I can see in your face that you are worried about possibly losing your leg. Let me assure you, that is not going to happen. It needs to be opened immediately and drained. Once it is, the pain will go away just as quickly. He gave Michael a supportive smile and then said, "Anyway, what is life without love? Love can sometimes be very painful."

The nurses had re-entered the room and were standing next to Dr. Canteras as he explained this to Michael. The doctor continued, "The fact that you are here in the middle of a war zone shows that you are no wimp. Shit happens! I wouldn't beat myself up over it if I were you."

He let that sink in for a minute and continued, "I have really sick patients at the University Hospital in León. The weather is terrible, and the roads can wash out at any time, so I need to get back there. You are in good hands with Dr. Agris, and he can manage this quite well. It is just a shame that with the shortage of good personnel, a valued member of the medical team will not be able to participate in such fulfilling work."

Dr. Canteras then turned to me, shook my hand, and left the room.

Michael grabbed the arm rails, pushed himself up in bed with an agonized expression on his face, and said, "What now?"

I responded, "We are going to proceed with what needs to be done. The same thing I told you yesterday, and that Dr. Canteras has told you today, before you do end up losing your leg."

Michael said, "I'm not really sure I want to do this."

I told him, "You have no choice, but you do have a little time to think it over. Since this is an infected, dirty case, we won't operate until the entire surgical schedule is completed, which won't be until midnight or 1 a.m. As to that other matter, the rules are there for a reason, and they apply to everyone."

JoAnne looked like she was ready to fire a response back, but then her expression changed. She said, "Michael, you're scared. I understand that. But you brought this on yourself, and the procedure will have to be done."

Carolyn looked at Michael and said, "The pain medications we've given you are heavily addictive, and our supply of them is very limited. I don't want you to get hooked on them but I know you will need some."

Michael nodded, saying, "Yeah, I get it."

"I will give you some medication just before the surgery," Carolyn added.

I could see that JoAnne couldn't contain herself, and as she was walking out of the room she looked over her shoulder, grinned at Michael, and asked, "Was it worth it?"

He answered, obviously humbled by the reality of his situation. "Things just snowballed. I didn't think about the outcome. I didn't care, as long as I was with her." JoAnne rolled her eyes and exited, and Michael lay there, tears welling up in his eyes. He said to me, "I came on this mission to Chinandega to help and be a member of the team. Then this...this bright light, Marta, appeared in my life."

I looked at him crossly, shook my finger at him, and said, "But you weren't honest about it until you had no choice. I don't like people lying to me. It just doesn't sit well with me."

"Well, technically I didn't exactly lie to you. I just didn't tell you everything."

"A lie by omission is still a lie, and you know it," I said, visibly exasperated by now.

Michael was about to say something but I held up my hand, stopping him before he could begin. The pleading look on his face was painful to see. He bowed his head in resignation and mumbled, "The rules."

I turned to walk away, saying, "The only way to get you and the whole medical team out of this mess is to send you home as soon as you are able to walk on that leg." I doubt that I will ever forget the sound of him sobbing as I walked out the door.

* * * * *

I checked on the other operating rooms, saw that each was progressing well, and got the usual thumbs-up from the staff members who weren't completely immersed in their tasks. I then went to my operating room where the two O.R. tables had been pushed against the side walls, leaving just enough room for myself and the other doctor to squeeze in to perform our procedures. The catch basins in the center of the room had been taken out and dumped, then quickly replaced to catch the rain that continued to leak from the ceiling. To my relief, I saw that at least for now, the plaster was no longer sloughing off the ceiling and falling onto the operating room floor.

As the evening progressed, the rain slowed and finally stopped, and the operating room ceiling didn't seem to be quite as likely to crumble down on us. It was almost midnight. I told the local nurses that I would like for them to contact the hospital administrator in the morning to see if he could get some carpenters in here and put up some supports to shore up the ceiling, so we would not lose the use of the operating room in the next storm. I suggested they work through Sister Esperanza, who seemed always able to get things done. There were many people in the town who wanted to help, and one of the nurses said she was sure that Sister Esperanza could have carpenters there in the morning.

I then gathered the entire team of nurses, residents, and local doctors – all but the students, who had gone home. Once everyone was assembled, we went from bed to bed, changing dressings, examining the children, and talking with the parents and instructing them in the care of their children after leaving the hospital. There would be two evening nurses on each ward until 7:00 a.m., so I knew the patients would be in good hands.

I looked at the team and saw the profound weariness in their faces. It had already been a long day, and my own eyes were heavy, weighted by fatigue. I allowed myself the momentary luxury of closing my eyes and dropping my head, my chin resting on my chest. After only a few seconds, I remembered that there were still matters that could not be left till morning. Snapping my head up and forcing my eyes open, I announced to myself as much as to the staff members who were gathered around me, "We are not done."

I knew Carolyn and JoAnne would need about twenty minutes to finish up, but told the others that they could go home. "Thank you for your help. I hope you had a good experience and an educational day. Now, go home and get some rest."

They all nodded wearily. We all shook hands, and the residents thanked me, telling me that this had been the most instructive and best part of their rotation. I bid them good night and watched them as they left for their homes and, I am certain, their waiting beds.

Carolyn said she was going to the pharmacy to fetch some morphine to put into Michael's IV before we started. I shook my head and said, "I'm not that forgiving."

She said she was going to do it anyway, and despite my disappointment in Michael, I couldn't bring myself to tell her not to. I told her that while she was at it, she might as well give him his evening dose of antibiotic. I then turned to JoAnne and said, "I need a surgical pack, please."

She responded rather abruptly, saying, "No you don't. You are not wasting an entire surgical pack on him." Apparently, I was not the only one who was really angry with Michael. She continued, "All we need is a scalpel, a package of sterile sponges, a towel to put on the floor, and a bottle of Betadine scrub to clean his leg with."

I looked quizzically at JoAnne and asked her, "What's with the towel on the floor?"

"We will need to hang his leg over the side of the bed, because when you lance the abscess, there is going to be a lot of pus."

I smiled at her and said, "Very practical. Let's get this thing done."

Carolyn had just finished putting the morphine and antibiotic into Michael's IV when JoAnne handed her the pack of sterile sponges and the bottle of Betadine. JoAnne put her gloves on, then swung Michael's leg to the side of the bed with a bit of a jerk that caused Michael to wince from the pain.

She looked up at him with a big Cheshire Cat smile and said, "Sorry. You want a leather strap or bullet to bite on?" Michael's expression was confused and perhaps a bit frightened. He obviously didn't know whether she was serious or just teasing him.

While Carolyn was scrubbing Michael's leg with the antiseptic solution, JoAnne had turned away, so that Michael couldn't see her affixing the scalpel blade to the handle. I put on my gloves and she discreetly passed me the scalpel. I gave a quick nod to both nurses, and we began what was not going to be the most pleasant experience of Michael's day. While Carolyn pressed hard on his thigh, JoAnne grabbed the ankle and held it gently but firmly. I brought the scalpel down quickly, stabbing the abscess directly in its center. Our patient didn't even have time to scream, instead letting out a loud, agonizing gasp. I actually had to jump back as the foul-smelling ooze erupted from my incision. As JoAnne and Carolyn continued holding tight, I took some sponges and applied pressure on either side of the wound until it was evacuated. I looked up at Michael, who was gripping the rails so tightly that his fingers had turned white, and said to him, "Breathe. Breathe."

After taking in a few deep breaths, Michael let loose with a relieved, "Wow! The pain is almost gone." With that, JoAnne and Carolyn loosened their grip and lifted his leg back onto the bed. JoAnne put a pillow under his knee to elevate it, and while Michael was still appreciating the relief from the pressure and pain, I stuffed a couple of sponges into the wound to keep it open so it would continue to drain. JoAnne then lifted his ankle again, and we wrapped a surgical bandage around the wound and returned his leg to the pillows. Michael looked up at us, saying, "That's it?"

I responded, "What do you want me to say? Now it's IV fluids, antibiotics, keeping the leg elevated, and rest. This is what Dr. Canteras had said was necessary, remember? You may not have enjoyed the way we did the procedure, but it was effective and accomplished what was needed. I could not take you to any of the operating rooms because this is an infected, dirty case, and I was not going to risk contaminating the children. That is also why it was done at the end of the day. Sometimes, even good surgical techniques seem to border on torture." Then, with what was probably a bit more enjoyment than was called for, I added, "It's the *rules!*"

Michael pulled himself up with the arm rests and leaned forward so Carolyn could put a pillow behind him, He licked his dried lips and said, "Please. I know you don't expect this or want to hear it, but thank you. I know it hasn't been easy for you, any more than it has been for me. It sucks, actually."

I responded, "And, your point is...?"

"I just wanted to say thank you."

I couldn't help feeling my anger at him begin to waver, But I knew I had to remain steadfast or risk losing the ability to continue on these missions in the future. "As I told you earlier, Michael, you are not a team member anymore. You are a patient and will be treated like a patient. I have those rules for a reason, and I have to uphold and enforce them. No exceptions." He offered no reply, probably knowing at this point that nothing he could say would change my mind. I turned and headed for the door, but paused, turning back and saying, "I meant what I said. As soon as you can put weight on that leg, you are being sent home." Then I opened the door and walked out.

Exhausted, I shuffled down to the end of the hallway, where I met JoAnne and Carolyn. I told them, "It's after one in the morning, and the streets are dark. I still have some matters I should attend to here, but I'm going to walk with you to your hosts' homes. I'm tired and need a break and some fresh air, anyway." They knew me well enough not to bother trying to talk me out of it, so they gathered their things and out into the night we went.

During the heavy rains, the water had flooded the streets, but the sidewalks were clear and the still night air was cool. It was a pleasant walk, and none of us felt inclined to break the stillness with small talk, so very little was said. The silence was short-lived, however, as it was beginning to rain again. Since they typically returned to their hosts' homes very late, the nurses had been given keys that allowed them to enter without having to disturb anyone. After seeing them safely inside, I turned up the street toward the home where I was staying. I had decided to blow off the minor matters at the hospital. They could wait until morning.

Unlike the nurses, I didn't have a key, and when I arrived, I didn't want to ring the bell and disturb the entire household. I knocked gently at first, then a little louder. In short order, Miguel, one of the servants, opened the door with a big smile and a glass of iced tea in his hand, and addressed me as if it were nothing out of the ordinary to be receiving guests in the middle of the night. "We saved you something to eat. Where would you like to sit?"

"On the veranda, if that isn't too much trouble, Miguel. I feel like watching and listening to the rain." For it had suddenly started coming down quite heavily again, and I found the sound pleasant and relaxing after such a long, hard day.

"Of course, doctor. Oh, I almost forgot! I have a message for you. I will bring it." Miguel put the glass of tea down on the table, and when I sat down, he ran back into the house. A minute later, he came back with the message in his hand.

Apparently, Olivia, one of the nurses who was staying about a mile away, had called because she was having stomach pain and was very uncomfortable. She was requesting medication. I told Miguel to waken the driver, Julio, quickly before the rain could again flood the roads. I went to my room and gathered up my emergency kit and several vials of medications.

When I emerged from my room, Julio was standing in the hallway in a torn pullover, shorts, and sandals. I told him where we had to go and why. He didn't appear too enthusiastic about going, and said, "The weather is not good." I responded that we'd best get going before it got worse.

The roads were good until we reached the edge of town, where they had already turned to deep mud bogs. Fortunately, the Jeeps we were using always seemed to get through this kind of obstacle without any problems. By the time we pulled up to the home, the rain was now coming down in sheets, and the wind had picked up to a low howl. I could see the button high on the side of the double gates, so I jumped out, rang the bell, and quickly climbed back in the Jeep. There was no response. I ran out again, by now completely soaked, and figured, *what the hell*. I just stood there, ringing the bell.

There was no response. Either the bell wasn't working or they had lost power. The only way in was to go over the wall. I asked Julio to drive the Jeep right up to the gate. I climbed onto the hood of the Jeep, and lifted myself to the top of the wall, only to discover that there was barbed wire stretched along the top. I took off my jacket, which like me was already soaked, and threw it over the barbed wire. My plan was to cross over the wire and drop to the ground below. The plan lost its allure when I looked down and realized that the ground was more than ten feet below. I thought to myself, *No way!*

I could hear dogs barking from somewhere on the grounds, but with the heavy rain and darkness I could not determine from where the barking was coming. After thinking about it for a few seconds, I realized that this was not going to work. I removed my jacket from atop the barbed wire, dropped it to the hood of the Jeep, and climbed down. I was soaked through and through, so I took my shirt off and wrung it out, threw the jacket and shirt on the floor of the Jeep, and then climbed back in.

Julio looked at me and shrugged his shoulders. I nodded, and with my thumb I pointed for him to go back while we could still get out of there. I could see by his face that he was pleased with the decision.

The rain struck the windshield with such force that Julio could hardly see the road, even with the wipers slapping back and forth frantically. He drove slowly and carefully until we reached the edge of town. We made it, and saw that the roads had water on them, but they were asphalt rather than mud, and the driving would be easier. When we arrived at the house, we both jumped out. He unlocked the heavy double gates, and as we swung them open they creaked loudly on their hinges. He then drove the Jeep into the house and onto the foyer, and we closed the gates behind us. I looked at my watch, and saw that it was after 2:00 a.m.

I told Julio that if the roads were reasonably clear in the morning, he would have to drive me back out to the house where Olivia was staying before we went to the operating room. He nodded, then asked, "What time?"

"Five o'clock, please."

He looked both surprised and less than pleased, saying, "You will only get three hours of sleep."

"That's the life of a surgeon, Julio. I can always get a quick power nap while they are cleaning the operating rooms and bringing in the new patients."

My back hurt and I wanted a hot shower. Then, my punchy state kicked in and I laughed, thinking, *I'm already wet. All I need is a bar of soap.* Of course, the shower I needed was a world apart from the one I'd already had. I opted for another one, hot this time, and out of the wind.

After my shower, I went to the kitchen, gulped down a Coke, wiped my mouth, and returned to my room, where I plopped immediately into the bed. In what couldn't have been more than a few seconds, I heard someone knocking at the door, followed by Julio calling out, "Get up, Doctor. It is five o'clock!" I mumbled, probably somewhat resentfully, "Okay. I'm up."

I struggled out of bed, still not believing that I had slept for almost three hours. But even this brief slumber felt good. I rubbed the sleep from my eyes, washed quickly, and put on my O.R. clothes and white coat. I shoved the vials of medication into my right-hand pocket and exited my room, meeting Julio in the hallway. He said he had already gone out this morning and checked the roads, and they were clear enough to drive on. The rain had stopped and the water had subsided somewhat. Later I would find out that the storm had caused considerable damage and that there had been casualties, but in the area where we were, this was not evident.

In any case, we were on our way and arrived at the ill nurse's house in about ten minutes. I got out of the Jeep and began to ring the bell, again with no response. I tried banging on the gates, but there was still no response.

Determined not to have made another fruitless trip, I went to the back of the Jeep and grabbed the tire iron, which I began banging loudly against the metal gatepost. *That* elicited a response – an armed guard with an old shotgun slung over his shoulder. I climbed over the top of the hood and peered over the wall so he could see me. He recognized me and immediately ran to the gates to let me in. As the gates swung open, I started walking the cobblestone path to the house, when I heard the dogs barking again. And out of the corner of my eye, I spotted an extremely large and determined German shepherd running very purposefully in my direction. There was no way I could outrun that dog, and no place for me to hide.

CHAPTER 9
Mudslides And Bombs

As the big dog advanced towards me, the guard threw his shotgun to the ground and began running after the dog and yelling at him. I could just see myself being mauled by this 120-pound animal. The adrenaline kicked in and I sprinted away with every ounce of energy I had. I was almost to the porch when I saw another German shepherd coming at me from the other side. He leaped, clearing the porch railing as if it was not even there, landing just feet in front of me and skidding to a stop. His mouth was wide open in a toothy snarl, obviously ready to help himself to a tasty meal of surgeon. Just then, the front door to the house opened and a maid and a houseboy burst out onto the porch, screaming in Spanish at the dog, "Sit! Sit!"

The houseboy flung himself onto the dog's back and grabbed the animal's collar, holding him in place. Only a few feet away, the guard had done the same with the other dog, screaming for the dog to sit, and using every bit of his strength to hold on to the collar. I stood there, dead still aside from shaking from head to toe. The maid yelled at me and beckoned with her hand for me to come quickly into the house. I didn't hesitate. Anything to get away from these two monsters. The maid was stammering and trying to apologize for what had happened. She said they had told the guards again and again that before they opened the gates they needed to chain the dogs up. Obviously, they hadn't done so.

I was safe inside the house, and the shaking subsided as I caught my breath. I explained to the maid that I needed to see Olivia, the nurse who was sick. She took my hand and led me to a room in the back where there were several beds. With the racket that had taken place outside, everyone was wide awake. I sat on the bed next to Olivia, and she ran through her symptoms and discomfort, which had been increasing over the past 24 hours. It was obvious she had eaten something that severely disagreed with her. I gave her some antibiotic tablets and some Lomotil for diarrhea, and told her how to take each medicine. I instructed her to stay on liquids only, and told her that she didn't need to come to the hospital today, that one of the other nurses could stay with her.

She said that was unnecessary, as there were several housemaids and a houseboy, and they were doing a fine job of looking after her. The houseboy walked me to the door, and as he opened it, he cautiously put his hand on my chest, motioning for me to wait as he looked outside. The guard walked up to the door and told the houseboy that they had the two guard dogs chained, and it was safe to come out.

I couldn't help giving the guard a very nasty look. He jumped to attention and saluted me, and apologized for not having the dogs under control when I arrived. He escorted me down the gravel path to the front gate, slid back the heavy steel bolt, and pulled on the latch. As the gate opened, I got into the Jeep. Julio looked over at me with a very concerned look on his face. Then for some reason, he started to laugh. I looked at him, and he obviously saw by my facial expression that I didn't get the joke. He said, "I was just thinking what would have happened to you if you had climbed over that fence last night during the rainstorm when those dogs were prowling the grounds."

I said, "That didn't occur to me. Good point."

He smiled and said, "God was looking over you."

"Yeah, I guess I still have an angel on my shoulder." For years, Marvin Zindler and I had joked that we must have a guardian angel that watched over us and kept us safe as we ventured to dangerous places. But sometimes I wondered if it really was a joke, given some of the dicey situations we had encountered both individually and as a pair, and had come through relatively unscathed. I was certainly willing to accept any help offered, from this realm or the next.

Julio chuckled and responded, "Okay Dr. Angel. I'm taking you to the hospital. You have work to do."

On the way to the hospital, Julio helped me improve my Spanish vocabulary and sentence structure. He teased me good-naturedly about it, but admitted that I was getting better at communicating in Spanish.

The morning sun grew stronger as it rose higher in the nearly cloudless sky, and along with the cool wind, it promised a clear and beautiful day. But the beauty of the day seemed almost like a mockery when we saw the damage that had been done by the previous night's storms. I'd had no idea how bad it was until now. The scene that unfolded before us was quite distressing.

Miracles in Bedlam

Julio glanced left to right across the road as he drove. In the streets, we saw several carcasses of chickens, a dog, and a dead horse, still tied to a tree in front of a ramshackle house. All were victims of the flash floods that had come so quickly the night before. Pushcarts and small wagons remained stuck in the mud, awaiting their owners' return to pry them free from the muck. As we continued into town, we could see that a hillside had washed away and smashed into and demolished a bakery, as well as destroying a cluster of flimsy shacks. I was shocked to learn that many of the people who had lived in these structures had died in the mudslide. There were a number of sticks poking through the mud to mark the location of their remains. I thought to myself, *The emergency room is going to be full today.*

Sitting bolt upright in the Jeep and peering out the windshield, I was able to see all the way down the street to the market, where a cleanup was in progress. The marketplace was filled with shop owners, peddlers, street merchants, and women doing their early morning shopping. There were also a number of peasants from the countryside, all dirt-poor and visibly frightened by the presence of the police and military personnel who were lining the streets and assisting in the cleanup.

The scene before us now was filled not only with the cleanup efforts, but also with people going about their lives despite the previous night's catastrophic downpour. I saw a housewife carrying a chicken from the butcher shop, and workmen with tamales and tortillas wrapped in newspaper. I spotted one man carrying a six-pack of beer, and thought it seemed a little early for that. Then again, considering what he and his family had just lived through... An ornately adorned crew cart, painted a gleaming yellow and red, with the owner's name stenciled in green across the back, plodded along through the mud on its large wood-spoked wheels, barely squeezing past us and turning the corner.

An unusually tall, thin man, wearing workman's garb, a shabby thin coat, and a flat, Cuban-styled cap that was pulled down over his forehead, squeezed between us and the pushcarts that lined the street on our right. He tapped on our front fender to make sure we could see him. Then he glanced across the street, sweeping the hat off his head as if signaling to someone on the other side. For some reason this made me a little uneasy, but the feeling passed as we continued slowly past the market. We could see and hear pigeons murmuring softly amongst themselves, a subtle counter to the shouts of an organ grinder and his monkey, eager to play for anyone who would give them a few córdobas.

In the next block I heard the thump and whir of sewing machines, and my curiosity kicked in. I was eager to see the source of the sounds, and we had a few minutes to spare, so I asked Julio to stop. I climbed out of the Jeep with camera in hand. Peering through the spaces between a wall of wooden slats, I beheld a dimly lit space in which it seemed that the very presence of air was forbidden. I felt the oppressive heat oozing through the cracks, amazed that even at this early hour, the temperature inside must have been over a hundred degrees. I saw row upon row of women, huddled over their sewing machines, joylessly engrossed in their work. Even as the women toiled, children scurried wildly around and under the tables, playing in what could only be characterized as a sweatshop.

Through one of the larger cracks in the slatted adobe wall, I saw a balding man with a barrel chest and an even larger belly. Obviously unshaven for several days and in need of a haircut, he moved between the narrow rows, muttering at the women huddled over their machines. Moving along the wall, I came upon a small window, partially opened. It seemed this was the only airflow into the room. There were several small children sitting on the ledge who spotted me immediately; I waved my hand and made funny faces at them, and they began to laugh at the crazy old *gringo*. I wanted to capture the joy in their faces, even in this depressing place, and my camera began to click.

It didn't take long for the owner/overseer to amble over to where I was. His manner was cordial, his Spanish was clear and spoken slowly. He didn't seem to take offense at my presence at the window. I smiled at him, telling him I was taking pictures of the children at play, but I said nothing about his sweatshop or the women inside. He stood there motionless and looking at me hard for several seconds, then said, "You are the one they call Dr. Angel, the doctor who has provided care for some of the children in this room who really needed help."

Being recognized in this manner was a great advantage for easing the tension in this kind of situation and turning innately suspicious people into friends. Two of the women whose children had been operated on the week before came running out, children in tow. The children's cleft lips were healing well, and I could see by the smiles on the mothers' faces how pleased they were. Even the owner broke into a big smile as he put his hands on the women's shoulders. He looked at me intently, his smile even brighter, and said, "*Gracias. Gracias.*"

I pointed to the camera and then to the mothers and the children, as if to ask whether it would be all right for me to take a few pictures of them all together. They answered almost as one, eager to have their pictures taken. I took several shots, including one of the mothers and their boss. Before saying goodbye, I told the women to bring the children back to the hospital in the next day or two to have the sutures removed. As I turned to leave, I noticed that many of the women and children had their faces jammed in the window, waving to me as I left.

Back in the Jeep, we continued along Calle Central past the central park and toward the Iglesia de Santa Ana, at which point we would turn left towards the hospital. Leaving the market, the neighborhood was rapidly urbanizing; the homes were larger and all walled in. We passed the small local theater and the school, and then came up to the parish house before approaching the church.

Suddenly we heard a tremendous explosion, and the road in front of us actually rippled. I could see the steeple on the Iglesia de Santa Ana sway, and parish nuns in their full habits ran from the building. The building was surfaced with vitrified stone, which appeared to roll like waves in the ocean. I quickly remembered that we were in the volcanic lowlands. My first thought was that in the event of an earthquake, we would need to keep moving, on the chance that the tremors were a forewarning of an imminent volcanic eruption. Julio steered the Jeep to the center of the road, away from falling bricks and mortar that were crumbling down on either side of us. Then came a second explosion, and a hundred feet of the road in front of us writhed and shattered, sending huge chunks of blacktop, concrete, and dirt crashing against the Jeep. We both immediately dropped to the floorboards, realizing at once that this was no earthquake. It was a barrage of artillery fire, sent not by the volcanoes, but by the Sandinistas.

As I peeked above the dashboard, Julio and I nodded at each other. I gave him a thumbs-up, and he threw the car in reverse and floored the accelerator. Wheels spinning, he moved backwards about 100 feet and stopped. Climbing out of the Jeep, he leapt up onto the hood and surveyed the street in front of us, looking to see if there were any injured people that we could help. The street – what was left of it – was bare. He climbed back into the Jeep and turned toward me, saying, "Do you remember that tall, thin man we saw?"

"Yes, the man who tapped our fender."

"Do you remember he lifted his cap and waved as if he was signaling?"

"Yes, yes. Why?"

"I think we were the target, and he was marking us for the artillery to fire on the Jeep as we moved along Calle Central away from the more populated market area and vendors."

"Are you sure you're not letting your imagination run away with you?" I asked, although I had a sinking feeling that he was right. I knew there was a reason that man had made me so uneasy.

He responded, "That's how the Sandinistas would do it. You and the American medical team are the enemy. I know you are not combatants and you don't ask whether a family that brings a child to the hospital is a Contra or a Sandinista. You treat everybody fairly, but I don't think the Sandinistas see it that way. You are getting too much good publicity. And you represent the United States. Therefore you are a target."

Even though I couldn't quite accept it yet on an emotional level, I had to agree with the logic of what he was saying. I responded, "Then we need to keep moving. Obviously we can't get through this street. Turn here, zigzag around a few of the blocks, and keep zigzagging and circling until we get to the hospital. Don't take a straight course. If we are a target, we need to make it more difficult for them to hit us."

And on we went, not knowing what unpleasant surprises might await us around the next corner.

Joseph Agris, M.D.

CHAPTER 10
We've Got This

Julio swung the Jeep sharply to the left, hit the brakes, then cut back to the right. We barreled down the next street, honking the horn and causing several men carrying shovels and pickaxes on their shoulders to jump from the street to the narrow sidewalks to avoid being run down. Julio took another sharp right turn with his foot still on the gas, and the hospital appeared a half block up, on our left. Thankfully, it had not been hit. I thanked Julio for the ride, jumped from the Jeep, threw my satchel containing charts and schedules and my camera over my shoulder, and headed for the hospital's main gate. As the gate opened, the guard jumped to attention and saluted.

Behind me, two ambulance attendants were leading an enormous man whose head and face were swathed in bandages. The emergency room doctors were going to be working non-stop today, and I had a feeling that some of those patients – especially those with facial injuries – would be moved directly to us in the operating room.

I ran up the ramp to the second level and into the doctor's lounge. After placing my camera, the charts, and the schedules on the table, I looked out the window to the north, and then west to the lowlands across the Rio Acome. The valley behind was covered in water from the past several days' torrential rains. I could see mile after mile of flattened farmlands. There were occasional uprooted trees, and many of the small farms and the surrounding villages, churches, barns, and homes had been inundated by the floodwaters.

Turning and leaving the lounge, my first stop was to the small private room where we had isolated Michael due to his infected leg. One of the local nurses, a woman named Arantxa, was at his bedside. I opened the door just enough to observe, without either Michael or the nurse being aware of my presence, and I watched as she removed the packing from his wound. It was obvious that he was hurting. I thought I could almost see his heart pounding as the nurse continued pulling the packing away. Then he began to retch with the pain, but I was still too angry with him to feel sorry for him. I could also see from his facial expression that he felt powerless and angry at what the nurse was doing, but also resigned in the knowledge that it had to be done.

I leaned unintentionally on the door, causing it to open more, its hinges squeaking loudly. Michael flinched at the sound. Having been discovered, I pushed the door open and entered the room. I turned to Michael and said, firmly but with a good-natured smile, "Do what Nurse Arantxa tells you if you want that leg to get better. You do want it to get better, don't you?"

Michael responded tersely, "Can I get more pain medication?"

I answered, admittedly with a less-than-compassionate tone in my voice, "I'll look into it for you," then almost immediately added, "No, on second thought, we really can't spare any. You know that our supplies are limited." Looking directly into his eyes, I added, "For better or for worse, that's love."

I then turned to leave the room, and Michael shouted, "I'm not in a joking mood, Doctor."

"Neither am I, sir. We will talk tomorrow."

* * * * *

After all of the excitement on the streets this morning, and then having to deal with Michael's turmoil, I was more than happy to return to the operating room and devote my attention to the residents and students. I pulled the door closed behind me and quick-stepped it to the operating rooms. Poking my head into Operating Room 1, I announced, "Okay people, we are going to be especially busy today. Those explosions you heard were artillery shells or mortar fire coming into the city. They almost got Julio and me. And we may be seeing injuries from last night's storms too. I'm afraid that in addition to our regular schedule, we will also have to contend with any emergencies sent to us from the E.R."

I then entered Operating Room 2, where I would be working with Dr. Canteras. There was a new group of residents, interns, and students, and as I looked them over, I noticed that they seemed considerably younger than groups that had come through before them. Either that, or I was just rapidly getting older. I remember that even as a young doctor, it seemed to me that each new group of interns appeared younger than the last, and I've wondered more than once, and something less than sarcastically, how long it would be until we had grade school age interns and residents.

Miracles in Bedlam

Setting my grumpy old doctor reverie aside, I addressed the group, saying, "I am training surgeons here, not observers. Get to the scrub sinks and back to the operating room with gloves on." I then ran down the hall to check on Operating Rooms 3 and 4, relieved to find them already in progress without any problems. It was my turn to get to the scrub sink and then to work.

It was even hotter than usual in the operating rooms. An overhead fan spun away but barely moved the moisture-laden valley air that hung over the surgical team. The nitrous oxide gas was not exhausted from the space very efficiently, and seemed to cling to the sheets and the staff's and patients' garments.

But it was show time, with the only thing missing being the popcorn. A sense of humor would get us through the day. The nurse patted my hands dry with a sterile towel and slid on my surgical gloves. My breathing slowed and my muscles relaxed, my nerves finally calmed after this morning's incidents. I felt good. The room was animated by the typical O.R. banter of instructing the students and trying to initiate a discussion between them and myself. The new group seemed overly reserved at first, and I knew that I needed to do something to bring them into the fold. I turned to JoAnne and asked for the *pequeño machete*. A few of the students and residents looked startled. Others just giggled as JoAnne slapped the handle of the scalpel against my palm and said, "Scalpel, Doctor."

I talked for well over an hour, describing every step in the procedure of a difficult double cleft lip repair. I was frequently interrupted as the students began to ask questions or asked me to clarify a point. At one point, I turned to the young resident who had been assisting me. I licked my dry lips under the O.R. mask, shot him a glance, and asked him, "Do you know how to suture?"

We stared at each other for a few seconds while the resident seemed to be trying to figure out the meaning of my question. I interrupted his rumination, stating in a harsh tone, "I have no time for bullshit, mister. Do you feel comfortable suturing the patient's lip?"

He quickly responded, "*Si, si!* I will do a beautiful job."

At that moment, a nurse whom I recognized from the emergency room swung the door wide and shouted, "The doctors in the emergency room requested that you come as soon as possible!"

I turned toward JoAnne, and before I could say anything she said, "I've got this."

I followed the nurse down the hall as she rapidly walked to the emergency room. She led me into one of the examining rooms where the doctor was cleaning a series of facial lacerations. I immediately noticed it was the big bear of a man whom I'd seen earlier, the one who'd come through the gate just before I had, his head completely swathed in bandages. I approached the wounded man, removed my pocket flashlight, and examined his eyes. Bit by bit, he followed my instructions and moved his eyes against the clotted blood that had dripped into them. His vision was good. He blinked rapidly, only to have more blood drip into his eyes each time he opened them. I removed the pillow so his head would lie flat. He was hurting, and his overall demeanor told me that he was obviously overwhelmed with fear. I'm sure it was unnerving and uncomfortable for him to see all that blood. I thought to myself, *The big guys are always afraid of blood and needles.* My mind flashed back to a 400-pound lineman from the old Houston Oilers football team, who began getting agitated even before I injected him with a local anesthesia.

I told the nurse to irrigate the man's eyes with saline solution and to finish cleaning his wounds, then to apply a pressure bandage. It became clear to me that he was not going to tolerate local anesthesia, and that we would have to complete the wound closure in the operating room.

I left the emergency room and picked my way carefully down the poorly lit narrow hallway to the main ramp. Once I was again in familiar territory, I raced up the ramp toward the operating rooms and shouted to Carolyn, who was already placing the next child on the O.R. table, that we would complete this case and then bring in the gentleman from the emergency room. I asked the residents in the room to raise their hands if they had sutured lacerations before. Three of them did.

I said, "The next patient has facial wounds, likely glass and debris from the bomb explosion. Once he is asleep, I want you to place three stools around the head of the table, and all of you will be suturing at the same time. I will be instructing. It will be a good teaching opportunity."

JoAnne was writing down the man's name, age, the last time he had eaten food, and his statement that he had no allergies. But she too looked concerned by what she was hearing about his extensive facial lacerations. She looked up at me, and I asked her, "What else can I say?"

She responded, "I think you said a lot. I've got this." And then all fell silent for a few moments. I shot her an appreciative look, but she was frowning. I was pretty sure I knew why.

I tried to explain it to her. "I know we're here for the children, but we are going to have to deal with war injuries and emergencies as well. No time for pondering motives today."

She replied, "I don't know what to say."

I understood her hesitance perfectly, and in an effort to address it, said, "We'll just take care of them as we see them: triage in the emergency room and treat the most severe cases first. We've got this."

JoAnne nodded, apparently satisfied. "I appreciate that, Doctor, and I'll give you everything I have. So what's our next step?"

"For now, we'll finish these cleft lip procedures, then remove the glass, then debride, clean, and close the man's facial wounds as we go on to the next patient. Then we will return to our original schedule."

It was as simple as that. We had to be prepared for any and everything.

With the cleft lip repaired and the child extubated, he was removed to the recovery area. The large man was guided into the room by both nurses. He climbed onto the O.R. table without difficulty and lay back as directed. The I.V. was placed and the anesthesiologist had him comfortably asleep in a few minutes. The residents, who were grouped on one side of the room, took a few steps forward and were staring directly at their patient for the first time.

I told them, "All the pieces are there. I examined this gentleman in the emergency room where his wounds have already been superficially cleaned, but they are deep and painful. We will need to separate the margins and re-examine to make sure all the glass shards are out. Then you will close the wounds in two layers using an absorbable suture inside and running sutures for the skin. This will give the best cosmetic result."

The senior resident looked up at me. "I guess we all have to prove ourselves, every day."

"Yes, and all three of you will be doing that today, while helping this unlucky gentleman." I looked down, certain that my features looked a bit strained by the young man's candid assessment of the situation. I was about the say something else, but stopped, and with a wave of my hand, motioned for the residents and students to get to work.

I reassured them, saying as they approached their patient, "Remember three things. First, you have the experience and training on your side. Second, good things tend to happen. And third, I will be standing next to the anesthesiologist, guiding you through it. There are no alternatives in surgery. The rules are, *see one, do one, teach one.*" They all chuckled and seemed more relaxed and ready to get started.

The senior resident administered the local anesthesia as I directed, placing small amounts on either side of the forehead and facial wounds. The nurse reached up with a sterile lap pad and removed some beads of sweat from the resident's face. He was still a bit nervous, but his hands were steady as he administered local anesthetic around each wound.

One student said, "He is already asleep. Why are you bothering with a local anesthetic?"

I asked the others if there was anyone who could answer this, but they all remained silent. I explained that the local anesthetic contained epinephrine, and before I could say another word, one of the students said, "That's a vasoconstrictor. It will stop the bleeding."

I nodded, adding, "Excellent answer, but that is only half the reason." Once again, the room was quiet. I continued, "When he wakes up he will be pain free for at least four hours. He will be a much more cooperative patient postoperatively, easier for the nurses to manage. He might even be able to go home today, which is important because we need the beds for the children."

The students progressed slowly and carefully, but their hands were steady and they were talking amongst themselves. The epinephrine in the local anesthetic was peaking, and the wounds were virtually bloodless. I occasionally caught a student or resident backhanding a suture and corrected them.

The procedures were going smoothly, thank goodness, but the morning's stresses had taken more of a toll than I had realized, and I couldn't hide the evidence from the nurses who knew me so well. At one point Carolyn looked at me and said, "Look, Doc, we've got this. Why don't you take a break? Get something to drink and get off your feet."

I suddenly realized how tired I was now that the adrenaline in my system was finally wearing off, not to mention that I was thirsty. I would definitely like to sit for a while, so I nodded and headed off to the doctor's lounge. Once in the lounge I looked out the small window. It had been raining again, but the rain had stopped for a while, though dark and heavily moisture-laden clouds remained. I expected there would be another downpour at any moment.

I picked up a bottle of water from a table, turned the cap, and listened to the snap as the plastic band broke loose. You always needed to listen for that, because there was lots of bootlegged bottled water. Children would pick up bottles in the street and fill them from the water trough, then replace the caps and offer them for sale. That was a good way to get dysentery. But this bottle was okay, and I slugged it down and then took a seat near the table with my feet up on the adjacent chair.

A well-worn English language Bible sat on the table. I picked it up, turned to the Psalms and began to read through my favorites. Don't get me wrong: I'm not a very religious man, but those mortar shells and rockets had shaken me to my very soul, as I am sure it had shaken Julio. It wasn't the first time I'd been in a war zone, but that's something you never really get used to. My angel had definitely been on my shoulder today, I thought. I continued to read the Bible, and then I tilted my head back and closed my eyes for a few minutes. It was going to be a very long day and night in the operating room, and if I could just sneak in a little cat nap...

I had no idea how long I had been sleeping when one of the residents came in and shook me. I took several deep breaths, opened my eyes and rubbed the back of my neck, which was stiff. I slowly touched my feet to the floor and stood. Balance returned and I walked into the bathroom, where I splashed some water onto my face. Only then did it occur to me to check my watch, and I saw that I had only been asleep for about fifteen minutes. But it was so deep and relaxing, and apparently was just what I had needed.

At that moment Dr. Canteras entered the room and informed me that all the operating room theaters had cleared. He said that the next group of children was sitting on the wooden benches just outside the rooms in the hallway, playing quietly with the toys that we had brought for them. The boys were showing off their cars and trucks while the girls were quietly gathered in a circle, sharing crayons and coloring books.

Dr. Canteras sat down in one of the lounge chairs. Its stuffing protruded in various places but it was still very soft and comfortable. He glanced at the Bible that I had left open on the table and then at me. "Been doing some reading?" he asked.

I shrugged and said, "Maybe more people should read the Bible and practice the Ten Commandments – and maybe we wouldn't be dealing with ten years of Contra-Sandanista conflict and more than 20,000 dead, and numerous uncounted injuries and suffering." It occurred to me that I was coming across as a little self-righteous and preachy, but Dr. Canteras didn't look as if he disagreed with me. Instead he leaned back in the chair, folded his arms over his chest and closed his eyes.

After a moment he opened them, and there was an expression of resignation on his face as he nodded. Then he said, "I really can't believe you and the American medical team are doing this. You're all angels but I think those that call you 'the Crazy Texan' are closer to the truth. I heard what happened this morning to you and your driver. The hospital is guarded and protected and they will not fire on this building. You are safe here. But my advice to you is to stay off the street, lay low and get from Point A to Point B quickly, but not in any set pattern. You, as well as other members of your team are targets for kidnapping at the very least. Don't overwork that guardian angel of yours."

I said, "I just want to help out where I can."

Dr. Canteras replied, "I respect that, but my conscience would not be clear if I did not warn you that you and your team have become a target. I suspect that some of the others have been telling you this too. They're right. The climate has changed. You have to deal with that. It doesn't change what you are here to do but it does change how you will act and do it. The mission will be a lot harder now and I think that in your heart you know this. You will have to discuss this with the team and they will have to account for that. There are other ways to get the job done and be safe."

Dr. Baladares, the other local surgeon from Managua who joined us in Chinandega, had just entered the room and was listening to the conversation. He said, "It doesn't mean we are not grateful. But if you die in the process of helping us..." His voice trailed off.

I looked at him and tapped my shoulder, and the other two doctors began to smile, as did one of the nurses who had also come into the room with Dr. Baladares. She gave me a sly glance and said, "You may have an angel on your shoulder. I don't know if I do, but I can care of myself. I have a gun." We all looked at her in surprise.

Then I said, "Well, let's all get back to the operating rooms. There is still a lot of work to do."

Outside, I could hear thunder and lightning and the sound of rain once again pouring down on the tile roof. Fortunately, the carpenters had worked through the night to repair the operating room ceiling, and so far, there was no indication that we would have a repeat of our previous contaminated shower raining down on our patients. I silently thanked that angel on my shoulder and any other angel or deity who might be listening in, for I was grateful for even the smallest respite from the whims of nature and the bombs of unseen enemies.

CHAPTER 11
Social Pressures & Sandanistas

When I was personally invited – or summoned might be a better word – to a formal reception dinner and dance in Managua to honor Nicaragua's new president, Violeta Chamorro, I was both highly honored and a little nervous. My nervousness did not abate when I was informed that I was to escort Mrs. Chamorro's young niece, Maria Torres, to the event. I was well accustomed to political and social events in the United States, of course, and had been to numerous events in other countries as well. I could hold my own with presidents and prime ministers and royalty. But this was a little bit different. Not only was it a celebration of a true history maker, as Mrs. Chamorro was Nicaragua's first woman president, but given the ongoing civil unrest, and the bomb scares I'd already experienced myself, I was not at all sure that such a high-profile event would be the safest place to be. Granted, the election and the transfer of power had been peaceful for the most part, but in Nicaragua in those days there was always trouble brewing somewhere, and it frequently erupted in one way or the other, as I'd seen firsthand. And now I was to be responsible for the new president's niece as well. That was a lot of social pressure.

Nevertheless I couldn't decline such a prestigious invitation. I contacted Julio and told him that I would need him to drive Maria and me to the event. In response, he came right out and told me I should think twice about attending. "Well, Julio, I've already accepted, and I'm going," I said. "If you don't want to drive me I can find another driver."

"No, no, I'll be glad to drive you," he said. "I'm just warning you that it's risky."

"Practically everything we do here is risky," I said, and he didn't argue.

So on the day of the event, Julio brought the big black SUV around to the front of Don Roberto's home. The houseboy opened the heavy double gates as I left my room and walked around the veranda to the front entrance. The entire staff had apparently lined up for the occasion. They were checking me out – my hair, my polished shoes, and even my starched and well-pressed white shirt. Roberto himself stepped up and adjusted my tie and then shook my hand, saying, "You are a peace emissary at the end of this civil war. An American representative who adds credence to the election of Violeta Chamorro to the presidency, and a new democracy in Nicaragua."

As if I didn't have enough to be nervous about, there were those expectations too. Nevertheless I smiled and said, "I'll do my best."

Roberto's wife hugged me and gave me a kiss on each cheek, then whispered in my ear, "You will do fine."

Julio was standing there with the door open, and I stepped into the rear of the SUV, waving to everybody who had gathered in front of the house as we pulled away. Don Roberto's last comments left a lot for me to think about as we drove to the home of Maria Torres.

When we arrived, Julio walked me to the door and knocked. I expected the knock to be answered by a servant and was surprised when the door was flung open and the bright sunlight poured into the entryway, illuminating a beautiful young woman whose eyes were on fire with excitement. Maria was stunning, dressed in a long, off-white chiffon summer gown, decorated with the intricate embroidery that was typical of women's fashions in Central America. The sunlight splashing across the needlework gave it a lovely shimmer.

Maria's parents approached behind her and I greeted the three of them in Spanish, shaking hands with her father. Maria herself seemed a bit nervous as well as excited. "It's getting late, and it's a long ride, so we really need to get going." With that, we unceremoniously walked out the door with Julio leading the way.

As we all walked toward the car, Maria's father took me aside. "I understand they have made an attempt on your life. There are certain kinds of crimes that don't usually mix. The criminals who attempt to kidnap are not usually the sort who would threaten violence."

I looked at him quizzically. "Never?"

He replied, "I'm not saying never, which is why I want you to follow my instructions on the trip to Managua."

I hesitated, imagining grim warnings of the ride to come, and I expected that he was about to voice his strong opposition to his daughter attending the big event with me. I tried to put his mind at ease somewhat. "I know I'm only a doctor, but I've been very lucky so far. My driver Julio is also a bodyguard, and besides, I have a guardian angel. If all else fails my angel will get us through." I was smiling but even as I spoke, I realized how naïve I must have sounded.

Mr. Torres smiled briefly but immediately brought the discussion back to reality. "President Violeta sees you as more than a doctor. She sees in you a potential American emissary with strong influence; someone who represents America's desire for this civil war to finally come to an end, and for a democracy to form under her administration here in Nicaragua. And the Sandinistas fear this even more than the Contras' guns."

There were those lofty expectations again.

Maria was already seated in the SUV behind the driver. The door was still open and her mother was reaching into the vehicle, smoothing out her daughter's beautiful formal dress. I opened the front door next to the driver, feeling it would be deemed more proper for me to be sitting there. But before I could move to get in, her father put his hand on my shoulder and said, "No, no," and gently guided me into the backseat next to Maria.

Suddenly, Maria shouted, "Wait, wait!"

Her mother was as surprised as I was, and asked Maria, "What's wrong?" The mystery was solved when in that same moment, a maid came running out of the house toward the car, with a beautiful beaded mini purse in her hand.

I thought, *Women and their purses.*

Mrs. Torres must have sensed what I was thinking and explained to me, "It's a beautiful accessory and it completes her outfit." Then she leaned in close and I heard her whispering to her daughter, "Relax. Everything will be fine. You are going to have a good time. Just act accordingly."

Maria, obviously anxious and exasperated, said, "Am I supposed to bat my eyes at the doctor as if he were a suitor?"

Just at that moment, two more maids came rushing out with large horsehair cushions from the couch that sat in the entryway to the house. Maria's father was waving them towards the car. He walked around to the driver's side and placed one of the cushions between Maria's knees and the back of the seat. I could see from her facial expression that she was not happy with this. A few seconds later the houseboy jammed the second cushion between my knees and the seat in front of me.

Her father said to Maria, "I heard that last comment. You'll have to work that problem out yourself, but I would suggest that instead of batting your eyes at the doctor, you should keep down and hold that pillow in front of you during your ride. And I think you need another bodyguard too." He waved to Mambo, the gate guard, who came running over, and he motioned for the guard to sit next to Julio. The guard removed the shotgun from his shoulder, placed it between the two seats, and climbed in.

I could see that Maria was not happy with that big heavy horsehair pillow wedged in front of her, and to be honest, I felt the same way about mine. Mr. Torres read my expression and said, "I know these pillows are uncomfortable but they could save your lives. If someone tries to kidnap you, they will shoot the driver and the bodyguard. Between their bodies, the back of the seats, and the cushions, the bullets will be stopped before they can injure you." There was nothing more to be said, but I couldn't help wondering what would happen if someone tried to shoot us from behind or from the side. I decided it was best not to mention that.

Mr. Torres told Julio to wait a moment before starting the SUV. He walked through the gate and anxiously scanned the street, looking up and down the sidewalks, at the wagons and pushcarts, into the windows of nearby structures, and onto the adjacent rooftops. When he returned he said to Julio, "I can't see them, but I feel them." Julio nodded and slowly pulled out onto the street.

As we drove down the street, children were plastering posters on the empty walls and even to the sides of grocery wagons and shop windows when their owners weren't looking. All of the posters announced the event to celebrate Violeta Chamorro's presidency and her political party.

Suddenly I had another one of my uneasy feelings, and I told Julio that I thought we needed to get out of this neighborhood quickly. I had learned not to ignore those gut feelings.

"Why don't you sit back, try to relax, and let me drive?" Julio said good-naturedly. He glanced in the rearview mirror as he said this, saw the intensity in my eyes, and suddenly understood. Without saying another word, he accelerated sharply and began weaving his way through the dense crowd. This scenario was now feeling all too familiar.

Julio maneuvered the SUV through the mass of rushing people, carts, and wagons as safely as he could. The goal seemed simple enough: all he had to do was get us out of town and onto the main road to Managua, but that seemed at the moment to be a formidable task. He gunned the big engine of the SUV, and the few remaining people on the corner scrambled out of the way as he burst past them. Some couldn't move quite fast enough, and skidded on the greasy cobblestones of the sidewalk. One man who stumbled shook an angry fist at Julio as he struggled to get back on his feet, and as Julio continued weaving down the street, he shouted out an apology, even though the man most likely couldn't hear him.

As we rounded a corner we encountered another obstacle: an ancient wooden high-wheeled delivery cart, bearing a frightened-looking driver and being pulled by a sturdy little donkey. The cart was partially blocking our path, but this did not stop Julio. As carefully as possible under the circumstances he maneuvered the SUV up to the cart and gave it a little nudge, whereupon the driver frantically urged the donkey onto the sidewalk, dropped the reins, and leaped from the cart. At that moment the cart overturned, but the driver hit the sidewalk safely on his feet, and both driver and donkey seemed to be unscathed.

It was obvious that all of Julio's senses were now on overdrive, as if he were seeing, hearing, and feeling everything at once while he frantically maneuvered the SUV towards the outskirts of town. Or maybe I was just projecting, since my own senses were overwhelmed and the adrenaline was coursing through my body. Julio glanced in the rearview mirror at the overturned wagon behind us, and then tilted his head towards us and asked, "Is everyone OK?"

"I think so," I said, a little breathlessly. "You did great."

He shrugged. "I have been practicing my whole life," he said, and I believed him.

At that moment a loud explosion showered the SUV with glass from an adjacent building. Broken glass flew in all directions as dust and smoke gushed alongside the road from the shattered building, the front of which had been completely destroyed.

Mambo immediately brought the shotgun up to the side window and whispered, "Sandinista!" Talk about *déjà vu*...

Within moments people were rushing out from everywhere, clearly trying to escape the melee as they screamed, "Sandinista! Sandinista!" Julio did not look back or sideways as this latest mad rush of humanity filled the sidewalks and spilled into the streets; he was now staring ahead intensely as we sped through the swirling dust.

I was looking out the back window and saw that the bomb had blown a hole in the wall between two buildings, and had also damaged the apartments behind the buildings. I observed two men with automatic weapons jumping through that hole and advancing towards us, a development that did not go unnoticed by Mambo, who let loose with two rounds in that direction. There was no return fire as Julio made a sharp left and then right turn, zigzagging away from the bomb blast.

Police were already arriving on the scene, as were some uniformed military men. A couple of horses had apparently broken loose from somewhere, and were now barreling down the sidewalk as the air filled with the shrill sounds of sirens from fire trucks and ambulances.

Unperturbed, Julio drove on, an expression of grim determination on his face; he looked as if he could have bitten the heads off of nails as he made a beeline to the main highway to Managua.

Maria, meanwhile, had ducked down and buried her head against the thick horse-hair pillow in front of her.

I gently rubbed her shoulder and said, "Hey, are you okay?"

She lifted her head and opened her eyes, wiped her brow with the back of her hand, and with a sad little smile of resignation replied, "We've lived through this for more than ten years."

As I smiled back at her, she sighed in relief and even managed a giggle, albeit a nervous one.

I said sympathetically, "It must be hard to live in a state of constant fear. I've heard so many stories of things that have happened to people here and to their friends and families." Of course I was still thinking about the incident from the other day, and Julio's insistence that I was a target.

Julio, still looking grim, said, "The stories aren't exaggerated. And I think we got out of there just in time; it was dumb luck that we were not hurt or killed."

Maria broke in, saying, "I know that they would like to capture you as a hostage, Doc – and me also, maybe. But I really think they want you dead."

I patted her hand and said, "It can't be that bad. I think we all need to take a deep breath." I wasn't nearly as self-assured as I sounded.

Julio said, "Sorry I got you into this, Doc. Sorry I let you down. Maybe I should have taken a different route."

I tried to brush aside his concerns, saying, "You didn't let me down. And you had no way of knowing exactly when and where this would happen. You're a good driver, and I believe that you have just saved all our lives." Julio looked doubtful, and I reached forward and patted him on the shoulder, adding, "Don't worry. I can feel that angel on my shoulder holding on even more tightly. And she's looking out for all of us."

Everyone laughed, including Julio, but his laughter could not completely disguise his concern. He was silent for a while and finally said, "We have a saying about the Sandinistas: When they set their mind to something, *they never forget.*"

I didn't need to ask him exactly what he meant by that. I knew.

CHAPTER 12
Seeds Are Planted

As we drove on, we saw that the police, firemen, and military were already restoring order in the area. Julio reminded me that this wasn't surprising, as they had been through this so many times before, and things usually settled down quickly. Of course I had seen this phenomenon myself on several occasions, but it never failed to impress me. Even as the streets were being cleared of debris as well as pedestrian and vehicular traffic, other people had begun spilling out of their homes to gawk, adding to the congestion and the cleanup problem. *Typical human nature, rubber-necking at violence,* I thought to myself. In any case the scene was soon behind us and Julio was now moving rapidly, weaving smoothly through the light traffic on the Pan-American Highway, which was merely a paved road, toward Managua.

Julio pushed the SUV to its max, and I extended my hand over the seat and gently patted his shoulder, saying, "Hey, slow it down."

He relaxed somewhat as he looked over his shoulder with a slight smile. He did slow down a little, but immediately turned his attention back to the road, and his grim expression returned. I said, "Maybe you should have taken me up on my offer and let someone else drive today."

He responded, "Or maybe I should have listened to my gut and we shouldn't have tried to go to this event at all."

"Well, if you felt that way, why did you volunteer to drive Maria and me? I gave you a chance to back out."

"It was the right thing to do, even if it wasn't wise. But I am still skeptical. We haven't gotten there yet."

There was a moment of silence and then he added, "Maria is right. The Sandinistas want you, preferably alive, I think... but those last two attempts make me wonder." His eyes hardened with contempt.

I smiled, saying, "Look, I won't say that I'm not concerned. But sometimes we need to take action even if it is risky. And remember that angel..." Julio didn't look entirely convinced, but his expression relaxed somewhat, and more importantly, he was no longer driving like a maniac.

Deciding to change the subject to something lighter, I said to Julio, "I've been meaning to ask you something. Did you attend school in America?"

"Why do you ask?"

"You have an excellent command of the English language."

Beaming, Julio responded, "I wish that were really so. My accent still marks me."

"It's barely noticeable."

"Well, I have lived in America on and off for several years," he said. "I learned to speak and read English there when I was still young. After I came back home I still returned to the States several times to study. In those days it was much easier because the Nicaraguan currency was stronger and bought more."

"I heard that you are much more than just a driver and a bodyguard," I said. "I understand you help manage some of the farms and find work for men in need of jobs."

Julio replied, "Good men are hard to find, and their loyalty is as important as, if not more important than, the work they do." Then he added, "This is still a divided country, as you've seen."

Knowing that he was referring to the civil war again, I nodded, saying, "Of course. You know, I had read a lot about your civil war in our American newspapers, and I'd seen clips of the action on television, but our media never told the half of it. I've learned so much more since I've come here and had a chance to speak with those who are directly involved."

For the first time, Mambo interjected himself into the conversation. He spoke pretty good English, though more heavily accented than Julio's speech. He said, "But as you probably know, our country is divided in another way too – physically. The high volcanic mountains divide Nicaragua into an Atlantic Caribbean side and a Pacific side. They are very different. The people are different. The language is different, the customs and amenities – or lack of amenities – are different. In particular, medical care is non-existent on the Atlantic side. I'm from Puerto Cabezas on the Atlantic Caribbean side."

I looked at him with interest and he continued, "I'm a member of the Miskito Indian tribe. You are a good man, Doc. We need to stand together. And you need to go to Puerto Cabezas."

"Okay, I'm listening," I said.

"I think you can give hope to the Miskito Indian family. You can bring us medical care and more – maybe some perspective about what is really going on. The Cubans and the Russians who set up a clinic are still there. They are criminals who prey on the people's innocence. And if I may be quite honest with you, it isn't our experience that the Americans who have entered into our conflict here care about the innocents. But I think you're different. It is my feeling that the sooner you go to the Atlantic coast and meet with the Miskito people, the sooner they'll turn their support to America. Perhaps then, America will help in bringing an end to this civil war."

This statement left me nearly speechless, and it wasn't because of the praise from Mambo or the faith that he seemed to be putting in me. Rather, it was because he had just validated former President Reagan's statements that a communist Cuban organization with Russian backing was occupying Nicaragua's Miskito Indian Caribbean coast. It wasn't a stretch to think that his remarks also supported Reagan's accusations that Cuban Communists with Russian support had been behind the Sandinista movement in Nicaragua. Although President George H.W. Bush – Bush the elder – was now in office, with the Nicaraguan civil war seemingly forgotten for the most part by the U.S., these matters were still very much on my mind. Mambo's remarks got me thinking about them all over again.

Mambo continued, occasionally letting down his guard and reverting to his native tongue. He switched back and forth among heavily accented English, Spanish, and occasional words from the Miskito Indian language itself. I had to listen carefully to sort this all out, and Julio and Maria helped me when I didn't understand. But I was fascinated as Mambo shared some history of the Miskito people. "They are Nicaragua's indigenous culture – like the American Indian," he said. "But they have never received full electoral privileges, only continued setbacks and reversals, and have been in a continuous struggle for recognition and human rights."

With a smile on his face, his voice slightly raised, he said, "I meant it when I said you have to go. You need to bring a medical team and the TV people with you, and all of you need to see the Miskito Caribbean coast."

Of course I was extremely interested, and was already mulling over the logistics. As if reading my mind, Mambo continued, "Nicaragua has one air carrier and it has a small fleet of single-engine planes. They seat four to six people, and you can get some equipment aboard as well. I know some of the men who fly frequently across the mountains for a local airline. These small planes fly between Managua and the Atlantic coast. They do stop at Puerto Cabezas and also down the coast to Bluefields, and off the coast to the Corn Islands. It's inexpensive, about $80 American. Next week you must go."

I said, "That sounds feasible, but we can take more medical supplies and equipment if we drive."

He shook his head. "No. It will take four or five days to get across those donkey paths in the mountains and that is where the Sandinistas are hiding. They will find you. They will take your equipment and they will hold you for ransom. The only way to cross those mountains safely is to fly."

"I have to admit that you have intrigued me," I said. "This sounds like a great adventure. But even if we fly I would still have some hesitation because of what you just now said about the Russians and Cubans being there."

Mambo acknowledged that it was risky but that on the other hand, a powerful resistance movement had emerged. He explained, "A sense of unity and independence had already been growing among my people before the Sandinistas came to power. When they got into power the Sandinistas attempted to incorporate the indigenous Miskito tribes into their own organizational structure, but when we saw that their goals were not always consistent with our own goals, we made it very clear to them that we were not interested. To counter their influence we organized our own political groups and took up the fight.

"One group, which started out as ALPROMISU but eventually became MIS-URASATA, initially declared unity with the Sandinistas against foreign powers. But its main agenda was to obtain self-governance and advance the cause of the indigenous people, and this was not always in keeping with the Sandinistas' agenda. Whatever unity there was between the Sandinistas and us was short-lived. Several splinter groups have formed over the years as the Miskito resistance grew more powerful."

He went on to explain that unsurprisingly, the Sandinistas did not appreciate the resistance from the Miskito Indians, and they met the resistance with an organized military presence characterized by violence and oppression. Mambo explained that Miskito Indian leaders were rounded up and arrested. This only increased the Miskito community's hatred of the Cubans and Russians. Many Miskito Indians crossed the border to Honduras, where they began working with the Contras and the United States. The Sandinistas then began to forcefully relocate Miskito Indian villages into refugee camps outside of Puerto Cabezas.

Mambo said, "The American people know little of this fight. We need your help as a doctor and as someone who can tell our story to the world. The American television team is covering the presidency of Violeta Chamorro. You have the power to bring that team to Puerto Cabezas and the Caribbean coast, in the name of God and in the name of peace. You can be our ambassador who can help make big changes. Maybe you are our only hope."

I was flattered, but at the same time a little uncomfortable. "You might be putting too much faith in me," I said. "Don't get me wrong. I'll be glad to do whatever I can, but I'm not sure I can work miracles."

Maria responded, "As a doctor, you're already working miracles in the eyes of many of the people here. You can be an ambassador of peace as well. And what about that angel you said God has placed on your shoulder?"

I didn't have an immediate response to that one. Notwithstanding my willingness to joke about it at times, I believed in my angel for the most part, but even angels can only do so much. On the other hand, I've always been an adrenaline junkie, eager for new and sometimes dangerous tasks. Clearly Mambo was not going to let up on me, and neither was Maria, who added, "These people need you. The Miskito Indians have trouble even getting something as basic and simple as a clean shirt to wear. You and your medical team will be amazed by the need, and by how much you can do to help them."

That cinched it for me. The seeds were planted. I decided at that moment that I would speak to the medical team, as well as to Marvin Zindler, Lori Reingold, and Bob Dows. Lori and Bob would be attending this evening's event, and I was sure I could convince them to come to Puerto Cabezas and document the actual presence of the Cubans and Russians on Nicaraguan soil. This would be a first, a real TV news scoop, and it could even turn into a full-length documentary. I thought to myself, *How can they resist such an opportunity?*

Mambo continued, "With the Chamorro government the Miskito Indians are organizing themselves into an armed movement in support of her political party. They have already pledged to work with her in an effort to stabilize the Caribbean region and in turn, she and the new government promised to respect the Miskito Coast as a newly created area." He added that this had immediately earned her the respect of the Miskito people.

"So when you arrive there, Doc, you will not only be the doctor and the ambassador of peace, you will also further cement the relationship between the Chamorro government and the Miskito Indians. Puerto Cabezas is the last place along the coast where there is a Cuban-run medical clinic and where there are Russians."

My face must have betrayed my lingering doubts, and Mambo hastened to assure me, "I know your arrival will result in some local disturbances, but that can easily be handled. The Cubans and Russians will have to leave, especially when they see that the American TV crew is documenting their presence. I think this will put more pressure on them and who knows, it could even affect Cuban and Russian international relations with the U.S. In this one short trip you could change the entire political atmosphere – and at the same time administer to some of the Miskito Indian children."

I said to Mambo, "Look, you've convinced me. As I said earlier, I'm not sure I can work miracles, but my medical team and I can surely help the Miskito people. I'm in, but I have to discuss this with members of the team and get volunteers. I also think that Marvin Zindler and his TV crew will be all over this story, and maybe they really *can* work some miracles."

Mambo nodded, grinning, and said, "You will have full support of the Miskito administration for your peaceful efforts on the Caribbean side. Let me know if you need me to contact my pilot friends." Then he moved the shotgun aside, turned fully around and shook my hand powerfully as an even larger grin spread across his face.

Julio mumbled something nearly inaudible; it sounded a lot like, "Now you've done it."

Indeed it seemed that I had truly made a commitment, and there was no backing out now.

Maria turned to me then and said, with just a hint of flirtation in her voice, "Enough of this serious talk. Do you recall when we first met?"

"I doubt that we just ran into each other," I said.

"It was the first week when your team arrived on a mission a couple of years ago. I was one of the Ladies of the Hospital. I was assisting you and your patients at the entrance of the hospital with administrative tasks."

"As I said, I'm sorry but I really don't remember us running into each other."

"We were running, all right – both of us. There were over 350 children and their parents lined up outside, all wanting to see you."

I smiled and said, "Yes, I think it's coming back to me. But you sure look different."

Maria said, "So you do remember me now?"

"Yes, yes, I do remember. I didn't get much of a look at you in that dark hallway next to the administration area. But now I recall that you were in your very proper gray-and-white Ladies of the Hospital uniform and that very beautifully embroidered apron."

Maria smiled and said, "You *do* remember."

"But look at you now – in your splendid ball gown. Incredible, incredible."

She blushed slightly, then laughed and said, "Do you think we could stop and have Julio put these hot, heavy horsehair pillows into the trunk of the car? They are uncomfortable, they're ridiculous and they're of no use to us anymore on the open road."

I hesitated at this request, then shrugged my shoulders. "As long you don't tell your parents. Remember that I'm responsible for you."

Maria said, "It will be our little secret. If it got back to my parents I would never hear the end of it."

"And I wouldn't either," I said, smiling as I instructed Julio to stop and put the pillows in the trunk. He was hesitant but complied with our request. The task quickly done, we were again on our way to Managua to honor Maria's aunt.

CHAPTER 13
Meeting Madam President

We were now entering the city limits of Managua, and we drove in silence for a while. I was still a little nervous, not knowing what additional trouble we might encounter. Looking out the windows, we could see that the entire road was lined with parked cars and of course heavily armed military guards every few yards. There were tanks and armored cars on either side, and as we moved further along the road we came to a checkpoint, where two Jeeps, each with .50 caliber machine guns, were now blocking the road. Clearly they were taking all precautions.

We were running a little late, and the reception had already started. Julio brought the SUV to a sudden halt and lowered his window. Several military men approached and saluted.

Maria lowered the window on her side and placed her delicate, white-gloved hand outside, holding the colorful invitation.

A handsome officer came forward with a big smile, greeting her and asking how many were in her party. Maria responded, "*Dos personas.*"

With that the lieutenant placed his head gently into the window and looked across the seat at me. As he withdrew his head he turned to the men standing behind him and in almost a whisper said, "*Gringo.*"

Without the slightest hesitation Maria snapped open the door, and with a loud commanding voice declared, "I am the niece of the president, and we are late. Move those trucks."

Startled, the lieutenant turned and looked more closely at her. Her eyes bore into him. He suddenly snapped to attention, saluted and gently stepped forward, closing our car door. As he did, he yelled to the others to move the Jeeps that were obstructing our path.

Julio drove us slowly to the front of the building, and several military men approached the car and opened the doors for us. The area around the building was filled with large SUVs. Because we were so late, there was no closer place to park. We would walk from here.

Reaching into my pocket, I gave Julio and then Mambo each a handful of bills that I'd acquired at the bank the day before. "Get yourselves something to eat," I said. They grinned and thanked me.

Maria, smart woman that she was, instructed, "Park at the end of the road with the car facing out. Do not take long. I want you to be here if there should be any problems and we need to leave quickly."

It was a sensible precaution, given the volatile environment. We couldn't let our guard down.

Before I could make a move, Maria had opened her door and emerged from the car, where she stood waiting for me. I exited my side of the car, briskly walked to the front, and offered her my arm.

"Wait a moment!" Julio called out to me as he reached over the seat, grabbed Maria's beautiful beaded purse, and handed it through the window to me.

"Wow, that's heavy," I commented as I gave the handbag to Maria.

Maria whispered, "It's the pistol."

Alarmed, I asked, "Won't they have metal detectors?"

Laughing, Maria said, "In this country?"

"Then... won't they search us?"

"I am the president's niece. They won't touch me."

With the purse tucked under her arm and a tight grip on my arm, she gently prodded me forward up the steps and into the reception hall.

At the door we were greeted warmly. Maria flashed our invitation but it seemed she was correct; they all knew she was the president's niece. What was surprising was that they all seemed to know who I was as well.

This portion of the building had a high ceiling, and it and the walls were decorated with hundreds of flags. There was the obligatory red carpet, with military men in formal dress forming a line for the guests to follow into the reception area.

Soft music was playing in the background, and as we entered the reception room there was constant chatter from those in line eagerly waiting to greet the president. The line stretched out in front of us along the entire side of the room and then angled across the front. There must have been several hundred people still in line. As late as we were, I could see from those standing in the reception line that it would be at least another hour before we reached President Violeta and her party.

The floor was of highly polished wood, like the floors of a basketball court. Despite the formality of the occasion, I was wearing my trademark Western boots with metal taps. I began to regret my choice when those taps resounded every time I took a step, echoing throughout the room. I was embarrassed and tried, without much luck, to walk more quietly. Maria found this quite amusing and began to giggle.

As the reception line began to move, she urged me forward with a playful tug on my arm. Then the unexpected happened. Maria's giggling and the sound of my boot heels on the wooden floor had attracted the attention of the crowd. Many who had stood in the assembly line recognized the president's niece, but few at the time recognized the American in the Western style suit and boots. Almost simultaneously the people in the reception line whispered to each other, "*Gringo.*"

When more than a hundred people almost simultaneously whisper something in a room that has the acoustics of a gymnasium, it echoes off the floor and the walls as if amplified by a megaphone or microphone. "*Gringo, gringo.*"

President Chamorro and many in her entourage turned to see the cause of the disturbance, and Maria could not keep from laughing out loud when that happened. Her laughter only drew more attention to us, and I was becoming increasingly uncomfortable as Violeta started walking toward us.

Violeta was stunning in her flowing gown, but she was formidable as well. She had an arthritic hip and carried a beautifully hand-carved cane in her right hand; with each step she slapped the cane down against the wooden floor, and it echoed like a gunshot. The room went silent as she drew closer to us, her cane tapping out each step.

I looked quizzically at Maria, who, like the young girl she was, was still giggling at what was taking place at an event that would normally be quite stuffy. Then suddenly she tugged at my arm, and because the gesture was so unexpected I nearly slipped on the polished floor.

She tugged again and said, "*Ándale, ándale!*" We moved toward President Violeta, and as we reached her Maria was gushing, "Auntie, Auntie, it is so good to see you. You look beautiful tonight!"

There are not too many times in my life when I don't know exactly what to say or what to do, but this was one of them, so I just took Maria's lead. As Maria introduced us the president nodded, smiled stiffly and gave me her arm, and the three of us crossed the floor to the front of the reception line.

Glancing sideways as we walked, I could see by her facial expression that the president was annoyed. Seeing me looking at her, she whispered that she had been disturbed by the derogatory comments about me, the rumblings of, "*Gringo, gringo.*" She said, "That word has connotations – you know? I will not have that. America is a strong ally. You as a doctor are helping me change things. We will talk later."

She stationed Maria and me on either side of her at the front of the reception line, bringing her cane firmly down one last time on the wooden floor. The sound echoed throughout the reception room.

Introductions continued, and although I didn't recognize all of the faces, I was surprised by how many names I recognized – names of distinguished people who were now shaking hands not only with the president and her niece but with me. One very large gentleman stood out; he must have been at least 6'2" and perhaps 400 pounds. His hands were as big as baseball catcher's mitts and his grip was strong, but his hands were soft, indicative of someone who had never done any hard labor. Unlike many others in the reception line who chatted with me in Spanish, he looked down on me from his great height and said in English, "You are that doctor angel from Houston, Texas that we are hearing so much about and reading about in *La Prensa*." I nodded and smiled.

"You are becoming somewhat of a celebrity amongst the peasants and farmers that you are treating, the poorest of the poor," the large man said. They all have a lot of respect for you." He still had a grip on my hand. I shook his hand again and then tried to withdraw, but he held me firm in that iron grip. Finally he introduced himself. "I am Arnoldo Alemán."

It didn't mean anything to me at the time, but he was actually sending me a message, that he was to become the next elected president after Violeta Chamorro. And of course I didn't know it at the time, but the medical teams and I would be working with his administration. In fact, during one of our medical mission trips he came into one of the small villages where I was working and insisted that I join him on his "political stump." Later when he won the election, the team members and I were invited to his inauguration. But that's another story.

Right now, standing there in the reception line, I did not have a good feeling about Alemán. The angel on my shoulder was sending me unpleasant vibes.

Finally Alemán released my hand and moved on, and the reception line continued to move as well. I was surprised to see two men in full military uniforms approaching us; this was unusual because everyone else was dressed in formal clothes. The uniforms were dark grayish-blue, and one man's uniform bore bright red epaulets with four gold stars. On the left side of his chest were a myriad of ribbons and medals. He had thick, dark eyebrows and his black hair was slicked back and greased down. He spoke sharply like a military officer, and as he stepped forward he clicked his heels before stopping and shaking hands.

But when he reached Violeta and shook hands with her, her pleasant smile disappeared. As their eyes met, daggers were flying. The handshake was abrupt, and Violeta did not linger; to the contrary she nearly pushed him forward in the line, as if she couldn't wait to get him out of her sight.

He stopped in front of me and clicked his heels together again, hand outstretched.

It wasn't an ordinary handshake; his fingers did not mesh with mine because his pinky and ring fingers were contracted and folded into his palm. Clearly this was a soldier who had been injured – possibly a gunshot wound, or perhaps a pistol that he held had misfired.

His voice surprisingly was soft as he introduced himself: "Daniel Ortega." And with his left hand he pointed to the uniformed man next to him, saying, "This is my brother Humberto."

It suddenly struck me that I was shaking hands with Violeta's predecessor: the leader of the Sandinista army, the communist who for more than a decade had been ravaging his own country in this very deadly civil war. I could hardly imagine him in this reception line, first shaking hands with the new president, and now shaking mine.

I knew that Violeta and Ortega had a complicated history. At one time the two of them had been allies of a sort, following the assassination of Violeta's famous journalist husband, Pedro Joaquín Chamorro Cardenal, whose anti-government stance had often landed him in jail or exile. There was no such thing as a free press in Nicaragua in those days. In fact it was the murder of Pedro that sparked the Nicaraguan Revolution, a revolution in which both Violeta and Ortega played a role. Originally Violeta had supported the Sandinistas and was part of the provisional government established under the Junta of National Reconstruction. But when the Junta became more radical and signed agreements with the Soviet Union, Violeta resigned and returned to her newspaper, the famous *La Prensa*. Ortega developed into a Cuban-style Marxist, and he and Violeta had long since parted ways.

I now wondered to myself if this was a public display of reconciliation, and if so, did it mean that Daniel Ortega was declaring that the Contra-Sandinista conflict was finally at an end?

These thoughts were racing through my mind when Ortega said, "I heard about all the good works that you and your medical team are doing. My people have been in need of the medical care and supplies and equipment that you have brought us for many years now. You have become a symbol of peace and unity for this country, I am proud to have met you. Please continue your good work."

With that, I gently turned his hand over and made a quick examination of the contracted fingers.

I said, "I do a lot of hand surgery, I think I can improve this if not completely fix it. You should come to the hospital; it would be my pleasure."

But before I could finish the conversation, pain radiated from the instep of my foot into my ankle and up my calf. The point of Violeta's three-inch heel was pressing firmly into the top of my foot.

I made a short gasp for breath and thanked Daniel Ortega and then quickly shook hands with his brother. When they moved on I turned to President Violeta, who was now regarding me with nearly the same expression she had previously given to Mr.

Ortega.

Then she smiled and said, "My dear doctor, there are some people we simply do not talk to."

She removed the heel from my foot and I smiled back, saying, "My dear Madam President, a little bump with the hip would send the same message with a lot less pain."

Smiling sweetly, she ran her gloved hand across the side of my cheek. "I will try to remember that for the next time."

The reception line had been significantly reduced over the past hour, though there were a few stragglers still arriving, so I did not feel nearly so bad about having been late to the party. Clearly I was far from the only tardy attendant.

A very pleasant gentleman and his wife appeared in front of me. The man's English was meticulous, without even a trace of an accent, and he had a delightful smile. As we shook hands he said, "I am Enrique José Bolaños. There are great things happening in this country. There are big changes ahead. I want to establish good relations with America, but we must also unite all Nicaraguans and end this bloody civil war."

This time my angel seemed to be giving me very good vibes. I did not know it at the time, but Mr. Bolaños was to become Nicaragua's third democratically elected president eleven years later; he served from 2002 to 2007. At the time I could not anticipate what the future held for Mr. Bolaños or myself, but we were to become close friends, and on her 85th birthday, my mother and her husband, Leonard Rokaw, joined our medical mission team in Managua. President Bolaños invited us to the presidential palace, where I participated in a program for continued improvement in the medical care of the country. And at the ripe old age of 85, my mother worked in the hospital, attending to the children before and after surgery. She was particularly helpful in the burn ward with her loving kindness and the gifts that she brought for the children.

But I'm getting ahead of myself again. After Mr. Bolaños and his wife moved on, there were only a few more hands to shake. And then the announcement was made for everybody to leave the reception area for the dining area, where the orchestra had struck up a loud and cheerful salute to the new president.

I sensed that the next phase of my adventure was about to begin.

CHAPTER 14
A New Friend
And New Enemies

s we entered the dining area, the president and her entourage took their seats at the head table, at which point, everyone else was seated. Then the festivities began in earnest: the orchestra played lively and sensual traditional music as dancers in spectacular, multi-colored outfits swirled across the stage. One dance group was almost immediately followed by another, the colors and designs of the various troupes depicting the diverse cultures of Nicaragua and indeed all of Central America. The performances went on for a long time, but for me the time flew. I found the entire spectacle very upbeat and refreshing, thinking that it surely must serve as a balm for the scars inflicted by many years of civil war, and a welcome reminder that grace and beauty can survive even in violent times.

When the last of the dancers left the stage, the orchestra went into full ballroom mode as couples migrated to the dance floor. To my surprise, President Violeta looked over at the table where I was sitting, and our eyes met. She nodded subtly, just a hint of a smile on her face, and her niece, catching her meaning a moment before I did, abruptly prodded me to my feet. I walked slowly and a little nervously toward the head table and reached up to take the new president's hand as she descended the several steps to the dance floor. I was acutely conscious that she was sending a hell of a message to the room at large, and the message was that any disparagement of "Dr. Angel" would not be tolerated.

As we waltzed across the floor, everyone else stopped dancing and began to applaud. Violeta's eyes were bright and she was smiling fully now. I felt warm and I knew I was turning red as we whirled around the dance floor, but by the time the waltz ended and the orchestra had struck up another tune, I was much more relaxed. By the end of the second dance the president and I were laughing and chatting casually like old friends.

After that dance ended Violeta said she wanted to sit down, so I escorted her back to her table. Impulsively I decided to take the opportunity to bring up the project that was newly on my mind. My words came out in a rush: "Madam President, I have decided that I want to take the medical team and the American TV crew to Puerto Cabezas and the Caribbean coast. They need the medical help and care, but it will also be a powerful political statement on your part if you support our efforts."

Briefly I wondered if I had overstepped, but felt instant relief when Violeta replied, "I said earlier that you and I would talk, and that's one of the things I wanted to talk to you about. Please sit with me for a few minutes." She saw me glance over at Maria, still seated at our table, and she said, "Don't worry. My niece will be fine without you for a while." As if to affirm this, Maria caught my glance and gave me a beautiful smile.

We sat down at the table, with hundreds of eyes still upon us, but Violeta ignored the onlookers and got right to the point. "As you may have heard, Puerto Cabezas is far away from everything. It is connected to the Pacific Nicaragua coast only by semi-passable seasonal roads; there are no hotels and it will be a difficult trip. But I have already made some contacts for a pilot and a flight from Managua to Puerto Cabezas."

Wow, I thought. *This lady wastes no time.*

"You also need to realize we have no direct contact with this area," she was saying. "You'll be the only travelers in a town of about 50,000 Miskito Indians. There is a Red Cross station there, and before the war there was a constant stream of foreign medical volunteers, and they were always well accepted. But I want you to be prepared for the worst. The streets are nothing more than gravel and bare earth, connecting small neighborhoods within a jungle environment. People live in humble, simple wooden homes. Everything is built of wood, and built by hand. Many homes are on stilts with thatched or tin roofs. They are fishermen and local farmers. They have nothing."

I nodded. So far everything she was saying was consistent with what Mambo had told me during our drive to the reception. At that point I decided it was time to ask Violeta what was perhaps the most important question of all. "Madam President, before I leave I must ask you if you are serious about establishing the Caribbean Miskito coast as an autonomous region, in a show of respect for these indigenous people."

"*Si, si,*" she assured me. "I visualize it as a Miskito Nation, similar to what you did in the United States when you gave the indigenous people – the Native Americans – their Nations. I have read about that part of your history. Cherokee Nation, the Navajo Nation, the Apache Nation and others – all autonomous and self governing, but within the United States."

Again I nodded, though a little less enthusiastically. For the sake of diplomacy, I decided not to mention that while the idea of an indigenous nation within a larger nation might have been a fine idea on paper, in reality the United States was hardly a first-rate model for fair treatment of native peoples. But at least it seemed that Violeta's heart was in the right place, so perhaps there was reason for optimism.

I told Violeta what I had learned about the Miskito – their history, their efforts to displace the Sandinistas, and their desire for the Cubans and Russians to leave the area. She nodded as I spoke, then responded, "I'm glad you've been learning about this region and the people. You already know that this indigenous community has not seen doctors in a decade because of the war, except of course for the Russians and Cubans who support the Sandinistas.

"But I can't emphasize enough that this won't be an easy trip. Travel along the Rio Coco simply does not figure into the travel itineraries of very many people, not even Nicaraguans. You will be taking a single-engine plane, and it's about an hour flight from Managua to Puerto Cabezas. You will need at least three or four days in Puerto Cabezas and a few days more to go up the coast to treat the children in the nearby villages. Because all of the structures there are built with wood there is a sawmill in the center of town. As it happens the man who owns the sawmill is the mayor. I will give you a letter of introduction to him. He can arrange for your housing and food."

Once again fearing I might be overstepping, but eager to promote my new cause, I said, "If I may make a suggestion, Madam President..."

Her face expressionless, she said, "Go on."

"You might consider placing a few sentences in the letter to the mayor, explaining your desire to establish the Miskito Indian region as a newly created autonomous area. And also permitting them to participate in municipal and national elections. This will be important in bringing the Miskito Indian tribes into their own political realm. They'll not only reject the Sandinistas because of this but they will also apply pressure to encourage the Cubans and Russians to leave the Caribbean shores – not to mention that it will play heavily on the reasons that we are there, and will help ensure our safety. I've found that it's always good to have as many things in writing as possible." Detecting what looked like the beginning of a frown on her face I paused, trying to steel myself for a dressing-down.

But I soon realized that her expression was only an indication that she had been listening intently and considering my words. After a few moments she said, "Very well. I will have everything prepared in two days. When the time comes, my niece Maria will send a car to take you to the presidential palace here in Managua, and she will accompany you. I will inform the guards that you are coming. Use the back door and rear staircase, and you will be admitted immediately upon your arrival. And don't worry if you're told I'm in a conference. I will see you no matter what. This is too important, and your willingness to do this for our country is very much appreciated."

The relief on my face must have been visible. Violeta smiled and continued, "I will prepare not only the Miskito Indians but the whole country by having stories placed in *La Prensa* regarding your upcoming trip. The medical as well as the political implications will be spelled out. I will also let them know that Mr. Marvin Zindler and the ABC-TV team will film the historical trip, and that this story will be distributed not only in the United States but hopefully will be picked up as an international story as well. Thank you for what you are doing for me and for my country."

I said, "We'll do our best. But please hold off on telling anyone about Mr. Zindler's participation until I speak with him and with his producer and cameraman. The cameraman and producer are here tonight but I haven't had a chance to speak with them yet. And this is the type of trip they are going to have to volunteer for; I cannot just command them to do it, or even ask them outright. But I think they will say yes. And I'll also ask for volunteers from the medical team who wish to remain another week – not just to help treat the Miskito Indians but also for what I believe will be for them the adventure of a lifetime."

"Well, if the cameraman and producer are here, why don't you ask them now?" she asked. I smiled, thinking that here was a person who was as assertive – or pushy, some might say – as I have sometimes been known to be when I get my mind set on something.

"With pleasure," I said, and stood up to scan the room. I found Lori and Bob and some other ABC crewmembers seated at a table on the far side of the room. I caught their eye and waved, then beckoned them to come over to our table, whereupon I introduced them to Violeta. Then I told them about our proposal. To my delight but not to my surprise, they agreed to go with me to Puerto Cabezas and get the raw footage, with the goal in mind of turning it into a major news story or even a documentary. They also scheduled a one-on-one interview between the president and Marvin Zindler, which would take place in the morning. As they returned to their table, I said to Violeta, "Well, if there's nothing else right now, Madam President, I should get back to Maria."

"Oh, of course, of course!" she replied, her eyes twinkling as she looked over at her niece. "Don't let me keep you. I will speak with you tomorrow."

When I returned to the table Maria said, "Well, it looks like you and my aunt had quite a lot to talk about. I trust the conversation was productive."

"It was indeed," I said, smiling.

Miracles in Bedlam

* * * * *

It was almost 2:00 a.m. when the dancing and festivities finally drew to a close, and I walked Maria out of the dining area. Two guards escorted us to the SUV, which was stationed at the end of the road, facing outward, as she had directed. As we approached we could hear music blaring, and we saw that Julio was singing while Mambo was pounding out a rhythm on the dashboard.

I tapped on the window, and immediately both men sprang from the car and opened the back doors so Maria and I could enter. After he climbed into the driver's seat and Mambo had settled back into his position, Julio turned around to give me some money.

"What's this for?" I asked.

"The change from our dinner, that was so kind of you."

I said, "No, just keep it." Then I continued, "You seem so awake and alive and rested. It's after two in the morning!"

Julio said, "We *are* rested. Thanks to you we had a nice dinner, then parked the car the way we were ordered and took a siesta. So now I'm wide-awake and I'm ready to drive home. And it's a good thing we did get some rest, because you have to be very vigilant at this time of night. There is danger on the road from wild animals as well as livestock that have broken free. There will also be the drunks. Just about every family has lost someone in an automobile accident on these roads because that person swerved to avoid striking an animal or a staggering drunk. I don't want that to happen to us."

Mambo added, "And it isn't just animals and drunks you have to worry about. There is only one road that we can take from here through León and on to Chinandega, and there are thieves and guerrillas. A lone car moving at night is always a target."

Maria said, "Do you think we need to put those horsehair cushions back in place?"

Mambo replied, "They are of little value, Señorita, except for psychological value – reassurance for your parents. They would not be effective protection from either a collision or bullets."

"I know," Maria said, smiling. "I was just joking. I hate those old pillows anyway."

Once we had left the city lights of Managua, the road was pitch-black except for the high beams of the SUV. There were also two searchlights mounted to either side of the automobile, and I noticed that Julio had turned these on as well. He was not taking any chances.

I closed my eyes and leaned my head back. I was exhausted, but my mind was going non-stop. All I could think about was a trip to the Caribbean coast and Puerto Cabezas. I'd gotten Lori and Bob to agree to go along and shoot footage, but would their bosses at the Houston ABC station, and their bosses' bosses at the national network, understand the significance of our project and realize that they had the makings of a major story? And equally if not more important, would the other members of the medical team be willing to volunteer? For that matter, would Marvin be interested in going with us?

The president had said she would have everything ready in two days, including the letter of introduction to the mayor of Puerto Cabezas. That really didn't leave much time for me to get ready. But as concerned as I was about details and the dozens of things that could go wrong, I knew that somehow we would pull it off.

If that had been all I had on my mind, it would have been enough. In the back of my mind, though, I knew that upon returning to Chinandega I would also have to deal with Michael, his leg wound and his relationship with Marta. He was going to be sent home immediately, and I was not looking forward to being the one to remind him of this, but it was my duty to do so.

And on top of all of that, there was also the day's surgical schedule. We wouldn't reach Chinandega until at least 4:00 a.m., and the first surgeries were scheduled for 8:00. That would give me only a few hours' sleep once we got back there. Perhaps I should try to get some sleep now. I closed my eyes, but the thoughts of Puerto Cabezas and the plans I needed to make and execute kept soaring through my mind, making sleep seem impossible. After a few minutes I opened my eyes and stared out the window for a while, my thoughts still racing.

Finally I started to nod off, but just before I closed my eyes I noticed a cluster of little homes and other buildings, on what seemed to be a small farm. A single porch light was burning at one of the little houses; otherwise there was no illumination. For some reason I had a feeling of foreboding. Trying desperately to adjust my eyes, I peered down a dark road that bisected the small farm. I could see nothing, but the foreboding wouldn't leave me. If there was any time that we needed that guardian angel, I thought, it was on this ride back to Chinandega tonight.

It was becoming steadily clearer to me that my presence in Nicaragua with the medical team and the TV crew – and particularly my attendance at the festivities for President Chamorro – exasperated some, unsettled some, and angered others. From the beginning I had been an object of curiosity with my "Crazy Texan" persona, but evidence was mounting that I was also a target for various parties who felt threatened.

La Prensa had been running stories almost daily about the team and I and our medical work, and I was beginning to realize that this exposure had the potential to harm as well as benefit all of us, and me in particular. And now there was no telling how many hostile eyes had observed me talking and laughing and dancing with President Chamorro. I sensed I had a new friend in her, but there was no telling how many enemies I'd made as a result.

I didn't think it was unreasonable to speculate that the Sandinistas who were still active in the area might wish to harm my team and me. Perhaps they viewed us as a threat to their very existence, I thought. And tomorrow, no doubt, the newspapers would have details not only about the event to honor Violeta, but very possibly about my new role as a peace envoy as well. Violeta had just told me that she was going to alert *La Prensa*, so no doubt the news stories would provide details about the medical team's planned mission to help the Miskito Indians, and the efforts to guarantee the establishment of an independent, autonomous region. That would not set well with some people.

Thoughts of Violeta's predecessor, Daniel Ortega, also hovered in the back of my mind. He had been nothing but civil to me in the reception line, but I had no reason to trust him and many reasons not to. What sort of plans might he – or at least some of his lieutenants and other loyalists – be cooking up with the Sandinistas? Might they be plotting ways to sabotage not only our nascent mission to Puerto Cabezas, but also our team's overall efforts in Nicaragua? Was it even possible that Violeta's niece, and Julio and Mambo as well, were right when they said that I was in danger of being kidnapped or killed? I didn't want to think about this, and certainly didn't want to be paranoid, but the nagging worries wouldn't leave me.

We drove on through the darkness as I continued to mull over these matters. There had been no conversation for a long time; Maria was very quiet, as if lost in her own reverie, Julio was concentrating on his driving, and Mambo was working the searchlights back and forth across the road. His vigilance, along with the double-barreled sawed-off shotgun sitting on his lap, gave me some comfort.

We were all startled out of our respective reveries when a blockade of branches and logs suddenly appeared under the glare of the searchlights. Judging from the smell they had been doused with gasoline, and just as we approached them, they burst into flame while thick black smoke began to envelop the area. Julio immediately shut off the air conditioning and lifted his pistol from his shoulder holster, shouting at Maria and me to duck down.

He didn't have to tell us twice.

CHAPTER 15
An Angel On Overtime

Mambo rolled down the window and had his shotgun at the ready, as was to be expected. But as I looked over the seat I saw a puzzled expression on his face. He immediately shut off the searchlights and the headlights as well, leaving us in pitch darkness. Between that and the smoke, we could see nothing except the roaring inferno in the middle of the road.

I could hear Julio hit the electric door lock buttons to make sure that they were all locked. Then the glass behind us broke and I heard Maria's terrified scream; her back was pressed against the seat cushions, and her face was white with shock.

A man clambered over the rear trunk and materialized in the area of the broken window. He had a grimy face with a thick unkempt beard, and he clinched a stiletto in one hand and an army revolver in the other. Fortunately he wasn't pointing either one at us at the moment, but was using the pistol to clear the glass along the edges of the broken window. But his dark little eyes were fixed on mine, and I just reacted spontaneously: I landed a punch with all my force along the side of his nose. I could hear it crack as he fell back, managing to pull the trigger on the revolver. But he was unable to take good aim, and the slug merely grazed my neck. That angel on my shoulder was still apparently looking after me, and putting in some serious overtime hours. Even so, I felt a searing pain where the bullet had grazed me.

Maria screamed again. I whispered to her, "Hey, it's going to be okay. We'll get out of this. Julio and Mambo will get us out. Hang tight." I wasn't entirely convinced myself, but my words seemed to calm her a little.

We couldn't see anything but the conflagration ahead of us, but Julio knew one thing: we had to get around this barrier before they trapped us. He took a chance and turned on the driver's side spotlight, then almost immediately switched it off as bullets and gunshots echoed in the direction in which the light was aimed. Then we noticed that there were low brushes along the side of the road, and that they too were beginning to catch fire. We were now feeling the terrible heat from the fire, and Julio saw that he couldn't get through the flaming barricade in the middle of the road. "But I think we can maneuver to the left of the flames," he said. As he gunned the big engine, I realized that he had more than enough to do handling the SUV, so I reached forward and grabbed the automatic pistol from his lap. He didn't protest as I did so, and I pointed the pistol out the broken rear window, peering through the thickening smoke.

The man I had punched was struggling to get to his feet, and now we had something else to worry about: several others had burst through the smoke and had rushed to his side. My adversary had lost the knife in his fall but had pulled a pistol from his belt. Mambo turned around, shouting a warning to me, and I lowered my head; the next thing I heard was the roaring of his shotgun as he released both barrels at once. My hearing was instantly gone, but there was nothing wrong with my other senses. I could see two men falling to the ground, and I could smell the gunpowder as Mambo quickly reloaded the shotgun.

Then Mambo surprised me. He opened his side door and jumped out of the SUV, maneuvering behind the blazing inferno in front of us and covering our escape. Julio drove the SUV off the road and around the flaming blockade, through the brush that lined the road to our left.

Yet another attacker suddenly appeared in the haze and smoke. He tripped and staggered beside us as the wheels kicked up sand and gravel at him. Mambo tackled him too, clamping a big powerful hand on his ankle and dragging him towards the flames. The man swung but Mambo dodged that and slammed him with the butt of the shotgun.

I was tempted to climb out the back window to help, but thought better of it when I realized that Mambo had his situation under control. The man's sleeve was now burning and he was screaming as Mambo grabbed his opposite shoulder and dragged him to the ground. He tried to wiggle loose but Mambo placed a heavy boot on his neck and put the shotgun to his temple. I lost sight of them as the SUV cleared the burning barrier, but moments later I could see that Mambo had grabbed the intruder's foot and was dragging him along the road towards us. Cinders flew from the man's burning clothes; his back was scraping along the gravel and his head was bouncing on the road as Mambo approached us and with one powerful arm threw him up against the back of our vehicle. Looking out the broken back window, I was amazed when he got to his feet and still made a run for it.

Julio quickly threw the big SUV into reverse. As the vehicle inched towards our attacker, ready to crush him, the man made a surprise move: he bent his knees and pushed himself with his uninjured hand onto the back of the vehicle. He seemed exhausted and beaten, but he still had some fight in him. Foolishly he reached into his boot and pulled out a knife, and Mambo raised his shotgun and hit him with it, hard, knocking him unconscious. The man's arm jerked convulsively as he rolled off the back of the car, and on to the road. Then Mambo came around to the front of the SUV and got back in.

By now we were shrouded in the thick smoke from the gasoline-infused fire, but that was actually working to our advantage. Still, it was anything but pleasant, for we were all gasping and coughing from smoke inhalation. And we still weren't out of harm's way.

As Julio began to inch the car back onto the road and away from the flames, several more shots bounced off the front right fender. Mambo spotted the gun flashes and let loose with two blasts from his shotgun. Then all was quiet. Julio stopped the SUV, and I sat up and took stock of our situation through the rear window. I was breathing hard, gasping to fill my lungs with air, and the spot on my neck where the bullet had grazed began to throb. I was reminded again of what a close call I'd just had.

Maria remained crouched on the floor unharmed, though clearly frightened. But she gave me a weak smile as I carefully exited the vehicle with pistol in hand. I walked back to examine the unconscious man, and saw that his stiletto had fallen and lay beside him. Not wanting to take any chances, I pocketed the stiletto as well as his pistol.

Mambo soon joined me. Looking down at the man with utter contempt, he asked me for the knife I had in my belt. I thought he was going to kill him right there, but Mambo walked to the side of the road, where he located some big vines and cut them down. Dragging them back, he tied our assailant's arms and legs behind him. Next he took one of the long vines and showed me a trick that I already knew, having learned it from my Vietnam days. He made a noose at one end, dropped the noose around the man's head and onto his neck, then pulled his feet up against his back and tied the other end of the vine to his ankles. If our attacker tried to make any significant movement to escape, the noose would tighten and he would strangle himself. It was a very effective way to immobilize someone.

Then Julio popped the trunk, and Mambo and I took the big horsehair pillows out and placed them in the backseat. Maria, seeing the pillows, rolled her eyes. Together Mambo and I lifted the unconscious man into the trunk and closed it, then calmly climbed back into the SUV as if nothing had happened. Maria looked at me questioningly. "We are going to take him to the hospital," I said. "I will start an IV and antibiotics, and we will treat his burn wounds, just as we would any injured patient."

Julio added, "We need him alive. We need to find out who is behind this. We need to bring an end to these attacks on you and the American medical team."

Mambo, still with a stiletto in his hand, said, "I could just kill him and save you a lot of trouble."

I replied, "I don't think that will be necessary. Let's proceed with him as our prisoner – one who will, I hope, provide us with some valuable information under the right conditions."

"I know how to make the right conditions," Mambo growled. "I will borrow some of your tools, Doctor, and he will talk to us quickly."

"Mambo, look, I know you are upset but we are all okay, thanks to you and Julio. And we will deal with this in the morning."

Mambo said, "But you're bleeding from your neck, Doctor, so it seems you are not okay."

With that statement Maria, for the first time, got a good look at my wound. Her beautiful, fine-featured face turned pale as she leveled her gaze on my neck and then on my shirt, which I suddenly noticed was stained with blood. Then she surprised all of us by smiling and saying, "Mambo is right. You have been wounded, and it looks like your neck is still bleeding."

"It's just a scratch," I said, although with the throbbing pain, it was beginning to feel like a little more than that.

"Shouldn't you be going to the hospital yourself?" she asked, and immediately she removed her beautifully embroidered handkerchief from her handbag and began to apply pressure to the side of my neck. "That's all I can offer for now."

"Well, we are going straight to the hospital," I said, "and I'll have someone look at it when we get there." I have to say that despite the pain I was in, the solicitous attention from a beautiful young woman took the edge off more than a little bit.

We were now moving rapidly toward León where, I suggested, we could stop at the police station, but Julio would have none of that. He was adamant that we would go on a few more miles to Chinandega to the hospital there, and then to the local military establishment – but not to the police. "The police are often part of the problem," he said. "You do not know who to trust anymore."

At last we reached Chinandega and made a beeline to the hospital, where I jumped out of the SUV, burst through the door and roused the emergency room doctor and several orderlies. Seeing my neck, the doctor and a couple of the orderlies hustled me into the ER and began treating my wound.

Meanwhile Julio and Mambo dragged our prisoner in and threw the hapless man on top of a gurney. He was conscious by now, but in no condition to complain or fight back. Working quickly, Julio and Mambo cut the noose from the prisoner's neck, and he immediately started to struggle a little. With the help of one of the orderlies, they lashed his arms and legs to the gurney. Then Julio pulled a roll of tape off of a shelf and wrapped it multiple times around the man's chest and waist until he and the gurney that he lay on were one.

I could see what was going on from the emergency room, and I shouted at one of the orderlies to put an IV into the man and start an antibiotic. The orderly obliged, asking about pain medication. I said, "No, I first need to determine our prisoner's state of consciousness and the blows to his head and face. I'm sure he has some fractures and a possible concussion." As the orderly worked to get the IV in place, Mambo, Julio, and I gave a quick summary of events to the emergency room doctor and the staff.

My own treatment completed and the prisoner being attended to, I told Julio and Mambo to take Maria home. I also suggested that she not wake her parents to discuss what had taken place tonight, but to get some sleep, and she agreed that this would be best. Finally I asked Julio to take the SUV to Managua in the morning for repairs. "I'll cover any expenses," I said.

"But what about you, Doctor?" Maria asked. "Aren't you coming with us?"

"I'm just going to bunk here for tonight," I said. "After all, I have to be in the O.R. at 7:00 tomorrow morning... well, *this* morning." We said our goodbyes and they left, and I stumbled to the doctor's lounge and found a couch on which to plop down.

* * * * *

I arrived at the O.R. at 7:00 a.m., exhausted but glad to be alive, and with my adrenaline still pumping like crazy. Gathering my surgical team, I told them we would make rounds in the children's ward and that I wanted to start the first surgical case by 8:00 a.m.

Barrett Phillips was there that morning, and in a loud booming voice he said, "That must have been a hell of a party last night. I can't help but notice that you have an enormous bandage on your neck."

Not to be outdone, I nonchalantly said, "Cut myself shaving." Everyone laughed.

In fact, by the time I got to the O.R. that morning, the story of last night's events had already been told and re-told many times.

But I had no time to dwell on the previous night's adventures, because there were patients to see. The post-op children were all doing very well. We changed dressings, answered parents' questions and dispensed medicine as needed. Then Kimberly passed out discharge slips with return dates for suture removal.

That afternoon the assistant administrator, Cardenas, said I was needed in the administrative office. I told the surgical team members to set up the operating rooms and bring in the next group of children, and I would be there in a few minutes. Cardenas escorted me to the administrative office, where his boss, Miguel Perez, stood just outside the closed door. As Perez opened it, I was a little taken aback to see that the room was packed. Reporters filled the small office and were lined up wall to wall. There were also several military men in full uniform standing next to the administrator's desk.

They all began to clap. The captain was the first to speak; standing at attention, he saluted and said, "You have brought us a prisoner. He will talk. We will find out who is behind this, and your stay in our country – and your medical team's stay as well – will be safer and without future incident. I promise you that."

I smiled and thanked him, but I guess my face betrayed the fact that I was not entirely convinced that our troubles were over.

The captain continued, "I know you are concerned, but I assure you that my men and I are doing everything we can to secure your safety and that of your team." I nodded, and waited for him to say more.

"We have found out quite a lot so far," he continued. "The bad news is that I feel that the group who attacked you on the road last night was considerably more organized than some of the previous groups have been. We have already gone out to the site and examined it. You were lucky.

"But the good news is that even though your attackers were more organized they were also stupid. They piled the rocks and the branches in the middle of the road and set it afire, but fortunately left enough room for you to bypass on the left side. They were also stupid to saturate the brush pile with tar and gasoline, which provided you with a smokescreen. It seems, Doctor, that the 'angel on your shoulder' that some of the news stories have talked about is still looking after you and your surgical team. You are again front-page news, not only in Nicaragua but throughout Central America. I understand the news services may carry the story to the United States as well."

Then he went on to praise me, with the reporters in the room busily taking notes. I was a little embarrassed by the praise, and finally interrupted the captain to ask, "What have you found out so far about the man that we took as a prisoner?"

The captain replied, "We have reason to believe that he is the leader of that little band that attacked you, and we have considerable information about him and his still-active Sandinista unit. Rest assured that we will continue to get more information from him."

"Were there any others found at the scene?" I asked. "I believe that my bodyguard Mambo's shotgun blast killed at least two men; they appeared to be dead on the road. And when Mambo fired into the underbrush we could hear cries. They were either killed or wounded as well."

The lieutenant spoke up. "When we examined the scene the road was blocked by large rocks and hot embers and coals from the fire. There was blood on the ground behind that as well as to the right side of the road. They must have returned and retrieved the fallen. They were obviously familiar with the territory. They did not leave their dead and wounded behind."

"That is all, Doctor," said the captain. "Now we will let the press ask you their questions. I am sure they have many."

At his cue the members of the press who filled the small office began shouting questions. They were all talking over each other, and it was impossible to understand anyone. Quietly I asked Administrator Perez if he and Cardenas would deal with them because I had children to take care of in the operating room.

Cardenas said, "No, Doctor. Mr. Perez can deal with the press, but I am taking you to the emergency room to get your bandage changed. You are bleeding again and it is getting messy." Perez nodded.

As I exited the office I turned to the reporters and the military, saying, "Return in two days, and I will have an announcement for you that will make headline news." Then I quietly whispered the words, "Puerto Cabezas," and winked. *Always leave 'em wanting more,* I thought to myself as I left with Mr. Cardenas.

As we were walking down the musty corridor to the ER, Cardenas said to me, "You know, you are a very good doctor and definitely an angel in our eyes. But I have come to the conclusion that that 'Crazy Texan' nickname fits you very well too." Then he looked at me a little anxiously, as if fearing that he had offended me.

I laughed and put him at ease. "You are certainly not the first person to tell me that," I replied, "and you most likely won't be the last." As we entered the ER I smiled and said to him, "But you know, I wouldn't say that I'm crazy, exactly. I take some risks that others might think are foolish. I have an unconventional way of doing some things. And most of all, I want what I want – when I want it."

Apparently emboldened, he looked at me with a stern expression, saying, "I have learned that. And if I may be honest with you, it has not always pleased my boss, Sr. Perez." Then he began to laugh, and he patted me on my shoulder and left me there to get my bandage changed.

I thought about our brief conversation as my wound was being treated. Crazy I might be, and determined to get what I wanted, but it wasn't just about getting my way. And it wasn't just about me, either. My team and I were actually making a difference here, achieving our goals of creating a little bit of order out of a great deal of chaos. So far, the rewards had richly justified all of the risks.

My wound freshly cleaned and re-dressed, I stood up to proceed with my day. There was one task ahead of me that I wasn't exactly looking forward to, but it was time to do it. If I were going to spend the day in the operating room, I knew I first needed to examine Michael's leg, and then deal with the "Marta problem." The sooner I got this done the better off we would all be.

Joseph Agris, M.D.

CHAPTER 16
The Rules Are The Rules

Before entering Michael's small isolation room, I put on a pair of surgical gloves. Michael looked up as I entered, and seemed surprised to see the bandage on my neck. I said, "You were not the only one who incurred a life-threatening injury on this trip." But that is all I said, and he did not ask me to elaborate. It was quite possible he had already heard the story from the staff.

Turning to the matter at hand I saw that the swelling in his leg was gone, along with the soreness. It looked pretty much normal. The local surgeon had visited Michael earlier and had given him a clean bill of health. I decided then and there that Michael would be released today and arrangements for his flight home made immediately.

"So what now?" Michael asked.

"You are going home on the next available flight."

Michael pressed the bed sheet against his face and began to sob into it. When the sobs finally subsided, he wiped his face dry and slowly sat up, taking deep breaths, his chest still heaving. He looked down, his features full of guilt and misery. "I don't want to leave the medical team."

"Look, Michael, we've already discussed this. Did you think I would change my mind? You are no longer of any good to me, to the team, or to our patients. I understand that you are dealing with a lot for a young man. You shouldn't beat yourself up too badly. Marta is beautiful and intelligent. But I cannot risk you compromising the effectiveness of our efforts."

He pulled himself up in the bed, wiped his face again, and looked like a little boy lost in the world. Averting his gaze downward for a moment, Michael whispered, "I don't have a clue what I'm supposed to do." Then he looked up at me again, and when I met his eyes with a blank stare, he immediately looked away.

"Just forget it, Michael. You're young and you made a mistake. Young people always do. The only real harm that came to you was an infected leg. Your leg is doing much better, and you will ultimately figure things out once you put this immediate despair behind you."

I leaned forward and extended my hand, and Michael sat up and shook it. It was time to go. The discussion was over, and the operating room was waiting.

As I turned and made my way to the door, Michael said, "Look, Doc. I came to Chinandega with good intentions. I came to be part of the team. I came to help. I didn't know anyone and no one knew me. And then this bright light appeared, and for following it, I'm banished. It doesn't seem fair."

I turned back around and saw that he was glaring at me. I returned his angry look, and said again, "The rules are the rules!"

He responded weakly, "What the hell does it matter now?"

"Goodbye, Michael," I said. "Safe travels home." I exited his room, closing the door slowly behind me and mumbling, "The rules are the rules," my voice conveying an anger I didn't really feel. Perhaps it was more a feeling of disappointment in someone I had trusted. As I began my walk down the hall I could hear Michael shouting, "It's a lot more complicated than that! What do you want me to say?" His tirade faded as I quickened my steps on the way to the operating rooms. I had a feeling that the story of Michael and Marta was far from over, but this chapter was definitely ending now.

* * * * *

Looking into the first operating theater, I saw that there was a procedure in progress and everything was okay. The second operating room was mine, and nurses JoAnne and Carolyn were prepping both little patients on adjacent tables.

When I looked into Operating Room 3 the surgical procedure was already underway, with Marta working tableside with the doctor. I entered the room, walked up to Marta and whispered into her ear, "Michael will be leaving tomorrow morning. When you complete this case you can go say your goodbyes." She nodded, and I thought I detected a hint of tears, but she continued her work like the professional she was.

With everything going smoothly in the other rooms, I joined Barrett Phillips and the circulating nurse, Arantxa, at the scrub sink. They pelted me with questions in rapid succession about the reception for President Chamorro and the incident that followed. As they spoke, they kept looking at the large bandage on my neck. Finally, I said, "Stop staring at me. You've seen bandages before. I'm okay. Let's get in there and get to work."

The surgical procedures progressed in an orderly, straightforward fashion, just the way we liked it in the operating room. There were burned, contracted little hands and fingers that were released, and skin grafts applied. A flesh burn that had come in the night before was cleaned and debrided and then we applied silvadene cream, a new topical drug developed by the Brooke Army Medical Center and donated by the Houston Methodist Hospital. I later learned that this was the first time it had been used in Nicaragua, and over the years it proved to be a breakthrough in postoperative burn treatment. There were the requisite number of cleft lips and cleft palate procedures performed as well.

The emergency room brought us a child with a severe hand injury that occurred from a threshing machine on the farm. According to Nicaragua law, young children could not be employed, but farm work was considered a completely different circumstance, and farm work-related injuries in both children and adults were all too common.

We also had an older gentleman, a goat herder in his 60s, on the schedule. It was an interesting case, and it had us all baffled. We thought he might have some form of cancer due to what appeared to be multiple tumors in the palms of his hands. His fingers were contracted, and he complained that he was having difficulty milking his goats, which threatened his livelihood. I brought the resident doctors in to see him but they did not have a diagnosis, either. Two of the local doctors looked in as well, and they said they had seen a problem like this on occasion, but couldn't put a name to it.

This was one of those teaching experiences that were a big part of the reason we were here. After a lot of discussion, head-scratching, and research, we finally came up with a correct diagnosis: the patient suffered from Dupuytren's contracture of his hands, which manifests as multiple painful palm nodules that, left untreated, would only get worse with time. It was a totally correctable problem, and proper treatment would allow this gentleman to get back to herding and milking his goats, affording him the ability to have a relatively profitable and infinitely more comfortable life.

Under normal surgical circumstances in a well-equipped hospital, we would use a pressurized arm tourniquet for the procedure, but no such device existed in Nicaragua, much less in Chinandega. If we were going to attempt the procedure and help this man, we were going to have to put on our best thinking caps and get innovative. But that is what Third World MASH-type teams do. You work with what you have, you innovate, and you succeed.

Of course there was no microscope available to help us see and dissect out the very small nerves and vessels of his hand, but we did have three- and five-power loupe magnifiers, which would be adequate. The only question that remained was the type of anesthetic to be used. The patient was an elderly man, but thin, muscular, and very active. I discussed this with my anesthesia colleagues and we decided we would use either an axillary block or a wrist block with local anesthesia. He would not be put to sleep. With the equipment gathered and the necessary modifications made, we then sat down with the goat herder and his family and reviewed the possibilities, potential complications, and realistic expectations.

After we had finished explaining, the man looked up at me, tears in his eyes, and said, "It's in your hands and the hands of God."

His wife stood and put her arms around me. She was thin and frail looking, but the hug she gave me betrayed a surprising strength.

"His hands are our livelihood. That is all we have. If you think you can fix it, we want you to try. I will go to church and pray that good fortune and your skill will prevail."

I explained to her that in this heat, we did not want to risk the children getting dehydrated, so their surgeries would be handled first. Her husband would have to abstain from eating and drinking until after the surgery, which wouldn't happen until ten or eleven o'clock that night. She understood and agreed, and we started him on an IV and assigned him to the adult male ward area. Nurse Dixon, who was fluent in Spanish, continued explaining the pre-operative procedure and answering any of the patient's questions as he led him to the ward. The man's wife had tears on her cheek as she proceeded to thank and hug me again, as well as the other nurses.

She put a colorful scarf over her head and gently tied it under her neck, then removed a string of prayer beads from her purse, wrapping it around her wrist and tucking the ends into the palm of her hand. She smiled at me and said, "I must see the priest. I am going to church. I will spend the day there. Prayers and candles for everyone. I will return tonight in time for his surgery, but I will have to go home first and take care of the goats. It is a long walk for an old woman, twice in one day."

Dr. Canteras, who was standing next to me, looked up and we nodded, the same thing occurring to both of us. He reached into his pocket, removed some money and offered it to her. At first she refused, but he pressed it into her hand and told her it was important that she be strong and in good spirits when she returned. He told her she should have one of the rickshaw taxi drivers take her to the farm, instruct him to wait while she tended the goats, and have him bring her back to the hospital tonight. "Besides," he added, "it is not safe to be on the roads alone at night."

She looked at him with a quizzical smile and tears on her cheek, and said, "Who would bother a frail old woman like me?"

He looked down at her hard-callused, muscular hands, chuckled, and said to her, "You have milked a lot of goats in your time, and have taken care of a farm. You are not someone anyone would like to tangle with. And, Mamma, when you're in church, don't beat up on the priest."

We all laughed as she walked away, and Dr. Canteras and I returned to the operating room. It had been a long and successful day, and I noticed that my neck wound was not hurting at all. As a matter of fact, it was actually numb.

All the cases were completed except for the old man with the Dupuytren's contracture of his hands. None of the students or residents had left. They all wanted to participate in – or at least be in the operating room for – this procedure. I told them to decide amongst themselves who would be first and second assistants and who would be acting as scrub and circulating nurse for the procedures. The others could rotate around the table to observe and ask questions as the surgery progressed.

I noticed that Marta did not participate with the group, and had left the lounge area. That was no surprise since Michael was going to be on the first flight out. I wondered how their farewells would go. Months later I heard about it from Michael and Marta, but right now I could do no more than imagine, and hope for the best for both of them.

* * * * *

After finishing her last case, Marta went directly to Michael's room. When the door closed behind her she drew the rather ornate carved mahogany rocking chair closer to his bed and sat down, resting one hand on the side rail while Michael placed his hand on top of hers.

Marta began the conversation. "I was told you would be leaving in the morning. It's okay. I'm here to see how this is going to play out."

Michael, still bleary-eyed from having just awakened when she walked in, looked surprised by her comment. He glanced at her, then towards the door as if someone was about to come in. But nobody was there.

Looking intently into Michael's eyes, she continued, "Let's talk about the present. What do you want me to say?"

He let out a long breath as he pondered her question.

With a big smile on her face, she continued, "You must be the luckiest guy in the world."

Michael wasn't smiling back. "You trying to be funny?"

He struggled to sit up, and Marta stood, then reached under his arm, hoisting him into a sitting position and fluffing the pillow behind him. She stood up, pulled the rocking chair even closer, and sat down again.

Michael blinked his eyes and looked her up and down. "Why do you say I'm lucky? Because I sure don't feel lucky."

"Several reasons. Because you came here, risked your life in this war-torn country and did have several days where you helped the children. You unfortunately got a scorpion sting, but you were treated successfully. You have no broken bones or permanent injuries, which means that when you fully recover you'll be able to walk, run, and do everything else normally." Then she interlocked her fingers with his and squeezed his hands, still smiling. She almost laughed out loud as she added, "And of course you met me."

Michael felt a tug deep inside. "What can I say to that? You became a shining light in my life."

Her eyes grew moist with tears, and he squeezed her hands even tighter. She tried to reassure and comfort him, saying, "I'm good. I am here to try to figure out how to conclude this."

Michael, still tightly grasping her hand, sat back against the pillow and closed his eyes. "Why do we have to 'conclude' anything? Do I have to leave you? Do I really have to go back home?"

"After what happened, Michael, it's the only way. We both knew the rules and we broke them. I'm accepting responsibility for what happened."

Filled with both sadness and confusion, Michael asked her, "What does that really mean? At first I thought it was infatuation, but I fell in love with you. It's a responsibility we share equally."

Marta said nothing, and Michael drew in a long breath and licked his dry lips. "You are more to me now than ever. You're more than just a beautiful woman... you are fun and smart, and we hit it off like I've never experienced before. We worked together well in the hospital, but then we broke the rules... but so what? We rejoined the surgical team early each morning and did our jobs well."

"I couldn't agree with you more, Michael, but that's not why I'm here. The decision has been made; you have to leave. What I want to know is this: are you wanting to make future plans, or do I just say goodbye and wish you good luck?"

Michael jerked his head up, meeting her gaze, then let his head fall back against the pillow, breathing hard. "I want you! I want to be with you!"

"Then you will follow the rules, like Doc said, and you will leave tomorrow. Time will heal your leg and it will heal this incident too. It's only a two-hour flight to Houston. I will get a passport and a visa. And of course, you can always return here."

He knew she was right. She leaned over the bed rail, drawing in close, and pulled his face to hers. They kissed for a long time.

"Get some rest. I will see you in the morning before you have to leave. We have our whole life in front of us. Let's do it the right way."

She got up then and walked across the room, hesitating only a moment before she opened the door. She turned back around to look at Michael. The single fluorescent bulb cast shadows across the room, but she could see the tears on Michael's cheek, and knew she had to leave now. She could not look at him again this way. She wanted to hold the images of him laughing, of making love, and of doing all the important but meaningless little things that lovers do – not the image of a man seemingly broken by his love for her.

Michael closed his eyes and let his mind wander back to their more pleasant times together. He knew in his heart that there would be a new beginning for them. It was the only thing that helped him set aside the despair that filled him.

His leg was better, but now it was time for the real healing to begin.

CHAPTER 17
"As You Wish..."

It was almost midnight when we started the surgical procedure for the goat herder. Even at this late hour the operating room was packed. Everyone wanted to see and learn from this operation. The patient was already positioned on the table with his hand stretched across a wooden board that extended from the table, and a row of stools had been placed around the board.

The wrist was washed and a local anesthetic injected. We waited for a few minutes for the anesthesia to become effective and the hand to become numb. At this point, his arm was wrapped from the fingers to above the elbow with a makeshift pressure cuff consisting of a piece of rubber tubing. As I've said: when necessary, improvise.

The anesthesiologist gave the patient some IV sedation so he would be more relaxed and comfortable. As we began with the actual procedure, I began a discussion with the residents and students who had perched on the stools or were standing and looking over our shoulders. I briefed the group on the history of Dupuytren's contracture, and posed a series of rapid-fire questions, to see how much they knew about the diagnosis and its preferred treatment regimen.

I handed the marking pen to the senior resident and guided him to outline the path of the curve linear incision of the palm and then the multiple z-plasties extending into the fingers. Once the incision area was mapped out, I instructed the nurse to give me the scalpel, whereupon I made the initial incision along the dark blue lines we had drawn on the patient's palm. With my magnifying loupes in place, I began to lift the skin from the contracture and vessels and nerves below. The resident and nurse secured the flap of skin away from the wound with small hooks.

The upper arm tourniquet I had applied was working well, and because there was no bleeding into the hand, visibility was good. I estimated that we had two hours of working time, but thought we would complete the case in an hour and a half or so, using our improvised rubber tourniquet.

I then gave the scalpel to the senior resident and told him to repeat the procedure on the opposite side. As we discussed the anatomy of the palm, I was trying to teach the surgeon and observers to anticipate the strictures we would come across before actually encountering them. The senior resident was a little shaky at first, but as the procedure continued, his confidence built, and he did well.

The nodules that had been limiting the patient's function were now exposed. I released them near the wrist, and began a dissection from the wrist toward the fingers, so that the tendons, nerves, and arteries could be more easily identified.

The other resident who was across the table from me now had his turn to complete the dissection of the nodule-like tumors and fibrous palmar contracture to the base of the finger. Here the vessels were much smaller and entwined in the scar tissue, and with my magnifying loupes in place, I finished the dissection of the palmar fasciectomy. This was a perfect time to review the anatomy, since all the structures of the palm were exposed to view. I irrigated the wound and directed questions to the student nurses and residents, and found them to be well versed in their anatomy. I had a feeling that before coming into the operating room this evening, they'd all had their noses buried deep in the anatomy books, but that's what this was all about.

Next I described how we would interpose the skin flaps of the z-plasty and put in what are known as palmar corner sutures in between the flaps. After showing them how to do this, I handed the needle holder to the senior resident and told the nurses to cut the ends of the sutures as he progressed.

I explained that reconstructive surgery such as hand surgery, cleft lip, cleft palate, and burn reconstruction requires additional training and long years of experience to make the right decisions. But I also felt it was crucial to emphasize that it was not just a surgical procedure we had just performed on this man. Everyone in the room who was watching this operation needed to know that we were literally giving him his life back, and by extension, enhancing his prestige, his standing in the community, and his means to earn his living and care for his family. Being able to return to goat herding, to milking his goats and making and selling the cheese, made it possible for him to care for his family and be an active participant in the community.

He would go to church and be able to put a few córdobas into the straw basket when it was passed around. In fact, he would probably put even more in, to help those who were less fortunate than he. Thus, the good that one man received would be multiplied, well after he was no longer under our care.

Social lesson completed, I turned our attention back to the surgical task at hand. "Irrigate it out, close it up the way I taught you, and I will be back in and we will have a lesson on splinting."

Thirsty and exhausted, I exited the room to the doctor's lounge. I sat down, propped my feet up, grabbed a bottle of water, put my head back, and closed my eyes for a few minutes. It didn't seem nearly long enough when a knock came at the door. "Señor Doctor, it is time to put the splint on."

I returned to the operating room, where they were all gathered around the table. The circulating nurse asked if I needed a plaster cast. In Nicaragua, cast material came in its most basic form – a powder that was mixed with water, with cheesecloth dipped into the mixture to form the bandage. I had brought the American version, which was a prepackaged roll of cloth impregnated with plaster of Paris powder. They had never seen this before, and were quite impressed with the fact that all we had to do was pop the roll out of the sealed aluminum foil package, dip the plaster roll in water, wring out the excess water, and apply it to the hand after a stocking-like bandage had been applied to his arm and hand. I put a palmar splint on with the man's fingers fully extended and the tendons a little stretched to begin countering the effects of having been contracted for many years.

Once the splint had been applied, I turned back to the group and said, "This man will have full function of the hand in four to six weeks. He will be strong and powerful again, fully sensate, and the tendons will stretch back to their proper length."

I asked Carolyn to get a pillowcase and some safety pins from the hall closet and make a sling. The patient being awake, he was able to sit up on the table while the sling was positioned and adjusted. With a student on either side for support, he stood and walked out of the operating room to the recovery area. As he was leaving, I asked him if he had any pain, and he smiled and responded, "*Nada, muchas gracias, nada.*"

The surgical procedure was over, and I thanked all of the participants and told them to be back at 7:00 the next morning. We had another full schedule and another fourteen-hour day planned.

I was exhausted, but before leaving I asked JoAnne and Carolyn if they would make rounds in the children's wards with the residents and students, and meet us out front to return to our gracious hosts' homes.

JoAnne reminded me that Maria Torres would be coming with a car at seven o'clock the next morning to take me to Managua for a private meeting with President Violeta Chamorro. As if I could forget... but the past day and a half had really flown by, and I hadn't had nearly enough time to prepare, what with all of my other duties.

I simply nodded and told JoAnne that Dr. Canteras and Dr. Baladares would be in charge. "Just between you and me," I said, "we're going to do things a little differently tomorrow. As you know, we usually take on the most difficult cases in the morning, but I'm going to change the schedule so that tomorrow morning, you'll begin with the simpler ones. Then when I get back in the afternoon we will start the more complicated cases. I know this is a reversal of what we usually do, but under the circumstances I think this will be safer."

JoAnne nodded in agreement and left the operating room. The other nurses began to remove the instruments and did a final cleaning so the room would be ready in the morning.

* * * * *

The car arrived promptly at 7:00 the next morning. As I'd expected, Maria was in the backseat. I was pleasantly surprised to see my companions: Julio was driving and Mambo was up front as usual, with his trusty sawed-off shotgun draped across his lap. I climbed in the back, and Maria handed me a bag containing a large hot homemade meat tamale, one of my favorite treats.

The streets were already crowded with rickshaws, motor taxis, donkey wagons, and lots of people on foot. Julio maneuvered skillfully through the crowds and traffic, past the market and onto the main road towards León. The ride to Managua was uneventful, a welcome relief after some of my recent excursions. As we drove up to the presidential palace, Maria waved at the guards, the gates swung open, and they immediately passed us through. She instructed Julio to drive around to the rear of the building, and when he did, she popped the latch, swung the door open and jumped out. As she got out, she turned back and told me to wait.

Several of the guards approached and greeted her, "Maria! Maria! *Buenos Dias.*"

She smiled, responding, "I have the doctor with me, and we have an appointment with Violeta."

"Si, Si. We know. She is in conference, but she told us that as soon as you arrive, we are to take you through the back entrance and up the stairs to the rear of her office and knock. She said she will dismiss whoever is with her, and that you and the doctor take priority."

Maria asked them, "Can I leave the driver and bodyguard? They are armed!"

"Si, si. They can park by the far wall, but they need to remain in the automobile. I will tell them."

Maria returned to the car and motioned for me to follow her. The guard at the door came to attention, saluted, and greeted us, and we climbed a poorly lit narrow, winding staircase to the second level. It seemed very strange to me. At the top there was another guard who, after coming to attention and saluting, turned and gently knocked on the door to what I assumed to be Violeta's office. He opened the door a crack and said something, then closed it and asked us to please wait.

In less than a minute, the door opened and there was President Violeta standing in front of me. I went to shake hands, but instead I got a kiss on each cheek and she guided me to a beautiful hand-carved rocker beside her desk. Maria took a seat next to me. Whoever Violeta had just been conferencing with was exiting the room, and I could see that there were fifteen or twenty people seated outside her office waiting.

I felt a bit like an intruder, and started to apologize, saying, "I can see you have a busy day, and that many people are waiting for you."

She brushed my discomfort aside, assuring me, "They can wait, they *will* wait. You have priority."

Dr. Agris, with President Violeta in her home garden.

Then without hesitation, she began, "We have to talk about your trip to Puerto Cabezas and your visits with the mayor, as well as the elders of the Miskito tribe. As we discussed the other night, this has become more than a medical mission. You are a symbol of peace to come and, I hope, a true peace emissary."

I nodded. So far, no surprises.

"Have you selected who will be traveling with you? Are the TV people going? This is very important."

"Yes, Jose Dixon, who is a senior scrub technician and fluent in Spanish, will be with me. Also, Barrett Phillips."

Violeta asked, "And that tall black basketball player that you brought with you – will he be going too?"

Chuckling, I replied, "That's Barrett. He is tall and likes to play basketball, and everyone here thinks he's either a member of the NBA or my personal bodyguard. But in truth, he is actually a very good surgical technician. However, he is enjoying his image as a basketball star when he's shooting hoops with the kids, as well as being mistaken for my bodyguard at other times, so I'm not going to correct anyone's misconception." She smiled and we all laughed, and I continued, "JoAnne and Carolyn are my most experienced nurses; they will have to decide which of them will accompany us, as the plane is too small to take them both. I spoke to Mr. Zindler, and as you know, I've already spoken to his producer, Lori Reingold, and the cameraman Bob Dows. Marvin is still a bit hesitant, and frankly I don't think he will be going, but that doesn't really matter. His producer and cameraman are eager to go. They see this as an international scoop and an opportunity to produce material that could win them an award. Thank you again for the opportunity."

"No," she replied, "I thank you for what you've done, and for what I hope you will do." The preliminaries out of the way, she continued, "Let me better prepare you for your trip. As I told you the other night, in Puerto Cabezas there are no hotels, but I have arranged for your accommodations. I have sent a messenger to the mayor, who can accommodate several of you, and the Red Cross compound will accept the others.

"Remember that this is a land of simple people. Fishermen and farmers. Beaches will be lined with dugout canoes and small wooden boats. There will be nets hanging out to dry. It's an easy walk to anywhere in this small town. The water edge is shallow and rocky. If you go further down the coast it is jungle that is full of snakes. But you should worry less about the slithering kind than about the two-legged snakes, the Cubans and Russians who have joined with the Sandinistas along the coast. In order to earn money, they have begun a drug trafficking operation that is slowly destroying the social norms of the Miskito. I know you have survived the attacks you have sustained and everyone says it is because of the 'angel on your shoulder,' but you may very well be closer to trouble there than you've been elsewhere. Due to the remoteness of the region, you will be on your own. We cannot go in there and extract you. Also, as we discussed, if things go well in Puerto Cabezas, I would like you to visit some of the towns and villages north and south of Puerto Cabezas as well."

Again I nodded, and she continued, "You must also understand that the church is very important. The people, including the Indians, of Puerto Cabezas are more Moravian than Catholic. The elders of the Moravian Church know you are coming and support your arrival. They want the Cubans and Russians gone. In the Barrio El Cocal, north of town, I suggest that you make an appearance and attend the Sunday Moravian Church service. Also visit the Catholic church in the center of town, and visit the school too. Never forget that while this is a medical mission trip for your team, you are also being viewed as a representative from my central government to the Moravian coast.

"There will be few guns and no bodyguards, and you will have to use your wits. There are more guns in the hands of the people of Puerto Cabezas than I like, but I hope they will stay in their homes while you are there. My government has sent a proclamation to the Moravian church and their Yatama organization, guaranteeing self-rule and first-class citizenship for all minority groups. And they are permitted to use English or the tribal languages as they wish. The proclamation tells them that they will have a vote in the development of the Caribbean coast and its resources. There will be no attempt to disrupt their cultural roots or identities as Moravian Indians. You are my representative to support this and to begin the health and education programs.

"But as with any group, there are some internal feuds relative to leadership and rivalries that are not to concern you. They will settle these amongst themselves, and it seems to be going well with the help of the church. Amongst the leaders I want you to emphasize that I have officially created an autonomous region for them, and to let them know that this cannot be changed."

She paused, as if waiting for my reaction. I said, "I feel confident that I'll be able to accomplish our medical mission, and of course I'll do my best to represent you and convey your wishes for this region. But how do we get the Cubans and Russians out of there?"

"They are already nervous that this has become an autonomous region and that the Miskito are wholly apart from the Sandinista movement. The Cuban clinic and the few Russian military people are basically isolated. The only choice is for their superiors to come and remove them. Diplomatic letters have been sent to that effect. It could happen at any time now. Your arrival will hasten that. I only hope it will be a peaceful evacuation."

"You could be putting my team and me into a very difficult and dangerous situation," I said. "Don't get me wrong. I'm not trying to back out of the trip – after all, I was the one who broached the subject to you, even though you had already started planning for it before I approached you. But today you've brought up some issues that I hadn't fully considered or wasn't aware of. Coming to Nicaragua in the first place has its risks, and I accepted that years ago. But it seems that those risks might be compounded in Puerto Cabezas."

"Yes, I know. I'm sorry, but there is no other way. Keep emphasizing that you are a medical team there to help the local people, and an ambassador sent to establish peaceful relationships. Hopefully, enough of the Miskito tribe will be convinced, and their guns will stay at home." It made me a little uneasy that she felt it necessary to repeat the point about the guns, but I said nothing more for the moment.

She continued, "Please try to avoid certain areas to the south where drug cartels have begun to infiltrate. This is a result of former President Reagan's desire to keep communism out of Central America. Your Congress foolishly cut off funds to the Contras. They were willing to do the fighting, and all your country needed to do was supply them with guns, ammunition, and training. Your President Reagan saw the need. The military saw the need. But as usual, the political arm, your Congress, lacked the *cojones* to do the right thing."

I said nothing, and she paused for a few moments and then continued. "Just remember that you are there as a physician, not a military man. You are also my peace emissary – I know I am repeating myself, but I cannot stress it enough – and hopefully you can be persuasive enough to convince the Cubans and Russians to remove themselves from my country. Then the few remaining Sandinista forces will see that they are leaving and, I hope, will put down their arms." Again she paused, as if waiting for my response.

I thought a moment and said, "So. That's all?"

We all laughed. I was mulling over what she had said, and also, of course, remembering the Iran-Contra affair that had rocked the U.S. during President Reagan's second term. Violeta glanced at me, an expression of mild concern on her face, as if she feared she might have offended me by making critical remarks about my country. She needn't have worried.

I said, "I am very familiar with some of the political issues around the Contra-Sandinista insurgency and your civil war. Political imperatives are what have driven the conflict, not only in your own country but also in mine. You can't fight a war by telling the resistance forces, in effect, to be careful not to shoot first when they contact the Sandinistas. Especially after our Congress stopped funding and forced the Contras into the position of either crossing the border into the safe haven of Honduras, or returning to fight in Nicaragua without adequate weapons and ammunition. That put the Contras in a position of having to choose between suicide and betrayal."

Violeta said, "Then I see that you and I are in agreement about these matters."

"In my opinion, this was and is a particularly despicable trend in our Congress. The Congress didn't understand it was dealing with institutions and people who were profoundly different from those to whom they were accustomed. Our legislators have never dealt with, much less understood, the day-to-day problems of your culture. The only way to really understand the depth of the differences in cultures is to physically go to other countries and experience them first-hand, and most of our Congressmen and women have never ventured that far from their safe and secure halls. Organizational structures are very different, and the ways of doing things and interrelating are not only unknown but incomprehensible to most people in the North, yet the U.S. Congress acted like a group of know-it-alls." Violeta smiled.

"Every day I spend in your beautiful country," I continued, "I come to more fully appreciate the cultural differences in the different areas, as well as the contrasts with, and surprising similarities to, the culture in my own country. Hopefully, with this experience and God's help, I will find a way to be that peace emissary you're looking for."

Violeta replied, "Perhaps with that angel on your shoulder, you will somehow magically change their hearts."

I responded that it was interesting that she put it that way, because it was my understanding, from what I'd learned about them, that the Miskito Indians had strong beliefs and deeply rooted practices in magic and witchcraft. Those beliefs exposed the existence of enormous cultural gaps among the Miskito Indians, the Contras as we know them, and the United States. Our Congress wrongfully assumed that our national interests no longer required that we support the Contra resistance, but President Reagan saw otherwise, and his conflicts with the Congress were legendary.

"Even though Iran-Contra happened just a few years ago," I said to Violeta, "it seems that many people have all but forgotten that the Cold War was still in full swing at the time. The Berlin Wall was still up, and the Soviet Union was a clear and present danger. Moscow was still on the air spreading their propaganda, all day, every day. And though many Americans were aware of the communist threat, Congress was backing away. Now these issues are all but forgotten. America has moved on. So I feel a strong obligation to do my best for you, for your people, and this country, to right the wrongs done by my own country that have allowed this problem to continue and fester."

Lest anyone reading this thinks that I am in any way condoning the illegal actions of the Iran-Contra principals, that's not the case at all. I simply believed then and still believe that neither the majority of U.S. politicians nor the public really appreciated the Contras' struggle for what it was. I explained as much to Violeta, and she said, "Of course. I understand."

Apparently deciding that we had covered everything we needed to regarding the mission, Violeta changed the subject abruptly. "I heard about the small problem you had with one of our nurses. I want to apologize for that. I understand one of your male surgical technicians, I believe his name was Michael, has been sent home. Young Latina women are very pretty and quite outgoing. Your young technician is not the first to be entranced by them, and will not be the last. I hope that this is not a bigger problem in your mind than it actually is."

"Madam President, my team has a set of rules for behavior. I reviewed those rules with everyone. Relationships of a romantic or sexual nature are specifically prohibited between team members and locals. So Michael is going home. But his being sent home is more than just punishment for his engaging in a romantic relationship. He was stung by a scorpion, and had developed a severe infection in his leg. We treated the infection surgically, and he has done well, but he needs to go home and finish healing. As non-team members, Michael and Marta will be free to reestablish their relationship in the future, and it is my understanding that they plan to do so."

Violeta smiled, saying, "As a woman, I have to say that your no-romance rule can at times be difficult, and maybe even distressing. We cannot control the wings of the heart, particularly in young men and women. Do you not remember when you were younger?"

I did my best to feign outrage, proclaiming, "Madam President, are you calling me old?" We both burst out laughing, and Maria, who had been silent throughout our exchange, was smiling too. I was glad for a moment's comic relief to offset the serious tone of our discussion. But I also sensed that it was time for me to take my leave.

"Madam President, we have taken up enough of your time. I need to return to Chinandega. The surgery teams are working, and will continue well into the night. In addition, I have assigned people to gather medical supplies, drugs, and equipment, and begin packing for our flight tomorrow. And just to reiterate: at present, the tentative list is myself, Mr. Barrett, Mr. Dixon, and one of my nurses, either Carolyn or JoAnne. From the ABC television crew, I expect writer and producer, Lori Reingold and cameraman, Bob Dows aboard the aircraft. But probably not Mr. Marvin Zindler." She nodded.

Maria and I stood and turned toward the front exit, but Violeta took my hand and said, "Not that way. There are many people waiting outside. You need to exit the way you came in, through my secret back door." She then leaned in, kissed me on the cheek, and whispered in my ear, "Your Spanish has improved, but with a bit of pillow talk, I can envision great improvements." As soon as she said this, she began to laugh.

Grinning (and, to be honest, feeling) like an embarrassed but intrigued younger man, I responded, "Violeta, is that a presidential order?"

"As you wish. *Vaya con Dios*," she said. Then she turned to Maria, and said, "My niece, I thank you for your efforts in this endeavor as well."

When we exited the presidential palace, I saw that Julio had turned the car around, and when we approached he already had the door open for Maria and me. As I settled into my seat next to Maria, my mind was reeling with thoughts of the upcoming mission. I was feeling several emotions at once: I was excited, of course, but also uneasy, and more than ever I was also beginning to feel the weight of the responsibility that Violeta had placed on me. So much was at stake. I couldn't help thinking of the line in the old poem about fools rushing in where angels fear to tread. I wondered where a "Dr. Angel" might fit into this scenario, and knew I was about to find out. And

Violeta's words, "As you wish," echoed in my mind.

CHAPTER 18
Mixed Feelings

Maria and I were now on our way back to Chinandega on our favorite egregiously mis-named thoroughfare, the Pan-American Highway. The part we were on now had but one lane in each direction, and was in need of significant repairs due to the damages from the war.

As we settled in for the long drive, Maria asked me, "So, what do you think of our meeting with Violeta?"

I thought a moment and then replied, "I think she was very truthful with me, and of course I'm very excited about this project... but I still have some worries. This will be a major undertaking for my medical team and myself, and it's a little nerve-wracking."

Maria nodded. "I can understand that," she said, and waited for me to go on.

"It's not just the normal risks I'm worried about," I continued. "My team and I have been in other parts of the world that are also very dangerous. But there's a lot at stake here. Our meeting just drove that point home for me, and now it all seems more... well, more real."

My voice cracked with emotion and I had to pause a moment. Maria nodded again, and her eyes were full of sympathy as she waited for me to continue.

Collecting myself after a moment, I said, "But in spite of my worries, talking with your aunt gave me inspiration. She is a very strong woman. Her strength will help me accomplish my mission – and hers. And I think that she, more than anyone, appreciates the depth of the commitment my team and I are making."

Maria said, "You already have a lot of things working in your favor. As Mambo said the other day, and as my aunt said too, you will have the support of the Miskito people. With the Sandinistas leaving, the Miskito are becoming the owners of their own struggle. And now they have Violeta's support and her proclamation that they are an independent state. So I really do not see the *piricuacos* as a threat to you or your team on the Miskito coast."

I stopped her and asked, "Wait, what's that word you used just now?"

She laughed and said, "Oh, you mean *piricuaco?*" I nodded.

"That is the Contras' slang term for their Sandinista adversaries, which means 'rabid dog.' It comes from one of our Nicaraguan dialects and combines *piri* – dog – with *cuaco*, which means rabid."

"Well, that's another new word in my vocabulary," I said, smiling.

"A very offensive word, too," Maria said, "but well deserved in my opinion. Anyway, I don't think they will be a problem for you."

"As my mother has always said, 'from your mouth to God's ears.'"

Though I smiled as I said that, I was still worried. Military actions could be mounted by the few remaining Sandinista guerrilla forces, carried out not so much as a military operation in itself, but as a tactic to intimidate my team and those who supported us, and to throw a little political weight around. If the Cubans still had any power or influence at all, my arrival with an American medical team would obviously threaten that power and might lead to retaliation.

Whether our arrival could actually change the balance enough to exert a final blow to the Sandinista movement in that part of the country and truly end the war was, of course, debatable. I am by nature confident – some would say overly confident – but I didn't want to inflate my own importance too much. Nevertheless we did have a chance to exert a positive influence, and without a doubt we were taking a risk. And clearly I was being asked to provide strategic guidance and leadership, as well as to add credibility to Violeta's reform efforts.

As I pondered these matters some more, my worries for my own safety took a back seat to my excitement about the mission and my concern for the people whom I hoped to help. They lived with risk every day, and most of the people in whom they had placed their trust had simply abandoned them.

Both Maria and her aunt had given me insight into the local medical doctors who had lived in Puerto Cabezas and along the coast. These doctors were a little better off than their patients, but most of them had done exactly what many other Nicaraguans of any means had done: they had fled for their lives and the lives of their families. Their exodus had provided the Cubans, with Russian backing of course, with the opportunity to move in and establish the clinic to which the Sandinistas had lent their support.

The mayor was obviously in no position to provide the political, much less the military, leadership and resources needed to successfully remove the Cubans.

To me this situation highlighted the significant – and age-old – disconnect between policymakers and those who are most affected by those policies. The Sandinistas, the Cubans and the Russians had intimidated not just the local doctors, but even more significantly, the politicians who, fearing for their own lives, had concentrated on saving themselves and subsequently failed the very people they were supposed to serve. To make matters even worse, the U.S. Congress had contributed to this leadership disaster. It was the same story I'd seen over and over again, and not just in Central America: Congress making policies based on its characteristically arrogant know-it-all attitude, without benefit of the type of information that can only be gained by having boots on the ground who are familiar with actual conditions and attitudes.

I was always amused by the way Washington-based officials referred to the Contra resistance as the "directorate." Yes, there was a "directorate" in place for years, but as far as I am concerned they were never the essence of the resistance. For me the essence – the very backbone – of the resistance was the army in the field, the *campesinos*. These were the people who really knew what was going on, and who fought bravely for their most basic human rights while their own leaders fiddled and clueless U.S. politicians continued to interfere.

Thinking about this prompted me to mull over the annoyance I'd long harbored regarding the elitism I had seen for years on both sides of the aisle. It was displayed by legislators and other Washington officials who not only put themselves above the "commoners" but also had the arrogance to equate English-language skills to intelligence. While there is a little more diversity in Washington these days, as well as celebration of diversity in the culture at large, the brand of elitism I'm talking about still persists, and was certainly a factor when I was in Nicaragua in the early 1990s. In Washington's eyes those who did not speak English were either poorly educated or intellectually deficient. Unfortunately, this type of elitism – or xenophobia, if you will – is shared even today by many ordinary Americans, most of whom rarely bother to become proficient in a language besides English. Without language skills you are doubly disadvantaged: you do not know your neighbor and you do not understand your enemy.

And I believe that it was this fundamental lack of understanding that made U.S. policy in Nicaragua so faulty, along with the fact that very few folks in the Congress and the rest of the U.S. government had any understanding of guerrilla warfare – how it is fought and how it will be won.

Looking back on it today, I understand now more than ever that the Nicaraguan Contra resistance was not a creation of the U.S. government, although of course our government did become entrenched in the battle in some rather infamous ways. All considerations of the Iran-Contra scandal aside, the Contras began as an indigenous movement of the people. They had stood up against the Sandinistas long before the

U.S. came on the scene. The Contras were a come-as-you-are force of farmers, merchants, and fishermen, all motivated by economic injustice. That was certainly true of what took place on the Caribbean coast with the Indians.

By the time we arrived in Chinandega I was feeling a little more optimistic, an optimism fueled by a renewal of my drive to get something done. Perhaps with a little friendly but firm encouragement, the Cubans and Russians would decide to pack up and leave – a peaceful resolution with no loss of life. Then the indigenous people could return to their farms and their fishing, their families, and their churches.

* * * * *

I returned to the hospital with more determination than ever. I went to the doctor's lounge, made a quick change and did a walkabout through the crowded hospital wards. The nurses were hustling to and fro with their little carts, changing IV solutions, giving medications, and assuring parents that their children were doing fine. The temperature had soared to over 100 degrees by now, and I ordered cool sponge baths for some of the infants. I also asked that bottled water be distributed to all bedsides.

Feeling that the situations on the wards and clinics were in control, I went to the operating room. The operating team members were working well together, their routine well established and smooth. Equipment and supplies were still plentiful because of the quantity we had shipped, and everyone was in good humor. There were no major problems on the horizon, but then again, it was still fairly early in what would be another very long day.

I ran into Marvin Zindler, Lori, and Bob on the veranda; they were there with the TV crew, shooting the before and after pictures of various patients and filming interviews with their parents. A little while earlier, Marvin had confirmed to me that he would not be accompanying us on the trip to Puerto Cabezas. He said it was because he had plenty to do in Managua, and he was confident that Lori and Bob could get the footage he needed for his story, but I know he was also justifiably concerned about the risks. That gave me some pause, because Marvin was pretty much fearless. But I wasn't about to back out now.

Marvin was wearing his typical white suit, starched and impeccably pressed white shirt, and his signature wide red tie that threatened to cover his entire chest. In the center of the tie was a single stickpin, another typical bit of Marvin flair. He had selected a child in a family in the far corner of the big room, away from the noise. I watched his approach. The camera was rolling as he glanced across the room and smiled at the mother. She wore a colorful yellow blouse with pleated puff sleeves that covered her shoulders; the blouse was stained with the rice cereal she had been attempting to feed to her child. Her skirt was floor-length, full and pleated, and over this was a typical apron with colorful, hand-embroidered designs along the edges. She was barefoot.

Miracles in Bedlam

The infant was confined in what looked like a miniature cage with steel bars, chipped and bent in places but still functional, protecting the child from himself and the environment. The IV had been removed and the child was started on soft foods, which in this part of the country meant either rice cereal or a corn mash to which sugar was added.

The mother was holding a white porcelain bowl, decorated with a local Indian design. Like a waiter, she had a well-worn, well-stained towel over her other forearm, with which she would occasionally wipe the baby's face. She was young and obviously inexperienced at feeding a child. Beads of perspiration dripped down her face and over her arms, and although her efforts were repeatedly frustrated, she persisted in trying to get some rice cereal into her child's mouth. But the cereal continued to flow down the infant's chin and onto her apron; clearly she was spending more time cleaning the child's face than providing sustenance.

Marvin stood there quietly observing, then stepped forward. He didn't speak a word of Spanish, but Marvin was never one to let a minute detail like that stop him from talking. Oh, how that man loved to talk. He began talking to the mother – in English, of course – supplementing his words with a pantomime of how she should feed the child. I was utterly fascinated; it was too good a show not to watch. I stood back, tapping Bob on the shoulder, and he nodded as he rotated the camera to capture the action.

This young mother began to chat with Marvin in Spanish, explaining that no matter what she did, she couldn't get the baby to take the food. Marvin continued to speak with her in English and pantomime the proper feeding technique. She tried again with the same poor result. In frustration she turned to Marvin, the spoon in one hand and the dripping rice-soaked bowl in the other. And then very carefully, she shook out the rice-covered towel and placed it over his arm.

Marvin stood there as he and the mother looked at each other and he contemplated the situation. He didn't pull a typical "Zindlerism." His voice remained quiet and level as he stepped forward to confront the child, whose little fists had tightened around the bars on either side of the crib, and whose big eyes were wide open, staring at this stranger.

Marvin had five grown children and was busy with many grandchildren at this stage of his life. But how was he going to react in this situation? We were soon to find out.

He placed the spoon in the bowl of rice cereal, filled it to overflowing, and withdrew it. In my mind I could just see the baby spitting this out all over Marvin's immaculate white suit. Given Marvin's extreme vanity about his dress and appearance, this might not have the most pleasant outcome. Yet I couldn't help it; a smile crossed my face.

Marvin probably had two things working in his favor: the fact that the child was hungry, and the child's obvious fascination with this stranger. In any case the little boy opened his mouth, and Marvin didn't hesitate a second. The spoon went in and

Marvin tilted it upward against the child's lip, gently placing his other hand under the chin. The little one had no choice but to take the food, and as the spoon was withdrawn Marvin kept gentle pressure on the chin until the child had swallowed it all. Marvin repeated this three more times and was very successful.

Meanwhile Marvin kept quietly talking to the mother in English, and she replied in Spanish as the smile spread across her face. While neither understood a word the other one was saying, it was clear that the mother did understand the feeding technique Marvin had showed her – and even more importantly, she understood his kindness. He gently placed the spoon in one of her hands and the bowl in the other, and draped the towel over her arm. He then prompted her via pantomime to feed her child. She followed his example, and the food went down. She turned and faced Marvin, and gave him a big hug.

When she stepped back, she realized her mistake, and so did the rest of us as we beheld Marvin's perfect white suit, now covered with splatters of rice cereal. He became a little flustered, grabbing the towel from the young mother's arm and trying in vain to clean the front of his jacket. Bob and I found it difficult not to laugh, and Bob was having trouble keeping the camera still, because more cereal was being deposited on the suit from the towel than was being removed.

Finally Marvin gave up on his efforts and for a few moments he just stood there, not saying anything. Finally, he tapped the mother on the shoulder, gave the towel back to her and gently turned her toward the baby. As he walked back toward us, he said to Bob, "Did you get all that?"

Bob said, "I don't know if I'm supposed to cry or laugh."

I added, "I think if you do use that segment you will get both responses from the audience. But it did show Marvin's humanity and dedication, so maybe you should use it."

Marvin glared, which I took as my cue to leave.

* * * * *

On my way down the hall I met Sister Esperanza, who told me she was going to the storage room, where several of the sisters and a few of the nurses were packing, labeling, and preparing the equipment and medications for the trip to Puerto Cabezas. She handed me a list that they had prepared, and I reviewed it, making a few additions. I told Sister Esperanza I would personally select the surgical instruments at the completion of the last case that evening. I explained that Mr. Dixon and I would carry the surgical instruments in our luggage, separate from the rest of the supplies.

With that completed I was on my way to finish the rest of the long day in the operating room. I was focused on our work, but the adrenaline was really beginning to build now, in anticipation of tomorrow's flight to the Miskito Coast.

PART 2

The Miskito Coast

CHAPTER 19
No Turning Back

After a restless night, I was up very early the next morning, more than ready for our departure. Maria had provided the car in which the team and I rode to Managua, and another family had loaned us the truck that carried our equipment. Awaiting us at the headquarters of La Costeña, which at the time was Nicaragua's sole domestic air carrier, was the single-engine prop plane that would transport us across the mountains to Puerto Cabezas. The team members would occupy the passenger seats, and I volunteered – or perhaps insisted would be a better word – to take the co-pilot position. This was somewhat selfish of me as I wanted to shoot photos from the aircraft when we flew across the mountains, and the co-pilot's seat would provide me with the best vantagepoint.

Despite having been informed in advance about the type of aircraft we would be taking, I had some concerns now that I was actually looking at the plane up close and personal. Not only was I worried about whether there would be enough room for the team and all of our equipment, but I was also concerned that we might exceed the small aircraft's weight capacity. At the same time I was keenly aware that I was playing for an audience and, cognizant of the public relations at stake, I walked boldly up to the plane and stood next to it, hoping that the smile on my face would disguise my anxiety. My fears were alleviated somewhat as I saw that each piece of equipment was being carefully weighed, and when that task was completed we were given the go-ahead to load.

The load-out

As I'd expected, the newspaper reporters had been tipped off about our departure, and as our group left the terminal the reporters had swarmed around us, wanting to take photos of us by the plane. I caught Barrett Phillips' eye, and his expression clearly communicated his sense of absolute confidence: *We've got this.* Tall, broad-shouldered and handsome, Barrett was resplendent in his white coat and O.R. scrubs, and right now he was helping to keep the reporters at bay until I was ready to speak to them. My conversations with Violeta had left me feeling that I was amply prepared to deal with the press, but nevertheless I was very glad to have Barrett as reinforcement.

As the clamor died down, Barrett turned and nodded to me, and that was my cue. "Ladies and gentlemen of the press," I began, "I am going to make a short statement and then take questions." I leaned back across the aircraft and planted one arm on the wing, hoping it gave me the proper look of authority and confidence.

"As you know, a trip has been planned to Puerto Cabezas. I don't know exactly what you have heard, so I'll explain it. First of all, this is a medical mission trip. That is our primary objective. We are going to replace the Cuban clinics and hopefully their Russian and Sandinista protectors, and we are going to do it peacefully.

"I am also traveling as a peace emissary for your new President Violeta Chamorro, and to help reassure the Miskito Indian organization that the Chamorro government will make every effort to stabilize the region and establish an autonomous Miskito entity with their own political parties and elections. It is hoped that with this promise the Miskito Indians and the Catholic and Moravian Churches will join in my efforts as an ambassador of peace to the region."

I paused a moment, then continued. "I want you all to know that a lot of the credit for this idea belongs to my bodyguard Mambo and my driver Julio, who brought this issue to my attention. They felt that if I as an objective third party were to intervene, a peaceful solution could be achieved. Their insight and commitment are key to this effort.

"But your president should also get a great deal of credit, for some of these issues have been very much on her mind as well. I have had meetings with her to discuss this trip, and I want it to be known that she provided advice and moral support, but left the logistics and financial arrangements to others, in order to counter any suspicions of political opportunism. The trip is being solely sponsored by myself, the Children's Foundation and ABC-TV, along with Mr. Marvin Zindler. I've pondered the possibilities; I have weighed the complications and expectations of such an undertaking. I have discussed it with my medical team and I want to introduce my volunteers: Mr. Barrett Phillips, Mr. Jose Dixon and my senior nurse, Carolyn."

There were nods and murmurs of approval throughout the small crowd of reporters.

"Finally," I said, "as risky as this undertaking may seem, I feel the political climate is right. We have made contact with the mayor in Puerto Cabezas and we have his support as well. And we have also been in communication with the Red Cross center in Puerto Cabezas."

I felt it was important to include this information in my little speech, as I have always been a stickler for communications through "proper channels." That's the best way to avoid miscommunications and misunderstandings, not to mention potential diplomatic crises. My meetings with Violeta herself before leaving, and my communications with the mayor and the Red Cross in Puerto Cabezas, had been a very necessary part of our preparations. It was important to let the press know that I had indeed followed proper communications protocol, so they wouldn't think that the team and I were overstepping in any way.

And yet, even with my attention to protocol, there were still plenty of unknowns. At this point, who knew what disruptions the medical team's arrival with the ABC news crew would cause? What if, in the midst of pursuing peaceful negotiations, the team and I found ourselves in a real war? The grim fact was that being a by-the-book doctor and medical team with high aspirations would only take us so far. We were ill equipped to deal with serious threats to our safety. There were no real security measures available; that angel on my shoulder was going to be pressed into even more overtime service, for all of us.

Then it was time for questions from the press, and they were pretty easy on me, all things considered. After taking a few questions I said, "Ladies and gentlemen, it's over 100 degrees out here on this hot tarmac, and my team and I are going to have to leave. There are cold drinks, sandwiches, and cakes inside for all of you. But before you partake, let me say that we truly appreciate being given the opportunity to meet with the press. It is most important. *You* are important. We need you to understand not only the medical mission but also our role as peace envoy to help bring this civil war to an end, and, hopefully, to remove the Russian-Cuban influence from your land. Please know that I do not claim to be speaking for your president, but I really believe that your understanding of what we're trying to do is important, and I think that communicating that understanding is your patriotic duty as members of the press. You really can make a difference in Nicaragua's future." I had learned early on how important it is to inspire friendly feelings from the media if you want your message to be passed along in the context intended.

As the final photos were taken and the small crowd of reporters began to disperse, the pilot said to me, "Are you ready to board now?" I nodded and gestured to the others, and they began boarding. After helping Bob Dows with his heavy camera into the aircraft, I buckled myself into the co-pilot's seat, put on my earphones, and adjusted them. I placed my Nikon camera with its telephoto lens on my lap, then turned around to Bob and Lori. "So, guys, how do you think that went?"

Lori said, "I think you did a good job of communicating with the press about what you hope to accomplish – both the medical mission and the peace initiative. You were clear and focused and you sounded pretty confident." Bob nodded in agreement. Then Lori added, "But just between us, are you really as sure that this is going to work as you seemed out there?"

I smiled ruefully. "Hey, there are no guarantees, but so far, so good. We have President Violeta's blessings and it looks like we have the support of the press as well, so let's hope the story they present will be positive. I think it will be."

Lori said, "My gut feeling is that you're right. The press loves the idea of 'Doctor Angel,' the man who has survived several attacks and credits it to divine help. That plays well here. But really, you have to be sort of a lunatic to be going to Puerto Cabezas, knowing the conditions we'll most likely incur."

"Wait. *I'm* the lunatic? Aren't you in this aircraft with me?"

At that Bob and Lori exchanged a glance, and we all burst out laughing.

As our laughter died down I said, not just to Bob and Lori but to the medical team members who were also listening, "I only know President Violeta slightly, but I feel pretty certain that her heart is in the right place. And so are ours. This is a good thing we're doing, and I want to thank all of you again for volunteering. Let's just bow our heads and say a prayer, and hopefully this bucket of bolts will get us to Puerto Cabezas. We'll deal with whatever we need to deal with once we get there."

We had our moment of silence, and at its conclusion I actually did feel a sense of peace and calm. Then the pilot revved the engine and began taxiing out onto the field. Through my headphones I could hear the chatter between him and the tower and he was given clearance for takeoff.

There was no turning back now.

Miracles in Bedlam

* * * * *

The day was clear and sunny, the conditions perfect for me to get some great photographs as we soared over the mountains. It was quite an eye-opening journey. Leaving Managua and heading towards Nicaragua's Atlantic coast, we could see how population pressures and the swelling cattle industry had pushed agriculture frontiers inland and towards the Atlantic side. The effects of deforestation were evident as well. That problem was destined to get worse in the years to come. Overall, Nicaragua lost about 21 percent of its forest cover between 1990 and 2005. One contributing factor was that American, Canadian, and Asian logging companies inundated the Atlantic coast, intent on exploiting the country's hardwoods. This became quite a political and personal focal point for the Miskito Indians who inhabited these forests but who had no say in, nor benefit from, the lucrative timber concessions that foreign companies negotiated over the years with the Sandinistas and, later, with the central government in Managua. This injustice and the deforestation itself were some of the matters that Violeta had pledged to address, but she would soon find that there were no easy solutions.

As if political and business conflicts didn't present enough of a threat to the environment, Nicaragua's pine forests later faced ecological pressure by the invasion of the pine bark beetle, which bored into trees to feed on their resin. The resulting loss of ground stabilization that the trees had afforded had caused rivers and streams to change their course, and often stopped their flow altogether. Violeta had also promised to address environmental problems by actively replanting clear-cut hillsides and introducing less-destructive agricultural techniques. No doubt about it, she had some challenges ahead.

As we crossed the volcanic mountain ridge that divided Nicaragua in half, plumes of steam drifted up from the open hearts of the volcanoes. Nicaragua is rife with volcanoes, several of them active, some of them dormant but "restless," and a few that haven't erupted in thousands of years. This latter group might be considered extinct, but then again, you never know. Seeing the volcanoes from above provided a poignant reminder of what a fragile and vulnerable jewel Nicaragua really is. Indeed, it was a reminder of the fragility of the entire planet: even if our own species can manage to keep from destroying itself, Mother Nature has the ultimate power not only to create but also to destroy.

And how eerie it is to be staring right into the mouth of a volcano as you fly only a few hundred feet over its rim. It is an experience I'll never forget.

I wasn't the only one who was taking advantage of the phenomenal photographic opportunities. Bob had his big TV camera pressed to the window, and Lori was busily scribbling notes. The others were also staring out the windows, mesmerized by the spectacular and ever-changing vista.

Almost before we knew it, we had crossed the mountains and were beginning a descent along the coast toward Puerto Cabezas. As we drew closer to our destination I couldn't locate an airport and wondered just where we would land. The pilot flew low over the town of Puerto Cabezas, tilting his wings right to left, and then revving the engine as we gained altitude. He made a circle over the mostly one-story wooden homes with tin roofs, which reflected the sun into our eyes, nearly blinding us. Then he made another circle.

It was then that it occurred to me that I was hearing nothing on my headset but noise. I pointed to the set and shrugged my puzzlement to the pilot, but noticed that he had removed his set and placed it around his neck, so I did the same with mine. Now I could hear what sounded like an air raid siren. *What the...?!!* Were we going to be attacked even before we reached the ground?

Now the pilot was making a third pass over the town, but this time he dropped low. I could see people scattering to either side of the main street, and others gathering children in their arms, or tugging at donkey carts, as the plane's wheels struck the red sand on the main street that was now, apparently, our runway. The pilot cut the engine and the propeller slowed, then he applied the brakes, and soon we were coasting onto a gravel lot, where he gently turned the aircraft around to face the direction from which we'd just come.

A bit surprised if not shaken up by the experience, I turned to the pilot and said in a voice that was a little higher and squeakier than I had intended, "There is no airfield?"

"We landed safely, be happy. No one is hurt. You are not hurt. Let's disembark."

I looked at him quizzically and asked, "How the hell do we get out of here when we get ready to leave?"

"The same way we got in, except in the opposite direction."

Sometimes I can do without a smart aleck. Trying to keep my exasperation under control, I said to him, "You do understand the deal, right? You are being paid to stay with the aircraft day and night until we leave. You are to gas it up and have it ready at a moment's notice."

He looked me in the eye and said, "Yes, that is the deal, and if there is trouble I expect a bonus!"

I said, "You got it. Just be here and ready to take off at any time."

"*Si, si,* I understand. Now let me help you unload your equipment. That is the mayor's truck coming down the street, and I can see there are two donkey carts behind to carry your supplies and equipment. I suggest that if you do not want them to disappear onto the black market, they get locked behind the stockade at the mayor's lumber mill, or you place them in trust with the Red Cross, which is directly across from there."

"Thank you for your advice," I said. I had already known to take special precautions with our equipment and supplies, because here, as was so often the case in the countries my team and I visited, there was a thriving black market. Few items were safe; any and everything could and likely would disappear if proper precautions were not taken.

Our landing had upset a cluster of bats that were now flying high overhead. The pilot, noticing my worried expression, said, "They will return to their roost high in the trees in a few minutes. Do not be concerned."

Adding to the chaos of our welcome were the throaty cries of the howler monkeys that were eating leaves and fruits high in the tree branches. Our flight had also disturbed them, and they were letting us know about it in no uncertain terms. Their utterances were not really howls in the sense that wolves, coyotes, and dogs howl; they sounded more like those Tibetan Shartse Dro-Phen Ling monks who specialize in "throat singing," except they were much louder and more obnoxious.

"After a day or two, you'll be used to them and the sound will not bother you," the pilot reassured me. "And they are not dangerous. However, I must warn you that if you have a shiny object like a pen in your pocket, one of the monkeys may drop from the tree to your shoulder and in the blink of the eye pick your pocket and disappear back into the forest. Tell the ladies not to wear any sparkling jewelry or earrings, or they may find themselves in a tug-of-war to keep their possessions, not to mention their earlobes."

I thought to myself, *Great, just great. What have we gotten ourselves into?* Somehow, though, I suspected that the howlers would be the least of our worries.

At that moment the mayor arrived with a small entourage. Introductions were made and handshakes exchanged, and then the equipment was quickly unloaded into the donkey wagons and the truck. The mayor was very cordial, inviting Jose Dixon, Mr. Barrett, Bob Dow and me to stay in what he called the men's quarters at the sawmill, behind a high-walled compound that looked like a fort in an old Western movie.

Across the street was a similar compound, two stories high, with a huge Red Cross logo painted on the roof and sidewalls. This was where the mayor had arranged for the ladies to stay. I thanked him for his kindness and hospitality.

The Red Cross compound

"We're glad to have you here," he said. "And because there are really no restaurants in this town, we will take care of all your meals as well. Most of the meals will be served in the Red Cross cantina. Also, there are several ladies in town who volunteered to wash any clothing while you are here. Please give them something for their efforts."

"Not a problem at all. We will be very happy to do that."

The mayor continued, "New patients are already arriving at the Red Cross center and at the old clinic in the center of town. People have stayed away from the Cuban clinic, knowing you are coming. The Cubans and their Russian and Sandinista overseers have remained aloof and quiet, and have not ventured into town since they heard that an American team with a TV camera was coming. The Cubans and Russians in particular do not want this to become an international political problem."

"Well, that sounds encouraging," I said.

He nodded. "Yes, and word about your arrival has put tremendous pressure upon them. We have information that they have requested a boat for their evacuation from the Caribbean coast. We have not yet been able to verify this information but if it is true, it seems that you have already won without firing a shot."

"I like the sound of that," I said, "though I know we have to be careful and we can't take anything for granted."

"That's right. We will have to proceed carefully. But we are grateful for your efforts. Also, I have taken it upon myself to give you a tour of the coastal area this afternoon after lunch, so you can meet with the different village and tribal elders. They have their own language, but since the English inhabited this coast hundreds of years ago, almost everybody speaks enough English to communicate easily with you."

"That's good," I said, "because my Spanish is shaky at best, to say nothing of my proficiency in the various dialects."

The mayor smiled and said, "You have nothing to worry about. You will also meet with the Catholic priest in town, and visit the small Moravian churches along the coastline so you can meet their clergy. This will unify the locals around your peace mission, which I feel is going to be very successful."

The ladies and their personal items were taken to the Red Cross facility so they could wash up and relax before going to lunch, while the mayor took us men to the sawmill. Upon entering the gates, we all climbed a rickety wooden staircase to the second floor, where each of us was assigned a small room. In my room was a little window, which the mayor opened for me. There was a small handmade wooden bed with a thin mattress, and in the corner was a washstand with a basin and pitcher. Just the basics, but I could get by. Our host proudly announced that he had an electric generator so there would be lights on in the evening, and he added that there was also a generator at the Red Cross. He stated that most of the rest of the town would be completely black at night.

Then he pointed down from the balcony to show me where the pump was. "There's a shower there as well," he said, and when I looked at him in confusion, he laughed and explained that the metal post coming out of the ground below us brought water up from the well when the pump was turned on. "It is cold – extremely cold," he warned me, "but believe me, in this heat you will enjoy it." He added that some of the workers, upon leaving the sawmill for the day, would just go under the shower fully dressed. Others would strip to their underwear. Then, he added, there were those who took it all off. Seeing my doubtful expression, he laughed and said, "I will put a plastic curtain on that metal rim to give you some privacy, but just remember that from the second level of the house or the sawmill, there is no such thing as privacy."

As if to demonstrate that last point, at that moment a large woman, with massive, pendulous breasts, stepped into the shower, dropped her blouse to her waist, and turned on the pump switch to let the cool water pour over her. She looked up and waved, obviously unfazed by being so clearly on display, and the mayor waved back. "That's your cook at the compound. She likes to be called Amy. You are all too skinny, but she'll fatten you up." With that he took one hand and rubbed his protuberant belly, snapping the straps of the suspenders that held up his work coveralls. Clearly he was having a good time.

He said, "Now, put your things away; they are safe here. Wash up and let's go over to the Red Cross cantina, where they have prepared your lunch."

A few minutes later Barrett, Dixon, Bob, the mayor, and I strolled over to the Red Cross compound. I was surprised to see that there were more than a hundred folks inside the compound walls. The mayor whispered, "Word travels quickly in a small community. Most of these people are patients who are waiting to be seen. Many are Miskito Indians, and they want nothing to do with the Cubans and Russians. They only want to be seen by the American doctors, and their expectations are high. Notices have been sent out to all of the tribes, and if you listen carefully you can hear the drums sending the message along the coast and through the mountains that Dr. Angel and the American medical team are here. As I said, expectations are very high."

Not for the first time, I worried that we might not be able to live up to all of those expectations. But the team and I were committed to giving it our best shot. And there was definitely no turning back now.

CHAPTER 20
Cubans And Russians

My concerns about the gravity of our mission were abated somewhat as I found myself seduced by the enticing aromas of the food that had been prepared for us. I hadn't realized how hungry I was. We were all seated on benches around a hand-carved wooden table, and were served a simple but delicious lunch of rice, beans, boiled chicken, yams, and plantain.

Following lunch, Barrett and Mr. Dixon, with the help of the Red Cross volunteers, brought the medical equipment and supplies into the Red Cross clinic. The Red Cross volunteers arranged an orderly and continuous flow of patients through the clinic for the remainder of the afternoon. The clinic went well and lasted into early evening. We could not have done it without their help.

Lori Reingold and Bob Dows were driven by one of the mayor's assistants through the town and into local villages, as well as along the Caribbean coast so they could get some atmosphere footage for the TV program. Before they left I asked Bob to take a telephoto lens and get pictures of the Cuban-run clinic, as well as any Russian guards or Sandinista military that might be there. I asked him to also take footage of the pier that was several hundred yards west of the clinic, so we could determine if there was any unusual activity or any new boat arrivals.

The mayor approached me late that afternoon as I was taking a rare break, and repeated what he'd said to me earlier: that the Cubans and the Russians had not been seen since before our arrival. I was glad he broached this subject again because it had been a nagging worry since he had first mentioned it, and I wanted to talk to him about it.

"Where do you think they really are?" I asked.

"If they haven't evacuated yet," he replied, "then I assume that they are holed up behind the walls of the clinic compound." He said he had stationed several tribal policemen in the area as lookouts. The lookouts had reported that they saw one Cuban medical doctor and some personnel exit the clinic for a few minutes. With a pair of binoculars they were also scanning the pier and the water behind the clinic. The Cubans then quickly ran back inside. But that was the last they'd seen of the Cubans and Russians. I was certain that the mayor's earlier prediction had proven accurate, that they had grown nervous with the arrival of the American medical team, and were likely waiting for someone to smuggle them off the Caribbean coast.

One of the tribal police did say that a cattle boat – more like a flat-bottom barge – had come in the night before. Such vessels would typically unload and leave before dawn the next morning, but this boat was still at the pier.

We were seeing the last of the patients for the day when Bob and Lori returned. I suggested we go to the mayor's home across the street and review the footage they had taken of the clinic and surrounding area.

I took a minute to thank the Red Cross volunteers who had done such a good job of maintaining order for us at the clinic. I asked that they be back by 8:00 the following morning. I was told that not only would they be returning, but several more volunteers were planning on meeting at the clinic as well to handle the expected surge of patients.

Sister Maris, one of the Red Cross volunteers, stepped up, took my hand and said, "God bless you. You have risked your life, you have all risked your lives to help the Miskito people. You should get a Nobel Prize for this humanitarian and peace effort. Sadly, I cannot grant you such an honor. All I can offer is to go to church tonight and pray for you and your Children's Foundation. God – as well as the Puerto Cabezas citizens and the Miskito people – bless you." I can't describe how good that made me feel.

The medical group walked across the street, and a guard at the sawmill opened the heavy wooden gates so we could enter. The mayor was sitting in a rocking chair on the second floor porch waving to us. As we ascended the stairs, I could hear him call out to his wife to bring cold drinks for everyone.

I asked Bob if he had been able to use his telephoto lens to photograph the Cuban clinic and the surrounding shoreline. He said, "I didn't want to stop the Jeep in front of the clinic, but I had no problem photographing it from the back of the Jeep as we drove slowly by. Then we drove down along the beach, and I photographed the piers and the boats that were anchored there."

I responded, "Anything suspicious? Anything the mayor should know about or see?"

Bob said, "The camera has a good screen, so we can all see it." He pushed the Play button on the camera, and we huddled around to see what he had captured.

The footage he got was interesting, and it wasn't too difficult to come up with a likely description of what they were doing. A thin, dark-haired man in a clinic uniform was walking out of the Cuban compound, looking around attentively, clearly alert to any threat. A few seconds later, he nodded back toward the doorway, and a group of Cuban medical personnel emerged cautiously from the doorway, then hesitated and looked like they were on the verge of running back into the building. The thin man seemed to be staring right into the camera, but at that distance, I doubt he could have made out enough detail to know for certain that he was being observed. Judging by the nervous look on his face, I figured he must have seen the Jeep moving slowly across the sand. He pulled a timepiece from his pocket, glanced at it, then shoved it back in his pocket. He looked around again as the Jeep, with Bob still filming, disappeared into the forest. With head down and shoulders hunched, he set off briskly toward the dock.

Bob began narrating the action on the screen. "Once we were in the cover of the forest, we had little trouble staying out of sight and continuing to film the man as he worked his way down the bulkhead to the shoreline, then suddenly darted to the water's edge."

At that moment, the tape showed a boat turning into a space between the two piers and slowly approaching the Cuban. The boat looked to be a Cigarette, a very fast, streamlined craft that was quite popular with wealthy socialites and drug smugglers. The mayor said, "These boats are commonly seen in these areas delivering provisions to the villages from the larger ships that are anchored offshore."

As we watched, the two men tied the boat up to the pier and then raced ashore. A close-up revealed them to be fair-skinned and fair-haired, with blue eyes. Their manner of dress did not blend in with the people of the Miskito coast, and they were apparently not accustomed to the tasks at hand, as they climbed awkwardly from the water's edge to the apron of the dock. The Cuban from the clinic reached out and offered his hand to help them.

In a startled voice, the mayor said, "Those are Russians! I do not recognize them."

Once the men had disembarked, the boat quickly backed away from the pier, turned around, and sped out to sea.

"Now where are they going?" I mumbled, more to myself than to anyone else.

The mayor heard me and answered, "Out of there, before they are fired upon by the tribal police if they've got any sense."

"Is there a Coast Guard or Navy vessel nearby that we can call up?" I asked.

The mayor responded, "Oh, we have dugout canoes, rafts, a small outboard motor driven fishing boat or two – really nothing. There is still a livestock boat with tall slatted sides at the pier, but none of these could ever catch that speedboat."

The last part of the film showed goats, pigs, and cages with chickens being unloaded from the boat, and the deck hands herding them along the pier toward the market.

I said, "Bob, that's great footage. It provides us with good evidence that the Cubans, the Russians, and Sandinista military personnel are holed up behind those high clinic walls. Clearly they're afraid, and it does seem that they are planning to evacuate as soon as possible. I think it's very interesting that the two men who arrived were not in military uniform and didn't have any visible weapons. They looked to me like political attachés who are probably here to arrange for a quick and safe evacuation of the Cubans and their staff. You know, I really would like to believe that we've won this war without firing a shot, but I don't think it is over yet."

At that point, two men came up the sawmill stairs. We were introduced to them and told they were cousins who were in the freight business and knew the waterfront and the merchant ships that docked in Puerto Cabezas.

The mayor explained that the cousins hated the Cubans and Russians, and as we talked it was easy to see why, for they conveyed several stories of Cuban and Russian atrocities that had been committed against their families and others in the Miskito tribe. I could tell by their attitude that they didn't want to allow the Cubans and their medical staff, and especially the Russians, to escape so easily. I explained to them that I was here as a medical doctor and a peace envoy, and I couldn't let my mission turn into a vigilante lynch mob.

But I had an idea. I asked the cousins if there was a way we could get a better view of the clinic and what was taking place behind those high walls, perhaps by photographing it from above. They conferred with each other for a moment in the Miskito language, then turned toward the group and said, "At the end of the pier and directly behind the Cuban clinic there is a tall gantry crane that is used to raise and lower the docks with the changing of the tides so it can align with the barges and boats that arrive here. It can be extended thirty feet or more into the air. It would be easy for one of us to climb the gantry, perch on top and see the entire coast, and certainly to see over the wall into the Cuban clinic. We could even take photos."

"With the arrival of the two Russians, we need to know what is going on behind those walls," I said.

"It's still light out," the mayor replied. "Our Jeep is parked outside. Why don't we get into it and take a look at that gantry? I also know how to work the gantry, by the way. Besides, it will be safer if we go as a group."

Bob and Lori made it clear that they were not going to miss this part of the story, either. So in short order, all three Jeeps took off down the red clay main street, and turned toward the water's edge. As a precaution against being seen, we all stayed under the cover of the large palm forest and banana trees that reached almost to the edge of the sandy beach.

Once we got to a good spot, but still out of sight of any of the group we were to observe, we parked the Jeeps. Bob hoisted the big TV camera to his shoulder, but remained seated in the back of the Jeep with Lori beside him acting as a spotter. The mayor, the two cousins, and I walked out to the pier adjacent to the tall gantry. I ran to the end of the float pier and began to climb the rusted old gantry. The cousins unlocked the winch mechanism, rotated the large steel disc, and repositioned the gantry to face the Cuban compound. Then they raised it, with the hand crank whining and grinding with each turn of the handle. The long shadows of the late afternoon gave way to evening, and the fog was starting to roll in, colluding with the coming darkness to shroud the clinic and hide it from our view.

I started to climb back down when I suddenly realized I had been looking in the wrong direction. Apparently the breeze had shifted, and the fog was being blown in the opposite direction., away from the subject of our observation Whether it was God's will or good fortune, I wasn't going to complain. An opening appeared in the fog bank, and I counted eight men in the courtyard of the Cuban clinic, with large canvas duffels scattered around them. As suddenly as the hole in the fog had opened, it now closed and we could no longer see into the compound. It was getting dark as I slowly and carefully climbed down the gantry. As we reached the floating pier, I shouted, "Here come more goats and pigs and some cows."

As the animals stampeded down the gangway to the livestock pens, their heads were tossing from side to side, their horns threatening. The cousins jumped to safety behind the iron gantry as the animals exited the pier.

"We can't do any more tonight. They are preparing to make a run for it. It would be nice if we could somehow confiscate some of their supplies and medical equipment," I said.

One of the cousins said, "Any paperwork left behind could be of even greater value."

I reminded them, probably more sternly than necessary, "I'm not here as a military man or a spy, and I won't endanger my mission by pretending I am one." They nodded in somewhat begrudging agreement, and we picked our way carefully along this pristine beach and returned to the Jeeps before the tide came in and the fog enveloped us.

"Bob, did you get all that on film?"

Bob replied, "Some of it, but as the fog came in. I was getting worried, I couldn't even see you on top of the gantry."

Gesturing dramatically, I proclaimed, "God parted the fog bank and gave me a few minutes to see over the Cuban compound walls. I think they are packing to make a hasty escape. Perhaps this really will happen without a shot being fired."

Bravado and suggestions of divine intervention aside, I knew that anything that could go wrong in a situation like this very probably would go wrong.

The mayor said, "Well, enough of this, we are having a celebration tonight. A barbecue is being prepared, Miskito style, and we hope it is as good if not better than your famous Texas barbecue. Lots of cold *cerveza* and no more talk of Cubans, Russians, or Sandinistas. Rest, wash, and change into some comfortable clothes. Many of the town's leaders and Miskito tribal elders will be here to meet you."

I put my bathing suit on, grabbed a bar of soap and went down to the pump. I turned the switch, and the cold water came up from the well below. It took a few seconds to get used to it but it felt great as I soaped up in my bathing suit under the shower. Several five and six year olds ran in and out of the shower around my legs. A mother called but they were not about to heed her. They were playing, laughing, and giggling, clearly having a good time at the expense of the lathered-up stranger.

I rinsed off, slipped into my sandals, and walked across the hard packed red clay to the stairs that wobbled a bit as I reached the second floor porch. The mayor was in his favorite rocking chair. He reached down to an ice chest filled with *cerveza*, popped the top off using the edge of the wooden rail, and handed it to me with a broad smile. "It looks like you could use this."

"I can indeed," I said. I figured I might as well party tonight, because given the plan that was formulating in my mind, there was no telling what tomorrow might bring.

CHAPTER 21
The Bearer Of Gifts

More than one hundred people were in attendance at the barbecue behind the high ramparts of the mayor's house. A surprisingly cool and comfortable breeze was now coming in from the ocean. A side of beef was being roasted over coals on a crude rotisserie, and next to it a goat was being roasted in the same manner. Covered in white cloth, and with wooden benches on either side, the long table stretched as far as I could see in the dark. There were large crocks of steaming beans and vegetables, and near the center of the serving table, in one of the largest cast-iron pots I've ever seen, were at least ten pounds of cooked brown rice. Behind each pot stood a young man or a young lady; all were dressed in colorful local outfits with clean, starched and beautifully embroidered white aprons. Each held a large ladle in his or her hands, waiting to serve the guests.

The mayor walked the medical team and me through the crowd, introducing first the dignitaries, tribal leaders, and the council of the elders, and then his business associates, followed by his friends and neighbors. After everybody had a chance to eat and drink, the mayor beckoned me and gathered some of the tribal leaders and the council of elders and asked us to follow him up to his study.

Meanwhile the celebration below got into full swing, with numerous guitar, banjo, and accordion players providing lively accompaniment for a lone but very talented singer. People were getting into a festive mood and beginning to dance on the hard-packed red clay, and we knew that we would not be missed for a short while.

After more formal introductions, some of us sat in a circle in rocking chairs while the others stood behind us. I was thanked profusely for bringing the badly needed medical supplies and holding a clinic at the Red Cross center. The people's distrust of the Cubans and their Russian overlords became very obvious, as did their dissatisfaction with the way medicine was practiced at the Cuban clinic, which, unlike ours, was not free. In fact, some of the men in the room insinuated that they thought the Russians and Cubans were here to poison their children.

I tried to reassure them by telling them about climbing the gantry and looking down into the Cuban compound to see the occupants packing to leave. I said the Cubans obviously saw the American medical team and the TV people as a threat, and that it seemed clear that they and their Russian sponsors were preparing to make a quick exit.

What I didn't mention was that we didn't yet know by which means they were planning to leave – would it be by boat or on a seaplane? That uncertainty still bothered me a little bit, but overall I was satisfied with the intelligence we had gathered. It had been widely suspected that the Cubans and Russians were involved with the Sandinistas, but we now had definitive proof on film. And both the Russians and Cubans knew that exposure of their continued involvement in Nicaragua's civil strife was a major international incident in the making.

That's when I decided it was time to raise the subject of the plan I'd been formulating. I told the group that I would actually like to meet with the Cuban doctors as medical men, with no politics involved, since all of us had supposedly come here on humanitarian missions. At this, a cacophony of murmurs and sharp individual conversations immediately filled the room, mostly in the Miskito language. I raised my hand to quiet the disturbance.

The mayor said that it might be possible to hold a meeting with the Cuban doctors, but he didn't feel it would gain us anything. He suggested that we ask each of the Miskito council members individually, so that everyone could have his say. I nodded in agreement, and he began by turning to the man on his immediate right. Then he went around the circle, and each of the council members and elders was allowed to make a short statement of his feelings about a possible meeting between the Cubans and myself. The feelings were definitely mixed, but the consensus was that it would not accomplish much and that no matter what, the Cubans and their Russian masters had to go.

I listened carefully, and when everyone had spoken, I mentioned the arrival of the two men on the speedboat that afternoon who were dressed more like diplomats than physicians, and were definitely neither Cuban nor Sandinista. I said I felt that if they were from the diplomatic corps, their presence might open the door to a conversation that would result in a peaceful exit of the Cubans within the next few days.

As the men appeared to be considering my words, I said, "I appreciate hearing from all of you. I have made my decision. I am going to go alone to the Cuban clinic at seven o'clock tomorrow morning, as soon as the sun comes up, and before I attend the medical clinic at the Red Cross center. I will not be armed. There will be no TV cameras. I have some medical textbooks and equipment that I will offer as a gift to the Cuban doctors – a peace offering."

One of the men shouted, "Cubans and their Russian masters do not understand *peace offering!*"

Murmurs continued around the room. The mayor interceded, "You're really planning to go alone?"

I said, "Yes."

"I cannot allow that. You are too important to us and the peace initiative."

I made it clear that there would be no negotiation on this. "I am going alone."

"O.K. go alone, but the local Indian police force will be watching you from the jungle and we *will* be heavily armed. I also request that you try to draw the doctors outside the wall in the open area and hold your conference with them there. Give them the gifts outside the walls. Do not enter the compound. You could easily be kidnapped or worse. Then we *will* have an international incident to deal with."

I smiled at him, saying, "I was hoping to do just that. I think the doctors at the Cuban clinic will be comfortable enough to meet with me on neutral ground in front of their clinic."

One of the council members chimed in at this point, saying, "There are two five-ton Russian military trucks parked to either side of the road at the clinic. They have not moved in weeks. I have scouted them and they are empty of arms and other equipment. I will place our men inside and behind those Russian trucks, and it will be up to you, doctor, to coax the medical staff out. May I suggest that you tie a white handkerchief to a stick and carry it with you as a declaration of a truce when you approach the clinic in the morning?"

The mayor responded, "Good idea. I can go along with that. But tonight I'm giving a party, with dancing, drinking, and good fellowship. There will be no more of this talk." At this, everyone stood up, and some came over to me and shook my hand, while others patted me on the back. The mayor and I exited the room and the group followed, pleased to set aside serious matters until *mañana*.

It was a wonderful celebration of dancing and music, with more than enough food for all to eat their fill. Then, close to midnight, one of the guards whose job was to oversee the lumberyard and equipment came running up to our table. He seemed agitated and spoke quickly to the mayor in the Miskito language.

The mayor turned to me and said that he had just been informed that there were several hundred people marching down the main street chanting, "*Americans stay,*

Cubans go! Americans stay, Cubans go!"

It seemed that the locals had decided to take this matter into their own hands.

"We cannot allow vigilante action," I cautioned. Violeta's emphasis that I was here as a peace envoy played loudly in my mind. "I don't want this trip to fail."

The mayor responded, "I will gather some of the elders. Also, many of the Miskito police deputies are here at the party. They will come with us. The crowd is marching toward the Cuban clinic, but we need to get there first. Please instruct your nurses to go to the Red Cross center and stay there. That's the safest place for them. I strongly suggest you do the same."

"No! I will be with you, Mr. Mayor."

At that moment, Barrett and Dixon jumped up, saying as one, "If you go, we go." I knew there would be no arguing with them, so I didn't even try.

The mob was now passing in front of the mayor's home, and their shouts of, *"Americans stay, Cubans go!"* could be clearly heard. But weapons were now being fired into the air as well. Not a good sign at all.

The mayor shouted, "We are going to go through the lumberyard and out the back gate. We will then be ahead of these mobs. We can form a line in front of the Cuban clinic. Hopefully, the crowd will be willing to listen, but this is a very rowdy crowd, many of whose bravery I suspect has been fortified by an evening of drinking. Firing their weapons only serves to further embolden them."

Then the mayor led us through the darkened lumberyard, out the back gate, and across an open field toward the Cuban clinic. We followed the coastline until we could see the spotlights on the Cuban clinic wall. Several of the mayor's men blocked the road at this point with pickup trucks and Jeeps.

The vigilante mob kept coming, continually bellowing their chant, *"Americans stay, Cubans go!"* Their guns were still being fired in the air, but so far only in the air. We knew, however, that if we weren't able to disperse the crowd, this could change in a heartbeat.

More spotlights suddenly went on along the walls of the Cuban clinic, illuminating the grounds outside the walls as well as the surrounding area. We did not know what types of weapons or how much ammunition they had, but it was very obvious that if they fired on a crowd this size, they would lose. Any angry crowd is difficult to control, and if the Cubans began killing the marchers, the crowd's anger would turn to rage, and they would either climb the walls or blow holes in them, then swarm inside and take their revenge.

The crowd came up to our barricade and stopped. I stepped forward with the mayor, with Barrett and Dixon following at our side and a step behind us. The mayor and I held our arms up and out in a gesture of peace, bidding them to stop their chants. A hush finally came over the crowd, with the exception of several boisterous men who were obviously intoxicated, and still continued shouting. We stood there silently, eye-to-eye and only a few feet apart. Fortunately, the men who were still shouting were not the ones with weapons. The mayor started to speak, but I quickly cut him off.

I said, "I heard your chants, your cries of 'Americans stay.' Our medical team is willing to stay. We are willing to work for free. We have supplies and equipment to help you and your children. I see that there are women and children in this group. As a physician I do not want to see anyone hurt. We will begin clinic again at the Red Cross Center at eight o'clock tomorrow morning. But, if this demonstration continues and you put the American medical team in jeopardy, we have our aircraft waiting and can be gone in five minutes. We don't want to have to do that. Think about your children."

Children were crying, and the women were now raising their voices to the men standing around them. One of the women shouted, "My child needs to be seen in the clinic tomorrow! You cannot leave!"

I responded, "Then tell the men standing next to you and the others around you to turn around and go home. Nothing good will be accomplished here tonight."

At that, the women started pushing and pulling their men from the crowd, taking their babies into their arms. Then I started shouting, "The Cubans are leaving! The Cubans are leaving!" Barrett, Dixon, the mayor, and others joined me.

Thankfully, the crowd began to disburse. I began moving through the crowd with the mayor, Dixon, and Barrett, shaking hands, patting people on their shoulder, and kissing a baby here and there. The drunks who stubbornly remained were quickly grabbed by the Miskito tribal police, placed into the Jeeps, and taken away. I let out a big sigh of relief.

The lights on the Cuban compound blinked several times and then went dark. I removed the white handkerchief from my back pocket and waving it high above my head, walked toward the Cuban clinic entrance. There was a large, rusty, iron knocker in the center of the door. I pounded on it several times. No response. I repeated the pounding. Several floodlights at the front gate flashed on.

A voice on the other side shouted, "What do you want?"

"I am the American doctor."

"You are the one they call Doctor Angel?"

"Yes, yes."

I was surprised when the answer was, "Thank you for what you have done tonight."

"I am a physician and I did not want to see any lives lost due to a vigilante mob."

"We are leaving. The will of the Miskito people in Puerto Cabezas is very apparent."

"I will come here tomorrow morning at seven o'clock, alone and unarmed. I would like to meet with you in front of the clinic," I said.

"To what purpose?"

"Doctor to doctor, humanitarian to humanitarian, And I would like to present you with some gifts to take back with you when you leave."

"I am Dr. Jose Hortez. I am the senior physician here, and I will meet you at seven o'clock. But no tricks, no hidden agenda."

I responded, "I am here as a physician and a peace envoy, nothing else. And I too would like to see you depart peacefully."

Dr. Hortez replied, "We will see you in the morning, then. Perhaps I could offer you a gift as well; a few of our country's best cigars. And again, we all thank you."

I laughed, and shouted back, "I don't think anyone in my country would refuse such a gift. *Hasta mañana!*"

With that, the spotlights around the Cuban clinic went dark, and Barrett, Dixon, the mayor, and I began our leisurely walk along the empty streets and back to the mayor's home. The mayor turned to me and put his heavy arm around my shoulder, saying, "The time for *cerveza* is over. I have an old bottle of very good scotch and several bottles of Flor de Caña rum. It is time for a real drink. You have earned it. Tonight you are not Dr. Angel; you are that Crazy Texan I have heard about."

* * * * *

It was a little after 6:00 a.m. and the sun was just coming up as I dressed in my operating room scrubs and my Western boots. I put an eight-inch stiletto in a pocket in the left boot, and a loaded semi-automatic pistol in a pocket in the right. I was not crazy enough to go in there unarmed, for I was all too aware that in spite of the friendly exchange the night before, this could be a setup.

I put a freshly washed and starched white lab coat on over my scrubs, and noticed that it was already getting warm. I donned one of my colorful red operating room skull-caps that I had acquired on a mission trip in Bolivia. It was not native but I thought it would impress. Then I tied a surgical mask around my neck and let it hang to my chest.

I tried to open the door to my room and depart quietly, but the squeaking hinges gave away my exit strategy. As I stepped out onto the second floor porch, the mayor was already in his favorite rocking chair with a steaming cup of coffee. He looked up at me and said, "The men are in position around the clinic. They left when it was still dark so they would not be discovered. I will walk you to the main road. You will go to the far end and make a right turn, and you will be facing the clinic in minutes."

We walked side-by-side, me with a backpack slung over my right shoulder.

"You are the bearer of gifts," the mayor observed.

"Yes, as I promised, I'm giving them some new medical textbooks, some that I wrote. Also some new American medical instruments that I don't think the Cubans have. I have duplicates of all of this so it is not a sacrifice to our medical team or to our patients."

"Do you think they will accept it?"

"I don't know, but the doctor I spoke with last night seemed agreeable. Besides, my mother always taught me that you don't pay a visit without bringing something."

"Always a good gesture."

When we reached the road where I was to turn, the mayor stopped, shook my hand, and wished me good luck.

I grabbed the edges of my white lab coat, unbuttoned it, and pulled it open, saying, "So they will see that I am unarmed."

The mayor looked at me, his concern evident in his expression, and said, "Unarmed?"

I smiled, gave him a wink, and started walking toward the Cuban clinic's front gate.

CHAPTER 22
Firefight

As I approached the Cuban compound, the heavy metal door set into the foot-thick wall began to open. At first, I didn't slow my stride, but the warnings I had gotten against going inside the compound echoed loudly in my head, and I slowed down unconsciously.

The door opened further and a voice called out, "What are you waiting for?"

"An opportunity to talk some sense. Come out. Please, come and sit with me."

The Cuban doctor, Dr. Hortez, was a short, thick-necked man with a barrel chest and an even larger belly. He filled the front door, almost blocking it. His black hair was slicked back, and he was clean-shaven, except for a very full, thick mustache curled at the ends. It was trimmed so precisely that it looked as if he had just walked out of the barbershop. With a beaming smile, he waved for me to come forward.

As I stepped forward, the ocean breeze caught my white lab coat and parted it. I made no motion to hold it closed, as I wanted him to think that I was unarmed. At once, my sense of caution, as well as the admonitions I had gotten against going inside the compound, were overruled by that adrenaline rush with which I'd grown so familiar over the years of my travels.

Against everybody's better judgment – including my own – I entered the Cuban compound and stepped between burlap sacks, packing boxes, and file cases that I had not seen from my perch on the gantry the other day. This told me they had been busy and were hurriedly packing to leave, and now it seemed more certain that the Cubans and their Russian masters had decided they were out of business in Puerto Cabezas.

I shook hands with the Cuban doctor, placed my backpack at his feet, and nodded. The two blue-eyed, fair-skinned suits approached, and I again gestured to the backpack.

In halting Spanish I told the doctor that it was a gift for him, as I had promised the night before.

He laughed. "A bomb?"

I laughed with him. The two Russian suits stopped in their tracks, whereupon we both laughed even harder. Then Dr. Hortez reached down and lifted up the backpack. The Russian suits looked nervously on as he unsnapped it and pulled out the books.

"Do these medical books have some importance?"

"I wrote them. Something to remember me by."

"What else do you have for me?"

"Some new medical instruments. Micro instruments. I helped in their design. You will find them useful when you return home. After all, we are still in the same business of helping people and saving lives."

The two Russians, obviously from the diplomatic corps, as I had earlier speculated, remained standing several feet away. They were standing next to a large wall calendar, a promotional gift from the Russian government, but what caught my eye was the statement under the calendar, *Tell it to God*. That surprised me.

The men took a few steps closer and one said to the other, "He has nice boots."

I had picked up a little Russian in my travels. (In fact, over the years my medical team made eleven trips in and out of Russia, even taking the Trans-Siberian Railroad all the way to the Ural mountain towns of Perm and Kungur.) At this point I knew enough Russian to understand what he had said, and with a big smile I responded, "Thank you," in my best formal Russian. They froze where they were standing, and I continued in Russian, "The Cubans must go quickly."

The Cuban doctor turned toward the two Russian diplomats and gave them a look, and then he turned back to me and said, "Different men for different tasks. I must apologize. If it were different times and a different place, as physicians we could have been good friends. As physicians I would like to think we have the same goals but we live under completely different systems, with different type of politics. Impossible!"

I said, "I can't believe we are having this conversation. You and these two Russian diplomats are not equal partners in the decision making."

Dr. Hortez nodded, saying, "I get it. I feel like an idiot too. They told me not to say anything to you. In any case, tomorrow, at the very latest, there will be a boat here, and my medical staff and I will be leaving."

I nodded, smiled, and said, "Be sure to take those two with you!"

"They just arrived the other day. Mostly as advisors. But I had already made the decision to leave. While I was stationed here, I always tried to stay behind the scenes and avoid the limelight. I knew that we could not assimilate. We did not fit in with the Miskito inhabitants of this coast."

"So you are telling me that you were a spy here at the highest level," I exclaimed.

"Not a spy, a doctor. I really did try. I was in some ways an off-stage operator stationed at this Godforsaken clinic. Even our leaders back home in Cuba forgot about this outpost. I really did try to help the locals. But I always dodged cameras in the interest of remaining incognito. I knew full well the threats that were out there. We were few, and the Miskito Indians were many. Thank God they are peaceful people. But it is time for me to leave and see to the safety of my doctors and other clinic comrades. As a doctor I never wanted any trouble. I always preferred to go around an obstacle. Now my big concern is, where the hell is our boat?"

I could hardly keep from laughing.

Then one of the Russians said to me, in heavily accented English, "It is humiliating to have been sent here and to confess ignorance of what has taken place. Aside from that, I feel a curiosity mingled with admiration for you, having caught wind of the work you are doing, not only here but also in your travels to Russia. Extraordinary how you have finally found your way straight into the lion's den."

I said, "I don't see it that way." I paused a few moments and then continued, "Have you noticed a sudden quiet in the town of Puerto Cabezas? There is little activity on the streets, in the market, and at the saloon. You all owe me your lives. That vigilante crowd wanted to hang all of you from the doorpost or pin your flesh to your compound wall. The mayor, the local Miskito police force and I saved all your lives last night. Things have quieted down since. I would like it not to become an international incident. I am here with the medical team to help these people, not to see them get shot. I am also here of my own volition, and with the authority of the newly elected democratic president of Nicaragua, to help her bring a peaceful end to the conflict here on the Miskito Coast, and to see you leave safely."

In Russian, one of the men answered, "*Dasvidania.*" ("Goodbye.")

I then turned away from the Russians and approached Dr. Hortez again, putting my hand out to him. He was hesitant, first looking over his shoulder at the Russians, but finally he turned back to me, smiled, and took my hand, saying, "*Vaya con Dios, mi amigo.*" ("Go with God, my friend.")

I was sure the local Miskito police and other members of my medical team were getting anxious outside the compound walls. I walked briskly through the gate, hands outstretched and waving to let the sharpshooters who were stationed behind the Russian military trucks, and in the area behind the trucks, know that everything was okay.

I walked triumphantly down the road, arm in arm with the mayor, to the Red Cross station. The clinic was already in progress, and there were what looked to be hundreds of people lined up outside, waiting to be treated. The Miskito Indians were getting their wish: the Americans would stay, and the Cubans were going home.

Joseph Agris, M.D.

* * * * *

The day was overcast and foggy, very humid, and miserably uncomfortable. It wasn't supposed to be like this at this time of year, but the current weather was certainly bucking that trend.

I was tired, but was still functioning normally. Because I don't tend to show my weariness, many of the people I've worked with seemed to regard me as something of a machine. I'm sure that on that day, I did appear to be somewhat cold and robotic, but I was determined to maintain a good bedside manner with the patients in the clinic. To the staff, I probably seemed like my old perfectionist, workaholic self.

Yet beneath my seemingly unperturbed exterior, my gut was lurching and my nerves were fraying. Despite my professed eagerness to be a part of the peace mission, and my bravado in approaching the clinic, I really hadn't liked being put in the position of having to confront the Cubans and their Russian masters. After all, I was here as a doctor on a medical mission. With my added diplomatic responsibilities, however, I felt the weight of the world on my shoulders. This "peace emissary" role was rapidly getting old.

I sat on the edge of the operating stool and stretched my legs. My hamstrings were tight. My lower back was aching, and was even tighter than my hamstrings. I felt that if I could just narrow my focus to this next surgical procedure, it would be okay. That was primarily what I was here for, after all.

All of a sudden, there was a flash of lightning, followed immediately by a deafening crack of thunder. The rain fell in huge drops, more like buckets full, against the tiles on the roof, but at least the ceiling and plaster were not crumbling down on us as they had done at the hospital in Chinandega.

The thunder continued and the rain lashed the windows. I half closed my eyes and my thoughts focused on the Cubans. I wanted to say something but couldn't find the words, so finally I raised my head and looked at the anesthesiologist, who gave me a thumbs-up. It was time to go to the scrub sink and get ready for the procedure.

This little patient had suffered a bad burn, and his arm and hand were contracted into a useless ball. The release of the burn contracture went forward quickly, without any problems. Skin grafts were taken from his thigh and transferred to his little hand and arm. I asked for the skin clips, which were something the nursing students in attendance had not seen before, so I instructed this new group of students in the proper technique of applying the clips.

I asked Carolyn to oversee the application of the dressing and splint, and left the operating room for the small doctor's lounge. I walked over to the far wall, put my back against it, and stretched. My neck was stiff, and I began moving my head from side to side like the beam in a lighthouse to try and alleviate the stiffness.

After a while, Carolyn came in and handed me a cold bottle of water. She hovered over me, looking uncertain and a little nervous.

Thinking it was the storm that had her feeling uneasy, I tried to reassure her, saying, "It's been a deluge outside, but it will probably stop pretty soon, as quickly as it started."

"That's the least of our problems," she responded. "Right now, I'm more worried about you. You are obviously overworked and exhausted, and I think you're also dehydrated. I want you to drink this water and take some salt tablets."

I reached up and pulled off my surgical cap. I knew that my hair was mussed, and no doubt I was looking somewhat disheveled and distraught. Carolyn, her eyes full of sympathy and concern, said, "I know that this trip has been stressful for you, especially that situation with the Cubans. It's dangerous, and I don't think the danger is over yet, and I know you don't either. It could still get us all killed. But I knew that when I volunteered to come here. We all did."

Then she smiled. "But for now, Doc, you need to lighten up. I think I know what will help to brighten your mood. We need to get you laid!" Clearly she was trying to make me laugh. A big smile crossed her face and she began giggling as she walked out, slamming the door behind her.

Instead of laughing, though, I balled my hands into fists and slammed them down on the table, then took a deep breath and listened to the rain beating down outside. At the moment it seemed that I'd never seen this much rain before in such a short time, even in Houston, where flash flooding is not uncommon.

Then I got to thinking about Carolyn's semi-facetious parting comment, and the word *chocha* just popped into my mind. *Chocha* means different things in different regional dialects of Spanish, so there's no universal interpretation, but in this instance, it could be summed up as a crude slang word for female genitalia.

My train of thought jumped quickly to the situation with Michael and Marta, and how *it's all about the rules – my rules* on these trips, immediately followed by the thought, *rules are made to be broken. But not by me...*

Suddenly, Barrett burst into the doctor's lounge without knocking. "They are on the move," he shouted. "They're on the move!"

"Who?" I asked, though I thought I knew the answer.

"The Cubans!"

I quickly followed him out of the doctor's lounge and to the front of the compound. Just as we reached the gate, a few of the mayor's men who had been watching the Cuban compound arrived to verify that the Cubans were indeed moving out. One of them blurted out, "I could see it for myself. The Cubans were shooting glances over their shoulders as they went. They began frantically removing burlap sacks, packing boxes, and wooden crates. The two Russians, however, were cool customers, just sitting on a rock outside the clinic gate while everyone else scurried about. We also recognized the Cuban leader who you had met, and who over the years has failed to understand or appreciate the Miskito people and their culture."

Another man said, "Word is spreading rapidly in the town. Whatever the Cubans had stolen or smuggled into the clinic has caught the attention of many young locals. Now that the Cubans are leaving, I do not want the locals to destroy the clinic or the supplies that would be useful to your medical team."

The mayor said, "These items will become fair game for the young Miskito warriors. We cannot let that happen."

I put on my white coat and Stetson hat, and without thinking I reached into the pocket of my right boot. Of course the Glock was still in there. The mayor's driver and his men were waiting outside, and we jumped into the waiting car. The locals were pouring out of their homes and shops and moving quickly toward the Cuban clinic building.

Suddenly an ear-splitting whistle split the air. Several more Jeeps with local Miskito police caught up with the mayor's vehicle, then pulled up to block the road in front of the Cuban clinic. Jumping out of their Jeeps, they stood statue-like and defiant, their weapons poised. Then a shot rang out.

There was no way to know which group shot first, but that single shot triggered a fusillade, and the mayor, my team and I found ourselves in the midst of a shooting war. Bullets splintered the stockade that surrounded the Cuban clinic and shattered windows on the second floor. Bullets ricocheted off the cobblestone walks and the Jeeps that we were now hunkered behind. The bullets were all being fired well over our heads and into the clinic. This was obviously a release of the locals' long, pent-up anger, brought to a head by their desire to see the Cubans and Russians move out even faster.

The Cubans were better armed than we'd anticipated. Automatic fire continued; men were jerking triggers nervously but not hitting anyone. They were spraying lead high overhead in hopes of slowing the assault. I thought it best to let them get it out of their systems or at least run out of ammunition.

But they continued to bang away like our Fourth of July, and I realized this could continue for a while. They were reloading their weapons with a speed that only comes from military training and extensive practice, likely in combat. The two Russians rushed into the doorway, which was much too shallow to offer them much protection from the gunfire. When there was finally a lull in the shooting, they took it as an opportunity to make a break for it. They dropped to their bellies and slithered away from the compound, hugging the cobblestones with one hand and trying to shield their heads with the other, pulling themselves along using their elbows.

I thought to myself, *If ever a man was out of place, and if ever he could use an angel, it's now.*

CHAPTER 23
Pistols And Puppets

Exiting the compound, the Russians pivoted sharply behind the stockade wall, which was now protecting them, and ran for the pier where a boat was docked, finally catching up with the fleeing Cubans. At that moment, a bullet nicked my sleeve, reminding me that while I was reasonably safe behind the barricade provided by the Jeeps and trucks, there was always the danger of being struck by a ricochet.

Then, the return fire suddenly stopped, and several of the police, the mayor, and I ran to the cover of the stockade wall as what we hoped was the last Cuban employee exited, carrying a large burlap sack in one hand and a suitcase in the other. The mayor extended his massive gorilla-like arm and caught the man by the neck, dropping him to the ground. The man staggered to his knees, and then with an unbelievable agility and probably a significant adrenaline rush, sprang to his feet, leaving his belongings behind and sprinting toward the pier and the awaiting boat.

Almost immediately, a loud clamor erupted, and I could barely hear the mayor over the roar of people shouting and the booming of double-barreled shotguns being fired. The crowd of young men who had accompanied us literally stampeded in all directions. Apparently, another party had joined our little get-together. Local militiamen were driving directly at the crowd in a small military-like convoy, scattering the young vigilantes. When this impromptu gun battle stopped as abruptly as it started, I figured that both sides had exhausted their supply of ammo.

I ran into the clinic and climbed to the second floor. Peering out the back windows, I saw the police chief pulling away from the wharf in a fast-moving skiff. Something about that struck me as odd, but then, the chief had given off bad vibes when our team had met him shortly after our arrival in Puerto Cabezas. We'd noticed that he really wasn't all that friendly and welcoming. On the other hand, I had anticipated that even some well-meaning people might be suspicious of us at first, so I had wasted little time worrying about the police chief's behavior. And I had no time to think about it now that the worst appeared to be over, and there was work to be done. I had the mayor and his men secure the Cuban clinic, and then we began searching the premises. We found a supply of medications and medical supplies and sacks of money that also needed to be secured and accounted for.

After seeing to the gathering of the supplies and cash, I went directly to the Red Cross compound, thinking there would be many wounded awaiting us, but no casualties had reported in. No one wanted to create an international incident. They just wanted to convince the Cubans and the Russians that it was time to leave Nicaragua.

The volunteers from the Red Cross compound brought everyone into the central area and held a short prayer vigil. With the disturbance over, the volunteers told the mothers to take their children home and return in the morning for the clinic. There were a few stoics who stubbornly remained, and we proceeded to treat them as if nothing had happened. What else could we do?

That evening, the streets were packed as if for a festival. The evening air was blessedly dry and cool. Hundreds of people from the surrounding countryside came into Puerto Cabezas, escaping for awhile from their airless wooden homes to celebrate the victory and to enjoy the coolness of the evening. Colorful banners began to appear along the main street. Of all things that I wouldn't have expected, a puppeteer set up a small stage on one corner and began performing, and it was only a few minutes before a crowd of children began to gather. People spilled off the sidewalks into the streets. Peddlers appeared, pressing the crowd to buy their food, drinks, flags, and other souvenirs. Traffic of course was at a standstill.

Carolyn, Dixon, Barrett, and I strolled amongst the celebrants, wearing our white lab coats. I have to admit to being a bit pissed off that I had a bullet hole in the sleeve of my favorite white lab coat, but then again, it wasn't in my arm. So there was that.

Groups of wandering musicians entertained the crowd along the main street, and a commotion caught my eye. Across the road, I saw the mayor, his arm in a sling, staggering alongside the local police and pushing through the crowd.

I said, "Mr. Mayor, were you shot, injured?"

The mayor began to laugh, his protuberant belly jiggling. "I straight-armed that Cuban with that burlap sack full of money as he was running from the compound, and my arm took the hit pretty hard, but it's just some muscle pain. I put it in the sling to rest it."

I responded, "Nevertheless, I expect to see you in the clinic tomorrow morning for a checkup!"

People began to gather around, and the mayor proclaimed, as mayors are often wont to do, "What a fine night."

Carolyn looked at me with her mischievous grin, whispering, "You look recovered from your troubles. Maybe it wasn't sex that you needed, but a successful gunfight to get your adrenaline going."

I grinned back, shrugging at her comments, then turned to watch the marionettes. I noticed that some were dressed in Cuban military uniforms. "What is the puppet show tonight?" I asked the mayor.

"I think it's pretty obvious," he said. "Like you and me, my friend, the puppet soldiers fight the communist Cubans, who then retreat back to their home country. Truth mixed with fantasy is the marionette's tale." Then he moved on.

I was tempted to move on myself and stroll through the crowd, enjoying the pleasant evening, when I spotted Bob Dows approaching with his large TV camera resting on his shoulder. He had been wandering through the crowd as well, shooting footage, with Lori Reingold directing the shots. No doubt about it, they had their exclusive now. A hell of a story, but would the station dare run it? I could just imagine the lead-in, and our own government's reaction to the story: *Cubans, Russians, Sandinistas, Miskito Indians, and a crazy Texas doctor, smack dab in the middle of it – the instigator in freeing the Miskito Indians and sending the Cubans packing.*

Bob Dows began filming the puppet show, which was clearly a re-enactment of the drama on the Miskito Coast: brightly costumed local vigilante marionettes flailed at the Cuban puppets in their gray stylized uniforms. Everyone was clapping, laughing, and singing as the marionettes were manipulated by rods and strings hanging from the curtained bridge above the stage.

Lori remarked to me, "Those are pretty violent little puppets. You'd think they were fighting for their lives."

I replied, "Well, in a sense they are. They're fighting for honor, justice, faith, and their right to self advocacy."

She murmured, to nobody in particular, "They seem to be doing better than we are at the moment." By that I assumed she was referring to humanity in general, but I didn't ask her to elaborate.

"This is definitely a case of art imitating life," I said to her. "Think of the puppet master as the Russian overlord, pulling the Cubans' strings."

"Yes," she agreed, "though puppets can't see who is pulling on the strings."

"Well, much of the time humans can't really see who's pulling the strings either," I pointed out. "Or maybe they just don't want to see." I added teasingly, "That's the whole point of that metaphor, you know."

"That's true," she said, smiling. "But yes... the Russian puppet master is on top, the Cuban followers below, backed by the Sandinista enforcers, with the local Miskito Indians in their colorful outfits vanquishing them. It's totally appropriate. The only one the puppeteer doesn't have is you – physician and liberator, the true hero, backed by the most powerful force in the world."

I couldn't tell if she was making fun of me, though I rather suspected she was. Maybe she was just getting back at me for my subtle taunt about the puppet metaphor. Ignoring her gentle dig about my supposed heroism, I said, "So, by the most powerful force in the world, you mean the U.S.A., I suppose."

Lori laughed before responding, "No, Bob's camera, with Channel 13 and ABC News behind it – that's the most powerful force. It shows the world what is happening here. It's a case of free speech, and the free press, not only reporting but also feeding these people's desire to live free."

Whether she was making fun of me or not, she did have a point.

The mayor had circled back around toward us and was waving from a distance with his good arm. I suddenly realized that I was totally exhausted, so turning to Lori, I whispered, "I'm going to call it a night soon. Busy day today, you know, and likely an even busier one tomorrow." I turned to leave, but the mayor caught my eye as he approached, signaling that he wanted to speak with me. Yet as he reached us it was Bob to whom he spoke, with a smile dancing across his full face. He asked somewhat mockingly but good-naturedly, "Tell me the truth now. What was it really that brought an American TV crew to Puerto Cabezas? Do you have a death wish like the doctor here?"

"What do you mean?" Bob asked him, and I could tell that he was wondering if perhaps the mayor had had a little too much to drink. After all, the mayor was fully aware by now of Bob and Lori's purpose for being here. If he was trying to ferret out some hidden agenda, perhaps he really had over-imbibed.

But he had a serious expression on his face as he replied to Bob. "I am worried for you. There are too many people in the street now. I don't want you to get hurt."

Attempting to dismiss the mayor's concern, Bob chuckled and said, "They're innocent civilians, celebrating."

The mayor was dead serious with his response. "I am beginning to think that you are naïve enough to really believe that."

Bob was obviously stunned by the gravity of the mayor's words and demeanor. "Meaning what?" he asked.

"This is the Miskito Indian coast. Despite what happened today, the Sandinista influence is still here."

"But these people are barefoot peasants having a good time," said Bob.

Lori, sensing an element that would add depth to her story, quickly interjected, "Mr. Mayor, I would like a short interview with you while we have this crowd as a background. As their mayor, what are you going to do for them?"

"I will find them work, and that will feed them. I will use the money that we recovered from the Cubans to buy more supplies and medical equipment, and to reopen the clinic. In fact," he continued, looking at me, "I want you to hold the first *free* clinic there, tomorrow morning at seven o'clock, and begin treating patients. We have taken down the Cuban flag. I am placing a Nicaraguan flag and an American flag in show of solidarity above the clinic."

Lori said, "That's only a start."

The mayor responded, "You need to understand that I am not a real politician. I am a simple lumber mill operator who happened to get elected mayor."

I piped in. "Use some of your own money, put in more effort, and use your talents. Look, you have been a successful businessman in Puerto Cabezas for a long time. You know how to organize. You might even consider organizing the Miskito Indians into a national political party."

The mayor looked puzzled at this, having obviously never set his sights beyond his little town. "National?"

I saw the glimmer in his eyes at the notion of such an opportunity to see his own importance increased.

Encouraged, I continued, "Why not? This can be the end of the Sandinista military and their atrocities. It also ends the Contras' well-documented brutality. The Sandinistas and Contras will no longer be coming to the *campesinos* to take what they want at gunpoint. The Sandinistas have lost both the election and public support. True, some Sandinistas have rejected the peace accord and continue to strike out from their hiding places in the mountains and jungles, but most have been disarmed and have gone back to their lives as fishermen and farmers. This is the beginning of the end of their ideology and geopolitics."

The mayor nodded.

"Most important of all," I concluded, "Violeta Barrios Torres de Chamorro is now your president. I trust her and support her. Her strength, charisma, and talent as a leader will guide Nicaragua through a period of reconciliation and rebuilding. The Chamorro government has created an autonomous region for the indigenous Miskito people, and you should work with the indigenous people's organizations on the Atlantic side to further your goals in Puerto Cabezas as well as theirs. Think on it, Mr. Mayor."

"Well, from what I've seen," said the mayor to me, "you've been able to accomplish a lot just in a few days. Maybe you should stay here indefinitely."

"Mr. Mayor, I'm glad to help out where I can. But I am, first and foremost, a physician. And I also know that the government in Managua has for decades considered us aliens, and perhaps it still does."

"You just changed that, and all in one night," said the mayor.

But I wasn't so certain.

Joseph Agris, M.D.

* * * * *

Now that the Cubans had apparently deserted their clinic, we took it over. As the mayor had promised, the Cuban flag was indeed gone from its place atop the building, replaced by the Nicaraguan and American flags. The way the flags were silhouetted against a glowing sunset was a sight I will always hold dear in my heart. The medical team and I were proud to look up and see those flags flying every morning when we went to the clinic, and I often found myself recalling the sound of the locals chanting, "Americans stay! Cubans go home!"

I was very thankful for the relatively peaceful departure of the Cubans and Russians. No one was killed or badly injured as far as I knew, and the only "casualties" were the bullet wound to the sleeve of my favorite white lab coat, and the mayor's little mishap with his arm. Just another day in Puerto Cabezas.

Nevertheless I was on high alert. A few mornings after the Cuban exodus, I heard the rustle of boots and the creaking of the floorboards outside my room at the sawmill. I sensed motion as the sunlight coming through the window was momentarily obstructed by someone passing by outside on the second floor veranda.

I had an ominous feeling, and ran to the window just as someone bolted in the opposite direction. I could hear footsteps rapidly descending the staircase at the far end, and saw the shadow of a man as he headed towards a cluster of houses away from the sawmill. The sun was so bright it gleamed off the metallic band on his cap, so it was easy to track him visually as he veered through the narrow alley between the buildings, using them for cover. He then sprinted into a clump of trees where he disappeared. Yet I had a feeling that he was hiding there, waiting... but for what? Or whom? I quickly pulled on my trousers, slipped into my cowboy boots, and instinctively pulled my Glock from the right boot's pocket.

Releasing the latch on the door to my room, I cursed the creaking of the old rusty hinges as the door opened. But I guess the noise didn't really matter, because the intruder was clearly not there anymore. I walked quickly down the stairs and proceeded in the direction he had fled. Approaching the trees where I was sure he was hiding, I heard his labored breathing before I saw him. And then for first time, I saw his face, dark and barely visible under the metal-banded brim of his hat. His eyes were focused on me, and with his arms extended outward, his legs bent and body coiled, he looked as if he were preparing to spring forward.

A sudden rush of adrenaline nearly overwhelmed me. Then my muscles snapped into action, seemingly of their own accord, as my finger found the trigger of the Glock. We made eye contact for a second. My eyes were darting at any hint of movement, and my own breathing had become deep and rapid. Suddenly the intruder turned and began walking away. Looking back at me once more he broke into a run, disappearing at last into the thick brush and trees.

A bit shaky but relieved, I returned to my room. At this time of the morning, the streets were empty and store owners were just arriving. The market had not yet attracted the early morning crowds. As I looked over the second floor railing and scanned the street below, I saw several of my resident doctors and nurses heading toward the clinic, accompanied by two of the sisters from the local Moravian Church. I waved to them and they waved back. "Did you see anyone or anything unusual as you were coming in this direction?" I called out.

One of the young doctors replied, "No one. Most people are still asleep or having their breakfast. We are going to the clinic to help set up so we will be ready when you arrive. We are planning vaccinations and polio preventive treatment in addition to any medical or surgical cases that might show up. One of the sisters wants to talk to you. Would you mind coming down for a minute?"

I started down the staircase, and then realized I was not wearing a shirt; I'd been out on the street in my trousers, with a pair of Western boots on my feet and a Glock in my hand. It occurred to me that I must have looked completely out of place, but just as quickly, I wondered, *did I really?*

I turned and ran back up the few steps, pulled on a shirt, and slipped the pistol back into my boot. Then I returned to the street below to meet with the group.

The senior resident doctor said, "We have everything under control. The morning will be busy, and you have your work cut out for you. But you should have some free time in the afternoon to visit the surrounding villages for polio and other immunizations, and to examine any children to see if any of them will need to come in for surgery or other treatments."

As our group continued on toward the clinic, Sister Maria took me aside and said, "I was checking the pharmacy during the last two days, and it seemed like more medications are gone than what I would have expected for the care and treatment of the patients." She added that she was worried that someone had gotten into the pharmacy in the evening and removed some of our medications and supplies.

I asked the sister for the names of those who had pharmacy access. Other than the sisters and the pharmacist who had been there for many years there were only two others. It appeared that we had a mystery on our hands, one that needed to be solved quickly, before the situation got any worse.

Joseph Agris, M.D.

CHAPTER 24
Bigger Fish

There were two delivery people who had access to the pharmacy. One was my Jeep driver, and the other had worked at the Red Cross center for many years. I told Sister Maria that I would discuss the situation with the mayor, and that we would take immediate action. "Please leave this to the mayor and myself," I cautioned her, and she nodded.

As we walked on towards the clinic, I concentrated on slowing my pounding heart by listening to the birds that flitted among the trees on either side of the road. I watched with casual interest the people going about their daily lives as the market opened for business. Green and yellow wagons, pulled along by bored-looking donkeys, clattered by. A local policeman passed, tipping his hat to the shopkeepers and ladies. I was still somewhat hyper-vigilant from my early morning encounter with the unknown visitor, my eyes panning from right to left, noticing every detail along the street as we walked.

The morning schedule would consist of giving physical exams and updating vaccinations, and I was certain I would see patients with farm injuries, war injuries, and burns, all of which had come to take up fully half of our time. And of course, there would also be a number of patients with cleft lip and palate defects.

I kept thinking to myself, *The black market brokers are getting bolder everyday. I'm sure they were involved in the disappearance of the medications from the pharmacy.* There were only two likely suspects, and the "new guy" was obviously at the top of the list.

Walking towards the clinic, I was once again struck with pride when, from a distance, I saw the Nicaraguan and American flags flying proudly atop the building, where the Cuban flag had so recently been. I once again felt relief that the Cubans had left. Yes, there had been some gunfire, but no casualties. That was a good thing.

I think all of us were surprised at how quickly the Cubans and their Russian masters had left, and how smoothly the young Violeta Chamorro government was managing the return of their independent territory to the Miskito Indians. And as for the clinic itself, it was now free and open to all. Body searches or ID cards were no longer required in order to receive treatment, and patients no longer had to pay the doctors. It was so different from the way the Cubans ran their facilities. What more could I ask for?

As we strolled through the neighborhood, I observed that it seemed to be in the process of urbanizing – or as close to urbanization as was possible in the small town – with a new church, school, and parish house. Yet these newer structures were still surrounded by shanties and barnyards filled with goats, pigs, and chickens.

When we finally reached the clinic, there were at least 50 families in line in the courtyard waiting to be seen. I put my weight against the heavy metal door, pushing with all my might until it finally began to swing open to the grating sounds of its old, rusted metal hinges. I then moved a folding chair against the back wall, and wedged the chair between the door and the jamb to keep the door open.

As we entered the clinic, I spotted a man on the emergency room gurney, struggling with the team. The apparently exhausted middle-aged farmer was gasping for breath and looked like he was on the verge of a heart attack. His clothes were soaked in sweat and he seemed delirious, or perhaps merely panicked. He was desperately trying to get something out of his right front pocket. I asked the group to step back a minute. When they did, the man pulled his ID card and the sweat soaked contents of a tattered coin purse from his pocket.

We were able to get his name from his ID card, but otherwise had no interest in the card, which the Cubans had required for admission to the clinic. The man removed a sheet of paper from the leather pouch and carefully unfolded it. The paper was so soaked in his sweat it was almost falling apart. There was only one word written on it, MALARIA.

I smiled at the patient and gently patted him on the shoulder, "*Comprendo, comprendo.*"

The man relaxed, lying back on the stretcher, and his previous agitation seemed to almost completely disappear.

I handed the note to the senior resident, who showed it to the others. With an all-knowing smile, he said, "We can handle this. Start an IV, introduce the anti-malarial drugs, and give him something for his fever and something to relax and calm him if you think he needs it. I think now that he knows that we understand what is wrong with him and knows he will be receiving treatment, he will relax."

Miracles in Bedlam

I wasn't really surprised to see a malaria patient. When you bring a medical team into a war zone, there is always the possibility of getting shot and certainly of dealing with gunshot wounds in patients, but in actuality, we are far more likely to be affected by one of the local infestations such as jungle rot or malaria.

Two of the nurses were walking down the poorly lit hallway with charts in hand, along with Carolyn, who was acting as my team organizer today. When she saw me, she beamed a big smile and said, "Good morning, Doctor." I smiled and returned her greeting.

"All the patient rooms are filled," she continued. "I'll walk you to the first one." Clearly this was her nice, gentle way of hinting for me to get going. Once again, the Red Cross volunteers provided us with excellent help, as did the medical students and residents who had joined us in Puerto Cabezas. And of course there were always the Sisters from the local Catholic and Moravian churches, who never seemed to tire, despite the oppressive heat.

I would like to say business was booming at the clinic. Then again, it was a free clinic and everyone working there was an unpaid volunteer. In fact, as I'd explained to the Nicaraguan press before our departure, the American medical team had used their own money to purchase the airline tickets to get here, which is so often the case with these medical missions. We also had help from various philanthropists who believed in our cause. God bless the Houston philanthropic community.

Sometime around mid-morning, the mayor and police chief came by to see how everything was going. I told them about the disappearance of some of the medical supplies, in particular a large amount of critically needed antibiotics, from the Red Cross pharmacy. I gave the police chief the names of the two men who were the only ones, other than the Sisters who worked there, that had access to the pharmacy. They both agreed to look into the matter. But once again I was getting those uneasy vibes from the police chief. What was it with this guy?

I reminded the mayor that one of the men was my Jeep driver, and that he was going to pick me up in the afternoon to visit the small towns and villages where we would be giving immunizations and Sabine polio vaccine cubes. I asked that he let me speak to the driver first.

Then on impulse I asked the police chief, "What do you do when you arrest someone? Is there a jail?"

When I addressed him, he put his shoulders back, stood tall and in a strong heavily accented voice made an effort to speak to me in English. "You will have to come this afternoon and see our lovely jail."

When the mayor heard this, he burst into such raucous laughter and stamped his foot so hard that it was contagious, and all of us around him began to laugh as well. I didn't know what to make of his reaction and asked, "Are you serious? Do you really have a jail?"

The mayor said, "Of course. It is air conditioned and we serve three meals a day on a checkered table cloth. Whatever the prisoners want!"

This time, the laughter was almost riotous. They made their point. I got the idea. There was a jail, but it was not some place you wanted to end up. I got the impression from what they were saying that a few days in jail was a harsh sentence all by itself.

As the laughter died down, I turned back to the police chief and said, "Later this afternoon, after we complete the clinic and before my driver takes me to the outer villages, we will visit this palace of a jail that you have just described to me."

Barely managing to not burst out laughing again, and gesturing as if holding a dainty cup with his pinkie outstretched, the police chief said, "You will have to give me time to get a table and a white linen or checkered table cloth so we can serve high English tea."

This apparently struck everyone's funny bones even more than what the mayor had said a few minutes ago, and they broke into another chorus of laughter, slapping each other on the back as if to force each other to breathe between guffaws. I turned to the police chief and with a straight face, thanked him for the offer of high tea but assured him that a tour of the jail facility would be adequate.

As the two men were leaving, I heard the police chief whisper to the mayor, "I hope he brings a nose clip with him."

* * * * *

The nurses pre-screened the children and other patients who came to the clinic. Those who were here for immunizations were dealt with quickly and efficiently, their charts recorded, and immunization cards given to the parents. Those requiring more thorough examinations or who had a definite physical problem such as a cleft lip or palate, burn, or other injury were directed to my examining room.

Later, I was surprised to learn that we had seen almost a hundred patients by 2:00 p.m. The team approach, and everyone's willingness to serve, were paramount to the incredible efficiency. But when I thought about it a bit more, I had to recognize that some credit went to the fact that we were not hindered by the unnecessary paperwork and the extensive entries into a computer system that are commonly required in America. I'm no technophobe, but in reality the computers added little to the patients' medical care except long waits, unnecessary forms, permission slips, and privacy act compliance confirmation. Needless, non-medical related obstructionism is the result of the American legal system, local governments, state governments, and the overpowering federal government, made even worse by the fact that hospital administration is typically run by lawyers. Doctors can't simply practice medicine due to these restrictions. Add in the insurance costs, and you have a big reason that the American medical system is a mess, despite having the best facilities, the most up-to-date equipment and procedures, and a vast, highly trained pool of medical professionals.

One of the great pleasures of working on a medical mission trip is that you don't have to put up with any of that extraneous effort, because there simply isn't any need for so much needless documentation. Everyone works with what little we have, and our only interest is in the care of the patient and the patient's safety. As medical professionals, we make every effort to provide the best care we can, without the worry about some pencil-pushing bureaucrats creating work that serves primarily to justify their existence, but does little if anything to benefit the patient.

If you've read some of my previous books, you already know that this is one of my pet peeves. While I am of course profoundly appreciative of the advances that have been made in medical science, and certainly of our state-of-the-art hospitals and clinics in the U.S., the medical profession could learn a lot from the purely pragmatic methods to which we often have to resort on these mission trips. If medicine could be practiced in the same fashion back in America, the cost of medical insurance and medical care would be a fraction of what it is today.

* * * * *

My driver arrived promptly at 2:00 p.m. The Jeep, which had been covered in mud from the rains a few days earlier, was now washed and spotless. The canvas top had been retracted because Bob and Lori would be joining us, and an open vehicle would aid in filming as we traveled. There was an extra five-gallon jerry can filled with gas and lashed to the right rear fender. On the opposite side, I strapped our heavy red plastic medical container, filled with immunizations for the children and some basic medical supplies such as suture materials and local anesthesia that might be needed.

I sat in the front passenger seat with my camera. Bob, hoisting his customary forty-pound TV camera and another thirty-plus pounds of batteries, climbed in behind. The driver was being quite the gentleman, tilting the driver's seat forward to allow Lori to climb into her seat in back. I noticed one of our medication cases clearly marked with the yellow mission tape in the well below the driver's seat. I didn't say anything about it at the time, but I felt I had an answer to the disappearance of the medications from the Red Cross pharmacy. I didn't need to be accusing anybody just yet, but more importantly, I didn't want to anger the driver who would be taking us from village to village along the seacoast for the afternoon. I just made a mental note to check it out at the first opportunity later in the day.

With everybody settled in their seats with their shoulder harnesses locked in place, I told the driver the first stop was to be a visit to the city jail. He looked at me quizzically. I ignored his unspoken question for the moment and said, "I get antsy sitting around. Let's go!"

I then told our driver that the mayor and police chief had visited the medical team at the Red Cross clinic, and that out of curiosity, I had asked the police chief what they would do, should someone be arrested in Puerto Cabezas. I told the driver that I had been surprised when the chief told me they had a jail. I added that my colleague Mr. Dows wanted to film the town, including the jail.

That seemed to put the driver at ease. Apparently satisfied with my explanation, he gunned the engine, spinning the tires on the gravel road as he pulled away. He made a rather sharp turn in the middle of the main street and was proceeding at a brisk pace when, only three minutes after leaving the clinic, we got hung up in market traffic, and the driver had to slow down considerably. Fortunately, it didn't take us long to clear the market, and soon we were barreling along at a decent but still leisurely pace through the verdant countryside.

I couldn't have asked for a better day. The sun was high and bright, and the sky was clear and deep blue. Bob Dows' camera was rolling, and I was clicking away with my Nikon. It seemed like everywhere I turned, there was a photo begging to be taken.

I wondered to myself what Marvin Zindler was doing in Managua at that moment. I could just see him sitting poolside under a shady umbrella with an iced tea, or strutting about in his white suit, engaging people in friendly conversation as only he could. Days like this, in places like this, often lead one to better appreciation of the beauty and blessings in life, and I remember thinking that Lori, Bob, Marvin, and I had the best of both worlds here in this remarkable country.

The wound on my neck had long since closed, but it still ached as we bounced along the rutted red clay road. As we drove, Lori and I began discussing Violeta Chamorro, commenting on the interviews that had taken place so far between the president and Marvin, and reviewing the list of progressive reforms that Violeta was planning. Both Lori and I were impressed with Violeta's clear interest in women's and children's health, as well as her stated commitment to improving the education system and making it affordable to everyone. She had plans for improving roads, bridges, and other parts of the country's long-neglected infrastructure, as well as ambitious plans to increase the country's productivity and raise everyone's standard of living. On camera, she had promised Marvin and me that she would have an ambulance for each hospital, and I had suggested that since the country has a long coast on both the east and west sides, that she consider a water ambulance for each of the coastal areas. She liked that idea, remarking that it seemed to be "an unusual but very practical consideration."

The driver, looking over his shoulder for a second, entered the conversation. "The word is, Doctor, that you already have a big influence with President Chamorro. She trusts you and your advice. Many articles and photos about what you have done so far are appearing in the newspapers almost daily, not only here in Nicaragua but throughout Central America."

I mumbled some modest reply, and the driver, still smiling, added, "We were all invisible men in this country. You and the television crew have changed that. We are willing to work for our new president and her programs."

As we passed through the market, people moved aside to avoid the Jeep, but the curb was crowded with shoppers and lined with three-wheeled rickshaws, donkey wagons, and an occasional ox pulling a flat bed laden with farm produce.

Further down the road there were stacks of burlap sacks containing peas, beans, and other dried foods for sale. We then entered the fish market, which I could smell some time before I could see it. Fresh fish hung from hooks, un-refrigerated in the afternoon heat. Dried anchovy and other small fish sat atop woven baskets. There was fish stock for cooking and big bars of green lye soap. I calculated the advertised price of the lye soap from the sign to be about five cents per bar, American. I knew I was going to get some of those on our way back. It reminded me of the soap my grandmother and mother had used, although mainly for cleaning purposes rather than hand washing and bathing.

A little further along this dusty red clay road we made a right turn, and the road came to a dead end. The driver pointed to a building some ways ahead and said, "Jail – jailhouse."

The jailhouse was located at a dead end, away from the town and away from the people. It was a ramshackle wooden structure with a rusting tin roof. There were small windows but they were barred with, of all things, wooden slats rather than iron bars. It looked as if you could put your shoulder to them and they would snap and crumble away.

What paint still remained on the jailhouse was peeling. It didn't look as if there had been any maintenance performed since it had been built, obviously many years before. A ditch extended from the jailhouse toward an uncovered culvert and in this heat, the odor was, to put it nicely, quite unpleasant. I now thoroughly understood the police chief's comment about the need for a nose clip.

The driver got up, moved his seat forward and reached for Lori's hand to help her get out, and I again saw one of our medical boxes in the seat well, still closed with yellow tape. Lori stepped out as the driver dropped his seat back into its upright position. For an instant, Lori caught my eye and nodded toward the floor of the Jeep.

I responded with a shake of my head, and she got the message. We would have to deal with this matter later. In a manner of speaking, there were bigger fish to fry for the moment.

Right then I had no idea just *how* big, but I was soon to learn.

Joseph Agris, M.D.

CHAPTER 25
Danny Two Shoes

*L*ori and Bob walked around to the front of the jail to continue filming, while I circled in the opposite direction. I asked the driver to stay with the Jeep since we had left camera equipment, batteries, and personal items aboard. I figured that we could trust him with those items, even if we did suspect him of stealing from the pharmacy. Taking my camera, I walked across the street and into the side alley, looking about to see that no one was watching. From this position I was able to get the entire jailhouse into the picture. I scanned the thick adobe walls and heavy metal roof, but I was still puzzled by the bamboo bars that crisscrossed the windows. Maybe they were stronger than they looked, but it still seemed strange that the windows weren't blocked with steel. My curiosity ultimately got the best of me, and I approached a window with the intent of testing to see how secure the bamboo was.

When I drew close, I peered into the dark cell behind the bars, and was startled when a gruff voice bellowed from the shadows, demanding, "Who the hell are you?"

I said, "The doctor."

The prisoner shot back, "What have you been drinking?"

I answered, in Spanish, "*Cómo te llamas?*" ("What is your name?")

He replied, "I speak English, and everyone around here calls me Danny Two Shoes, because I dance on the street for money."

Danny was shirtless, with beads of perspiration dripping down his face onto his neck and chest. He was dressed only in a pair of filthy three-quarter-length baggy slacks that some refer to as Jamaica pants. He was also, despite his moniker, barefoot. Wherever his two shoes were, they certainly were not on his feet at the moment. Danny was missing a few teeth, and the teeth that I could see were stained brown. I was certain that he was dehydrated; his lips were cracked to the point of bleeding in a couple of places. His shoulder-length hair was unkempt and looked as if it hadn't been washed for a very long time.

Danny approached the window and gripped the bamboo bars with large, powerful hands. His breath smelled of garlic and his hair reeked of fish. At first, he looked at me with contempt, but his visage suddenly softened, and he began to speak with an air of dignity that belied his appearance. "I can read. They give me the newspaper, and I've seen your picture in it. You are the doctor they call *Dr. Angel.*" At this, he began to laugh.

We held each other's gaze for a moment, and I smiled, saying, "It's a long story. Can we talk about you?"

He responded, with a tinge of irritation in his voice, "You are on the outside and can do what you want. I'm not going anyplace. I could use the company."

"What put you on the other side of those bars?"

He responded with a curt, "The usual."

"Since I'm not from here, could you explain what you mean by *the usual?*"

"I drink too much, I get arrested too often. I sober up for a few days in jail and then they let me out." He continued, "I have some information for you. Information that could change a lot of lives. People think I'm stupid and drunk, but that has not affected my hearing. I remain quiet. I listen. And they foolishly talk as if I were deaf or stupid."

I had heard the same kind of ploy from drunks in many countries over the years, and didn't want to waste the time hearing it again from him. I turned and started to walk away, and he shouted, "Where are you going? Don't you want to hear the information that I have? I'm not trying to sell you something. I really mean that my information has national implications."

I still wasn't convinced, and intended to dangle a bit of my own bait in order to escape without becoming further entangled in his little game. "Let me check on my friends and I will be right back."

"Promise?"

"I promise," I said, though I was filled with that all too familiar sense of unease. I went back to the Jeep and gave some money to the driver, telling him to get some bottles of water and juice, some bread, sausage, crackers, and anything nourishing he could find. I told him to use all the money and bring the food and drink back to me.

The driver looked puzzled, asking, "What is this for?"

"Do as I ask, please. I will be right here when you get back."

Somewhat against my better judgment, I returned to Danny Two Shoes and asked him, "What is this information you want to unburden yourself of?"

Danny began with icy clarity, stating, "First you need to know that the sheriff is a card-carrying member of the FSLN. In fact, he was part of the Sandinista Special Forces, and is very unhappy with Violeta's election to the presidency."

I said nothing. I hadn't had much contact with the sheriff, but I knew whom he was talking about. I waited for Danny to continue.

He was again gripping the bars tightly, glaring at me. For a few seconds, he didn't say anything. I tried to gain his trust, saying, "Don't be afraid. What we discuss will stay between you and me."

"I'm not afraid! I'm *angry*."

"When did you get this information, and is it reliable?"

"Ask anyone in town, even the mayor. Everyone knows the Sandinistas appointed the sheriff and that he made life quite difficult for many in Puerto Cabezas. He is the one who needs to be in this jail!"

I waited for a moment, and he continued, "The Sandinista Special Forces were criminals. Like most criminals, they stuck with what they knew best and what had worked for them again and again: extortion, beatings, kidnappings, and worse. He should be inside this prison."

"Let's say that for now, I take your word on this. I will check it out with the mayor and others that I have met at the Red Cross center and the clinic."

"Check all you want, you will find I speak the truth."

Just then I could hear footsteps on the gravel path along the alleyway. I signaled to Danny to move back into his cell. As I turned I could see my driver carrying a package under each arm as he approached. Walking up to meet him, I took the packages and told him to return to the Jeep. He looked at me suspiciously, but I waved him away with no further comment.

The bags would not fit between the bars so I removed the items one by one and passed them in to Danny. As soon as he grabbed the cold bottle of juice, he popped the top and gulped it down. I then handed him some bread and dried meat, bottles of water and more juice.

He looked at me through the bars, raised a bushy skeptical eyebrow, and said, "You truly are Dr. Angel." His face was suddenly aglow. "You now have to hear my whole story before anyone comes back."

With a laugh I said, "I have my own ulterior motives here. We have more than enough patients to take care of without you being sent to the clinic because of malnutrition, dehydration, and heat exhaustion. The temperature in your jail cell must be well over 100 degrees."

"I've survived a few days in here before. I will survive it again. They will probably let me out tonight or tomorrow morning, but you need to hear this now. It might be our only chance to talk."

He took a drink from a bottle of water and wiped his mouth with the back of his hand. "It is an interesting world you have entered into, now that the civil war is finally drawing to a close and the Miskito Indians have been given their own tribal territory. But the end of the war does not mean there will be peace. Quite the contrary. I might drink too heavily on occasion, but I can read and write, and I have tried to educate myself. If what I have heard is true and if it takes place, pandemonium will rain throughout Nicaragua and extend into all of Central America."

"You have my attention, Danny Two Shoes."

What he said next took my breath away. "They are planning on assassinating President Violeta Chamorro!"

I stood there, peering through the bars in shock. My mouth dropped open but no words came out.

Danny again repeated, "There are plans to assassinate Violeta Chamorro."

"How do you know this? Why do you tell me this?"

"They brought me here several days ago, not so much because they thought I was drunk, but because several of the merchants complained that I was dancing on the street near their establishments and interfering with their customers. I was dancing, panhandling, playing my homemade flute and not bothering anyone. Children were laughing at my antics and running up to me with a coin or two. I did not dispute the police when they came and said I was drunk and I would have to spend a few days in the local jail. I knew it was better to go along with them rather than fight. I had not made enough to even purchase a drink yet, anyway. Two nights ago, there was a meeting of the sheriff, the police chief, and several others. I could only hear voices, no names, but I recognized their voices. They were discussing an assassination plot sponsored by the FSLN and the Sandinista Special Forces. I lay on the floor listening. They thought I was in a drunken stupor or asleep. I just listened."

"Why do you tell me this?" I asked him again, calmly, though my mind was racing at Danny's mention of the police chief.

The earlier intensity returned to his eyes, and the corners of his mouth turned up gently as he continued, "You are Dr. Angel and I truly believe that God has sent you to us. You have the people's hearts and minds. Don't disappoint them."

Releasing his hands from the bars, he spread them wide, then gave me a curt look as he continued, "I have a feeling you are going to wish you had never visited this jail and engaged in this conversation with me."

I really couldn't argue with that.

"I know you are only one man," he continued. "But, obviously, an important one. More importantly, you brought the American press and TV, and they will carry the day."

"We're trying," I said. "But there are no guarantees."

Then Danny asked, "Who sent you to the jail? Who sent you to me?"

"I just wanted to see what the jail in Puerto Cabezas consisted of. Just a feeling inside me that told me I should make this visit. I cannot give you an actual explanation. A feeling." Even as I spoke I could see how in Danny's mind, this sequence of unlikely events had all come together in a singular moment of truth – of serendipity.

Danny took his time responding, and when he did it was a little cryptic, but meaningful nonetheless. "In silence we are not safe," he said. He then reached over and drank some more water, this time more slowly and deliberately, but his eyes never left my face. We stared at each other in silence for a long time.

Finally I broke the silence. "I will think on all this."

"It is not the time for thinking, but for action. I will be released tomorrow, or at the latest the day after. Thank you for the food and the drinks. It was very kind of you. I will see you in a few days. I am in your debt. But now you are in mine, too. And in Nicaragua's debt as well. She needs your help to prevent this from happening. When we meet on the outside, I will bring a priest and a Bible. I will swear to you with my hand on the Bible that I have spoken the truth. Until then, I want you to think about how we should proceed."

At that moment, I heard Bob Dows calling for me. As I turned to leave, I said goodbye, and assured him, "Danny, we will talk again." And this time, I meant it.

I walked from the alleyway onto the main street where the Jeep was located, and the driver handed me a cool bottle of water. Bob asked, "Where were you? What were you doing?"

"Just looking over the jail facility and taking some photos. I've never seen anything like it. Bamboo bars on the windows."

I climbed into the back seat, and we started down the coast, stopping at a couple of nearby villages and small clinics where children waited for their immunizations and Sabine polio vaccine cubes. Other patients were examined and diagnosed, then referred to the Red Cross center or the clinic the following day.

It was getting late, the sun was setting, and we were all exhausted. As we entered a fishing village on the coast, there was a big commotion, with people running from the village toward the beach. The driver stopped the Jeep. We all got out and began walking with the crowd to see what was going on. My driver spoke to a woman who was carrying a basket on her head and a butcher knife in her hand. He asked her in the local dialect if a boat had come in with fresh fish.

The woman replied, "A miracle, a miracle."

After listening to much excited chatter I was able to piece the story together. One of the elderly tribal fishermen had been gone for almost a week, and his family and friends had been worried about him. It seemed that the fishermen usually returned the same night or the next morning, but this one had been gone a week, and everyone had feared the worst. "We have been going to church and praying for him," one of the women said. "We feared he was dead or lost at sea. God has answered our prayers and he has miraculously arrived only minutes ago."

I went back to the Jeep and grabbed my camera. Bob already had his video camera in the ready position on his right shoulder as we trudged through the sand and threaded our way around the palm trees that lined the beach. We arrived at a very chaotic scene, with what looked to have been thirty or forty people gathered on the shore, including some who had children swaddled in cloth and tied to their backs. Many of the people had their hands in the air and were yelling, "*Hallelujah!*"

And who knows, maybe it *was* a miracle. Given what I had just learned from a bedraggled inmate at the city jail, I hoped that miracles would not be in short supply here. We needed them now, more than ever.

CHAPTER 26
The Madam

Back at the sawmill, with darkness falling, I stripped down and put on a bathing suit, then grabbed a bar of soap and a towel and headed downstairs and outside. The steps creaked as I descended, and the railing shook as I gripped it to get support. I was relieved when my sandal-clad feet finally touched the red clay at the bottom of the stairs. Walking over to the well pump, I threw the switch and turned the handle to allow the shower to function.

I drew the "privacy" curtain, but frankly, I was too hot and too tired to worry about my privacy. I just wanted to feel clean. As usual, the well water was freezing cold, and at first I shivered from the shock. But as I stood there my body became accustomed to it, and I was soon enjoying it as if I had taken a dip in the most luxurious pool in the world.

In order to get the red clay dust out of my hair, I soaped with the bar of lye soap I had purchased for a nickel in the market, then rinsed and soaped a second time. The soap was rough and actually felt good on my itchy skin, but did not lather very well, what with the high mineral content of the well water.

I was actually enjoying myself. Looking up, I could see more stars than I could ever remember seeing before. I found myself searching the heavens for Orion, the Big Dipper, the Little Dipper, and all the constellations that I could remember learning about as a member of the high school astronomy club. The tenuous situation we were in and my worries about it faded, and I felt like a new person. I flung open the shower curtain and threw the lever to turn off the pump, then took my towel and dried off. I wrapped the towel around my waist and slogged through the water-soaked clay surrounding the immediate shower area, then shuffled across the hard, dry clay, and climbed the rickety stairs back up to my room. As I reached my door and was about to enter, I saw Nurse Dixon approaching below, dressed smartly in a clean white shirt and slacks, and dragging a large, obviously heavy cooler.

He called up to me, "Hey, Doc! I'm going across the street to the Red Cross cantina for dinner. Will you join me there? The mayor and some of his people are coming a little later."

"Give me a few minutes to change," I said, "and I'll help you with that cooler." He nodded gratefully and said he would wait for me.

Though we'd been here for only a short time, the medical team and I had already become "regulars" at the cantina, since we took most of our meals there. After our initial visit, the mayor had suggested to us that it would be appreciated if we provided some of the refreshments, since many of the people who brought our meals did so out of their already meager food budgets, and couldn't really afford to also provide the refreshments we all liked. In response, some of the team members had borrowed a cooler at the sawmill and had gone to the local grocer, where they were able to get some ice and local beer. Every evening at dinnertime, they dutifully toted their bounty to the Red Cross cantina and shared it with everyone. It was apparently Dixon's turn for the *cerveza* run tonight.

I was glad the mayor was going to be at the cantina, for I was quite anxious to let him know what I had heard from Danny Two Shoes at the jail that afternoon, and I'd been hoping I would get a chance to do so tonight. If what Danny had told me was true, I didn't think it could wait. Danny's story might be a total fabrication, but then again it might not be, and the implications were ominous, to say the least. I simply couldn't take a chance.

Taking a cue from Dixon, I decided to dress up as well, and I unpacked a beautifully embroidered gray guayabera shirt and black slacks. A few minutes later I joined Dixon, and together we toted the heavy cooler of *cervezas* across the road to the Red Cross compound. The guard at the gate saluted as we approached.

"*Abrir la puerta, por favor,*" I said. ("Open the gate, please.")

"*Si, Dr. Angel, si, si.*"

The heavy steel gate groaned on its hinges as he maneuvered it just wide enough for Dixon and me to pass through and enter the compound. As we walked towards the main building where the cantina was located, a sense of uneasiness overcame me. Was I getting a message from above? I tried to shake off the feeling as Dixon and I approached the door of the cantina and were greeted by one of the Red Cross volunteer women.

214

At that moment we saw Barrett approaching us, still wearing his operating room greens and white coat, with his O.R. mask hanging loosely around his neck. He looked quite professional and handsome. We invited him to join us, and the three of us entered the cantina with the ice chest, stopping just inside the door and giving the room the once-over.

The only lights in the place were from small bulbs hung from exposed wires in the ceiling and open fixtures along the walls. Curtains had been drawn over the windows, shutting out any light from the central area of the compound and the street itself. There were cast iron lamps on each table and small candles burning within. This atmosphere was somewhat romantic and tended to conceal the shabbiness of the cantina and everything that was in it. Despite being rough around the edges, it offered at least a hint of hominess.

In the far corner of the room, in the area closest to the kitchen, was a small table, on which sat an old-fashioned Victrola, with records stacked alongside it. The turntable was rotating, and an old ceramic groove record bobbled on its surface, playing soft dinner music. The music seemed to vary from hour to hour, depending upon who was willing to get up to select and replace the record when it was needed.

Dixon, Barrett, and I decided we would take the closest table we could find against the rear wall. In situations like this we always liked to have our backs to the wall, as it gave us a clear view of most of the interior of the room, particularly the entrance.

The mayor entered alone a few minutes later and took his usual table near the door, a position that offered him a good view of anyone coming in or out of the cantina. On his heels but not with him were several elite Miskito Indian policemen, who took the closest table they could find, which was adjacent to the restrooms. The only question that remained was whether or not the police chief would arrive for his usual evening meal. Given what I'd heard from Danny, I suspected he wouldn't.

I nodded at each of these groups and they returned my nod. Then I walked over to the ice chest, took out a bottle of the local *cerveza*, popped the top, and carried it over to the table where the mayor sat surveying the room.

"Mr. Mayor," I said, "I need to talk to you in private."

He said, "This is private enough. With all the noise in here, no one else will be able to hear us."

I nodded, but continued in a low voice, if only to suggest the importance of what I had to say. "I heard something very disturbing this afternoon. It might be just a rumor, or the ramblings of a drunk, but I need to share it with you."

"Go on," said the mayor, leaning close to hear me above the din.

I briefed him about my conversation with Danny Two Shoes, wondering if he would take Danny's claims seriously or dismiss them as an alcohol-fueled fantasy. But the look on his face indicated that he was taking it very seriously indeed.

When I was finished, the mayor said, "What is the phrase that you Americans use?

Cutting to the chase?"

"Yes," I responded, not knowing quite where he was going with that.

"Well, we are doing that here, but very slowly and very carefully. A slow-motion chase, you might say."

Seeing my puzzled expression, he explained, "I too have been hearing the rumors, and I have people watching out for any developments. Thank you for telling me what you heard. Believe me, we will not dismiss any of the stories, no matter who tells them, without investigating. We are taking it all seriously. Please do not hesitate to tell me anything suspicious you might see or hear; I don't care what time of day or night it is."

"You got it," I replied.

The mayor added, "One of my informants may be coming tonight; I hope you get to meet this person." Once again I looked puzzled, but the mayor simply laughed and said, "Go back and join your friends. Have fun. We'll talk again later."

Just as I turned to go back to my table, the door to the cantina opened and a striking woman entered. The proverbial hush fell over the room for a moment, and I instinctively glanced over at the mayor, who winked at me. *Was this his "informant?"* I wondered to myself. But beyond that wink, the mayor's demeanor gave no clue.

As the chatter of the crowd resumed I stared, as discreetly as I could, at this newest arrival. She had bleached blonde hair, brushed tight against her skull and pulled into a knot high on her head. From where I sat she looked to be in her fifties, and though she was very well proportioned, it didn't appear that she was anywhere close to starvation, and I am being charitable in my description. She wore a bright red velvet dress that had a scooped neck and was off the shoulder to one side, complemented by ornately designed stockings and high-heeled shoes. She wore bright red lipstick and way too much rouge on her cheeks. Under her arm was a small dark dog with a rhinestone-studded collar.

She looked very out of place – not because she had a dog, for several of the regulars thought nothing of bringing their little dogs with them to dinner – but because of her ostentatious dress and makeup. However, almost as soon as she entered the cantina, one of the Red Cross volunteer ladies came up to her and engaged her in conversation. I was intrigued. This woman, who looked like a stereotype of a madam at a brothel, had to be a regular; I wondered why I hadn't seen her before.

She pointed to a table adjacent to ours. The Red Cross volunteer led her to the table and pulled out a chair for her as if she were the most honored guest there. The little dog, which looked to me like an extraordinarily tiny Yorkie, suddenly yapped loudly, and our entire group turned in its direction. The madam shushed it, after which it sat quietly in her lap, for a while, anyway.

Before long, others entered the cantina for their evening meal, at least half of them with small dogs. Several of them stopped to talk with me. The madam's tiny Yorkie barked again several times, and I playfully barked right back at it, to the apparent amusement of those seated nearby.

As more people flowed into the room, Dixon and Barrett jumped up, went to the ice chest, and began carrying beers to everyone. They were greeted with waves and smiles, and were instantly the most popular guys in the room.

Meanwhile, the mayor ceremoniously unwound a gold-covered cord from around the top of a velvet bag and extracted a bottle of Nicaragua's famous Flor de Caña rum. Barrett, Dixon, and I had previously experienced some of that formidable concoction with the mayor, and while I couldn't presume to speak for my companions, I wasn't sure I was up to it again so soon. It was a very smooth rum, but a bit too much on the sweet side for my tastes, and had a kick that I wouldn't soon forget.

Catching my eye, the mayor held the bottle up, gesturing toward our table and grinning. "Join me!" he mouthed.

I was tempted but resisted, and hoped my team would follow my lead and refrain from imbibing as well. I felt that it was more important than ever for all of us to stay alert, and if we were going to do so, no one should be indulging in hard liquor. Besides, we would have clinic, a line of patients, and many surgeries, all of which would begin early the next morning. I didn't want to dictate to my staff, for after all, they were all adults, but I was relieved when Barrett and Dixon and the others who had joined us declined the mayor's kind offer.

I was feeling a little hungry by now, though, so I turned to one of the volunteers and asked, "Do you have any plantain chips tonight?"

"Si, si, of course. It is a favorite of everyone. I will bring you a basket."

A few minutes later, baskets of warm plantain chips were placed on each of the tables. On the first night we'd eaten at the cantina the mayor had proudly announced, "The plantains are locally grown and we make the plantain chips ourselves." They were worthy of his boasts, and quite addictive.

The tiny Yorkie began to bark, and when I turned to look at it, the woman said to me in heavily accented English, "He likes plantain chips."

Well, I could take a hint. I reached across and offered the little Yorkie a plantain chip, which the dog quickly devoured.

"Is that an adult dog or is he a puppy?" I asked in Spanish.

"So, you speak Spanish," she responded, this time speaking in her native language.

"The dog is so small," I said, as I fed it another plantain chip. At the same time, I took another discrete look at the woman. She wasn't quite as old as I'd originally thought, at least forty-something, but definitely not any older. It seemed clear that she'd had a tough life here in Puerto Cabezas.

"Good things come in small packages," the lady said.

"So they say," I replied, then asked her, "Would you like a *cerveza?*"

"You are very kind," she said in English.

I took a beer from the ice chest, popped the top, and handed it across to her.

"Thank you," she said.

"My pleasure," I responded, as I fed the dog another chip.

The door to the cantina opened again, and everyone turned simultaneously as a woman wearing an absurd hat and several pounds of costume jewelry around her neck and on her wrists marched vigorously across the room and took a table on the far side. The mayor waved to her. *She must be another regular*, I thought, though she was another one I hadn't seen previously.

The mayor held up his bottle of rum in her direction. She nodded, a big smile on her face. The mayor took the bottle over to her table, poured a small glassful for her and placed it in front of her, and she rewarded him with a kiss on the cheek.

As the mayor returned and passed our table, I found my resolve melting, and pointing to the rum bottle I said, "Let me have just a little bit of that." Smiling broadly, the mayor acquired another glass from one of the volunteer ladies, filled it, and passed it across the table to me.

I took a very small sip, and as I did, the madam spoke to me again. "How long have you been in Puerto Cabezas?"

"Just a few days. We leave soon."

"You are all with the American medical team?" she asked, and I nodded.

"I have heard the chanting at night. *Americans stay. Cubans go home.*"

Dixon replied, "Yes ma'am. I hope that has not kept you up at night."

She smiled at him. "I recognize the man sitting next to you, Dr. Angel. Dr. Angel and the story of the miracle baby. It has been retold many times on the radio here. We all support the American medical team, and have wanted the Cubans and their Russian masters gone. Your medical team has impressed Puerto Cabezas. Is it true that you do not accept any money from those that you treat?"

Mr. Dixon nodded, and replied, "No money needed. It is totally free for the people here."

Just then, one of the Red Cross volunteers came to the table and asked what we would like to have for our evening meal. Then someone walked over to the record player and put on a more upbeat series of local songs, in Spanish of course.

In short order, dinner was being served, and it was the same for everyone: chicken and rice, plantains, and boiled yucca. I found myself chuckling at the volunteer's insinuation that we had a choice. But the food was fresh, wholesome, and delicious, and the conversation was lively across the tables, and throughout the room, for the next several hours. At one point, the mayor motioned for me to join him at his table. When I had seated myself next to him, he said in a voice low enough that only I could hear, "Obviously our esteemed police chief is not coming to dinner tonight."

"I wonder what spooked him," I said. "It seems he is on the run now, or at least preparing to depart very soon."

"I've come to the same conclusion," the mayor responded.

I couldn't shake the feeling that another shoe was about to drop, that something big was in the works. Yet I couldn't just sit in the cantina all night, waiting. Finally I said to the mayor, "I'm going to have to go back to my room soon and get a few hours of sleep. We have another long day at the clinic tomorrow. But I have a feeling that we have significant surprises ahead, and not only in the clinic."

The mayor responded, "I understand. But remember what we talked about. If you hear anything, I want to know immediately." I nodded and walked back to my table, and as I did the madam's little Yorkie yapped again. I took that as a sign that the dog wanted more plantain chips, which I of course provided.

It occurred to me that I had been feeding the dog, but hadn't even asked the woman what its name was, an oversight that I quickly corrected. She told me that its name was Miss Maggie. I petted Miss Maggie's head, then took the half-eaten basket of chips and placed it at her table. "It was nice talking to you," I said.

"Yes, it was," she replied. "I thank you for all your kindness, and so does Miss Maggie. Most important, thank you for all you have done, are doing, and will do for Puerto Cabezas. And not least of all, Miss Maggie thanks you for the plantain chips."

"My pleasure."

I went back to our table and asked Dixon and Barrett if they were ready to leave, and they answered by immediately rising from their seats. I said, "First let's stop by and say good night to the mayor." But before we could even step away from the table, another group beckoned us over to their table, and as we were talking with them I noticed out of the corner of my eye that the madam got up from her chair, still carrying her tiny dog, and ambled over to the mayor's table. *Curious*, I thought, but quickly realized that I might be reading more into her actions than was warranted.

When we finally extricated ourselves from our conversation, we went over to the mayor's table, and by then the madam had settled back at her own table. The first thing I noticed was that the mayor's cheerful demeanor had changed to one of concern. As soon as we reached his table, the mayor said, "We need to bring everyone back here to the Red Cross compound for their safety." I reminded him that Lori Reingold and Carolyn were staying within the Red Cross compound. He nodded curtly and said, "I mean all of you need to be here."

"Why?"

"Because I think this place is about to explode. The only question is when. You need to contact your pilot and remind him to be ready to depart at a moment's notice. I suggest that you have everyone keep their personal things in their carry-on bags, and to be ready to board the aircraft immediately if necessary. Possibly tonight. Maybe tomorrow."

I mirrored his hard look and said, "Where did you get your information?"

The mayor replied, "From the lady you were talking to all night."

"The madam?" I blurted out. Apparently I was right about her being his "informant."

"Well, a madam in a manner of speaking. Officially, she owns the biggest local bar at the far end of the main street. That is not a place that I would take you or your medical team members. Too many drunks, and what you would call 'loose' women, and fights occur almost every night. Not just drunken fistfights, either. Sometimes knives or machetes come out and leave their ugly marks." I knew what he was talking about. I'd recently treated a man who had been in a machete fight; the poor man required 100 sutures.

We were silent for a few moments, waiting for the mayor to continue. "Knowing her has its advantages. The madam and her girls see and hear it all. They report to me. In turn I overlook the barroom brawls and don't get involved in her business. I see it as a fair exchange if I do say so myself."

"What did she report?" I asked. "Can you tell us?"

"The madam reported to me that trouble is in the wind." Clearly that was all he was going to tell us. But I knew enough by now to take such a warning seriously.

"Thank you, Mr. Mayor, for the warning, and we will follow your advice. I will discuss this tonight with the team members and will notify our pilot."

With that we left the Red Cross compound for the sawmill, hoping that its high walls, the tops of which were impregnated with broken glass, would provide a measure of security. But at this point, I had my doubts.

The most pressing problem now, as far as I could ascertain, was twofold. First, we needed to figure out where the police chief was hiding, because he was obviously at the very center of the threats we faced. Secondly, we needed to find out what level of threat the American medical team in Puerto Cabezas was facing. I hated the idea of cutting our trip short, but I couldn't justify keeping my team in harm's way if there was a credible threat. I recognized now that with the seemingly benign exit of the Cubans and Russians, I had become somewhat complacent about the potential for danger. And I also realized that we had no way of being certain that all of them were gone, or if they were, that their absence would guarantee a peaceful process for our peace mission. In fact, their departure could well be the beginning of yet another phase of a war we had thought was over. I had learned long ago that every act, no matter how well meaning and how beneficial, could have dire, unintended consequences. Complacency was folly in a country that was still a war zone.

When we reached the high wall that surrounded the lumberyard, we had to pound on the heavy steel gates, for there was no bell. We waited a few minutes, and finally a natty man in his early twenties, with a dark full mustache, slid the heavy iron bolts back. The steel door slowly began to swing open.

Miracles in Bedlam

I was worried. If the American team was forced to leave in the next few days, who would take care of the medical needs of the people at Puerto Cabezas? There were very few local nurses, and as far as I knew, no local physicians to recruit. I was also aware that under the circumstances, medical personnel from elsewhere in Nicaragua would be very reluctant to come to Puerto Cabezas and the Caribbean coast.

My thoughts were interrupted by Dixon as he walked me back to my room. "Doc," he said, "I found two local nurses while I was visiting the market today, and they would like to join our group at the clinic tomorrow. I took the liberty of inviting them."

He handed me a small piece of paper with their names scribbled on it. Examining the names, one seemed familiar to me. "A very interesting discovery, Mr. Dixon."

"Do you want them?" he asked.

Instead of answering him, I grabbed him by the arm. "We need to talk to the mayor, and we need to talk to him *now*," I said. Dixon knew me well enough to not question me when I had my imperative face on, but he also knew that I would tell him everything as soon as whatever crisis had arisen was over. Together, we rushed back out through the heavy steel doors, which had not yet been bolted back in place, and high-tailed it back to the Red Cross compound.

CHAPTER 27
Watching And Waiting

I was hoping the mayor was still at the cantina finishing his meal, and luckily, he was. Gasping for breath, I handed him the slip of paper with the names on it. Dixon, also out of breath and still visibly befuddled by my reaction, just stood in silence with me as we waited for a response.

But the mayor seemed in no hurry to even look at the paper, opting instead to take another bite of food and chew on it for a minute. Finally he glanced down, and the moment he did, his eyes widened. He took a long gulp from his beer, then sat it down noisily on the wooden tabletop and looked up at Dixon and me.

"What is this list?" he asked.

Dixon explained, "These are the names of a couple of local nurses I talked to at the market today. They want to join our group at the clinic tomorrow, and I invited them to do so."

There was a moment of silence, and Dixon, looking from the mayor to me and then back to the mayor, said, "You know, I'm beginning to get the feeling that I messed up big time."

Both the mayor and I hastened to assure him that he had done nothing wrong. I said, "I do owe you an explanation, Mr. Dixon. You haven't been privy to all of the conversations that the mayor and I have had about the Cubans and their influence on the locals. The other day the mayor mentioned some names to me, names of people who might possibly be colluding with Violeta's enemies. One of them is on this list. You had no way of knowing, of course."

"Which one?" Dixon asked.

"Anna!" the mayor and I chimed as one.

Now it was Dixon's turn to look shocked. "What did Anna do?" he said. "She seemed so nice when I talked to her, so sincere in her desire to help us."

The mayor said, "As I have mentioned before, when the Cubans and their Russian masters arrived, some of our fellow Puerto Cabezians were, shall I say, not unhappy to see them. Some of the population in fact was convinced that Castro was their savior. And what few nurses we had joined in the work, volunteering their time at the Cuban clinic."

Dixon nodded. "I see," he said, though it was clear that he didn't entirely understand yet.

"But some were doing more than just working with patients," I said. "Some were actively collaborating with the Sandinistas and the Cubans."

"And we have very good reason to believe that Anna was one of them," the mayor said. "She's one whose name I mentioned to the doctor here. She joined the Cuban clinic staff, and about a year ago they sent her to Cuba for training."

"She was a collaborator," Dixon said, stunned.

"So it would appear," said the mayor.

Dixon said, "You seem to know quite a bit about this Cuban clinic and its volunteers, Mr. Mayor."

The mayor raised his bottle of beer and took another long swig from it, then said, "Well, it is my job to keep up with what's going on here. But keeping up with the Cubans also became sort of a hobby with me. The more I learned, the more worried I became. But I always knew in my heart that the Americans would come, and here you are."

I said, "In light of some of these newer developments, it seems that our celebration of the Cubans' and Russians' exodus may have been a little premature."

The mayor said, "We do have cause to celebrate, but it's not over yet by any means. There are those, including me, who believe that the major battles between the Contras and the Sandinistas *are* over. Only small local pockets of Sandinistas remain, and the Cubans and Russians had been hoping to stay under the radar for the most part. But that hope ended of course when they learned that you and your TV crew were coming. They realized they could no longer keep their presence hidden from the world."

"That makes sense," Dixon said.

"Yes, but as I said, it's not over yet. There may still be some Cubans and perhaps even Russians hiding out somewhere nearby – perhaps hiding in plain sight."

Dixon asked, "You have evidence?"

"I hear things," the mayor replied simply.

I thought about the madam I'd met earlier that evening, who was now nowhere to be seen; she must have left soon after we had. And I thought again of Danny Two Shoes, and what he had told me, not only about the police chief but also about the Sandinista-appointed sheriff.

The mayor continued, "But I don't want to make it seem as if all is lost. Dr. Angel and all of you have accomplished a lot in the very short time you've been here."

"Don't sell yourself short, Mr. Mayor," I said. "You have played a big part too, and you know it."

The mayor was clearly pleased by my acknowledgment and smiled, but then his expression became serious again. He said, "Besides this collaborator who wants to join you at the clinic tomorrow, there is still the matter of the police chief; nobody seems to know his whereabouts. And I can tell you that while the Cubans didn't trust many of the locals, they did seem to trust the police chief completely."

Dixon murmured, "I did notice that he wasn't in the cantina tonight. I didn't think anything of it until just now. Where do you suppose he is?"

"Our illustrious police chief may – or may not – have joined the Cubans in their exit from here," the mayor said. "That is a matter of great concern for us now."

"Why do you think the Cubans trusted him?" Dixon asked. I looked at the mayor, and he nodded, so I quickly filled Dixon in on what Danny Two Shoes had told me that afternoon about the possible assassination plot against Violeta Chamorro.

"That's pretty disturbing," Dixon said. "On the other hand, this Danny fellow was just a drunk in a jail cell, so..."

The mayor interrupted him, a little curtly. "I have heard similar things from other sources," he said.

"At this point," I added, "we have to take all such rumors seriously, just like the Secret Service does in the U.S. when there's a threat against our president."

"I understand," Dixon replied. Then he added, "Do you think the Cubans and Russians are deserting Puerto Cabezas because they truly believe that the war is lost?"

"Mr. Dixon, I think it more likely that the Cubans heard what the locals had in mind for them after that demonstration the other night on the main street," said the mayor.

"Hanging?" Dixon asked, grinning.

I nodded and said, "Or a bullet to their heads, or a machete to their necks. Take your pick." It wasn't that Dixon and I were glorifying potential violence or making light of the very real threats. Still, there was a small sense of gratification in knowing that the people had made their will known, and that most of the Cubans and Russians seemed to have actually paid heed.

The mayor said, "I have no doubt that they were intimidated by the demonstrations, but they had already been on notice. As I told you when you first arrived here, the Cubans and Russians obviously felt pressured when they first heard that an American medical team and a TV crew were coming. I've since found out that seven Russian collaborators left before you even got here. But the few who may still remain might be the most dangerous ones of all."

"I'd like to believe that they will all be gone soon," Dixon said. "But on the other hand, what other options do they have? What do they have to gain by staying here?"

"Well, think about the Cubans," said the mayor. "In returning to Cuba they could be found guilty of desertion, and the penalty for that would most likely be death or at best, life in prison. Deserting their clinic here in Puerto Cabezas could be more dangerous for them than staying and fighting."

"Not to change the subject, Mr. Mayor," I said, "but do you have any idea where the police chief could be hiding?"

"I'm not sure, but as I said, I wouldn't be surprised if at this moment he was packing to leave. But there's no telling where he might be going, and with whom he might be meeting to advance whatever it is they're plotting."

The mayor and I locked eyes for a moment.

"When I spoke with President Violeta in preparation for this trip," I said, "she warned me about some of these possibilities – not a plot to assassinate her, of course, but about various threats to our own safety."

"Are you beginning to regret coming here?" the mayor asked.

"Not at all," I said. "I knew it was risky, and my team did too."

"But knowing there may be danger and actually facing it are two different things," Dixon admitted. I gave him an alarmed look, whereupon he hastened to add, "Still, I'm glad we came."

"Well, I'll say again how very impressed I am with all of your efforts," the mayor said. "And Doc, you have... what do you Americans say?... gone above and beyond the call of duty."

"I'm just a simple doctor," I said.

"I can't tell if that's genuine modesty or false," said the mayor, "but it is obvious that you have a cause here beyond your medical mission, and perhaps even beyond Violeta's peace mission. You seem to have taken a very personal interest in Puerto Cabezas."

"I won't deny it," I said. "When I learned about the history and plight of the Miskito Indians, and Violeta's plans for their autonomy, I knew I had to do something. That's why I proposed the mission to her in the first place, though it seems she already had something like this in mind. I've always had a soft spot for the underdog, and it seemed that here was a situation where I really could do something."

The mayor nodded, smiling. I continued, "And getting back to the police chief... part of this is 20/20 hindsight, but I have to say that when some of my team members and I first met with him after we got here, we sensed that he was a little uneasy, almost nervous. He didn't seem to be happy with our presence here, and I got the feeling that he was holding something back. Now, that feeling we had makes perfect sense."

The mayor said, "I am very disappointed, especially since I was the one who appointed him to his position."

"That's understandable," said Dixon.

"I am going to find him," the mayor continued. "And when I do I will arrest him and charge him with collaboration in the assassination plot against President Violeta. Once he is in my hands, I will get all the information I want from him."

"What will ultimately happen to him?" I said. I was a little concerned and noticed that Dixon was too. Surely a man couldn't be charged, and certainly not convicted and sentenced, without evidence... but this was not the United States, and I suspected that there might be a big difference in the two countries as to what constituted evidence. Were the whispers of a jail inmate and a madam and her girls sufficient here?

"You Americans have a phrase, 'need to know.' And with all due respect, Doctor Angel and Nurse Dixon, I don't think you have the need to know what will become of the police chief."

Neither Dixon nor I said anything, and after a while the mayor added, "Let me just ask you this. What would your reaction be if I told you that after we obtained the information we are seeking, that I intend to see that he is shot as a collaborator?"

I considered my reply very carefully before answering, "I don't think I would like how that would reflect upon me or the medical team. The team has a strict set of rules, one of which is to remain apolitical. And as medical professionals, we are bound by an oath to do no harm."

"But you just told me earlier tonight that my chief of police plans to assassinate the president."

I responded quickly, perhaps to remind myself as well as inform the mayor, "I'm a physician, I save lives."

"And that would stop you from helping me find him, arrest him and put him in prison?"

"The way you were talking, Mr. Mayor, it sounded to me like you intended to put a blindfold on him, stand him up against the wall, and shoot him."

"I must uphold the law. To be honest, my hope is that when we go to arrest him, he will resist, and I – or one of my men – will be justified in shooting him. If that doesn't happen, the police chief will be tried and most likely found guilty, and will probably be sentenced to thirty years to life in prison. We are a Catholic country, and there is no death penalty in Nicaragua."

I replied, "I have no problem with you trying him as a Cuban collaborator and putting him in one of your prisons. As you know, I just visited your jail today. And I've heard stories about some of the other prisons in this country. I imagine they are all hellholes, and no one could be likely to survive even twenty years, most especially a corrupt police chief."

"But you would be reluctant, Doctor, to have him shot or hanged?" the mayor challenged. "Even if it were proven beyond a doubt that he was part of a plot to assassinate the president? Even if he actually assassinated the president himself?"

"Mr. Mayor, I guess you are right. There are some things doctors just don't have the need to know."

The mayor quickly retorted, "Yes, you wouldn't want to be the one to have him shot or hanged, because you are a medical man. You took an oath." I didn't reply. He was mocking me, but gently and not maliciously; he was simply emphasizing that his priorities and responsibilities were of necessity different from mine and Dixon's. I was glad I was not in the position of determining the police chief's fate. While I was committed to doing what I could to help the mayor, the chief of police was now a local problem for him and the Miskito Indian elders' council to deal with once they captured him – if they captured him. I really didn't want to hear what happened after that, at least not beyond knowing that he could cause no further trouble.

Dixon, echoing my thoughts, said to the mayor, "Of course, you first have to find and catch the police chief. Doc and I will do what we can to help you find him. But from there it is out of our hands."

The mayor replied, "My sentiments exactly. I have to catch him first. Then he will go before the council of elders and they will make the decision. They know more about handling this than anyone else."

"Well," I said, "I really don't have anything to add to that."

"I don't expect you to add anything, doctor. I just wanted you to understand my position as mayor of Puerto Cabezas, and to be aware of the possible outcomes when we capture him. In the end, it will be up to the council of the tribal elders. And now, is there anything else I can do for you and Mr. Dixon?"

"Possibly," I answered.

"Anything – just ask."

I thought about it a moment. Finally I said, "Actually, I don't have anything specific right now. I can't say for sure exactly what we will need before this is all over, but I do want to make sure you have our backs, as we have yours. And I also trust that you will convey our farewells to the elders and to everyone else if we have to leave suddenly. We're taking that warning you gave us earlier tonight very seriously."

"As well you should," said the mayor. "And yes, you have my support and I will do whatever I can to provide you with whatever you need. We understand each other. We are friends for life. But enough talk. It's time we toast this moment with a glass of Flor." And he lifted his trusty bottle, handed a glass to Dixon and one to me, and filled all three glasses to the brim. We clicked them together and then the mayor raised his glass, saying, "A toast to our President Violeta Chamorro and an end to this civil war!"

If it hadn't been clear before, it was abundantly clear at this moment that the mayor was a strong ally. We sat for a few minutes and finished our drinks. Finally and somewhat reluctantly, Dixon and I excused ourselves and walked back towards the sawmill. Our need for sleep was urgent, though the prospect of getting enough, or any at all, was dwindling rapidly.

We were more than halfway back to the sawmill when it occurred to me that I hadn't followed up with the mayor on what, if anything, he wanted us to do about Anna, the nurse whom Dixon had invited to tomorrow's clinic. It was clear to me that despite reassurances from the mayor and me, Dixon was quite upset about learning that she was most likely a collaborator – not just because he had issued the invitation, but also because he had misjudged her so badly. I almost turned back towards the cantina but then thought better of it. We had dealt with enough tonight, and if we had any hope of getting sleep we had to get back to our rooms as soon as possible. We would, I decided, take care of the Anna problem tomorrow, provided she even showed up at the clinic. I actually doubted that she would.

Though it was quite late, there were still several small clusters of people milling about just outside the Red Cross compound and scattered along the main street. Some of them seemed to be demonstrating; there was nothing open or overt, but we did hear occasional shouts of, "Americans stay! Cubans go home!" That was encouraging but also a little disturbing. Far more disturbing were the gunshots that rang out in the night, closer than we would have preferred. They may have been merely celebratory gunshots, but then again...

"No, this isn't over by any means," Dixon muttered. We wasted no time getting to the sawmill and behind the high stone walls of our own compound, though the walls didn't do much to muffle either the shouting or the gunshots. We climbed the rickety stairs to the second floor balcony, and Dixon's face contorted as he sucked in great gulps of air after the climb. Then we stood still, straining to listen and make out what was being shouted in the street below. We noticed that there were some other chants besides the familiar "Americans stay, Cubans go home," but we couldn't quite make out what was being said.

Dixon said, "Our only hope of getting out of this place safely if – when – the time comes is to pull together. I think we all need to team up with this goal in mind." Though he seemed to be stating the obvious I knew exactly what he meant.

"You're right," I replied, "and I'm laying down some new rules. For one, we must always travel as a group. And we also need to..."

The sudden creaking of the rusted old hinges on a door being opened interrupted me, and Dixon and I nearly jumped out of our skins. Our conversations with the mayor tonight had put us into a state of hyper-vigilance, and without thinking I reached for the Glock in my boot.

But it was only Bob Dows, who joined us out on the balcony. "You two look like you've seen a ghost!" he said, grinning. Dixon and I smiled gamely, weak with relief but far from relaxed. Then the three of us stood watching the small spectacle below, listening, and...waiting. We weren't quite sure what it was we were waiting for. What did seem certain was that the shouts were growing louder.

"Well, at least there haven't been any riots tonight," Bob observed.

"That could change in a flash," replied Mr. Dixon.

And Bob and I both knew he was right.

CHAPTER 28
Secrets At The Old Port

As the people below us seemed to grow rowdier and the gunshots rang out a little more frequently – or was it just my imagination? – I grew more uneasy and sensed that Dixon was too. But Bob seemed unfazed, simply saying again, "Nope... no riots tonight."

Dixon, sounding slightly annoyed, remarked, "You seem a little disappointed, Bob."

I jumped in, ribbing Bob, "Well, you know the old journalism slogan, 'If it bleeds, it leads.'"

Bob smiled, and didn't challenge my statement. He just shrugged and said, "Nothing that happens would surprise me at this point. I understand that the mayor is still worried. But whatever occurs, riot or not, I'm going to try to get footage. That's why I'm here, after all. I should probably go back to my room and grab my camera, just in case."

I held up my hand, gesturing for him to stop, saying, "The safety of our medical team is more important to me. That's what Mr. Dixon and I were talking about before you joined us." It wasn't my intent to cramp Bob's journalistic style, but he needed to know about the potentially serious threats we now faced.

"Keep in mind that we can't depend on outside help right now," I said. "Marvin, thank goodness, is safe in Managua for now, and although he knows where we are, even a miracle worker like Marvin can't get us any immediate help if we really get into trouble. We have Violeta's support, but we have no way of communicating with her right now, and she couldn't do anything to get us out of a tight spot either. Presumably we have the support of the Nicaraguan press, but what can they do? Even with all of that moral support, we're more or less on our own."

"That's kind of a gloomy way of looking at it," Bob said.

"It's a realistic way of looking at it," I answered. "Violeta warned me of the hardships we would encounter. She warned us we couldn't really trust the police and wouldn't have any backing from the army. But despite what I told the mayor a little while ago, she didn't really tell me everything, in all likelihood because she just didn't know it all herself. Remember, she's had very limited communication with this area. To tell the truth, if I had known about everything that has been taking place here on this coast, we might not have made this trip."

This comment obviously stunned Bob, who blurted in response, "I beg your pardon?" Dixon looked similarly surprised, especially after my having just told him and the mayor that I didn't regret my decision to come here.

Bob was obviously weighing his response, then finally spoke again. "Doc, I've never known you to back away from a challenge, even a big one."

"There's sometimes a fine line between a big challenge and a foolish, unnecessary risk," I retorted. "But now that we're here, my task is to keep the team safe and to get us out quickly and safely if need be."

"Fair enough," Bob said. "Do you really think we're going to need to go sooner than originally planned?"

"After some of the things the mayor told us about tonight, I'd say there's a good chance," I replied. "As you recall, I'd already instructed the pilot to be ready to get us out at a moment's notice. And the mayor told Dixon and me just a little while ago to make sure that the pilot and the plane really are ready. For now, I'm thinking about sending the entire medical team to the Red Cross compound, since that is considered neutral territory. The mayor suggested we do that."

Dixon was nodding his agreement as I spoke, but Bob stood there, still looking a little stunned. Finally he said, "I guess we don't have as many friends here as we thought."

"Not as many as I'd like," I said, "We've done all we can with the local officials, but most of them are corrupt. Especially the police chief, who seems to have disappeared, and the sheriff, who's reportedly a Sandinista sympathizer. The only ones we can really depend on are the mayor and his staff, whom I trust implicitly, and some of the Miskito police force and the tribal elders who are aligned with the mayor.

"Still, whatever the outcome of our peace mission, our medical mission has accomplished a lot in these few days, and our team has done much better than the Cubans did in the many years they've been here. And that has earned us the support of most of the local residents."

"True," Dixon said.

"But again," I said, "Our safety is paramount. The locals for the most part have turned on the Cuban doctors, not on us. It was the Cubans and the Russian support staff who needed to run for safety. But that doesn't mean we can take our own safety for granted. To put it bluntly, we can't be sure that all the Cubans and Russians are gone, or if the ones who left are gone for good. There's still plenty of potential for conflict, and I don't want our team to get caught in the crossfire."

Dixon added, "And we're not even entirely sure that all of the local residents support us, or will continue to do so. They could turn on a dime. The people were going after the Cubans this week, and maybe most of the ones down there tonight are targeting the Cubans, but what if we're the targets next week? The situation here is very volatile."

Bob said, "It is confusing."

"That it is," I replied.

Nodding, Dixon added, "I guess one of the things that really frightens me is not knowing exactly what is in the hearts and minds of all of the demonstrators we've been seeing – especially those we've been seeing and hearing tonight. Before you came out here, Bob, Doc and I were listening to some of the shouting and chanting, and not all of it was 'Cubans go home.' We were straining to hear and understand some of the other chants but couldn't quite make them out. But we have to assume that there are some locals who resent us for various reasons. We've got to tread carefully."

A sudden gust of wind blew in from the ocean, causing the palm branches to make an eerie rasping sound as they rubbed against each other, and pelting us with sand carried aloft from the beach.

Bob interjected, "Looking at it from that perspective, I think staying here is like swimming in the bay, waiting for a shark attack."

"Maybe, maybe not," Dixon said. "I've been listening to the locals speaking among themselves at the clinic and on the street, and for the most part their anger has been focused on the Cubans. But at best, that means that we're left to pick up the pieces if the Cubans really do go away for good."

"I don't fancy getting trapped in the middle of a local revolution, if that's what's brewing," said Bob.

At that moment Dixon looked at the two of us and said, "I guess even revolutionaries have to sleep. Have you guys noticed how quiet it's gotten all of a sudden?" He was right. The shouting had ceased, as had the gunfire. Only a few people were left in the street, and they appeared to be finally making their way back to their homes. With the street nearly empty, it was very quiet, almost eerily so. I went to the balcony railing and looked out, straining to see the Cuban compound, but the angle wasn't quite right.

At that moment, Barrett appeared and joined us on the balcony. "Don't you guys ever go to bed?" he asked.

"Well, what are *you* doing up?" Dixon responded.

"It's so damn hot I couldn't sleep, and I thought I might catch a cool breeze out here." He paused a few moments and added, "But to tell the truth that's not the only reason I couldn't sleep. That conversation with the mayor earlier tonight, just before we left the cantina, has me a little spooked."

"You're not the only one," Dixon said.

With steel in his voice, Barrett continued, "Tomorrow I am going to get us rifles and ammunition. We can take turns standing guard."

"We are a medical team, not an armed military force," I said. "We have come here to provide medical care, and for as long as we are here, we are still representatives of Violeta Chamorros's peace mission."

"Being armed doesn't rule out being peaceful," Barrett muttered.

"We'll talk about that later," I said. "The rest of you go to bed. Get some sleep. I think we'll be safe here for tonight, and we'll make arrangements to move to the Red Cross compound tomorrow if necessary. Let me talk to the mayor some more. But we have a full clinic in the morning, and remember that after lunch the driver is coming to take some of us to the fishing villages along the coast again. We still have a lot of work to do there." The little group dispersed, and what remained of the night passed quietly and uneventfully, a fact for which I was immensely thankful.

* * * * *

As I left my room at the sawmill the next morning I was met by the mayor, who was chipper and almost lively, as if there were no trouble brewing at all. "You sure seem to be in a good mood," I said, "considering the conversation we had just a few hours ago."

With a big grin and a wave of his hand, the mayor said, "I'm in a fine mood. I just spoke to the madam a little while ago, and it seems that the situation isn't quite as urgent as it appeared last night – at least not for now."

"Um... okay," I said, my skepticism obvious. "What exactly does that mean for my team and me?" I was starting to feel as if I were on a roller coaster. First we were in grave danger, and then we weren't, and then we were again, and then we weren't... This was going to take a little getting used to.

The mayor replied, "Let me put it this way. I recommend that you proceed with your plans today as if all is normal. You should still remain prepared, of course – keep that plane fueled and ready – but for now I really do not see a need for you to have to pack up and leave. I do want you to let me know if the nurse that we spoke about last night, Anna, shows up to the clinic today. But I rather suspect she will not."

Clearly this was all of the information I was going to get, for when I asked him to elaborate, he simply winked and said, "Need-to-know, Doc, need-to-know." With that he clapped me on the back and we walked across the street to the Red Cross cantina for breakfast.

Shortly after we were seated and served our meal, the other members of the team began filing in and joined us at a long narrow table along the back wall. I quickly filled them in on the latest threat report, and reviewed our schedule, which I explained would proceed normally. Then the mayor, still cheerful, took the opportunity to give us a history lesson about Puerto Cabezas. As we ate our breakfast of fresh-caught fried fish and eggs, he told us that the indigenous Miskito and Mayangna peoples always referred to Puerto Cabezas as *Bilwi*, which he said means "snake leaf" in the Mayan language.

He said, "The port was first used by English pirates around the 1600s, and they referred to it as Bragman's Bluff. Then in the 1890s, the pirate stronghold, which had been ruled by an alliance of English and indigenous people for almost 200 years, was annexed by the Nicaraguan government when General Rigoberto Cabezas hoisted the Nicaraguan flag over the port city. The Nicaraguan government honored General Cabezas by naming the port after him. Puerto Cabezas became the capital of Nicaragua's enormous national reserve, which became known as RAAN, short for *Región Autónoma del Atlántico Norte*." (Today it is known as *Región Autónoma de la Costa Caribe Norte*, or RACN for short.)

The mayor took a minute to sip some of his coffee, and shoved a forkful of fried beans and eggs into his mouth all at one time, with some of the food landing on his protuberant abdomen. Ignoring the spill, he continued with our history lesson.

"Even though the Caribbean coast was under Nicaraguan control, a consortium of United States businesses, including the Bragman's Bluff Lumber and Fruit Company and Standard Fruit, began exerting their influence in the area. These companies siphoned timber, food, and fish from the Caribbean Coast, and no one complained. It was actually good for the locals because of the high-paying jobs offered by some companies like Standard Fruit.

"In addition, the Bragman's Bluff Company built a substantial pier, Muelle Viejo – which simply means, 'Old Pier,' that has withstood the elements to this day. The pier has a very interesting history and still sees plenty of international shipping – including by pirates and profiteers. Most of the profiteers these days come from Colombia and quietly arrive in the middle of the night, though some have actually been brazen enough for daytime arrivals. The Colombians bring their white powder cargo, which they off-load here, and then it is shipped north to Mexico and the United States."

The mayor stopped just long enough to spoon in another large portion of fried fish, eggs and beans. I've rarely seen a fellow who took such pleasure in eating. I took this opportunity to speak up about an issue that I hadn't really had a chance to talk about with him in any great detail, with so many other seemingly urgent matters on the table. I reminded him that some of our patients who came from one of the local fishing villages had told us they had seen a military vessel, flying the Cuban flag, and that it had been quite close to the shoreline at various times recently. The latest buzz, which we had just heard yesterday, was that it was now around the vicinity of the Old Port. "Maybe this port is hiding secrets that need to be investigated," I said.

The mayor took another sip of his coffee, cleared his throat, and replied, "I have also received word of the latest sighting. I believe they are here to remove more of the Cubans and some of the Russian and Sandinista allies. I also have more reason than ever to suspect that the police chief, who as most of you may now know was trying to arrange the plot to assassinate President Violeta Chamorro, is hiding someplace along the shoreline until the boat arrives. He will then try to make his escape, and they will give him sanctuary in Cuba."

A couple of the nurses who hadn't yet heard about the assassination plot looked alarmed, and the mayor said, "Don't be worried. The police chief does not seem to be an immediate threat to our president or to us. As the doc told you just now, you should all proceed with your plans for today."

At that moment I noticed Lori Reingold getting up from the far end of the table with Bob Dows, who was gathering his equipment. This was a hint to the group that we needed to get to the clinic at the Red Cross center. Just then, one of the nurses came through the door, telling us that there were at least eighty patients lined up in the clinic waiting to see the doctors.

I thanked the mayor for the interesting historical perspective of *Bilwi*, and asked him to have the two Jeep drivers ready to leave from the Red Cross center at 1:00 p.m. For now, there was plenty of work to do at the clinic.

* * * * *

I split the team between the three examining rooms so that we could proceed efficiently and quickly. With no air conditioning, the heat seemed particularly oppressive today, even though it was still early. The ceiling fans were running at maximum speed and it was still almost 100 degrees in the clinic. I gave some money to one of the nurses and asked her to go to the local grocery store and have them deliver several cases of bottled water and bottled juice for the children.

Just before we began our rounds, I whispered to Mr. Dixon, "Be sure to keep an eye out for Anna. We're to let the mayor know immediately if she shows up."

Dixon nodded. "Don't worry. That's one of my top priorities. I can't believe I was so easily fooled by her."

"Hey, man, let it go," I said. "You did nothing wrong. Just keep your eyes open, and I will too."

As the day progressed, Anna was nowhere to be seen. We continued seeing little patients and administering inoculations. Others – about fifty percent of those we had seen – required surgery for congenital defects such as cleft lip, cleft palate, or burns. Then there were the expected number of farm injuries and war wounds. As usual, arrangements were made for them to be transferred to the hospitals in Managua, León, or Chinandega, where they would receive the surgical procedures they required.

Everything was going well and in an orderly fashion for more than an hour when I heard a disturbance in the main waiting area, and I left the examining room with Mr. Dixon to see what was happening. One of the Red Cross volunteers told us that most of the patients wanted to meet or be seen by Dr. Angel. She explained, "Everybody is still talking about the miracle baby. There are some here who had actually taken the long overland ride through the mountains to Chinandega, with the hopes that they could see and pray next to the miracle baby, and that they could see you. When they were told that you were here on the coast, many came here. Some are even talking about a shrine to the miracle baby. Perhaps they are hoping for a miracle of their own."

"I have a compromise in mind," I said, smiling. "The miracle baby isn't here, of course, but I will meet and greet everyone who is in the clinic. And then Mr. Dixon and I will go outside and greet those who are sitting along the curb. We'll shake hands with family members and take a quick look at the children. We'll ask them to be patient and tell them that we will see them in turn in the clinic as quickly as we can."

The volunteer nodded, and I continued, "Meanwhile, we will hand everyone water and juice so no one gets dehydrated while they are waiting. This way everyone gets to meet with 'Dr. Angel,' and hopefully this will restore peace and quiet in the clinic." Fortunately the juice and water that my nurse had ordered earlier that morning had arrived.

Accordingly Mr. Dixon and I – he with his fluent Spanish, and I with my rudimentary grasp of the language – began making our rounds, beginning inside the clinic and then continuing outside, where long lines of people waited to see us. That small gesture went a long way, and the effect was amazing. Hugs, kisses, handshakes, and assurances that everyone who wanted to be seen would be seen did indeed ameliorate the situation.

Bob Dows, lugging his ever-present camera on his shoulder and the nearly as cumbersome batteries on his waist, had already sweated through his shirt and trousers. But he continued to move briskly up and down the line, photographing while Lori Reingold was taking notes and one of the Red Cross volunteers was helping with interpretation. This would be the first episode in a spectacular program that would continue for more than a week on ABC-TV.

Finally, Dixon and I went back into the clinic, and saw yet more patients. We had been hoping to finish by 1:00 p.m., but it was nearly 2:00 when the last patient left. The two Jeeps and drivers were patiently waiting for us outside the Red Cross compound to take us north to more of the isolated Miskito villages. It only took a few minutes to load our equipment and supplies with the help of the drivers, and the volunteer ladies from the Red Cross cantina had packed us a to-go lunch and some cold drinks.

I told Alonzo, my driver in the lead Jeep, that we were going to stop at the pier, *Muelle Viejo*, and then go north along the coast toward the Rio Coco, stopping at villages and treating the children. Alonzo seemed like a good man, and I trusted him. He had replaced the former driver, who seemed to have disappeared the day after Lori and I saw the stolen goods from the pharmacy in his car. The good news was that there had been no more missing meds or supplies since then, but I still wondered what had happened to that driver. I sensed that it was best not to ask too many questions.

Then we were off, and as we approached the pier I said, "Let's go for a walk!" I grabbed a cold drink from one of the coolers, and others followed suit. Bob Dows was the first to get out of the Jeep, and walked rapidly up the pier, signaling for us to wait. He then began to film as the medical team and I strolled along the wooden boards of the historic pier.

Lori said she had learned that during the civil war, both the Contras and the Sandinistas had received arms and ammunition that were smuggled in aboard boats that anchored at this pier. "And the town's prostitutes assisted the Sandinistas in this undertaking," she added. "Seems that they provided some useful services besides the obvious."

"Some things never change," I remarked, thinking about the madam and her girls, who had been busily supplying the mayor with the information that had been vital to the safety of the medical team.

About halfway down the 420-meter-long pier, we came to a security gate. Alonzo explained to the guard who we were, showing the man some paperwork that had been signed by the mayor. We were then granted clearance to continue walking to the end of the pier.

Bob said, "This pier's most historic moment was when Anastasio Somoza allowed U.S.-funded Cuban exiles to launch the Bay of Pigs invasion in Cuba. As we all know, the Bay of Pigs Invasion was a fiasco and failed utterly, but this was the site from which it was launched."

At the end of the pier I raised my binoculars and scanned the ocean. Yes, there was a military-styled boat flying the Cuban flag in the deeper waters just beyond the shore break, as the fishermen had reported to us.

As we returned along the wooden pier, I pointed to Bob and told him to check out the *pangas*, large fiberglass skiffs that were crumbled and half buried in the sand. These had been seized from narcotics traffickers and destroyed by the military – stark evidence of the illicit shipping lanes that were located just minutes from the center of Puerto Cabezas.

With cold drinks in hand, we all climbed back into the Jeeps, and I instructed Alonzo to continue north to the Miskito villages along the coast. But the sight of that military vessel with the Cuban flag weighed on my mind, and the familiar feeling of unease was returning with a vengeance. I thought again of the fueled-up plane that was waiting for us. At any moment, all I had to do was say the word, and the team and I could return to a part of the country where we would be at least marginally safer. If we had to, we could go back to the States.

But we had patients to see here, and I couldn't turn my back on them.

CHAPTER 29
Instincts

As we proceeded north toward the fishing villages, our driver pointed out La Bocana, an old pirate enclave at the river's mouth, just north of town. Unlike most of the beaches around Puerto Cabezas, which are more rocky than sandy and are not what one would picture as a place for a Caribbean vacation, the beach around La Bocana has more sand than rocks. Even so, it appeals to a different kind of tourism than you might expect. Instead of coming here to lie on the beach and soak up the sun, many people come here with metal detectors, looking for pirate treasures from the past.

We were headed towards the villages of Tuapi and Krukira, and if time allowed, we would continue on to Waspam and the Rio Coco. Perhaps, I thought, we could get a fishing boat to take us fifty kilometers offshore to the Miskito Keys, one of the many places in the area where traveling by boat was safer, easier, and smoother than traversing what passed for roads.

The Miskito Keys were at once a primitive paradise – with their stilted, thatched bungalows built over pristine turquoise water – and a haven for bad guys with their speedboats. The Keys were also a profoundly isolated community, where immunizations and the most basic medical care were virtually nonexistent. The people there were very much in need of our services, and my team and I were eager to accommodate them, but it was unlikely that we'd get to do so on this trip. Traveling to the villages along the coast would be a much more productive use of our limited time here.

As we went from village to village, I sat up front in the Jeep with several cameras clicking away. Each village had its own kind of simple beauty. They were all as poor and undeveloped as Puerto Cabezas, if not more so, with simple wooden homes whose tin roofs reflected the sunlight. Windows often didn't have panes of glass but instead had simple curtains on pull rods, and the curtains flapped constantly in the ever-present ocean breeze. The trees above us were home to thousands of chattering parakeets, seemingly mocking us as we passed below.

A "clinic" in a village on the Miskito Coast

The village children, all dressed in colorful but tattered and dirty shorts, were playing everywhere. There were dugout canoes pulled just above the tide line, and fishing nets hanging out to dry all along the coastal area. We arrived in Tuapi, a small village no different than all the others we had seen, and got directions to the clinic. The clinic was a one-room wooden board structure elevated on wooden stilts in an attempt to keep out the moisture and the bugs. The "windows" were actually just openings in the sides of the buildings, with shutters clipped back against the building so that the ocean breeze could pass through freely and provide some ventilation and cooling. The clinic had a 1940s era cross-linked steel examining table and a large, covered but almost empty supply cart in its single room. Basic supplies were minimal, and medications were virtually non-existent.

A woman named Ideta, who ran the clinic, said she was a practical nurse as well as a midwife, and was the only source of medical care in the region. She rang a bell that hung to the side of the open doorway, and within minutes children came running and mothers brought their infants swaddled in colorful papooses slung across their chests.

Ideta said, "We were expecting you. The drums told us the American doctors would be coming. Everyone is excited to meet the American team and the famous Dr. Angel. Everyone has heard about Chinandega's miracle baby."

The children were orderly and polite. They played amongst themselves outside until Ideta called them into the clinic with their mothers and family groups. I asked the children to come to the examining table one at a time, at which point I would immediately present them with oversized lollipops. Nothing like a bit of bribery to ensure that you have a quiet, cooperative child for examination.

Of the children we examined, several had symptoms of maladies both minor and significant. When we questioned the mothers, we learned that few of their children had received any form of immunization for polio. There was one child with ptosis, a form of congenital lazy eye, which presents as a drooping or falling eyelid. There were burns as well, most of which had obviously not been treated adequately if at all, and had been allowed to form scar tissue, resulting in contractures and limited use of fingers, hands, and arms. There wasn't much to be done for these patients onsite; I could only refer them to the appropriate hospital for surgery. Other than burns, the next most common injuries we saw at this clinic were from farm accidents, again treated inadequately if at all. Obviously, there was little we could do for many of them at this rustic clinic. But immunizations could easily be provided, as could topical medication for the various rashes and insect bites.

All things considered, the children were for the most part quite healthy and good-spirited. Food, though simple, was plentiful in the forms of fresh fish, chicken, and homegrown vegetables. They were actually a lot better off than many of the children of Nicaragua and other parts of the world.

As we worked, the loquacious Ideta told us there was an east/west road from Puerto Cabezas through the mountain valleys to Rosita that connected with Route 21 through the town of Siuna. She then filled us in on a little of the area's history. In 1880, Siuna, Rosita, and Bonanza were the center of a gold rush. Immigrants from as far away as

China and Europe, as well as those from North America and throughout the Caribbean, had flocked to the area hoping to strike the mother lode. Today most of these immigrants have left, and there are very few outsiders and virtually no visitors. But while the gold rush is long since over, there is still significant mining activity there, and Nicaragua in general is considered to be one of the best places to invest in gold and mineral mining, due to the government's lack of regulation over the mining industry.

The children who required surgical procedures were photographed and medical histories taken, and their names were added to a list that Ideta was compiling. The team and I donated several hundred córdobas to each of the families on the list, enough for them to get bus tickets and buy water and food along the way to Chinandega. Once there, they would be met by Father Marcus and Sister Esperanza and taken to the hospital, where they would be promptly admitted and treated, and would remain until they were healthy enough to make the return trip home. With the photographing and surgical patients list complete, we packed up our gear and prepared to board the Jeeps and head north to the next village, but not until we had received a lifetime's supply of hugs and kisses.

Our last stop was at the town of Krukira, at the southern end of the Reserva Natural Laguna Pahara, where the topography was changing to marsh-like coastal lowland. The conditions and medical problems we encountered there were similar to those we had observed in the other villages we had visited. The people there had also been made aware of our coming, and as we had encountered in our previous stops, quite a few patients were waiting for us when we arrived. The process there went smoothly and efficiently, but it was still late in the afternoon before we were able to pack up and begin the long journey back to Puerto Cabezas.

We had accomplished our goals in these coastal villages, and were now eager to return to Puerto Cabezas and the safety of the Red Cross compound. We had not been on the road for long when the sun was beginning to set, and we did not wish to be on the unlit roads at night. Beyond all the natural obstacles that would be more difficult to see and avoid in the darkness, I think that all of us were a bit nervous about the possible presence of any Cubans or Sandinistas who would probably love to find us so far from our base.

It was already dark when we reached Puerto Cabezas, and all of us were hot, tired, and hungry. All I could think about was that cold outdoor shower. We stopped first in front of the main gates to the Red Cross compound, where we left Lori and Carolyn. The Jeep then made a quick U-turn in the middle of the street, and Mr. Dixon and I helped Bob lug the camera equipment up to the second level. Each board seemed to creak more loudly as we trudged to the porch outside our rooms.

I went into my room, and within seconds, I had stripped down to my shorts, grabbed a bar of soap and a towel, and descended two steps at a time to the shower below. The shock of the icy cold water dissipated quickly, and within a few minutes all I wanted to do was stand there and let it run over my body and cool me down. When I looked up, the sky was filled with stars, and the evening was illuminated by an almost full moon. What a beautiful sight.

Then, out of the corner of my eye, a light bulb dangling on its cord and blowing in the evening breeze caught my attention. Standing under the light bulb with her hands on the second story balcony rail was the very large, buxom woman I had met several days before. Her children were with her. Once again she was unashamedly topless, apparently just having left the shower before I arrived there. Now she was grinning from ear to ear and waving at me. I'm a friendly guy. What else could I do? I grinned and waved back. Then I turned the lever to shut the pump off and the cool water stopped falling. As I wrapped myself in the towel I blew her a kiss with my one free hand. She began laughing so hard that I thought the railing she was leaning against would come apart and she would fall to the ground below.

As I started up the steps to my room, I encountered Mr. Dixon, his towel over his shoulder and a bar of soap in his hand. I whispered to him, "You have a friend on the balcony across from us who wants to say hello. When you get in the shower just look up."

I continued up the stairs, leaving him with a confused look on his face, and I could hardly keep from laughing out loud. I knocked on Bob's door, opened it a crack and yelled through, "Bob, I'm going to the Red Cross cantina. When you're rested and comfortable, please join Mr. Dixon and me there."

"Give me twenty minutes," he hollered back, "and I'll meet you there."

When I arrived at the cantina for dinner the mayor was at his usual table just inside the door, where he could greet everyone and view the entire room. Sitting across from him was the madam. The mayor had a fresh bottle of Flor de Caña on the table and motioned me over, pushing a glass toward me and filling it. Mr. Dixon joined us a few minutes later.

The madam, wasting no time with small talk, looked at me and said, "As you may have seen by the street protests of the past few evenings, our Miskito Indian population here remains as feisty and independent as ever. I am afraid that tonight's protest is going to be bigger and more dangerous for everyone concerned."

"Continue, please," I said calmly, trying to ignore the wave of anxiety that was washing over me. "What makes you think that tonight's protest will be bigger and that it might be dangerous?"

"For the past few nights, I have had more than my usual number of rabble rousers at my bar at the far end of the main street. They have been drinking a lot of homemade liquor, and have cleaned out my entire supply of rum. The more they drink the braver they become. The liquor loosens their tongues, and the young ladies who work for me told me earlier this evening that they have been hearing talk of plans for a march tonight down the main street to the Cuban clinic. Some said they are planning to set the clinic on fire, others say they plan to blow it up."

I was stunned. "Why would they want to blow the clinic up now, when it's clear that the Cubans have no more power there? The Nicaraguan and American flags are flying proudly, and our medical team has been seeing patients there. I understand that there is still some concern about a few Cubans who still might be in hiding, but I can say with reasonable certainty that they're not hiding out in the clinic!" I tried to keep my voice calm, but it was a challenge. That emotional roller coaster was definitely gearing up again.

The madam replied, "I believe you, Doctor, but it seems there are some people who are still not convinced. They want every last reminder of the Cubans and their Russian-Sandinista backers gone from Puerto Cabezas and the Miskito Coast. They are convinced that some are still hiding out and that even you may not be aware of it. You have to understand that even though your arrival with the TV camera crew, and the subsequent story of the miracle baby, have nearly elevated you to sainthood in the eyes of many of these people, they are still deeply angry about the Cubans. Evidently some of them realize that despite all of the good things you have done, there are limits even to your powers. They are convinced that you have not been able to rid the clinic of the Cubans, so they feel they must take matters into their own hands. Their anger is growing, and sometimes I think it is a miracle that so far no one has been killed or injured."

"Well, I do appreciate the warning," I said. Then I asked, "Is there any word about the police chief and his alleged assassination plot against President Chamorro?"

I was directing my question to both the madam and the mayor, but it was the mayor who spoke up. "I have put the word on the street that he is to be considered a criminal at large, but we have not received any information as to his whereabouts."

Then he raised his glass and said, "A toast to President Violeta Chamorro." After we clicked glasses and I took a sip, the mayor raised his glass again and said, "A toast to you, Dr. Angel, and your medical team." Again, glasses were raised and clicked. Then the mayor raised his glass once again. "And a toast to the remaining Cubans who have the sense to get out by tonight before the situation is beyond my control." Glasses clicked all around again, but this time my hand was shaking a little when I raised my own glass.

After taking a few more sips, I asked, as casually as possible, "Has anyone heard what happened to the boat that I saw from *Muelle Viejo* earlier today?"

The mayor responded, "That I do have reports about, from several fishermen that returned this evening with their catch. They reported two small dories had been launched close to the pier. Looks like they are preparing to retrieve the remaining Cubans and the Russian support staff."

"Okay," I said, and I'm sure the momentary relief I felt could be easily seen.

Then the mayor added, "I wish I could tell you with more certainty where our indoctrinated police chief really is. I am of course still convinced that he is hiding – not in the Cuban clinic, but somewhere very nearby. But I am not going on a hunt for him right now. It would be a bloodbath on both sides. For now I prefer to give him a chance to leave on his own, and I believe that when he goes, the assassination plot will evaporate as well."

"I prefer that outcome as well," I said, "although I wouldn't automatically assume that just because he leaves Puerto Cabezas he will abandon his plot." Though I had previously discussed this matter with the mayor, the uncertainties about the police chief's intentions were still bothering me. While it was possible that he would be spirited off to Cuba, in which case he might no longer be a direct threat to Violeta, I felt that if the police chief merely escaped to another location in Nicaragua, we couldn't be so sure that Violeta was out of danger.

The madam, seeing the worried look return to my face, took another sip of rum and looked across the table at me with a big smile, her red lipstick making her lips look even fuller and more sensuous. "Instead of running off to treat all these children, Doctor, I think that you should join in the popular pastime of Puerto Cabezas – drinking. It begins early in the morning. You need to get an early start too, as things can get a little rough later on." At that, she began to laugh. The mayor soon joined in and was pounding the table with one hand and throwing rum shots back with the other.

The madam then said to me, "I wanted to surprise you with something typical of the Caribbean coast for dinner. I asked them to make *pakru*. This is locally caught fresh fish and yucca baked together in banana leaves. The other dish I asked them to prepare is *auhpi piakan*, which involves mixing together plantains, a meat such as chicken or pork, and coconut. The name of the dish in the Miskito Indian language means 'a meal mixed together.'"

The mayor interjected, "You can't leave us without having authentic Miskito cuisine."

At that moment Bob entered with Lori and Carolyn. They took our usual table against the far wall. Mr. Dixon and I thanked the mayor and the madam for the drinks and the information, and then excused ourselves to join them and the other members of the medical team. I invited the mayor and the madam to come join us when the meal was served.

"*Si, si*," said the mayor, "and I have another bottle of Flor for the group."

As Dixon and I sat down at our table, I could hear someone running a wooden plank along the outside of the stockade, shouting, "Cubans go home, Americans stay!" I thought to myself that the first volley of the evening had just been fired. And I strongly felt that for our own safety, we needed more information before we made any decisions.

Just at that moment, one of the volunteer ladies came to our table and confirmed that they were preparing a special typical meal, as had been requested by the madam, but that it would be another hour before they would be ready to serve. She asked if anyone would like anything else to drink, and said she was bringing some calamari as an appetizer while we waited.

But I was restless, uneasy. I didn't feel like eating or drinking right now. I turned to Bob and, with a nod to Dixon, I said, "Bob, don't you think your story would be more effective if we got some more evening footage?"

Neither Bob nor Dixon needed any convincing. They both nodded, and the three of us got up almost simultaneously. We headed back across the street to the sawmill, retrieved the camera equipment, and then walked to the Old Pier.

The air had been cooled somewhat by a sharp wind blowing across the Caribbean Sea toward the harbor. Not only were the stars visible on a clear cloudless night; the few lights that lined the pier and formed the crescent around the harbor could also be seen for miles. Everyone was looking skyward at the beautiful array of stars, thousands of stars like we had never seen before.

While Bob was shooting footage I took the opportunity to take a closer look at him. He was looking pretty good, all things considered. He seemed alert and cheerful, his eyes sharp and sparkling in the glow of the moon. But then Bob usually seemed cheerful, and unless you caught him in an unguarded moment, it was difficult to ascertain what he was thinking. Right now he did not seem to be a man who was fearful of what might take place in the evening yet to come. But as we walked further out onto the pier he said, in a voice that sounded a little stressed, "I noticed you talking to the madam and the mayor. And you clearly have something on your mind. How bad is the situation?"

"I won't lie to you," I said. "It's not looking real good right now."

"In other words," Bob said, "We really can't rely on the locals for our safety."

"That seems to be the case," said Dixon.

As we walked out along the pier to the security gate, a sudden gust of cool wind buffeted us from the seaward side. Though it wasn't a particularly cold wind, I felt a chill nonetheless. We found to our surprise that the security station was unmanned. *Did the mayor order this?* I wondered.

Bob and Dixon and I had been partners on tough international trips before. We trusted each other as only people who have been in difficult and even dangerous situations together can trust. When push came to shove, we were each other's best advocates, and we had a deep faith in each other's instincts. Suddenly, we heard the guttural whine of an outboard motor and the slapping of the waves against a rubber landing craft, and our respective and collective instincts were telling us that this nighttime stroll might have been a huge mistake. Possibly even a lethal one.

CHAPTER 30
Vigilantes

I turned and whispered to Bob, "Whatever you do, don't turn that camera light on."

He whispered back, "Understood. The last thing I want to do is to make us targets."

Dixon mumbled something nearly unintelligible about the warnings we'd been hearing from the madam and others. I couldn't make out all that he was saying, but it seemed to be something about how we should have left well enough alone and stayed in the cantina. Then he whispered, much more clearly, "So what do we do now?"

"Haven't made up my mind," I said.

"Well, I know what we need to do," Bob said. "We need to get the hell off of this pier as fast as we can and return to the safety of the Red Cross compound. And we need to stay off the streets tonight. I believe I have enough footage."

That made sense. Without saying another word, we turned and began walking off into the darkness, moving as quickly and as quietly as we could, and half-expecting shots to ring out into the night. Fortunately, the silence remained unbroken, and once we were off the pier I said, "Okay, here's what we'll do. When we get back to the Red Cross I'll ask the madam, who seems to know our pilot quite well, to contact him and have the plane fueled and the engine running just before daybreak – not tomorrow, but the day after. I'll ask the mayor to have the air raid sirens go off with the sunrise on the day we leave, just like on the day we arrived, in order to clear the main road of pedestrians and animals. I will want us to board while it is still dark, and as soon as the sun comes up, our plane will be speeding down the 'runway,' which hopefully will be cleared. If all goes well, we'll be safely on our way back to Managua."

"So you think it's for real this time?" said Dixon.

"I think so," I said. "I really do believe that things are going to get rough – possibly tonight and almost certainly over the next few days – and we don't need to be in the middle of it."

"Makes sense to me," Bob said.

"But we're not going to abandon our patients. Tomorrow we'll complete the clinic in the morning, and then we'll go to more villages. But this time we'll hit the ones south of Puerto Cabezas, and we'll get to as many as we can."

Both Bob and Dixon nodded in agreement with this plan, and I added, "I'll tell the team when we get back to the cantina."

When we re-entered the cantina we saw that the crowd had really picked up. The room was noisy, almost raucous, and the whole place was filled with enticing aromas that made me suddenly realize how ravenous I was. The mayor and the madam were already at our table, and as Bob, Dixon, and I sat down, the first course was brought to us. It was the best meal I'd had in ages.

As we ate, I filled the team in on our latest plans, and related the mini-adventure that Bob and Dixon and I had just had. "I'm sorry we didn't get a very good chance to look at the boat," I said to the mayor. "We felt an urgent need to get the hell out of there while we could."

The mayor, clearly deep into his cups, just laughed and waved his hand. "No worries," he said. "Leave the mysterious boats to my men and me. Your job is to keep yourself and your team safe. Now, have another glass of Flor! Drinks all around, for everyone!" The mayor was as good as his word, brandishing an unopened bottle of Nicaragua's famous rum, then opening it and pouring until everyone at the table had a glass.

"A toast to the Americans!" the mayor shouted, and glasses were raised and clicked.

"And you will be glad to know," the madam said to me, "that the plans for a riot tonight – for burning down the Cuban clinic – have been cancelled again. Or at least postponed." With a wink she added, "That's according to some of my most reliable sources."

In ordinary circumstances I might have felt relieved by such news, but I was learning that I could no longer take anything for granted in this place. The rest of the night did pass relatively quietly, however, with only the occasional drunken shout from the street about the Americans and Cubans. Perhaps we had a small reprieve after all.

Miracles in Bedlam

* * * * *

Early the next morning, the Red Cross volunteer women were already at the clinic as usual when we arrived, and they had our little patients and their families waiting their turn to be brought to the exam rooms. The morning progressed uneventfully, and we accomplished a lot. A young child was there with his mother, suffering with a recent burn from boiling water. His wound had been cleansed, antibiotic cream applied, and the wound was bandaged. I had just completed interviewing the mother, giving her instructions for the child's continued care and emphasizing that a return visit to the clinic would be necessary, when Dixon came into the room and announced, "You have a visitor."

Our treatment completed, the mother and child left with one of the volunteer ladies to schedule her next appointment, and Dixon brought in a very attractive young lady. She spoke English, albeit with an exotic accent. In fact, everything about her was exotic. Well-cared-for black hair extended over her shoulders and glistened against her dark skin. Her high cheekbones accentuated her facial features. I figured that she was of mixed ancestry, probably English and Miskito Indian. She was an extremely beautiful and sensual-looking young lady, and it soon became clear to me that she worked for the madam. She stood in the doorway, unmoving, merely looking at me and waiting for something. I met her gaze, somewhat enthralled by her big beautiful eyes and her dazzling smile. Dixon came further into the room and motioned for her to follow, at which point she came forward until she stood beside us. She held out a meticulously manicured hand, which I took and shook gently, noting how long and delicate her fingers were.

Dixon pointed to a chair and said, "*Siéntase por favor.*" ("Please sit.") She sat, crossing her legs, which had the effect of making her short, tight skirt ride halfway up her thighs. I turned aside, trying to ignore her beauty and maintain my air of professional detachment. Sometimes this is more difficult than others.

Turning to Dixon, she said, "So you are Dr. Angel?"

Dixon said, "No, I am the doctor's surgical scrub nurse."

"Ah. And clearly you are an intelligent man, but you are not English. Why are you in Nicaragua?" Without thinking about it, Dixon began talking to her in Spanish.

I was feeling a bit uneasy with the familiarity – even intimacy – of their exchange, as if Dixon and the young lady were old friends or perhaps more. Suddenly, she stood, put an arm around Dixon's shoulder, and pointed to me, saying, "Then this must be the famous Dr. Angel – the man with the miracle baby that we have heard so much about." She leaned toward me, close enough that I caught the scent of her sweet perfume, and then she pursed her lips and said, "The madam sent me with an urgent message."

She was now standing very straight, her back arched slightly and her chin upraised as she drew in a deep breath. I was growing impatient, eager to hear the madam's message. The young woman's beauty – her facial perfection and the sleek silhouette of her body – had been distracting, but the apparent import of the message she was supposed to deliver brought me quickly back to earth. Finally, she said, "The madam wanted the doctor and the medical team to know that men have been gathering all day at her bar, fortifying their courage with alcohol and frequent outbursts of 'Americans stay! Cubans go home!'"

"Hold on a minute," I interrupted, not attempting to disguise my annoyance. "We've heard this before, several times, and then we were told that everything was all right again and not to worry." As I spoke I was silently recalling the old tale of the boy who cried wolf, but almost immediately wondering to myself, *but what if there really is a wolf this time?*

Looking a little downcast, the young woman said, "Forgive me, Doctor. The madam and I understand how difficult this has been for you. But the mood of the crowds is constantly changing and we have been trying to keep you updated. Things happen quickly here. And unlike on other days, the men we saw and heard today have all been armed with rifles, shotguns, pistols, machetes, and even pitchforks. We feel certain that they are just waiting for darkness to fall, and that they will then march on the Cuban compound."

"But why?" I said, the frustration obvious in my voice, as the madam and I had already been over this territory. "There are no Cubans there anymore!" She just shrugged, looking as if she didn't believe me.

My mouth suddenly felt very dry, and I needed to clear my throat. My chest felt very heavy and my breathing became shallow as I pondered what she had just said. Then I turned to look at her. She had backed up a few steps, one hand on her hip, one leg thrust forward, as if in a model's pose.

I said nothing for a moment, then mumbled, "Vigilantes."

The room fell into an awkward silence as we stared at one another. Dixon broke the silence, saying, "You sound worried."

"I'm not just worried. Scared senseless is more like it."

Dixon continued, "You're afraid you are mixed up in something over which you will have no control."

He was right, of course, but my fear ran deeper than that. "Wait here," I said, and left the young lady and Mr. Dixon standing there. I couldn't help myself. I was feeling a sense of panic, and left the clinic with my heart in my throat. I had to see the mayor. When I reached the iron gates in front of the sawmill compound, a guard met me. His manner was casual even though he had a rifle slung over his right shoulder and a machete affixed to a wide, well-worn leather belt. His dress was nondescript: red-sand-stained sneakers – the left one worn through, exposing his toes – and faded navy dungarees and an old pullover. He told me to wait there, and disappeared up the stairs to the second floor. I wondered to myself, *Why the intrigue? These people know me, so why am I being asked to wait here, rather than seeing the mayor immediately? What's really going on?* The guard's behavior amplified my sense of foreboding like nothing else had so far.

Moments later, the mayor came bounding down the stairs as if he hadn't a care in the world, and no indication that he knew about the vigilante-like mob that was forming at the other end of town. He walked up to me, smiling as usual, and we shook hands. I said, "Let's go back to the Red Cross clinic," and the mayor nodded. I wanted him to hear the news directly from the young lady the madam had sent.

When we got back to the room where Dixon and the young lady were waiting, she explained the situation to the mayor as rapidly and succinctly as she had explained it to us. After she finished, the room fell once again silent for a few moments.

Then the mayor said, "We will do what we always do. Soldier on. Fight the good fight." He went on to say he did not want a lynching in his town and would personally make sure this message reached everyone, including any Cubans who might still be hiding in the area. "My message to the Cubans will be very clear," he said. "I will leave them with no doubt that they need to flee for their lives, and the sooner the better. And you of course are welcome to share that message too," he added to the young lady.

She shook the mayor's hand, then mine and Dixon's, and turned and left. After she had gone, the mayor started toward the door, then stopped. Turning back towards Dixon and me, he said, "Let's not put off moving any longer. Tonight, your entire team will stay within the walls of the Red Cross compound. It's still considered neutral territory here, and you will be safer than at my home or within the lumberyard. Pack your personal things and bring them here."

Dixon and I nodded, and the mayor, seeing the look of concern on our faces, said, "You still have a little time. These vigilante groups do not get up the courage until they are drunk enough and until the sun has set. Continue with your clinic and your other plans. You are not in immediate danger at this time."

Then the mayor gave us a dazzling smile, and with a wave of his hand, abruptly turned and left.

"Well, Mr. Dixon," I said, "it looks like we have a very full day ahead of us – maybe fuller than usual. We'd best get busy."

CHAPTER 31
The Gathering Storm

As always, Dixon was ready to spring into action. "Please tell the other team members to have their personal things packed and brought to the Red Cross compound," I told him. "Tell them we'll be eating dinner and staying within the walls of the compound until we leave tomorrow morning. But our plan to go to the villages south of Puerto Cabezas has not changed. I'll join you as soon as I can."

Dixon immediately left and managed to gather the entire medical team in the Red Cross cantina. He later filled me in on the part of the exchange that occurred before I joined the meeting.

He had begun by announcing, "We've had a little trouble."

Carolyn asked, "What kind of trouble? More of the same?" My team was not totally in the dark, of course. They had been made aware of the various threats over the past few days, although few of them knew all of the details. And they didn't know about the latest warning from the madam's lovely messenger.

Barrett spoke up. "We want to know what is going on here. Are we in any danger?"

"We need to be very careful, Barrett. And yes, Carolyn, you could say it is more of the same, but it seems to be escalating. A vigilante mob is forming in the bars and bawdyhouses at the end of the main street. There's talk of burning the Cubans and any remaining Russian supporters out."

"Out of where?" Carolyn asked.

"Out of the Cuban clinic compound," Dixon replied. As members of the team began to protest, Dixon cut them short. "Look, I know what you're thinking. It's the same reaction Doc and I had. But many of the people here remain convinced that there are still some Cubans and Russians hiding there. And they have been talking about storming the place and torching it or blowing it up. So far it's been all talk, but we have new information that leads us to believe that the talk is going to turn to action - maybe tonight. There's a group that has been emboldened by alcohol, and most of them are armed not just with shotguns but with machetes and even pitchforks."

"Pitchforks and torches. Frankenstein would be impressed," one of the team murmured, attempting to bring some levity into an otherwise grim situation. But nobody laughed.

"Well," said Barrett, "I suppose it is possible that some of the 'enemy' is still hiding in the area, maybe not within the walls of the compound and certainly not in the main clinic building itself, but there are a lot of places to hide out around there. I guess we really can't be completely certain."

"In any case," Carolyn said, "The people here seem to want to take action based on what they believe is true, not what we believe is true. We can try to convince them otherwise, but we have to be prepared no matter what."

"Exactly," said Dixon. "And rest assured that Doc Joe has been discussing all of these matters with the mayor. The mayor had previously told the doc that for our own safety all of us - men included - should be staying here at the Red Cross compound. The doc didn't want to move anyone until we were more certain. But now we don't want to take any more risks. So, guys, Doc says that everyone should pack their personal bags and bring them over here. We'll all sleep at the Red Cross tonight, and unless things change again, we should be prepared to board our plane tomorrow morning before daybreak to go back to Managua."

"Wow, that sounds serious," said Carolyn, just as I was walking into the room.

"It's serious, all right," I said, "but our plans for this afternoon remain the same. Gather the remaining medical supplies and equipment, as well as the medications that we have stored in the pharmacy, and load the Jeeps. We are going south to the small villages along the coast to do what we always do: treat the children and their parents and administer immunizations. Of course you know to dress comfortably; it is going to be hot, and have good walking shoes, not sandals. Meet back here in thirty minutes. The Jeeps and the drivers are waiting for us."

Bob wanted to sit up front on this trip, taping our travels as we went. I took a seat in the back with Lori, who had her pad and pen, making notes along the way. Our first stop was a small community situated in a marshy area fed by the Likus River, a branch of the Wawa River. Its borders form the Laguna Karatá, which empties into the Caribbean Sea.

Miracles in Bedlam

We had been told that this area was probably the single hardest destination to reach in Nicaragua, and after that trip I wouldn't argue with that opinion. We'd also been warned that the area contained some of the poorest villages along the coast, and as a result was sorely lacking in medical care as well as clean water. We were advised to take malaria prophylactics, and despite the sweltering heat we were warned to wear long trousers and full-length sleeves as protection against being bitten by mosquitoes. We also brought mosquito repellent for all members of the team and our drivers.

The lack of facilities and basic medical supplies was a major issue throughout this region, and the lack of sanitation only made things worse, as the Rio Coco and the Likus and Wawa Rivers were also the sewer systems of the region. Despite the obviously septic condition of the waters, we often saw women along the shores of these rivers washing clothes, beating them on rocks, and hanging them to dry over the bushes that lined the rivers. In addition, young children and teenagers were sent to the rivers to get buckets of water to bring back to their villages for cooking. We were told that contamination was more severe as you went downstream from the town of Waspam, which was on today's itinerary. The infant mortality rate was high, the major cause being dysentery from these polluted rivers and streams. We were traveling with plenty of bottled water and colas, and would not be eating anything offered to us unless it was well cooked.

As I mentioned previously, in this oppressively hot and humid atmosphere, disease was arguably more of a threat than the Sandinista military and the drug traffickers who moved freely along the coast. But the Sandinistas and drug traffickers were also still a threat here; they utilized this area because of the small inlets and thick foliage that provided cover for their illegal operations. Of course, as a medical team we remained neutral to these matters, and traveled ostensibly unarmed, though I still carried my trusty Glock in my boot, and my driver – Alonzo again – was armed as well.

As we traveled, I was as usual photographing sites along the route, and was particularly impressed by the beautiful multi-colored bromeliad flowers that filled the trees. For a while I allowed myself to be steeped in wonder, my worries about the threats we faced momentarily forgotten. A trip to the Atlantic and Caribbean coasts of Nicaragua is not for everyone, but my team members and I were thrilled with the closer look we had been able to take by visiting these small villages in the heart of the Miskito Indian territory. As we drove, I thought again about how truly diverse Nicaragua is, and how different this coast was from the Pacific side of the same small country.

The humidity was in full force, and the clouds of red clay dust kicked up by the Jeeps formed a film on everything, including all of us. Still, we welcomed the warm if slight breeze; even a subtle hint of cooling was refreshing. The sun was still high in the sky, but inching its way west.

When we stopped in the village of Kambla, Alonzo pulled alongside some teenagers who were riding donkeys laden with coconuts that the boys had recently cut from the trees. We asked directions to the town's clinic, and with a wave of the hand they invited us to follow them. Within a few minutes, we arrived at a cluster of small wooden homes, elevated on logs serving as the cross beams that supported the floors. The roofs were tin, and like many other similar homes we had seen along the coast, the windows were simply square holes in the walls, with no glass or screens.

As had been the case in other villages we'd visited, it seemed that word of our coming had already reached this village. There were sixty children and their parents already sitting under the palm trees around the clinic, waiting for us. Similar to the clinics in other southern villages and those that we had visited to the north, these facilities were maintained with little if any supplies or equipment, and there were no medical personnel, only a lone midwife who provided all the medical care for the village. She spoke English, and told us she had received some rudimentary training in Managua before returning to her home here in Kambla. "No one here has seen a physician in many years," she told us. "I do the best I can with what I have." I was impressed with both her level of knowledge, given the minimal training she had received, and with her devotion to the well being of her fellow villagers, but I realized that the people's needs far outweighed her capabilities. My medical team was well organized and experienced, and we got right to work.

Mr. Dixon and Alonzo, speaking Spanish and Miskito dialects, were separating out those children who were in need of immunizations but otherwise healthy. Carolyn worked with the local midwife, administering the immunizations and answering any questions the patients had. Meanwhile, Barrett and I held our clinic outside under several large palm trees, where we examined children with cleft lip and palate and other congenital anomalies. And as had been the case in other villages, we also saw those who had been victims to burns and farm injuries.

It was here that, for the first time on this medical mission trip, we were introduced to war injuries resulting from mine explosions. In the 1980s, the Rio Coco was a heavily land-mined area. Under U.N. sanctions, many of the mines had been cleared, and areas known to have remaining mines still existed and had been cordoned off with ribbons and wire. However, over time in this jungle atmosphere, the colorful ribbons had deteriorated and trees had grown up quickly, destroying the wire barriers.

To make things worse, the locals, who thought they were helping, cleared some of the mined areas themselves, disposing of the mines by throwing them in the river, where they settled into the silt on the floor of the river. With the coming of the rainy seasons, the silt and mud – along with some of the mines – were washed downstream to rest in the shallows at the seashore. There they sat, waiting for a child to jump in for a cool afternoon swim, or a mother's helper to wade into the shallows to get a bucket of water.

I had seen the result of these mines in Honduras and Guatemala as well. The troops traversed the jungle trails in the daytime, and the enemy would mine the trails before the soldiers returned in the evening, resulting in devastating loss of life and limbs. There were hundreds of young men at the hospitals and the rehab centers who had lost one or both legs to these mines.

Many of the children could not be treated in this very primitive and limited facility. As we had done in the northern villages, we took their names, photographed them, and gave the mothers enough money so that they could travel to León or Chinandega, where we would be able to provide the surgical care they needed.

We were hot, tired, and thirsty, and were grateful when several of the young men climbed the coconut palms and with their machetes, sent a number of coconuts to the ground below. We then used a spiked spear-like stick placed in the sand to split the hard outer shell. Others used their machetes. The coconut milk was cool and thirst quenching, and most importantly it was safe to drink.

After Kambla, we continued south along the coast, stopping at a couple more villages. By this time, our bodies were covered as if we had been painted by the red clay dust that the delightful breeze from the Caribbean was blowing across our path. The fisherman were returning, carrying hand-woven baskets of freshly caught fish on their heads, and I enjoyed watching them as they hung their nets up to dry.

As we continued down the coast, there were small shallow streams, and the Jeeps easily forded these. But as we approached the estuary of the Likus River that emptied into the Laguna Karatá near the village of Karatá, our next destination, the banks of the river were too steep and the water too deep to cross with the Jeep. Alonzo drove parallel with the river for several hundred yards and then stopped.

"Are we lost?" I asked.

"No," said Alonzo. "I am surveying for a spot where we can cross the river." He drove a little further along this route, and then stopped again.

Two trees had fallen and their trunks lay across the river from shore to shore. They had been cleared of all branches. The trunks were not more than eighteen inches to two feet at the most in width, and they seemed solidly embedded in the red clay to either side. Turning to me, Alonzo said, "This is where we cross."

Seeing the puzzled expression on my face, he explained, "We will put the Jeep in low gear, then slowly bump onto the logs, and drive across to the opposite side. The other driver can follow my lead."

On this leg of the journey, Bob and I had switched places, with me riding shotgun and Bob in the back seat with Lori. Bob seemed very excited with the driver's plan, and exclaimed, "I gotta get this on film!"

Knowing better than to get between Bob and his intended shoot, I responded by saying, "Hold up! I'm getting out." I grabbed my camera and jumped from the Jeep without even bothering to open the door, barely in time to avoid being stampeded by our greatly inspired photographer.

Lori said, "I think I will join Dr. Agris on this side, and walk across the logs and meet the Jeep on the other side." She hesitated for a minute before adding, "Hopefully."

Alonzo geared down slowly, bumped the front tires about six inches off the ground onto the trunks of the two logs that lay across the river, and then gunned the engine as the rear wheels followed in a similar manner. He then put the pedal to the metal, accelerated across the logs, and suddenly stopped.

Lori and I sat on the far bank confused, but then we saw Bob climb over the seat. Alonzo lowered the windshield and Bob crossed on to the hood of the Jeep and then stepped onto the bumper and down to the ground. He walked about thirty feet away from the Jeep as it sat suspended on the logs over the river. I then realized what he was trying to accomplish. He wanted to shoot some video of the Jeep at ground level, showing the tires on the logs, the stream below, and the river flowing beneath. What a great shot. It was a classic Bob Dows maneuver. That's why he was such a great cameraman.

Bob was now lying parallel on the ground, camera rolling as he gave Alonzo the high sign. Alonzo gunned the engine, and the tires almost flew off of the logs and into the air as he came off the tree trunks several feet up, and then landed on the hard-packed clay with several bounces, hitting the brakes and swerving around Bob. But Bob didn't even flinch, and kept the camera rolling. Lori and I just looked at each other in amazement. I offered to take her hand so she could walk across on one log, with me on the other, helping to steady her as we crossed. She would have none of it. She tucked her notebook into her purse, slung her purse over her shoulder, and sat down on the log. In that sitting position she scooted herself across to the opposite side. We were smiling and then laughing as she progressed, and when she reached the far bank, Alonzo, who had left the Jeep, reached out and pulled her to her feet as she stepped off the log onto the red clay soil.

The driver of the second Jeep had watched closely and then followed Alonzo's example, driving carefully over the logs without incident. I'm sure this was much to the relief of his passengers. And my Nikon had been clicking away the entire time, getting still photos of our Jeep on the bridge and then Lori doing the scoot as she crossed. I had then slung the heavy Nikon over my shoulder and let it hang down my back as I climbed up on to the log. I'd gotten my balance and then quick-stepped across the bridge to the opposite bank. All I could think of was that we needed to do the same in reverse to get out of here, and that we needed to do it fairly soon so we wouldn't be attempting such a tricky maneuver in the dark.

Alonzo had clearly been enjoying Lori's and my antics as we crossed the log bridge. After he'd helped us back into the Jeep, he turned back to the group and said, "We are only minutes away from the town of Karatá." From there, we would continue south to our last stop.

Miracles in Bedlam

The area around the laguna was marshy, and insects buzzed everywhere. The foliage was thick and jungle-like. There were howler monkeys high in the trees, as well as what seemed like a million birds, including parrots with stunning multicolored feathers. It was a photographer's delight.

The bushes nearby rustled, and out of the corner of my eye I glimpsed something scurrying along the ground in the underbrush. I leaned out of the Jeep to try to take a photo, but the small animal – whatever it was – disappeared into the dense forest before I could get a photograph.

As the Jeep entered the center of the village, a crowd began to gather. The homes were very similar to those in the previous villages we had visited, but for some reason these seemed even more squalid than their neighbors. The buildings flanked the road in a semi-circle. The odor of wet charred wood from outdoor cooking fires hung heavily in the air. Clothes were drying on lines stretched between some of the wooden buildings and hung over low bushes to either side.

Alonzo had forgotten to put the windshield back up after Bob had stepped out to photograph the river crossing. As we disembarked from the Jeep, the crowd that had gathered was giggling and pointing at us. I looked at Alonzo and Bob, and they turned and looked at me, and almost simultaneously we began to laugh. With our faces covered by the heavy coating of red clay dust, we must have looked like something out of a Zombie movie.

Alonzo spoke in the Miskito language with the town's elder, who led us to an outdoor washing area where there were several concrete tubs filled with clear water. I was wearing a set of operating room greens, and since the Jeep had protected me only from the waist down, from the waist up I was a beautiful dark red color. I pulled off my top and washed in the sink, using it to remove the clay powder that covered my face and arms. I then turned the shirt inside out and put it back on. There was a broken pane of glass mirror hanging above one of the wash tubs, and when I looked into it, I saw that my hair was still thickly coated with the red clay dust. I'd sometimes wondered what I would look like as a redhead, and now I knew. I can't say that the look was really the best one for me, but washing my hair would have to wait until we returned to Puerto Cabezas, where I could again stand under the deliciously cold outdoor shower.

A strong wind was blowing from the coast, and the sky was full of dark, dust-laden clouds. "I'm afraid we are in for a heavy evening rainstorm," I said to no one in particular.

After greetings from the town council, we immediately went to the small clinic and began treating the children and some adults as well. Mr. Dixon and I did the histories, physicals, examinations, and when necessary, photographs. Carolyn and Barrett administered the polio vaccines and other immunizations. Meanwhile, Alonzo and the other driver washed the red clay dust off the Jeeps and refilled the tanks from the metal five-gallon gas cans that were strapped to the bumpers. As soon as clinic was finished, we would be on to our final stop only a few minutes' drive away, to the village of Wawa. We were now down to our last two boxes of medical supplies and vaccines, and I was hoping there would be enough to treat everyone in the small village just south of us.

Once our work was finally done, we got handshakes, hugs, and gifts of plantains, coconuts, and dried fish, all of which we gratefully accepted and placed in the empty containers in the back of each Jeep. As we left the village, a crowd of laughing, barefoot children ran alongside the Jeeps, waving and shouting to us.

The sky had darkened and the wind coming off the Caribbean had increased. The red clay dust was swirling around us, and I tied a bandana over my face, as did Alonzo. As we continued south along the coast, the wind began to buffet the Jeeps and the blowing red sand dust was obstructing our vision. The drivers were moving more slowly as they picked their way along this sandy, pothole-riddled track. The air grew increasingly humid as we continued through the delta of the Laguna Karatá. Then, the clouds parted momentarily, and we could see a break in the dense jungle that looked like a low-lying meadow of marsh grass.

As the heat and humidity increased even more, we were again covered in red clay dust. I fought to ignore the salty sweat that was running into and burning my eyes, as well as the mosquitoes that were buzzing around my ears. At this point, I was actually hoping that we would get a good thunderstorm to drive the mosquitoes away, but I was soon to be reminded of the maxim, "Be careful what you wish for."

The village of Wawa came into view, and our drivers closed the gap between the village and us quickly. We were greeted with an excited crowd, beating drums, waving, and shouting. Alonzo asked one of the locals if there was a covered area under which he and the other driver could park our Jeeps. We were directed to a wood storage shed that was usually used to dry fish but was empty at this time. Two young men pulled back the two large wooden doors, and we drove right in.

At that moment, a couple of bolts of lightning struck the metal sheets that formed the roof, followed almost immediately by an earth-shattering clap of thunder. As we exited the Jeeps, large drops of rain began to fall, and before long the area was being pounded by rain. A squall had drifted in from the coast, bringing with it puffs of cool air. While that afforded us some reprieve from the heat, the storm wasn't going to make it easy for us to get our work done. There was more lightning and another earsplitting peal of thunder, and the wind was now gusting all around us. Alonzo shouted over the thunder and bellowing wind for us to follow him. The storm was quickly growing worse, and as we gathered our supplies and equipment and followed Alonzo, I couldn't help thinking that if the Cubans or Sandinistas didn't nail us, and the mosquitoes didn't get us, the weather just might.

CHAPTER 32
Big Dogs

We each grabbed one of the plastic boxes with our needed medical supplies, ignoring the rain and running to the clinic. As we were running, the thunder echoed through the jungle and bolts of lightning lit up the rooftops over the village. Fortunately it seemed that the storm was passing harmlessly above us – for now, anyway.

As we ran, thunder echoed through the jungle, and another bolt of lightning reflected off the rooftops in the village. We were now beginning to slip and slide on the wet clay, which had become as slippery as an ice skating rink. As we approached the clinic, the thunderstorm raged on, and just as we reached the relative safety of the interior, Carolyn gasped loudly, apparently startled by something other than the storm. I turned to ask her what was wrong, but she had already dashed out the doorway into the storm.

Just as I was about to holler for her to come back in, I saw the little girl, frozen in her tracks, standing in the tempest, holding a plastic bucket over her head and crying. Apparently, one of our little patients must have gotten left behind or lost in the crowd as the rain started. Carolyn ran full tilt from the clinic to where the terrified girl stood and scooped her up, shouting, "You're not supposed to be out here!" Turning back toward the clinic, it only took Carolyn a couple of seconds before she and her little charge were standing inside. Even though Carolyn's face was drenched from the downpour, one look at her and I saw that it was she, and not the frightened little girl, who was crying now.

The clinic nurse pulled the hand-woven curtains across the windows to keep the blowing rain out. The clinic was packed, but everyone was in an upbeat mood, and the cool ocean breeze that accompanied the storm was very welcomed. The lightning show was incredible as it flashed across the sky. But it was scary as well; who knew where it might strike next?

I saw a few villagers running down the path outside the clinic, and asked the nurse where they were headed. She told us that they were going to a small chapel at the end of the road. The chapel had a steeple, which was the tallest structure in the area and had been struck by lightning in years past.

I parted the curtain and leaned my elbows on the window frame, gazing out at the storm. On impulse, I thrust my head and arms out into the rain, allowing it to wash the red clay dust from me. It felt delightful, and I found myself laughing at the simple pleasure. Then lightning flashed again, followed by a sharp thunderclap that drowned out the sounds of my laughter. Following this, a surge of electricity flashed through the air again, causing the wooden building to shake.

But the rain and thunderstorm were not going to discourage or dissuade us. We had taken an instant liking to these brave, independent, and openhearted people, and we were not going to be chased away by a thunderstorm. We weren't leaving until we had accomplished what we'd come here to do.

Carolyn and Mr. Dixon began lining the children up in a semi-circle around the perimeter of the clinic building, while Barrett and I began the routine of taking histories and performing examinations. We followed by taking photographs of children who would have to be sent to León or Chinandega for their surgical procedures.

The rain and lightning flashes began to subside, and the old midwife, who also acted as the village nurse, just shrugged, altogether unconcerned with the weather outside as she helped herd the children in an orderly line for their examinations and immunizations. She folded her ample arms across her chest and said, "Your work and kindness are much appreciated. You have taken a great risk coming to the Miskito Coast, maybe at the risk of your lives."

Mr. Dixon answered her slowly and deliberately in Spanish, "We felt it was the right thing to do. We believe that God is on our side."

The old woman looked straight into Dixon's eyes, and speaking softly, her voice quivering with emotion, she said, "We will never forget you for what you have done here! Never!"

Mr. Dixon was about to reply when the midwife put both arms around him, nearly suffocating him, then pinched him on each cheek, her face beaming with a delightful smile that made her, by any measure, beautiful. At that moment, I was overcome by my admiration for the woman and for the Miskito Indian people. Despite their profound poverty and the relentless assaults on their land and their culture, they held tight to the things that truly mattered, and did their best to not let their challenges dampen their spirit.

Carolyn broke my trance when she said, "Have a look outside."

The rain squall had stopped as suddenly as it had arrived, which allowed us to move some of our little patients outside to an adjacent small room, giving us the space we needed to work within this small facility. The clinic then progressed quickly, as Dixon and Alonzo fielded questions in Spanish and the Miskito dialect from anxious mothers.

We had just finished with our last patient when we heard a sudden racket coming from the laguna. Having grown up on a lake and having built a racing skiff, as well as owning a boat that we had used for water skiing, I was very familiar with the sound of high-powered outboard engines. Clearly the villagers were equally familiar. While the few remaining children remained playful and compliant, the facial features of the mothers and the other adults had suddenly changed to those of deep concern, even fear.

Looking out over the water, I could see a sleek fiberglass skiff barely skimming the surface of the water, heading into the laguna. They gunned the motor, then killed it as the skiff was run up onto the beach, and then everything went silent.

"We've got trouble," I muttered. I knew that the only people in this area who owned boats of this caliber were either drug runners or the gun runners who were still supplying the Sandinistas.

The day had become even hotter and more humid, and the sun had reappeared for the moment, although dark clouds were still threatening from the north. I noticed that the children were not playing hide and seek in the tall grassy fields, as children in these areas normally did, but instead were all playing along the banks of the river. Because of the rain, the river was high at this moment and had been turned red by the sandy clay that had been washed into it by the storm. My mind momentarily wandering, I thought, *The mothers shouldn't let their kids be playing so close to the river when it's so high.* I noticed that there were small rocky pools where some of the older children sat on the side and fished.

As if reading my thoughts, Alonzo said, "You can see that the water is red from the mud, and very fast moving. Several feet of fast water – that's enough to knock a person off his feet. The red clay is very slippery, and a person who is knocked over will not be able to get back up again. And a car attempting to cross it will lose traction and be swept away."

I replied, "We will stay until evening, and if the rain stays away and the sun comes out for any length of time, the roads should be drier and more manageable. If not, we'll just have to stay in the village overnight." Alonzo nodded and then walked a few yards away to talk to some of the locals.

Dixon and Barrett walked up to us just as I was making that last remark to Alonzo, and Dixon said, "But now we have a more immediate problem."

I nodded, and Barrett reached into his boot and to my surprise removed a 9mm Beretta. So Alonzo and I weren't the only ones who were armed. With his pistol in hand, Barrett drew the slide partially open and checked to see that there was a round in the chamber. His manner was quick and decisive. I raised my pants leg and revealed the Glock I had tucked away in my boot.

Dixon looked at Barrett and me with an expression that seemed to say, *What is this? The O.K. Corral?*

Seeing the expression on his face, I said, "We'll be all right. I really don't expect to have to shoot anybody; it's for self-defense."

Barrett nodded in agreement, saying, "Same here."

Dixon asked, "You really think we will need to defend ourselves? You think they'll have guns?" But he already knew the answer. Of course they would have guns.

"We're going to go meet them," I said. "We're not going to brandish our weapons, but we need to get the upper hand from the beginning." Both Barrett and I put our guns back into our boots, and the three of us began walking purposefully towards the laguna where the boat had landed.

"Clearly they've spotted us," whispered Dixon as we drew closer to the men.

"Of course," I said. "But let's stick with the plan. We have several things in our favor. We will surprise them. They don't expect Americans – much less a TV crew – to be way out here. These types of people like to remain anonymous. They are not looking for attention or anything that could result in international retributions. They are the big dogs here, and know that the wrong type of attention could take that away from them. The local villagers run and hide when they come. We won't. We are going to walk briskly, backs straight and heads held high, looking them in the eye. That's the one thing they are not expecting."

Dixon said, "They probably have automatic weapons, and all you two have are your little pistols."

"Our aggressiveness is going to be a façade," I said. "We're going to show strength and unity, and our words will be our bullets."

Dixon said, "I hope we can pull it off."

"No worries," I said. "We'll be fine." But I was not nearly as confident as I sounded. I knew I was knowledgeable and skilled, and had a pretty good awareness of what was really going on here. And I was typically quick to respond to any situation. But armed gunmen and drug runners were not the types of "situations" I was used to handling.

As we neared the visitors, I noticed that the beach was deserted of villagers. The locals had all disappeared into the jungle or fled to their homes.

I knew that whoever could control the situation from the start would prevail. I looked at Barrett striding alongside me. The tall, good-looking Barrett had no problem pulling off the assertiveness façade, with his muscular physique that made him look more like an athlete or bodyguard than a medical professional. Dixon was not so formidable looking, and I could tell he was very skeptical about the action we were now taking. He kept in step with Barrett and me as we approached the boat, but I could see on his face that he was nervous, to put it mildly.

As we approached, one of the men stayed in the skiff, his arm resting on the wheel, watching us intently. I noticed that his arm was wrapped in a bloodstained, dirty bandage, and that he had a scar across the left side of his face from his ear almost to the corner of his mouth. He looked scared. We could see he had a pistol tucked in his belt, but he made no moves to remove it. He was much younger than the other two men, and had a head of dark, curly hair and the beginnings of what he probably hoped would soon be a mustache.

The other two men were slowly approaching us. They unslung their automatic weapons, but carried them across their bodies in an unthreatening manner. One man was thin and hollow-cheeked; with high cheekbones and dark, deep-set eyes. There was an angry expression on his face... or was it mere puzzlement? I couldn't really say.

The man to his left seemed to be the *jefe* (the boss). He was a large, solidly built man who looked to be in his forties. His shaved head was shiny, high-domed, and sun-burned; his cheeks were full, and his brows were thick and bristly. As he approached us, he opened his eyes wide against the glow of the sun and stared directly at the three of us as we continued walking toward him. His feet sank deep into the loose sand, and his gait was that of a man accustomed to command and determined to remain in control.

We continued to advance. We must have presented a curious image to him, dressed as we were in our O.R. scrubs and white lab coats, and me wearing my customary pair of well-broken-in Lucchese boots and Stetson hat.

I was alert as a wolf, surveying and trying to read their body language and facial features. I was intensely aware of the potential volatility of our situation, and I had to make sure the confrontation did not turn ugly. I was tense, but determined not to lose my nerve as we confronted the visitors.

The big man re-slung his weapon, and a big smile appeared on his face. For a moment I thought he was going to laugh out loud; then he pointed to me and said, in broken English, "You are cowboy doctor."

Mr. Dixon answered him in Spanish, "No, he is Doctor Angel from Chinandega, the doctor with the miracle baby."

The two men suddenly stopped in their tracks, looking dubious.

We were now only a few feet apart from the visitors, who seemed to be contemplating their next move. Suddenly, the big man took two steps forward, then grabbed me in a huge bear hug, literally lifting me off the ground, whereupon he kissed me on both cheeks and set me gently back down.

Barrett took a defensive stand, but I waved him off.

"We listen to the radio and to the drums," the man said. "You are the famous Doctor Angel. Are these your assistants?"

Dixon took the lead and in Spanish made formal introductions.

The big man abruptly took the automatic weapon from his partner, and slid the strap over his shoulder, then pushed him forward to shake hands with each of us. He then waved us on toward the boat to meet the injured man.

As I walked across the sand toward the boat, I felt a stab of anxiety, and tried to remind myself why I was here instead of safely back home in Houston. But as we approached, the young man broke into a delighted smile. At the same time, he was staring at the three of us as if in a bit of a quandary.

The big man, the *jefe*, the boss, indicated for him to climb out of the boat, and when he did the boss made introductions. The young man told us he had been born on the Miskito Coast and knew every inlet and cove, and had therefore been given the position of the boat's pilot. His English was quite good, and he did not need Mr. Dixon to translate.

I could now see that the entire back of the skiff was filled with boxes and crates, with a tarp pulled over them, partially concealing the load. I immediately averted my eyes, but a sudden glare from the big man seemed to indicate that I had already seen more than I was supposed to see. Not for the first time on this trip, I thought, *Well, there's no backing out now.*

CHAPTER 33
The Man In The Door

Doing my best to ignore the glare of the *jefe*, I leaned back against the hull of the skiff and asked the young pilot, whose name was Juan, if he would like me to examine and treat his wound and apply a new dressing. He nodded, and as I examined the wound he talked about growing up on the Miskito Indian coast. He repeated that he'd been traveling this coast since he was a teenager with his uncle, and that he knew every cove, laguna, and rock on the coast for miles around. Now, he said, he piloted the skiff himself.

I was hesitant to ask him how he'd been injured, but he volunteered the information that he had been cut with a machete. Knowing the customs and traditions of this part of the world, I was aware of the cause of many machete wounds. I said to the young man, "Was she beautiful? Was she really worth it?" I couldn't help thinking of Michael and his scorpion sting. As the old song goes, "love wounds and mars." And it isn't always just the heart that bears the scars of love.

The others in our little group started to laugh, and I could see the color rise in the wounded man's cheeks. We had embarrassed him, but that was my intent in asking. It was a diversionary tactic that apparently worked, for the *jefe* was no longer glaring at me. The tension had passed for the time being.

The *jefe's* other companion said, "She was very young and very beautiful. Her father caught them, and Juan did not run fast enough."

Finding it hard not to laugh again, I said to Juan, "We need to get you to the clinic." Then I put my arm around him. But he had suddenly grown quiet and seemed anxious; clearly he did not entirely trust me yet. His companions, however, were now pushing him forward, and I continued to lead him toward the clinic with my arm across his shoulders. As I walked I told him, "I am not going to hurt you, I just don't want you to get an infection and end up having your arm amputated. You don't want that. Have you ever had a tetanus shot?"

"No, we don't have such things here."

"I have antibiotics and tetanus vaccine with me at the clinic in the village."

He still seemed hesitant; he stopped and rocked back on his heels a moment, but his two companions urged him on. I felt a surge of sympathy for him. He was so young, and he obviously did not know what to expect. He was a bundle of unchecked emotion: fear and doubt, not to mention embarrassment about the cause of his injury.

I said, "We have all been in that situation when we were younger."

His expression brightened a little and he said, "Even you, Doctor?"

I laughed, responding, "Sure, but I was able to run fast."

Juan said, "Are you serious?"

"Absolutely. Beautiful young women can make us crazy, but I have learned my lesson. I am an old man and can't run so fast anymore."

That broke the tension for Juan, and there was more laughter and back slapping as we approached the clinic. As we entered the clinic I stamped my feet to remove the sand from my boots.

Jefe commented, "Your boots are beautiful, I like them very much. I would take them for myself but they are too small for me."

I asked him if I should take that as a compliment or a threat, and the big man just smiled and patted me on the shoulder.

The other members of my team were still in the clinic, along with the village nurse and several of the children. They all looked up as we entered with the strangers. I motioned for Juan to sit in the chair at the far end of the room, and I told Carolyn that Juan had incurred a machete injury. I asked her to get the large scissors and cut off the dirty, bloodstained dressings. She said to him, "I do not mean to be indiscreet, but is the young lady okay?"

Juan replied, "I cannot say. When I saw her father with the machete I just ran. But not quite fast enough, as you can see." He looked a little embarrassed again.

"Any guess as to where she is now?"

"Home, I guess. She was probably given a beating with a switch."

After removing the dressing, we poured peroxide over the wound, which bubbled away the crusted dry blood. The wound margins were gaping, but there was no sign of redness or streaks extending from it, and it looked quite clean. I told Juan he was going to need some stitches, then turned and nodded to Carolyn. I motioned to the others to move aside, then removed a bottle of xylocaine – a local anesthetic – from the shelf and filled the syringe.

As I approached Juan I gave Carolyn another nod, and she gently but firmly grabbed his hand and forearm, holding it steady as I injected the anesthetic to either side of the wound. We are a good and practiced team, and it went so fast that he didn't realize what had happened until I had already removed the needle. Almost immediately, his pain was gone, and he kept touching the wound margins, which were now numb.

Carolyn explained to Juan that she was going to wash the wound and scrub it with surgical soap, and he was not to touch it anymore. She told him that if he did, she was going to tie his other hand to the arm of the chair. You could tell by looking at her face that she meant it.

He paused, took a deep breath, and said, "*Si, si.*"

I put on a pair of gloves, removed the scalpel from the surgical kit, and standing in a position that would block Juan's view of his wound, I trimmed away several millimeters on either side of the wound, creating clean margins. Carolyn then irrigated the wound several times. Since it had been untreated for three days, I sutured it first at the distal (far) end, then at the slightly inflamed proximal (near) end, leaving a small gap in the center so the wound could drain. Carolyn then applied antibiotic ointment and we dressed it.

When we were done, Juan broke into a delightful smile and began profusely thanking everybody. I handed him a small envelope with some antibiotic pills and explained to him when and how he should take them, warning him to take all of them without stopping.

As he and his companions left the clinic, several ladies came forward with woven baskets on their heads and offered the men plantains and dried fish. They took some items and gave the women some money, then continued back towards their boat on the beach. But as they retreated, the *jefe* turned around once more and gave me a look that, while not a glare, was clearly a warning. I gave him a nod and a smile that I hoped would convey the message that he had nothing to worry about. We weren't there to bust up drug rings. We were there to help and to heal. He apparently got my message, and smiled at me before turning back to his men. Very shortly afterwards, we heard the roar of the motor, and the boat sped away.

* * * * *

There were still storm clouds overhead, vying with the sun, which seemed to be losing the contest. The afternoon remained dark, gloomy, and threatening, but when I consulted with Alonzo, he said that he felt it was safe to leave. I was relieved, because I was still planning on leaving from Puerto Cabezas at daybreak the next morning.

We said our goodbyes to the tribal elders and gave the children all the remaining lollipops and small toys we had. As we were leaving, a few scattered drops of rain began splattering the windshields of the Jeeps. Looking at me, Alonzo said, "Don't worry. We should be okay." The Jeeps were once again bouncing over the red clay road. They rode high, and I knew we would be all right as long as we didn't run into another deluge. Nevertheless, Alonzo and the other driver were moving more slowly on the return. We all appreciated that, since these primitive roads were now very slippery, and a skid off the road would leave us stranded, with little hope of assistance.

The drive was uneventful until we came back to the dreaded log bridge. The Jeeps would once again have to bounce up on the logs and cross the narrow, fast moving river below. But this time, the logs were wet and the wheels of the vehicles were covered with slippery red clay. Though I kept these thoughts to myself, to say that I was anxious was an understatement.

Alonzo stopped just before the bridge. He backed up and then slowly began to move forward to align the wheels with the two tree trunks. I decided that I would like to get some photos of our Jeep coming across the bridge from the opposite side, so I asked Alonzo to stop, and told him that I would walk across the bridge and take the photos as the vehicles came towards me. Lori looked at the red mud and decided that she wanted to stay dry and remain in the Jeep this time, as did Bob.

I took my boots off and got out of the Jeep in my bare feet with my camera slung over my shoulder, stepping up onto the log and slowly inching my way across its wet surface. Then I continued another hundred feet, whereupon I found a grassy spot where I could kneel down and take photos.

Alonzo, now having lined the wheels up with the two tree trunks, backed up about ten feet, gunned the engine, and bounced the Jeep onto the logs. My heart seemed to stop for a moment when he did that. The wheels bounded up and landed successfully, centered directly over the two logs, and he proceeded across slowly. As he reached the far side, the nose of the Jeep dipped as it dropped almost a foot, back onto the clay bottom. I heard Alonzo down-shifting the gears until the wheels gained traction in the wet red clay. At once, it began to move slowly forward. He pulled up alongside of me and I climbed back into the Jeep. Lori found a rag under the seat, which I used to wipe the red clay from my feet before slipping back into my boots. Meanwhile, the other Jeep also made a safe crossing.

I took in a deep breath and slowly let it out. I had been really concerned about Alonzo's maneuver, to say the least, but he had handled it very well. Plus, I'd gotten some good photos as the Jeep inched its way across on the log bridge. It wasn't an adventure I wanted to repeat any time soon, but I was glad I'd gotten pictures. And we were now safely on our way back to Puerto Cabezas.

Upon our arrival, the drivers took us directly to the sawmill, where we unloaded the cameras and supplies. Then we men slowly dragged ourselves up the stairs to the second level, and went to our respective rooms, while the ladies went on to their quarters at the Red Cross center. I knew we would have to pack our gear and take it over to the Red Cross compound as soon as possible, but I needed to take a short breather. I sat in the rocking chair and stared out the window, but instead of relaxing, all I could do was contemplate the looming threat of another vigilante mob in the evening. I thought to myself, *Well, God willing, we will be on our way back to Managua before daybreak.* But the thought didn't really offer much comfort.

It was barely seven in the evening, but it looked like midnight. The rainstorm was coming in from the Caribbean coast, and the clouds were heavy and dark. *This could actually work to our advantage,* I thought.

My energy suddenly seemed completely sapped, and no wonder. We had just put in a sixteen-plus-hour day, dealing with precarious roads, dangerous weather, and potentially hostile drug runners, in addition to all the patients we'd seen and treated. Overall, I was satisfied with what we had accomplished in Puerto Cabezas and the villages to the north and south. I felt that for the most part, we had accomplished the objectives that had brought us here, and we had done so despite the tense and sometimes dangerous circumstances – not to mention the weather. So there was that.

I almost began to relax, but then, seemingly against my will, my brain hit the reset button and the troublesome thoughts of a vigilante mob popped up again. I gently rubbed my eyes and closed them, but even with my eyes closed, my mind did not turn off. If anything, it went into high gear, with my thoughts racing on even faster. There were some things we hadn't been able to accomplish. We didn't know if the Cubans were really gone. We still didn't even know where the police chief was, and we were no closer to knowing than we had been on previous evenings. I had the frustrating and downright creepy feeling that I was up against a wall.

I opened and closed my eyes again, gently rubbing them, then blinked several times. As I pulled my hands away, I noticed for the first time that they were still stained with the red clay from the Jeep ride back to Puerto Cabezas. There was no telling what my eyes looked like after all of that rubbing. I had thought my brain was overworked, which was probably the case, but clearly it was not anywhere near ready to shut down. That was just as well, as I knew I needed to get my things packed and over to the Red Cross compound. Despite the urgency of that task, however, my breathing finally slowed and I began to get lost in a fog. My exhaustion won out at last, and I fell into an uneasy, dreamless sleep.

My slumber was interrupted by a very loud pounding on the door. Before I could move, I heard the hinges loudly squeaking as the door slowly opened. Still in a fog, I wondered, *Am I dreaming this, or am I really awake?* I lifted my head and in the dim light of the room I saw the silhouette of a large male. I was awake, all right.

I dared not move. The room was dark, and the moonlight that would normally be shining through the window was obscured by heavy cloud cover. I could hear the wind howling fiercely as the rain pummeled the tin roof. Cursing myself for having let my guard down and drifting off to sleep, I returned my focus to the man now standing just inside the room, my hand slowly reaching for the Glock in my boot.

CHAPTER 34
The Last Night

With my vision limited by the darkness in the room, my other senses had shifted into overdrive, and a melange of aromas filled my nostrils, with the overriding smell being a mix of beer and sweat. Just as I was about to draw the Glock from its hiding place, the man stepped forward, close enough that I could better make out his features. To my great relief, I saw that it was the mayor. Just as I was able to make out his smiling visage, he handed me an ice-cold bottle of *cerveza*. I did not immediately take a drink. Instead, weak with relief but dripping with sweat, I ran the cold bottle across my forehead and down my neck. The mayor took a long pull from his own bottle, turned, and with his empty hand slammed the door closed behind him, which only slightly diminished the raucous sound of the rain and wind outside.

Sitting down in the rocking chair in the corner of the room and offering him the only other chair, I asked him, "Where are the others?"

The mayor sat down, took another long swig from his beer, and ran his sleeve across his lips. "Everyone has been moved into the Red Cross compound. You are the last one to leave. We will enjoy our cold beers together, and when the rain subsides I will help you move as well. You and the team will be safe there."

"You're sure we'll be safe?"

"As safe as you can be in these circumstances."

"What else have you found out?" I asked him, taking a swig from my own bottle. Fully awake now, I continued, "I'm thinking that maybe instead of spending the rest of the night at the Red Cross, we should just leave now, while we can."

"The pilot cannot take off in this weather," the mayor said. "However, rain squalls are short-lived, and in a few hours the skies should clear. I don't recommend leaving before daybreak as you had originally planned, but I promise you that with the rising of the sun we will have you aboard the aircraft and on your way back to Managua. For now, get yourself moved over to the Red Cross compound, and you and the team can all wait together."

I thought to myself that I was more than ready to leave. I was feeling antsy, and wished we could leave now, but knew that the mayor was right when he said we needed to wait. I offered up a silent prayer that God would see us home safely in the morning.

"How are you feeling now?" the mayor asked.

"Alive. That's about it. But I'll be fine after I get some rest. That short power nap really helped."

"You call it a power nap," said the mayor, "but anyone could have come in here and shot you or slashed your throat while you were napping. You're lucky it was me who intruded on your 'power nap.'"

I looked alarmed, and he laughed, indicating that he was at least halfway kidding me.

"*You're* lucky you made yourself known when you did," I told him. "I was just reaching for my Glock." At this, we both chuckled.

The rain had diminished to a mere drizzle, followed by a dense fog coming from the bay. I slowly lifted myself out of the rocking chair.

The mayor said, "I have never seen you look so exhausted."

"It's my neck wound. It hurts, but I have felt worse. A lot worse. I guess now that the rain has subsided, we need to get my personal items and the medical equipment together and move them to the Red Cross compound."

It didn't take long for us to pack the equipment that was in my room, since most of it was still in the medical cases, and with the exception of my cameras, my personal items were in my single carry-on bag. As we left the room, I noticed that the rain had stopped, at least for the time being, but the fog had set in, obscuring the buildings across the street. The mayor said he expected the fog to remain for some time, and added that we might see another heavy downpour before the skies cleared.

We crossed with the equipment to the Red Cross compound. The guard opened the gate and then took one of the boxes from the mayor and carried it the rest of the way to the cantina. The medical team was all there, chatting as they ate their dinner. When the mayor and I entered, everyone fell silent. Scanning over the group, I felt I needed to speak to them, to deliver another message about preparedness. I began forcefully, but still trying to project calm assurance, stressing the urgency of our situation and my desire to ensure the safety of the team.

As my little speech progressed, I started talking faster and more forcefully. I thanked the team for the long hours and hard work. And I thanked the mayor and Red Cross staff for making it all possible. I felt like a real firebrand, waving my hands as I spoke. I was getting a few strange looks, but I didn't care; it seemed more important than ever for me to convey not only my gratitude to the team and to the mayor and volunteers, but also to emphasize my concerns for our safety. I ended my talk by repeating that everyone should leave out a change of clothes for the morning, that they should have everything else packed tonight, and that they were not to leave the Red Cross compound at all, for any reason. They all nodded in agreement.

My speech complete, the mayor and I joined the team for a dinner of chicken and rice, plantains, yucca, and sweetened tea. And of course there were baskets of homemade plantain chips and plenty of good cold *cerveza*.

As we ate, the mayor thanked us all for the medical care we had provided for the children of Puerto Cabezas and the surrounding villages. Then he said, "You may not fully realize the extent to which have brought peace to the Miskito Indian Coast. Although we still don't have all of the loose ends tied up, as you Americans might say, most of the Cubans and the Russian masters have left. And more importantly, with their leaving, the Sandinistas have lost their strongest base of support, and they know it. I cannot stress how much you have contributed to bringing an end to the civil war. You are all very brave. You have risked your lives and while it isn't over yet, you have done a lot of good." Then he turned to me and said, "And you, Doc, have risked your life more than once. It is almost as if you are not afraid to die."

"Well, I don't want to die, of course. I don't want any of my medical team members to die or be injured, but we can't allow ourselves to be consumed by a fear of death. As doctors and nurses, we see and deal with it every day, but we have to assume that we are not yet finished playing our parts in the game."

The mayor said, "You put that angel on your shoulder to the test on this trip."

I said, "Yes, and she has come through for us so far. Look, I didn't anticipate many of the scenarios that took place. And yes, the team and I still feel like we are in the middle of it. But I don't do self-pity, and they don't either. And I don't sugar coat anything either."

Several members of my team nodded and laughed. I gave them a feigned stern look, and they laughed even louder.

Shaking his head, the mayor said, "I think I know one thing that really motivates you. You strike me as a person who doesn't like to lose."

It was my turn to laugh as I said, "You got me there. My brain is not wired to accept losing. My team is made up entirely of winners. In surgery, you only get one chance to do it right. It's the same in life, and people have to be held accountable for their actions."

The mayor's face suddenly brightened and he pushed back his chair and briskly left the cantina. Not knowing what he was up to, I shrugged and continued eating, suddenly remembering again that I was starving.

When the mayor returned in a few minutes, I studied him.

"What's wrong?" I asked.

"What do you mean?" the mayor said, all innocence and light.

"Why did you leave in the middle of our dinner?"

From behind his back he produced a bottle of Flor de Caña, and with some force slammed it down on the table, the sound echoing through the cantina. The mayor raised both hands and shouted, "You have no obligations in the morning. You will be leaving early. We are very pleased with what you have done. You have faced dangers and had a successful outcome. We will toast this success tonight."

He uncorked the bottle and poured the ice tea from his glass into an adjacent potted plant, then filled our glasses. He then got up and asked the Red Cross volunteers to bring glasses for everyone as he went from table to table with the bottle of rum, not taking no for an answer from anyone.

I was thoroughly enjoying myself, and my group clearly was as well. Tonight we had no qualms about indulging a little, as we'd had enough successes to earn a bit of indulgence. We had accomplished several important tasks, and despite obstacles and almost constant hazards, we had stuck to our mission and had come through, un-shot and mostly unscathed. Within a few hours, we would be on a flight back to Managua, leaving behind the subversive threats that surrounded us here in Puerto Cabezas.

But we would also be leaving friends, and right now, on our last night here, the mayor wanted to make a special toast. Even though my team and I were not heavy drinkers, tonight we had a good reason to participate. We deserved a party.

While we celebrated, we could hear people outside the compound chanting, along with the occasional burst of gunfire. It was a reminder that there was still much unrest, and that things could turn ugly pretty quickly. We wouldn't really be out of danger until we were safely on our flight out of here. Rarely have I so urgently wanted to leave a place, while at the same time longing to stay.

As the hour grew later, the ladies retired to their respective rooms, but Dixon, Bob, Barrett, the mayor, and I sat up and talked for a couple more hours about a return visit and other future plans. Finally, when the mayor could see that we were getting a bit bleary-eyed, he stood up and excused himself. It was time for him to return across the street to his home within the lumberyard.

I looked at my watch and saw how late it was; sunrise was less than three hours away. "I suggest we all try to get a few hours of sleep," I said. I walked the mayor to the stockade gate and thanked him, then returned to the cantina to find Bob, Barrett, and Dixon gone, and the cantina deserted. I put two chairs together, one to sit on and the other to rest my feet on. Maybe I could grab at least a couple of hours of shuteye.

Miracles in Bedlam

The unrest in the streets outside the compound continued until the wee hours. The much-threatened torching of the Cuban clinic compound didn't take place, but there had been enough noise and uncertainty to keep any of us from completely letting down our guard.

Yet as the streets grew quieter, I was finally able to drift off to sleep. Almost before I knew it I was awakened to the sound of an airplane propeller, which was soon joined by the blast of the air raid siren, as I'd requested. This told me that a plane was actively moving along the main street, warning the local citizens and any animals to clear the street. I ran and knocked on the doors to wake Bob, Barrett, Dixon and the others.

I was acutely uncomfortable; my bladder told me I needed to relieve myself, so I rushed outside to the latrine behind the cantina. Upon my return, the pilot had entered the compound and was waving frantically to me, shouting. "*Vamonos, vamonos. Andale, andale!*" ("Let's go, let's go. Hurry, hurry!")

I gave the pilot a thumbs-up, then headed back into the cantina, where I began to hustle everybody and their personal luggage out the door. The pilot already had the forward and rear luggage compartments open when the group arrived.

I retrieved my duffel bag and placed it in the front compartment, followed by Mr. Dixon's luggage. I also placed Lori's and Bob's luggage into the rear compartment and then offered to take the camera. Bob said he wanted to use it to take more aerial photos during the return trip.

Without the medical equipment and supplies, the compartments easily accommodated the personal luggage for the return trip. Minutes later we were all aboard and belted into our seats, while the air raid siren continued blasting its warning.

The pilot shouted over the sound of the engine, "I'm cleared for visual takeoff. The street is empty." He rolled the aircraft along the main street, increased power, and adjusted the flaps.

Then he increased the plane's speed rapidly, and from my seat I could see the trees at the end of the street coming at us far more quickly than I would have liked. My heart was pounding as we suddenly lifted at a sharp angle and cleared the buildings and the jungle in front of us – by only a very few feet, it seemed to me.

I turned to the pilot and said, "After that take-off I think we all need a drink."

He smiled and replied, "Sadly, I don't keep that stuff in the aircraft." He began to tune in the channels for the airport in Managua.

Ten minutes later we were cruising smoothly at about 20,000 feet. The pilot said, "This will easily take us over the volcanoes and mountain range below. Some of the volcanoes are smoking; you might want to photograph them through the side window." Bob paused to inspect and set his camera, and then began filming the landscape below.

I snapped a few pictures too, but spent most of the flight lost in my own thoughts and emotions. I was feeling a mixture of pride in our accomplishments on the Miskito coast, relief that we were all still in one piece, and profound sadness at having to leave this wild and beautiful region. But there was, as usual, plenty of work still to be done before we went back home to Houston.

* * * * *

I truly hadn't known what to expect when I first arrived in Nicaragua, and certainly the Miskito Indians' realm was an unknown quantity for all of us. What we found on the Caribbean coast was a stunning area that looked like an old Western frontier post, magically transplanted into a beautifully lush tropical rainforest. Big, wide porches with hand-carved mahogany rocking chairs. Wooden buildings raised on stilts with tin roofs. Thick jungle foliage that overtook everything. The unpaved red clay roads, and on dry days, the swirling clouds of red dust that coated everything. And the extreme isolation of the Miskito Coast and the small fishing villages. I know it was all very foreign and intimidating to some of my medical team members, especially those who had never before been to Third World countries.

But to a person, we all fell in love with the area, as we did with the entire country of Nicaragua, and most especially with the people. I do not think that I'm the only one on my team who feels that the Miskito Coast in particular has a way of getting under your skin and staying with you long after you've washed the red dust from your hair and returned to the "civilized" world.

PART 3

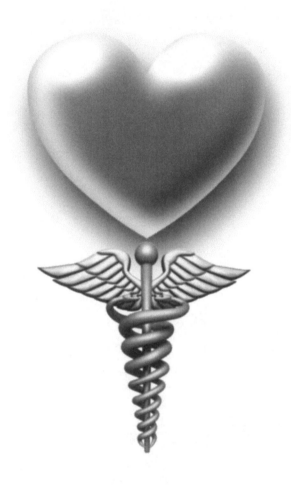

Love Wins

CHAPTER 35
The Unicorn Boy

In spite of my sadness about leaving Puerto Cabezas, I was relieved when at last we were landing safely, our adventures on the Miskito Coast behind us. As the flaps were at full and the pilot began to brake, I saw a black SUV sitting on the tarmac, its driver leaning casually against it and having a smoke as he watched the aircraft come in.

The pilot taxied off the runway and stopped only a few feet away from the SUV, then began his after-landing checklist and put in a call into the tower. A lineman ran out with flags in both hands, guiding him in even closer to the black SUV. The lineman then dropped the flags and ran to chock the nose wheel, as the pilot pulled the throttles to the shutoff position and the engine began to spool down.

Then the pilot climbed out of the cockpit and kicked down the folding stairs, allowing Bob Dows and me to de-plane. The SUV driver ran out and began unloading the luggage from the plane's rear compartment. We each grabbed one piece of luggage as well, and took it over to the car, where we left it for the driver to organize as he saw fit. As always, however, Bob insisted upon stowing his video camera himself.

When we were all seated and belted in, with me riding shotgun as usual, the driver turned and said, "Everyone is looking forward to your return. The doctors and students at the hospital are talking about nothing else but seeing you at work this coming week."

I nodded, and then without prompting from me, he added, "I saw Mr. Marvin Zindler at breakfast this morning and he is doing fine."

"That's great," I said. "I know he was worried about us."

"We will pick up Mr. Zindler at his hotel in Managua and then continue on to Chinandega. We should arrive there in about three hours if the roads remain open and we do not have too much traffic." He then mumbled something in Spanish about slow-moving donkey carts and wagons. I couldn't make out everything he was saying, but I could tell that his description was anything but complimentary.

I turned to him and said, "This is a much more comfortable ride than the Jeeps we have been in these last days, not to mention the red clay dust we have been covered with. Hugo and Haydee Holmann have always been very kind to provide us with the SUV for the trip to Chinandega."

"*Si*, and I am glad that Mr. Holmann and his wife sent me to pick you up. It is my pleasure to take the medical team to Chinandega. Doctor, just in case you were wondering, you will be staying again with Mr. Holmann's in-laws, Mr. and Mrs. Callejas, at their home in Chinandega."

I had been expecting as much and nodded. Then I asked him, "Do you happen to know how the other members of our medical team have been progressing while we were away?" While it may seem strange that I was asking a driver about what was going on with my team, I knew that he was privy to many goings-on around the hospital and clinic. In fact he was probably more aware than some of the hospital administrators of what was happening with the team and the mission. In my travels, I've found that you can never go wrong by making friends with drivers and bodyguards and other service providers.

And this driver did not disappoint me. In response to my question, he smiled and said, "*Si, Si*. I visited the hospital last week with Mrs. Holmann and a reporter from the *La Prensa* newspaper. The reporter was doing a follow-up story on the 'miracle baby,' as well as visiting with the post-op patients who had cleft lip, cleft palate and burn surgeries. I'm not a doctor but everyone seems to be doing fine. The children are fine and playing with each other. That's a good sign. Everyone is really pleased with the school supplies and toys your team brought. And they have a surprise for you, Doctor."

Having learned to be wary of surprises on these medical mission trips, I ventured a question, "May I ask what the surprise is? Will you give me a hint?"

"I'll give you more than a hint. They have a seven-year-old boy whose name is Eleazer Castillo. He is the most playful, energetic, outgoing, and smart child that I think I have ever met. However, he has a cleft lip, cleft palate and a tumor mass growing out of his forehead like a unicorn. No one seems to know what it is or how to deal with it. Everyone says that Dr. Angel will know what to do for Eleazer."

I asked, "Would you happen to know if they took any x-rays of the child's head?" Again I felt it couldn't hurt to ask him about this; he just might know. And as it happened, he did.

Miracles in Bedlam

"I heard one of your nurses, Kimberly I believe it was, suggest that," he said, "but there are no facilities for x-rays in Chinandega. Possibly at León, at the University Hospital. But I don't know if the radiology section is functioning or how well they can produce a film."

My mind was racing now. One of my areas of expertise in medical school and during my residency was in diagnosis. I always liked a good medical mystery. But at the Texas Medical Center, I had access to many diagnostic tests and different types of radiography, scans, and MRIs. In Chinandega, the diagnosis would be much less comprehensive, based solely upon the patient's history, a more rudimentary examination, and my personal experience. The diagnosis might only be a best guess.

I thought to myself, *We worked with the "miracle baby," and now I am being asked to produce another miracle with the "unicorn boy."* My bout of skepticism aside, I had to admit that I couldn't wait to examine little Eleazer. "I hope I am capable of solving the mystery," I said.

As we passed through the small towns and markets on our way to Chinandega, I turned my attention to taking more photos. The road, which paralleled the southwest side of Lago de Managua, bore witness to the effects of the rainy season, and the roadside was overgrown with bushes and a nearly unbroken treetop canopy.

The skies were clear and the temperature was continuing to rise, as was the humidity. Once again I found myself lost in the beauty of these jungle-like surroundings. I was so lost in my own thoughts and the loveliness of the countryside that I didn't realize some of my companions were trying to engage me in conversation until Lori startled me out of my reverie. I vaguely remember her asking, "What do you think?" Not snapping to the fact that she was talking to me, I said nothing, whereupon she leaned over the front seat and tapped me on the shoulder. I jumped, then glanced back at her.

"I'm sorry to have startled you," she said, "but Bob and I need to plan our schedule of filming and I thought you might be able to give us some idea as to what your plans are for the next few days in Chinandega and at the hospital in León."

"I think you should do an interview with Sister Esperanza and Father Marcus and the volunteer Ladies of the Hospital," I answered. "They've devoted their lives to these children and made our trip so much easier. In addition, I've been hearing a lot about the so-called 'children of the dump.' We really need to see these kids for ourselves, and to see if we can find a way to make things better for them. I'm sure that Father Marcus and the Sisters of the Church would be glad to help."

Our driver glanced over his right shoulder toward Lori and said, "No matter what you've heard about these kids, the reality is probably going to be more shocking than the stories. The 'children of the dump' are the poorest of poor. They sleep outside or wherever they can find shelter. They wait until the trash trucks come to the dump to unload. Then they gather semi-rotten food, vegetables, and other produce that has been thrown away, so that they have something to eat. These children are uneducated, and most of them have no families. Their clothes are tattered, torn, and filthy. It is very difficult to see. I have driven Father Marcus there. He distributes used clothing and some money. He and the sisters are planning to raise enough money to build a home for these children – an orphanage I suppose you would call it – where they can get proper clothing, safe and nutritious food, and an education. There are no words to describe it. I will speak with Father Marcus, and you can bring the television team as well."

Lori said, "It can't be as bad as you are telling us."

The driver said, "It's worse. As I said, there are no words to describe these children and the way they live like animals. In fact, our animals are better off than these children are. We care for our animals better than these children are cared for."

Bob, who was filming through the front window, suddenly stopped and said, "I would like to film it. You don't need words; the photos will be worth a thousand words. Photos might make it possible for us to raise the money to build a home for them, not only in Nicaragua but maybe also in Houston. It would be wonderful to help remove these children from such a horrible situation, and you know that people back home would gladly write checks once they've seen how these kids live."

I said, "I'll try to work this into the schedule at the end of the day." To the driver, I said, "Let us know when you can make arrangements with Father Marcus and Sister Esperanza to take the group. I would like for them to join us if possible, since they have a relationship with these children. Without their accompaniment, a group of strangers showing up with a TV camera might be intrusive and frightening to them, but with Father Marcus explaining why we are there, it will be a safer and more comfortable visit."

The driver nodded in agreement and said, "After we get you settled at the Callejas home, I will visit with Father Marcus and the sisters, and tell them of your idea; that you wish to see the children of the dump, to provide them with medical care as well as doing some fundraising on their behalf, both here and in Houston."

Lori asked me, "Do you know if we have any more toys and school supplies that we can bring with us?"

"I'm sure we still have some, and if not, I'd be happy to go to the market and purchase some to bring with us, as well as some fresh foods and candies."

Bob said, "I'll help you take care of that, since there's really not much for me to do until we get there and start filming."

Smiling and nodding toward our driver, I said, "We have a plan! And our driver here can set the time and place."

I turned and looked out the window, then placed my camera back on my lap. We were reaching the northern tip of Lago de Managua on Route 26, and passing through the town of La Paz Centro, where we would turn south and connect with Route 12, which would take us north into the city of León.

Miracles in Bedlam

Bob had his big television camera on his shoulder and the window rolled down so he could photograph several overloaded, high-wheeled wooden carts, each of which was pulled by a single burro. I felt so sorry for these little animals, struggling with such a big load. But their plight, I thought, was not much worse than that of many of the humans who lived around them. Most of these people had more than their share of burdens to carry, even if those burdens were not always visible. Plus, a family's burro would at least be fed regularly, even if the family was not. Our driver was right: many of the beasts in Nicaragua fared better than the humans did.

In years to come, the "children of the dump" received coverage from ABC-13 journalists, who did their part to let the world know about the children's plight. Many good people donated money and time to help these kids, including Rotarians in many Rotary Districts across the U.S., who adopted the "children of the dump" as their club's international project. But that's almost worthy of an entire book in and of itself.

Children of the dump

Father Marcus

Dr. Agris, Dr. Mark Urbach, and Marvin Zindler at a fundraiser to build an orphanage & school for the children of the dump.

Joseph Agris, M.D.

* * * * *

When Mr. Castillo and his son Eleazer arrived at the clinic, the room became very quiet. As he moved forward, the throng of people awaiting treatment parted, staring at the boy, then flowed back in place as Eleazer and his father passed, the din of their conversations immediately resuming at an even more animated pitch.

One look at Eleazer explained the increased intensity of the other patients' conversations. While Eleazer had a cleft lip and a cleft palate similar to a hundred other children we had seen at the clinic and the hospital, he also had a very prominent feature that was dramatically different from the other patients we treated. Unlike those others, he also had what is called an encephalocele. His skull had not completely closed after his birth, and a portion of his brain had pushed forward, distending his forehead on the left side. The medically uneducated personnel in the clinic did not know what his problem was, and neither did the patients filling the seats in the waiting area. As is common when uneducated people are confronted with unfamiliar phenomena, the people watching Eleazer as he walked through the waiting area were superstitious and afraid. They said nothing, but their faces betrayed their fears and unspoken questions: *Is this something my child can catch? Is this part of a disease, or something even worse?*

Eleazer was prescreened by the nurses just like everyone else, and they listed, "cleft lip, cleft palate, and tumor-like mass of the forehead." Many of them thought he had a cancer and was going to die.

When the local nurse brought Eleazer to the examining room, he had a broad smile on his face. He was not afraid. He was very grown up for a seven-year-old, putting out his hand and shaking mine. He was also smart, and while he was aware of his multiple, congenital problems, they had not stopped him from making friends, going to school, and doing all things that seven-year-old boys do.

Yet it was this very normalcy that scared me so much. Young boys climb trees and often get into places they shouldn't. If Eleazer fell and bumped his forehead, it could result in an intracranial bleed – blood filling his brain. It could kill him. The cleft lip and palate were the least of his problems.

I asked the father why he brought Eleazer to us. He replied that he had taken this child to several of the local clinics. "The doctors have all examined him and all have said there is nothing they can do," he said sadly. "They all told me that they didn't feel that he can even be treated successfully in Managua either. They said he will die!" The man had tears in his eyes, and my heart hurt for him.

Since Eleazer's situation had been presented as being so hopeless, the little boy was simply allowed to grow up with his cleft lip, cleft palate, and encephalocele left untreated. The father encouraged him to do "boy things," and did not limit him in any of his activities. As a result, Eleazer developed an outgoing attitude that allowed him to fit in, even with his bizarre combination of very prominent birth defects. As I've previously

288

indicated, such an accepting attitude is very unusual, particularly within this culture. These children are usually hidden away on the farm; they never get to go to school or interact with anyone outside the family.

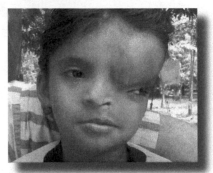

Eleazer, the "Unicorn Boy"
after excellent cleft-lip repair

I wanted to find out more from Eleazer's father about why he would bring Eleazer to us after being told by other doctors that there was nobody in Nicaragua who could fix the boy's problem. He responded, "Everyone has heard about Dr. Angel and what he did with the miracle baby. Everyone told me I should bring Eleazer to be examined by the American team and to ask Dr. Angel to see my son."

He paused for a moment and then added, "I have been going to church and praying that a miracle would happen for my Eleazer, just as it did for the baby. You are our miracle doctor. I always pray that our many volcanoes remain peaceful, and for the upcoming rainy season to be nurturing and not destructive. And so far my prayers have mostly been answered. I have also prayed for you and the medical team, and now you are here and these prayers have also been answered."

I discussed Eleazer's medical history in detail with the family and found that he had a sister, Mardian, who was normal in all aspects. It turned out that Eleazer's situation was anomalous: there was no history of a genetic background. The little boy was otherwise in good health and was very, very smart.

I explained to the Castillo family that I could fix Eleazer's defects, but I couldn't do it all at once. On this visit I would personally repair the left-sided cleft lip. The palate defect would be repaired at a separate time. The encephalocele, however, would need to be treated in Houston.

Then I brought Kimberly and Elia into the room and introduced the Castillo family and Eleazer to them. I explained that we would need to discuss visa arrangements with the U.S. Embassy in Managua, and that I would personally call Continental Airlines to convince them to provide free tickets for Eleazer and one parent to come to the Methodist Hospital in the Houston, Texas Medical Center for this extensive and complicated surgical procedure. I added that I would discuss Eleazer's situation with the famous Texas Children's Hospital administration, and request that they approve free surgical procedures and hospital stay for him.

I then reached down and put Eleazer on my lap, and asked if he understood what we were talking about. Eleazer had a big smile and said, "I get to go to Texas. I want to be a cowboy. Will you teach me to ride a horse? I want to see your guns."

I gave him a big hug and said, "What makes you think that I have guns?"

Without hesitation Eleazer answered, "You live in Texas. Everyone in Texas has guns. You need them to fight off the Indians."

We all laughed at Eleazer's statement. I figured that they watched too many John Wayne movies in Nicaragua. I explained to Eleazer that the Indians in Texas are friendly these days, and that cowboys don't fight them. I said, "I do have horses, though. I have a beautiful black stallion with a white star on his forehead. But he is pony-sized – he is what they call a miniature horse – and his name is Hero." Then I added that Hero was a gift to me from the actor Chuck Norris. Eleazer didn't respond to that, but his father's eyes grew big and he looked right at me as he said, "You know Chuck Norris?"

"Si, Si."

"Now I truly know my prayers have been answered. I know you can make this happen for Eleazer."

There's another Chuck Norris joke in here somewhere, but I'll leave that to others. In any case, there was no question that we would give it our all. When the situation involves children, my team and I go above and beyond providing direct medical care.

I told Kimberly and Elia to work with President Violeta Chamorro in arranging for a passport and visa for Eleazer and a family member, through the U.S. Embassy in Managua. "I will also take some Polaroid photos of Eleazer and send the photos and a letter to President Violeta," I said. "Things will go smoother and faster if we work from the top down."

With that completed, I sent Eleazer and his family to have his blood tests done and told them we would do the cleft lip repair the day after tomorrow.

The family was expecting a lot from "Dr. Angel," but I felt I was not making promises I couldn't keep. Even so, I knew that it could take several months to complete the paperwork and arrangements. Government and government personnel do not move quickly, even with the potentially life-threatening situation that Eleazer had.

Until arrangements could be made for his transport and surgery, we needed to keep him safe from falling and striking his forehead. I suggested we get him a football helmet to protect his head. Whether he would wear it or not was something else, though. Boys will be boys, after all.

Two days later, Eleazer underwent surgery for repair of the left-sided cleft lip. It went very well, in terms of both functional and aesthetic results. He would be out playing baseball again in two weeks – carefully, I hoped. Since baseball is a major sport in

Nicaragua, I couldn't expect him to abstain completely.

The cleft lip surgery was of course just the first of several surgical procedures to transform Eleazer into a functional and aesthetically handsome young man. The major brain operation and cranio-facial procedure would be undertaken at Texas Children's Hospital in Houston as soon as I could get an American visa for Eleazer, based on my letters of medical need.

Kimberly spent many hours working to arrange for a home for Eleazer to stay in during his time in Houston. The hospital in Houston promised to provide operating room time and post-op care as well. The procedure would require two surgeons and their assistants, so I contacted my good friend, Dr. Ed Murphy, a neurosurgeon at the Texas Medical Center, to assist in the procedure. He and I had made several trips together to provide medical care for children in Peru.

We were able to obtain a passport for Eleazer and a family member, and we also got a 60-day visa for medical care. This would provide more than enough time for the procedure and recovery.

And I am pleased to say that the surgery, which took place a couple of months later, went very well. I made the incision in the hairline so it would not be visible. Then I carefully exposed the defect in the skull with the protruding portion of the brain.

Dr. Murphy, the neurosurgeon, then came into the O.R. and expertly dealt with the non-functioning, protruding portion of the brain tissue – the "unicorn horn." He completed his procedure with a graft to cover the opening, but this alone would not be strong enough to protect the brain for the rest of Eleazer's life.

I re-entered the O.R. and constructed a plastic plate to close the defect. The skin was then meticulously closed over this plate in a way to minimize scarring, with the instant result that Eleazer's forehead now had a normal shape and contour. His peers would no longer call him the "unicorn boy." And his brain was well protected behind the strong plastic plate.

In a few weeks he would return to Nicaragua and his school. He would be reunited with family, friends, and classmates, looking just like everyone else. For the first time in his life he really would be just another student, and would be treated like all of the other kids. He'd be able to play sports with his peers without fear of sustaining a serious or fatal injury. And he would be easily accepted by everyone. Because of his outgoing personality and keen intelligence, Eleazer had actually adjusted quite well despite his deformity. But now there would be no limits for this little boy.

Eleazer stayed in Houston for several weeks following the surgery. A loving family provided a temporary home for him and his family member while he recovered. Then he returned to the small, quiet town of Chinandega, now just another little boy like so many millions of others, but also a living testament to the reason that the team and I do what we do.

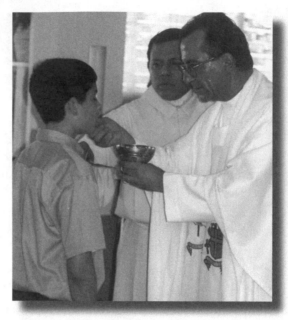

*Father Marcus of Chinandega
blessing one of the children
to whom he has devoted his life*

*My best friend, the late Marvin Zindler
with Father Marcus.
Both champions for the less fortunate
and the exploited*

CHAPTER 36
Affairs Of The Heart

It was mid-morning, a couple of days after our return from Puerto Cabezas, and the medical team and I were on our way to the hospital in Chinandega, after having visited some patients in neighboring villages. Marvin Zindler, Bob, and Lori had accompanied us. Apart from the usual medical duties, I faced a rather uncomfortable task that I'd been putting off ever since I had sent Nurse Michael back home to Texas. Although I'd had the obligatory stern exchanges with Michael before he left, my communications with Marta had only been cursory. Because I'd been so busy preparing for the trip to Puerto Cabezas, I hadn't yet had a chance to sit down with her alone for a serious conversation about her violation of "the rules." And during my first couple of days back in Chinandega, I was preoccupied with several other matters. But Marta was on notice that I intended to have that important discussion as soon as possible after my return from the Miskito Coast. It wasn't something I was looking forward to, and I'm sure she wasn't either.

The day was dry, and the sky was deep blue, with nary a cloud to be seen. Though by all appearances it was a lovely day, the heat was building rapidly. It is because of the extreme heat that Chinandega and some of the surrounding areas are often referred to as Nicaragua's Hell, and you won't get any argument from me on that assessment.

Small brick homes lined the road as we passed through the town of La Paz Centro and into a small village before turning north to Chinandega. The houses were shaded by mature trees, chickens ran free in the front yards, and an occasional donkey could be seen, tethered to a stake and lazily eating grass. The laughter of children playing could be heard in the dry, still air.

I waved out my window to a very old lady who was sitting in a rocking chair on her porch facing the road. She was built like a bulldog, obviously the product of decades of toil. Her face bore the marks of that toil, and her eyes spoke of the worries of one for whom even basic security was beyond her imaginings. She was watching the younger children who were playing in the front yard, and eyeing us suspiciously as we slowly drove past with cameras out the car's windows.

My body was also tired of sitting, and reminded me again that like the woman, I too was getting older. I stretched out my arms and felt the gratifying pop as the kink in my back was relieved. Then I wiggled my feet to improve the circulation. Marvin Zindler had just awakened and was looking around, but seemed lost in a fog.

I turned and said, "Mr. Zindler, we are approaching León, and should be arriving in Chinandega in about thirty to forty minutes."

Marvin, who knew all about the saga of our star-crossed lovers, responded, "I imagine that Nurse Marta is anxiously waiting to speak with you. I wouldn't want to be in your shoes for that conversation."

Almost everyone in the car burst out laughing, and those who weren't comfortable laughing just sat silently, but with smirks on their faces. I didn't comment. I just pushed myself more upright in my seat, pressing my back deeply into the cushion. Kimberly observed my posture and my silence and gave me a broad, pleasant smile. She said, "I've been around you long enough to know your moods. Would you like me to be there when you have your conversation with Marta?"

I continued looking out the front window, and without turning to face her, I said, "I would appreciate that very much."

We passed a group of young men, each with a bedroll under one arm and a makeshift pack strapped to his back. These were clearly migrants, landless laborers whose lives consisted of going from plantation to plantation, wherever there was paying work available, and moving on when the work ran out. They all hoped to receive better wages and to benefit from the opportunities presented by cross-border trade with Honduras and Costa Rica, as well as the United States. Some in the group were no more than teenagers, who worked in the fields alongside their elders, and received no formal education or medical care.

Traveling by car through a country such as Nicaragua reveals a great deal about the well-being of the country and its people. A variety of demographic figures provide valuable clues as well, and I'd done some demographic research on Nicaragua before coming here. One of the most reliable indexes is life expectancy, the average number of years a person in a given country or area can expect to live. The figures I found for Nicaragua at the time of my early visits varied (depending upon the sources to which I referred) from 69-71 years. That was slightly above the world's average, but among the lowest for the Americas. Interestingly, female life expectancy was and remains four to five years longer than that of males, even in this rural setting.

We were now entering León, where multiple roads converged into a large traffic circle. It was as hectic as you might imagine. Because of this convergence there were several gas stations, as well as a parking lot filled with eighteen-wheelers.

Across from that parking lot was a large open market and gathering place, with an array of sidewalk vendors. The market offered an abundance of used American clothing, and because of the nearby university there were many bookstands. But unlike other areas we'd visited in Nicaragua, the markets in León didn't display many local crafts. There were some handbags and textiles, but you had to go to Managua or other cities for a wide selection of locally crafted items.

León is laid out in the traditional Spanish colonial grid pattern, with the main cathedral and a park in the center. La Catedral de León is the largest cathedral in Central America. Construction was begun back in 1747, but it wasn't until 1860 that the cathedral was consecrated and given the title of Basilica by Pius XI. The cathedral is built in the Baroque style with a mixture of gothic and neo-classic architecture from that era, and its location in the center of town, along with the surrounding park, magnifies the church's grandeur.

La Catedral de León

León had not emerged unscathed from Nicaragua's civil wars; the Sandinista forces had attacked key locations in the city, and León was the first city in Nicaragua to fall to the Sandinistas. They had captured León after a vicious battle, and bullet holes could still be seen everywhere in the buildings along the roads we now traveled. León was further damaged when the dictator and then-president Anastasio Somoza Debayle responded to the Sandinistas with aerial bombardment, ordering the air force to "bomb everything that moves until it stops moving." In subsequent years, the city was partially restored, but the scars of the war remain to this day.

Traffic was heavy in this area, and our driver had to slow the vehicle as he maneuvered around the countless three-wheeled rickshaw taxis that spewed thick black and gray smoke from their exhaust pipes. As if dodging and weaving around the rickshaws weren't enough of a challenge, there were also donkey carts laden with all sorts of farm produce plodding along at their typically glacial pace, and large eighteen-wheelers filled with cattle and sugarcane, rushing north to the feedlots and refineries. Some of this cargo would be taken to Nicaragua's Pacific port, Puerto Corinto, for sea transport.

Taken as a whole, the scene was a photographer's delight, and Bob Dows was quickly changing the tape in the TV camera as we moved through this melee of humanity, farm animals, and assorted motorized vehicles.

A bustling market

Miracles in Bedlam

I was getting hungry, so I turned to the group and asked if anyone else was hungry as well. I received a resounding "yes" from everyone, including our driver, Julio. I asked Julio to take us to the central town park, which was appropriately named Parque Central. The park was surrounded by *fritanga* stands, which I had been told were the best and most fun places to stop and grab a bite. The word *fritanga* is a derivative of *frito*, or "fried." It's Nicaraguan street food at its finest. You couldn't exactly call it health food, as virtually everything served at a *fritanga* stand is fried, except the fresh meat, which is charcoal-grilled. One of the specialties I've always enjoyed is *pupusas*. Though the *pupusa* is originally from El Salvador, some of the best I've had were served in Nicaragua. The *pupusa* is a shaped like a pancake and made from a cornmeal-like dough. Similar to pita bread, it has a pocket, and that pocket is filled with cheese, chicken, pork, or a combination of ingredients. A *pupusa* is a meal in itself, and at the stand we visited that day, they were selling for the unbelievable price of about fifty cents.

My absolute favorite was *nacatamales*, which are similar to the classic Mexican tamale, except they're wrapped in banana leaves instead of corn husks. The best ones I've ever had are homemade by the cooks at the Holmann residence in Managua and at the Callejas home in Chinandega. But I was willing to try the ones at the *fritanga* stand, and I was not disappointed in the least.

Besides the array of tempting foods, there was an ice chest filled with bottled water, juices that were not often seen in the U.S., and the ever-present Victoria *cerveza*. We found an area where there were several very old but functional wooden tables with wobbly three-legged stools around them. This was where we would dine.

As I so often did, I let my more fluent companions and associates do the ordering; in this case they were Julio, Elia, and Dixon. After sitting for quite awhile, we decided to stretch our legs and take a mini-tour of the immediate area. Several of us went into the gorgeous cathedral, which to my surprise had a simple, carved wooden interior, rather than the ornate décor so typical of Catholic churches. The depiction of the Virgin Mary was exceptionally lovely.

When we went back outside to the Parque Central, our meals were almost ready. The friendly *fritanga* vendor from whom we'd ordered our lunch said, "Are you the American medical team I have heard so much about? Which one is Dr. Angel, the man associated with the miracle baby?"

Before I could say anything, everyone pointed toward me. The vendor reached across the cart and grabbed my hand firmly, vigorously shaking it until I finally managed to pry it loose. He stepped out from behind his cart and put his arm around me, then pointed to Bob Dows and asked that he take our photo. I handed Bob both my 35mm Nikon and the Polaroid. The vendor had obviously never seen a Polaroid photo, judging from his quizzical expression when I handed him the undeveloped print.

Elia explained to him in Spanish to hold it up to the sun and to wait about a minute. As the picture began to appear, the puzzled frown on his face changed to a big smile. I have never grown tired of watching people's expressions as they viewed the Polaroid phenomenon for the first time. For them it seemed like magic, and their delight was always magical to me as well.

After a moment, the vendor turned to me and said, "*No dinero necesito.*" I told him we had to pay for our food or we could not eat with him. He slowly nodded in agreement and continued preparing our lunch.

I paid the gentleman for the wonderful lunch and added a little extra for his attention and kindness. He was a bit stubborn and tried to refuse our money, but I pushed the córdobas into his hand, and he finally accepted them. As we left, I told him that if anyone in his family, particularly children, needed any medical care, they could come to the hospital and there would be no charge. I gave him one of my personal business cards and told him that it was a VIP ticket to the hospital should he need it. As we left he was waving and shouting, "*Vaya con Dios.*"

Our journey from León to Chinandega was a pleasant ride through farm country, interspersed with a few small villages. I don't know if I've adequately conveyed the fact that Chinandega is a gateway to some of the most breathtaking spots in the northwest corner of Nicaragua. It may be Hell, but it is a lovely Hell. That said, Chinandega was a spot that was rarely included on tourists' travel lists in those days. There were no hotels in the area back then, and you had to know someone so you could stay in their homes, as our group was doing on this trip. Things are different today, but in those early years of our missions to Nicaragua, we were very grateful for our accommodating hosts.

We were now halfway between León and Chinandega, passing through the town of Posoltega, where today there is a memorial plaque – delivered by President Bill Clinton – for the victims of Hurricane Mitch, one of Nicaragua's worst national disasters, which hit the area in 1998. The quiet little town of Posoltega was thrown into international fame as Hurricane Mitch poured more than two meters of rain on the slopes of one of the two volcanoes that were adjacent to the town. A gigantic wave of water and mud – nearly ten feet high – roared down the slopes of the volcano, obliterating everything in its path. Several small communities on the western slope disappeared instantly, along with 2,500 people.

Those who were not washed away or buried alive lost everything. News reports of natural tragedies often co-opt the phrase, "left only with the clothes on their backs," but one of the survivors remembered seeing children and adults pulling themselves out of the mud, naked, as the torrents of water and mud had stripped the clothes from their bodies. The survivor's expression as he shared the memory was one of a man who was reliving the experience anew, clearly haunted by the image that remained so fresh in his mind. "All you could see was their eyes. Empty eyes. Their naked bodies were plastered in black lava mud. As they pulled themselves from the mud, they looked like corpses rising from their graves."

He went on to describe hearing people screaming for help for days after the land-slide, because they could not free themselves from the grip of the mud, and there was no one to help them.

The president at the time was Violeta Chamorros's successor, Arnoldo Alemán. I had attended Alemán's presidential inauguration with my secretary and nurse, Jeannie, and other members of our medical team who were working in Nicaragua. President Alemán was impressed with Jeannie, who could speak five languages, including Arabic, fluently. Alemán made overtures toward her and even asked her out on a date, but that's a story for another time.

In my personal opinion, President Alemán did not serve the people of Nicaragua well during his six-year term as their president, and that is putting it politely. He actually reneged on his promise to help the survivors in Posoltega, merely because the town's leadership was Sandinista.

International efforts in subsequent years resulted in the establishment of new communities in the area, despite reports of mismanagement of the relief fund under the Alemán administration. The survivors had housing, but no productive work was available to those whose farms had been buried under ten feet of mud. With no means of making a living, many of the survivors eventually made their way to other areas in Nicaragua or illegally crossed the border into Costa Rica in search of work. In short, the natural disaster was horrific, and made far worse by a political fiasco during President Alemán's administration. But again... another story, for another time.

* * * * *

We entered Chinandega, stopping at the home of Roberto Callejas, so that those of us who were staying there could shower and change. After a quick shower and a change into my operating room greens and my white lab coat, I joined Jose Dixon and Barrett Phillips for the short stroll to the hospital.

As we approached the hospital I began to plan my day. I wanted to make rounds on the children's and adult wards so I could check that everything had been going well during our absence that morning. But I was acutely aware that by doing so I would only be delaying the inevitable: I hadn't forgotten that I also needed to meet with Nurse Marta for a discussion to which I was still not looking forward.

Still, I thought again about how good it was to get back into the routine at the hospital in Chinandega. Everyone was still buzzing about our adventures in Puerto Cabezas, talking about how relieved they were that we had returned safely. The news of the riotous demonstrators had quickly reached Chinandega; in fact, the newspapers throughout Nicaragua had carried stories of the incident, as well as reports of the Cubans' exit. Our medical team and the ABC-TV news team were being portrayed as heroes in the news reports, as it was being reported that all of the Cubans and their

Russian sponsors had left Nicaraguan soil. We, as well as the public, were hopeful that the Cuban presence had finally ended and that with it, the Contra-Sandinista conflict would abate. This was not merely local news; the rest of the world was watching, since the events in tiny Puerto Cabezas were being viewed with hope as a portent of shifting tides on an international scale.

Since it was late in the day, we entered the children's hospital through the guarded iron gate at the emergency room, passing through the ten-foot-high walls that surrounded the building. We walked through a small alleyway where the laundry rooms were located. Clotheslines were strung along the alleyway, laden with recently washed operating room gowns and sheets that were hung to dry in the sun. Back in the United States – especially in larger towns and cities – clotheslines are about as prominent as mechanical adding machines or manual typewriters, and are rarely if ever seen. In a less-developed country, however, this was the most practical and accessible means of drying laundry, and clothing and linens that have been sitting in the sun for hours to dry are almost sterile. I found the sight unusual enough that I grabbed the camera from its usual resting place on a strap hanging from my shoulder, and took several shots of what we in the U.S. would consider a relic of days long since passed.

Entering the hospital, we began with the post-op children's wards. Everybody was in a jovial mood. The toys, games, and school supplies that we had brought were clearly being put to good use; a play table had been set up in the ward with many games, puzzles, and coloring books on it. The children were gathered around the play table, and when we walked in, they wanted to show us what they had been doing. After Dixon, Barrett, and I spent a few very pleasant and enjoyable minutes with the children at their play table, we proceeded to visit each of the children in the ward, examining them and speaking with their parents.

I saw Marta changing a child's burn dressing, and asked her to meet with me when she finished. She looked up and nodded, but said nothing. I then returned to visiting the children with the team members, cleaning wounds, changing dressings, checking their intravenous lines, and speaking with family members.

After we completed our rounds, I met with Sister Esperanza, JoAnne, and Kimberly, and reviewed the schedules for the next day. I saw Marta walking toward the lounge area and asked JoAnne to join me for the discussion I needed to have with Marta. I remembered that Kimberly had previously volunteered to join me, but she was needed elsewhere, and I felt that the talk shouldn't be put off any longer.

JoAnne and I met Marta in the lounge area. When we entered, she turned and faced us with her hands on her hips, saying, "I understand you had a very successful trip in Puerto Cabezas." Then she took a deep breath and wiped her cheeks.

JoAnne leaned up against the wall, folded her hands across her chest, and quickly scanned Marta from head-to-toe, assessing the other woman's mood as only women can. Clearly she anticipated trouble, or at least awkwardness, but she said nothing, and waited to see how the conversation would proceed. Marta pulled one of the wooden stools away from the table and sank down upon it. Her eyes were now tightly closed, her lips pursed, and her fingertips massaging her forehead. It was obvious to us both that Marta was in sheer misery, with the flood of tears rolling down her cheeks attesting to the pain that filled her.

JoAnne went over to the counter, filled a glass with water, and handed it to Marta. Marta took a sip of the water, composed herself, and began telling us of her deep infatuation with Michael, and how incredible their relationship was. She ended by saying, "We had no choice. We fell in love." Silent again, she laid her head on the table, and her tears began flowing again.

It was time for me to respond, and I felt myself torn between my responsibility as medical team leader and my duty as a compassionate friend. I began from the perspective that didn't tug at my heart. "It's not true that you had no choice. Michael knew the rules and he chose to break them. Michael visited you at night, and that's when he got that scorpion sting on his leg. As you well know, he got a severe infection that required surgery and medical care. He could have lost his leg – or his life."

After an awkward, silent moment had passed, JoAnne spoke up and said, "The first time I married was for sex, and that didn't work out. The second time I married was for love. That didn't work out either. If I get married a third time it will be for money." This apparent non sequitur did the trick. The heavy weight had been lifted from the room, and even Marta had to laugh.

The administrative part of me was sorely tempted to further rebuke Marta, even to taunt her foolishness to drive the lesson home, but the compassionate part of me won out for now, and I couldn't quite bring myself to do it. Instead, there was another long and heavy pause, during which none of us said a word. However, a thin smile remained on Marta's face following JoAnne's comment, which had helped to lighten the difficult situation somewhat. After a few more moments of silence, Marta lifted her head from the table and looked me in the eye as she struggled to say, "All I can do now is say that I'm sorry."

There was another long pause, during which the three of us continued to exchange uncomfortable looks. Then for what seemed like a long time, Marta sat with her face in her hands, silently weeping. When her tears finally stopped, she wiped them away with her sleeve, took another drink from her glass of water, and sat up a little straighter. It seemed as if the initial shock was gone and she was ready to move on.

I took a deep breath, exhaled, and said, "Marta, you are one of our best nurses. You're doing a wonderful job assisting in the operating room, and you are so good at working with the children on the ward." I paused as I tried to find the right balance between being firm and comforting. I continued, reminding her of the importance of teamwork, which couldn't be effective or efficient unless everyone behaved professionally. I pointed out how easily that professionalism could be compromised when we allowed powerful emotions to intrude.

At times, Marta seemed to absorb the logic of what I was saying, yet a few seconds later she appeared to be struggling to grasp the thoughts that seemed to be in such conflict with her feelings. It was obvious to me that she was overwhelmed. She began crying again and wiped her cheeks. I wondered with some dread if this was an emotional meltdown.

In a few minutes, however, Marta gathered her emotions, and it was clear that her resolve was solidifying. Her eyes still red, she finally said, "Nursing has become my life. Especially caring for the children. Working here with the American surgical team... and seeing what you have accomplished here... is beyond anything we could have ever hoped for. It is like nothing we have ever seen. You have given these children and their families new hope and a new life in a country that offers so little of either."

JoAnne said, "Marta, never forget that you are also part of this team. Without you it would not be possible." She walked over and gave Marta a big hug, then broke away, adding, "If it is true love and it is meant to be, you *will* see Michael again. Dr. Agris is good friends with President Violeta, and can help get you a passport. You can also write a letter to the U.S. Embassy for a visa. It will probably take a few weeks, but it is all possible. We can even help you with travel arrangements."

Marta stood and gave JoAnne a hug. She then turned and shook my hand and said, "There are many children still waiting. I have work to do. Please excuse me." Turning away, she left the room.

JoAnne turned to me and said, "Now we need to go to the record room and complete some of the charts from last week, and then I need to get back to the O.R. to help set up for the afternoon's surgeries."

As for me, I was nearly weak with relief. What I had feared would be an altogether unpleasant confrontation had instead emerged as a meeting of minds, and the meltdown had been successfully averted thanks to the balance we had achieved between the need for "the rules" and the inescapable dictates of the heart. And I was more convinced than ever that the story of Michael and Marta was far from over. For now, as always, there was work to do.

Joseph Agris, M.D.

CHAPTER 37
The Girl With No Ear

It was 6:30 a.m. and the team was assembled in the children's ward at the hospital in León. Nurse Dixon and Elia were shuffling the charts in an attempt to get them in order, and making some notes. I paused for a second, my eyes sweeping up one side of the room and then down the other, a pair of thin gold-rimmed metal glasses hanging precariously from the end of my nose.

Today's goal was to see all the little patients on the children's ward and several adults upon whom we had operated the previous day. We planned to change all the dressings, answer any questions, and provide the needed medications, so as to be able to send home as many as possible, since every bed in the hospital was filled. We completed rounds and dressing changes, then gave out discharge notices on the children's ward. That completed, we turned to the few adults across the hall. On the men's ward, there was a young Contra soldier who had sustained burns in combat. Since we had applied his skin grafts, he had been gaining strength and endurance, evidenced by his improved appetite, which can be a good indicator of a patient's feeling more whole after having extensive surgery.

As we changed his dressings, which I knew was a very uncomfortable procedure, he was joking with us. This was a clear sign that he was regaining his stride. The grafts looked excellent, and Mr. Dixon and Barrett said they would complete the redressing, so the others and I could go to the operating room.

Although I had come to Nicaragua to treat the country's children, we were reminded every day that we were still in the middle of a war zone, and we were seeing young men with war injuries nearly every day. We had the equipment and the expertise to treat them, and felt it was our duty to do so. The medical team's "war" was not against human enemies but rather against disease and injuries, and I felt that we were winning in these brutally difficult cases.

However, these successes and the "miracle baby" continued to produce more publicity than we wanted. The medical team was still riding a wave of celebrity, with new articles about us being published every day, followed by a swelling stream of radio programs. The news programs were divisive at times, but overall were proving to be highly effective, praising the American team's expertise in the operating room, as well as presenting my team and me as peacemakers who treated all who needed it, with no questions asked.

I left the burn ward with my entourage: JoAnne, Elia, and Carolyn. We entered the operating room suite, hung up our white lab coats, and put on operating room caps, masks, and shoe covers. Then I turned and saw a group of local residents and interns, along with two of the local doctors. I nodded politely to them and shook hands.

"And you are all here from the university program here in León?"

With a generous smile one of the residents stepped forward and said, "That is true."

"Are you prepared for today's procedures?"

Almost in unison they all nodded and said they were.

"Very well, let's proceed. Welcome to another day in hell." I was laughing as I said it, but not entirely joking, and it was clear from the expressions on their faces that they knew it.

As usual there were two operating tables in each room, and the children were already anesthetized. The surgical sites had been prepped and washed, and the local nurses who were assisting had already draped the surgical areas. I went to the scrub sinks, followed by my nurses and the students, and once thoroughly scrubbed, I proceeded into the operating room.

On one table there was a young man with a moderate sized ganglion tumor on his wrist. The local general surgeon said he had done these before and would be happy to do this case with the help of a resident and an intern.

On the other table was a patient with a wide double cleft lip, which I would be doing. JoAnne stood on my side of the operating table right next to me, and would be instructing the student nurses during the procedure. Mr. Dixon took his position on my other side; he would be my scrub nurse as usual. Students and residents then gathered around, and one aggressive young man wedged himself into a spot immediately behind Dixon and me. He was thin and had wild, wiry hair.

The young intern stood timidly as if he had never been in an operating room before and said, in a squeaky voice, "Doctor, sir, I am William Martinez, a first-year intern."

I gave him a cursory nod, then craned my neck and scanned the operating room. I counted eleven students, residents, and interns tucked into this small space – and there was no reason to believe there wouldn't be more coming later. The students were there to learn and to assist at the operating table, in preparation for their own careers as surgeons.

At the second operating table, Dr. Baladares was gearing up, and behind him was another throng of eager students and residents. He was already beginning to ask his observers some questions regarding hand anatomy and the surgical procedure for the removal of the tumor.

I turned to Dixon and said, "Marking pen, please."

Before we began the repair of the cleft lip, I marked the lip and explained the structures that would have to be moved and rejoined. At the same time, I was firing questions at the intern Martinez, who had managed to push himself into a tableside position.

I turned to Martinez and said, "If you get a question wrong or miss a question, I want you to step back and allow one of the other students to take your place tableside. We will rotate on that basis. Answer the question correctly, and you stay. Miss a question and you rotate to the back of the line. Got it?"

Behind me, only inches away, I heard some giggling and whispering, but the tone had been set, and the giggling and whispering ceased immediately with one glare from me in the general direction of the perpetrators. In any case, that skinny little intern Martinez proved his mettle. He must have read up on anatomy the night before, as well as on this specific procedure, because he answered every one of my questions in impressive detail. Plus, he was fearless, and not intimidated by me or by his giggling classmates.

As every surgeon knows, the operating room is very serious business. To me, there is only one way and one time to do any procedure: the right way, the very first time. I felt it was particularly important to stress this principle when conducting my teaching on my medical missions in remote areas. I knew that you needed to know your stuff and present it in a straightforward way if you were going to be invited back. Accordingly, there was very little BS in my operating rooms, and rarely any humor. I do not tolerate casual repartee, tall tales, or jokesters. And today in particular, I was in no mood for small talk, not that any one of the interns or residents seemed inclined to engage me. To the contrary, they all dutifully asked questions and rotated tableside, paying close attention while I pointed out anatomical facts and surgical details as the operation proceeded.

One of the residents asked me, "How do you decide on the procedure of choice for this or other cases?" I managed a tight grin and said, "Sometimes it's a tough decision. I don't mind making tough decisions; that goes with the job." My grin became a genuine smile as I continued, "But in cases like this, the decision very often comes down to what works best in your hands – and that's a result of the surgeon's training and experience.

"This is why I want you to learn and become adept at as many procedures as possible, so that you will be able to make the best choices for each patient. I know this is a lot to ask in the limited time we have together, but that's exactly why we need to make the most of the time we do have." I felt that this was a way of easing any residual tension from my earlier gruffness. I ran a very tight ship, but I wasn't a tyrant (though I'm pretty certain that a few of the more thin-skinned students and residents I've worked with might tend to disagree).

The lip procedure was almost completed, and only the skin sutures needed to be placed. I relaxed my muscles for the first time in an hour, breathing deeply. Then I turned to the senior resident and said, "Have you sutured before?"

"*Si, si,* many times."

"I will put in the corner sutures and I want you to complete the closure with the six-zero sutures. Mr. Dixon will assist you and Nurse JoAnne will help as well."

Then I glanced over at the other table. The hand tumor had been removed and the team was now closing the wound. I called out to them, "Don't forget to put on a plaster splint, and use plenty of padding."

I was hot and thirsty and felt almost claustrophobic with the crush of students, residents, interns, and nurses that now filled the O.R. I pulled off my gloves and pushed the double doors to the operating room open, walking out into the hallway. It felt a bit cooler there, or it might have just been my imagination. Either way, the change was welcome.

Standing just outside the entrance to the O.R. was the administrator. I've learned from experience that this is rarely a good sign. As a rule, I've never allowed myself to get close to hospital administration personnel. It's not just their involvement in hospital politics that I dislike. I also hate their small talk about children, grandchildren, relatives, friends, and enemies, and have generally tried to avoid them as much as I could. As I said, the operating room is serious business – and to my way of thinking, that business extends well beyond the O.R. So when I first saw the administrator standing there, I felt the urge to brush past him as if I were in a rush to resolve some crisis. And with that urge came a fresh wave of claustrophobia.

But there was no escaping him, and he greeted me with a handshake and a big smile. Then he put his big arm over my shoulder and said, "I have someone outside in the waiting area who wishes to meet you." Another wave of uneasiness swept over me, but I brushed the feeling aside and gamely walked down the hall with the administrator, with neither of us saying a word.

As we entered the small room used as a waiting area for patients' families, the flooring creaked loudly under the worn and dirty red carpet. The administrator whispered to me, "This is a very wealthy and important political family from León. I want you to take excellent care of them."

I looked at the administrator with an expression that told the whole story. But just in case my expression wasn't sufficient, I whispered back, "I'm not interested in a patient's political or economic standing. I treat everybody equally. If they have a medical or surgical problem that we can deal with, I will be happy to help them." To myself I thought, *What a pathetic man.*

Standing together politely waiting for us were a mother and her daughter; the administrator made the introductions and then excused himself. I took a few moments to collect myself, then turned to the mother and daughter and invited them to sit down. They did so, and I joined them. Both mother and daughter were quite beautiful and well dressed, and I could not see any exposed defect on either one. I asked, "What is the problem? How can I help you?"

The young lady swept her long dark hair away from the right side of her face, and I was startled to see that she was missing an ear. I quickly noticed that there were no other scars in the area, so clearly the defect was congenital. She had been born with a rare condition of aplasia (missing) of the right ear.

The mother asked, "Can you fix this? Can you give my daughter an ear?"

Slowly I replied, "Total ear reconstruction is one of the most difficult and complicated procedures in all of plastic surgery. In the entire Texas Medical Center of more than 8,000 physicians, there are only two plastic surgeons who perform any significant number of these types of reconstructions, and I am one of them. It takes someone who is not only a good surgeon, but who also has the artistic capability to design and carve the ear."

I explained that the procedure would require the removal of at least two of the young woman's lower ribs. The rib cartilage would then need to be carved to form the framework to shape and build upon to recreate the ear. "This is not a single stage operation," I said. "It usually requires five to seven separate surgical procedures, which are usually scheduled six months to one year apart."

I was watching the two ladies closely as I spoke. You learn how to pick up on cues when explaining complicated surgical procedures such as this. The expressions on the faces of the patients and their loved ones, the glances they exchange as you're talking – all of these are important. But both mother and daughter seemed unfazed.

I continued, "We usually can complete a very satisfactory total ear reconstruction in five separate surgical stages approximately one year apart. The first procedure is the most complicated because it entails the removal of the ribs from the chest. It takes several hours to carve the rib cartilage into the shape of the ear framework, followed by the actual installation of that cartilage under the skin to form the first stage of the ear reconstruction. Your daughter would be under general anesthesia for the entire morning."

The mother asked, "Can you begin the procedure at the University Hospital in León this week?"

I rocked back in my chair and gazed at the ceiling, frustrated at her quick response. I said, "I have not heard from your daughter. Wouldn't you like to discuss this at home with her and your husband?"

"There is no one in Nicaragua who knows how to do this procedure, not even at this hospital," she said. "You are our only hope. My family is well positioned politically and monetarily, but we could never afford five trips to the United States for these surgical procedures."

Her eyes were red and tears appeared on her cheeks. Her hands shook when she said, "And I am doing this for my beautiful daughter, not for me!"

I said nothing, and neither did her daughter. After a few moments the mother continued, "We trust you completely. We have seen the before and after photos in the newspaper and in a recent television story here in Nicaragua. Then there is the 'miracle baby' – and everyone knows you have an angel on your shoulder."

I thought to myself that her expectations here were very high – perhaps too high. The procedure was, after all, very complicated, and required multiple stages. And since the family could not afford to travel, I would be undertaking the operations in less-than-adequate facilities and with minimal instrumentation. Yet I did not want to take away either the mother's or her daughter's hope. Being a man of few words in these situations, and not wanting to raise expectations any higher, I slowly said, "It is a possibility."

No one said anything for what seemed like minutes. Then I continued, "These are the conditions. You will go home and discuss this with your family. I will speak to the anesthesiologist. I will also review the instruments that the University Hospital has available, and we need to check with my nurse, Elia, to see if she brought my personal instruments for this particular type of procedure."

I took a few minutes to let this sink in and to gather my thoughts. Then I said, "Arranging for the proper anesthesia, having the appropriate instruments, preparing in advance with photographs, measurements, and ear markings... that's half the case right there. But I cannot get started unless I know I have full and informed consent from your husband as well as from you and, of course, from your daughter."

The mother's voice stayed strong but tears streamed down her cheeks. She wiped them away, then managed a smile as she said, "You make the preparations here. We will discuss this at home. We will meet again tomorrow when you finish surgery. I would like to invite you and members of your team to my home for dinner."

The daughter was looking at her mother in speechless amazement. Her beautiful eyes were also moist. Her voice quivered as she said, "We will do as you ask, Doctor, and please come to dinner tomorrow night with the members of your team." The expression on her face was one of desperate pleading.

I said, "Understand that I am not saying no, but I am not saying yes either. I am simply asking that you give me time to take this under advisement so I can determine whether or not we can do the procedure here safely and effectively."

At that I stood and shook hands with the young lady. The mother threw her arms around my shoulders and kissed me on both cheeks. Then all was quiet and still.

Finally I said, "You will have to excuse me. We have a very full schedule and I need to return to the operating room."

They thanked me and left. I sucked in several deep breaths and walked back towards the operating theaters, stopping in the doctor's lounge. Retrieving a long-overdue bottle of water from the refrigerator and gulping it down, I wondered, *What the hell am I getting myself into now?*

CHAPTER 38
Exhaustion And Elation

When I returned to the operating room, I saw there were two little patients who had been burned. They were both in need of skin grafts. Elia and JoAnne had set up the instrument tables and the patients were asleep. The local nurses were cleaning the wounds with a disinfectant solution, Betadine scrub, in preparation for the grafting procedure.

Looking around the room at the well-organized team as they finished prepping the patients, I thought again about what marvels the university and medical school in León were. This was a place of pride for those lucky enough to study here, and the teachers were tough and dedicated. As badly as the odds were against them in a country that was still recovering from civil war and was further crippled by a lack of development and multi-generational poverty, their successes were all the sweeter. And those who graduated from the medical school became a model for the younger generations that followed.

Later that day in the same O.R., I supervised and instructed residents and interns on a procedure to correct a congenital web finger defect known as syndactyly, or conjoined fingers. Following the separation of the conjoined fingers, skin grafts had to be performed to complete the covering of the separated fingers.

The procedure was straightforward and I had done many of these before, so I was relatively relaxed. I took this opportunity to discuss with the anesthesiologist the possibility of doing the young lady's ear reconstruction, most notably, the opening of the chest to obtain the rib cartilage grafts. The anesthesiologist assured me that they had all the equipment, drains, and suction tubes that might be needed. "They conduct chest surgical procedures here almost daily," he assured me.

I turned to the intern and the local scrub nurse who was standing next to Elia, and asked them, in Spanish, about the availability of instruments for such a procedure. The intern seemed hesitant in her answer, so I asked Elia to translate it into "a more formal Spanish." Everyone laughed as Elia explained that my Spanish was about a fifth-grade level. In fact there was now a running joke in the O.R. about that request I'd made for a *pequeño machete* when I wanted a scalpel. Though I was strict about procedures and protocol in the O.R. and didn't tolerate nonsense, I didn't mind the occasional joke at my expense. I'm the first to acknowledge my limitations in other tongues than my native English. (You should hear my Urdu.) Now I was taking Elia's comments and the others' laughter with good grace, but I was still determined to get an answer to my question, and Elia more than anyone else was aware of my determination.

After Elia's quick translation, the scrub nurse responded by telling me that she felt that they had the equipment and surgical instruments necessary for the chest and rib procedures. Nevertheless, she said, she would review the instruments in the surgical instrument preparation room and give me a definitive answer before the day was over.

Later that afternoon, Elia and JoAnne escorted me to the prep room. The chest instruments were neatly laid out on a stainless steel table. I adjusted my reading glasses and looked over the instruments laid out before me. Elia, smiling, added, "I went through the instruments that I had packed and found the small rib cutters as well as your carving instruments. Just on a hunch I had packed them, not knowing whether or not we would be doing any of these types of procedures."

With a broad smile I said, "It's that angel my shoulder."

Elia responded, "No, it's women's intuition. Be prepared."

"Well, Elia, you're an angel too."

I knew that undertaking this delicate and complex ear construction procedure was putting a lot on my team as well as on me. We were all working long hours and sleeping little, and I knew that the ear procedure would make our schedule even more hectic for a few days. A case that required this kind of planning would consume most of the morning. It needed to be scheduled as the first and primary procedure for the day. This meant we would have a backlog of other surgeries for a couple of days.

JoAnne said she had reviewed the schedule and could adjust it so the ear reconstruction procedure could be scheduled for the day after tomorrow. I looked at Elia, who responded with a nod. Then I said, "We have been invited for a late dinner with the young lady's family. It will be at approximately 10:00 tomorrow night. The last case scheduled for tomorrow is at 9:00 p.m., which should give us time to shower and change before we go to dinner. At that time we will discuss the surgery with the family in far more detail. But let's please keep this amongst ourselves until then. Thank you."

The day's surgical procedures went well and uneventfully, and the surgical teams worked until almost midnight. Some twenty patients had undergone surgery that day. By midnight the members of the surgical teams were all bleary-eyed and exhausted, and they still needed to make evening rounds on the wards before they could retire. That's just the way it had to be. Everyone was too exhausted to say much. The group went to the children's ward first. It held approximately forty beds, all of which were full, and additional patients were sleeping on the floor under blankets.

The team divided into two groups, each covering one side of the room. I could see Dixon tapping his fingers as he reviewed the chart at the foot of a bed. He was breathing slowly, and even that seemed painfully difficult. I went up to him, put an arm around his shoulder, and took the chart from his hands, saying, "We need someone up at the front of the hospital who speaks Spanish fluently. Get up there now and have them contact our drivers. Have them bring the Jeeps or the van to the front of the hospital; we will be ready to leave in ten minutes. We have the situation here under control. Go."

Mr. Dixon was too exhausted to refuse, and apparently too tired even to move. He just stood there, slack-jawed. I put my hand on his shoulder and said, "Go now, please." He just blinked, swallowed hard, and left the ward. I'd never seen the poor guy that worn out.

Most of our little patients were asleep now, with their mothers tending to them at bedside. The dressings were clean and dry except for the recently completed skin grafts, but some drainage from the grafts was expected. There were only a handful of patients that needed some attention, and once these were handled, the team was ready to leave. In the morning when everyone was fresh, we would discuss the possibility of undertaking the first stage of the ear reconstruction with rib grafts. But before doing that I would once again review with Elia and JoAnne the surgical equipment available at the hospital, as well as my specialized ear carving instruments that Elia had so wisely decided to bring. The complexity of the procedure we would be performing demanded that we check and re-check to make certain that all necessary preparations had been made, for both the success of the procedure and the safety of the patient.

The next morning, ward rounds began at 6:30 a.m. and the surgery schedule started promptly on time at 7:30 a.m. My team and I were in the midst of a very productive morning when I heard the unmistakable, mildly irritating, but not entirely unexpected voice of the hospital administrator in the hall outside the O.R.

Stepping out of the room, I learned that the administrator simply wanted to confirm that we were going to do the procedure for the total ear reconstruction, and that we were prepared. "Yes, we are," I told him. "It will be a difficult and complicated procedure, one that the students and faculty here have never seen. It will be an excellent opportunity for them to learn. I'm going to give a short lecture and then I'm expecting a full crowd in the operating room."

"So you're completely prepared? Do you have everything you need?" The man was a little annoying, but he was, after all, simply doing his job.

"I have gone over in my mind again and again the procedure and the equipment needed. It seems that what the hospital has available, combined with what I have brought with me, will be more than adequate." He nodded, and I added, "My nurse Elia was thinking ahead, and she brought the specialty instruments for carving the cartilage and reproducing the new ear."

The hospital administrator was beaming by now. He said, "I have to admit that I was excited but cautious about such an undertaking here in León."

"That's understandable," I replied. "It's a very difficult and delicate operation, or I should say a *series* of operations. But I knew that we couldn't do it at the Children's Hospital in Chinandega. The facilities here are better, and the safety factor is considerably improved. I have every reason to believe that the operation will go very well." The administrator looked relieved.

Perhaps you are wondering why we didn't recommend that the patient have the procedure done at the Medical Center in Houston, as was the case with the "unicorn boy." That's a fair question, but the truth was that this type of reconstruction procedure was a challenge even in an American hospital with impeccable American medical standards. In this case, there wouldn't really be anything to gain by going through the elaborate process of getting a visa and handling all of the other logistical details. We had the equipment and supplies we needed here in León, and I was confident that with the proper team assembled, the operation would be a success. I expected nothing less than excellence and efficiency from the teams I worked with, and I had a good record of getting what I expected in that regard.

Satisfied with my responses to his concerns, the administrator thanked me and left me alone with my thoughts. And there was a lot to think about, for it was no easy task that we'd be undertaking. But I had confidence in my own abilities and in those of my team. And what a wonderful teaching opportunity this would be. Interns, residents, and faculty were all planning to turn out to observe. As has been the case with every challenge I've faced, it was my intention that my team and I would exceed everybody's expectations.

I carried this confidence with me when, at the end of another long workday, the team members and I showed up at the young lady's home for supper that night. We were given a warm welcome and made to feel at home immediately. In the back of my mind I'd been wondering if the family might change their minds after a more in-depth discussion of the procedures and issues, but I needn't have been concerned.

Miracles in Bedlam

By the end of our evening together, after reviewing every detail of the operation and the risks involved, the patient and her parents were more excited than ever, and anxious to get started.

* * * * *

On the morning of the surgery, I stood with arms crossed over my chest as the nurse prepared the young lady for the first stage of the ear construction procedure. Contrary to what you might think, my stance was not one of those "doctor poses" intended to convey authority. It would be more accurate to say that my arms were crossed on my chest because there was almost no elbowroom in that O.R., which was jam-packed with observers.

My day hadn't gotten off to the best start. Profoundly worn out from the previous few days and nights, I had slept through my alarm, which was very unusual for me. I woke with a start at 7:45 a.m., which barely gave me time to take a quick shower and get to the hospital. All the way there I berated myself for being late for an important case. I may seem like a hard-ass at times to some of my team and medical students, but I'm always much harder on myself than I am on anyone else.

When I got to the hospital, I was told that most of the group had arrived early and everything was prepared and ready for my arrival. And indeed, as soon I had scrubbed up, donned my operating room attire, and passed through the O.R. doors, I saw that the entire team was ready. I also saw that the room was packed with interns, residents, local staff, and surgeons who had come to see the operation. None of them had ever seen this procedure in León, or anywhere else in Nicaragua.

There is an old saying in the operating room that nothing moves forward until the surgeon arrives. Now here I was in my greens, white coat, skullcap, and Texas boots, and it appeared that we were about as ready to move forward as we were going to get. Nevertheless, as I assumed my position at the table I did a last minute check of everything and everyone around me. I had to reassure myself that everything was in order and that we really were ready to proceed.

Kimberly and JoAnne were assisting me at the table that morning. JoAnne, seeing me looking around the room once again, and being aware of my obsessiveness about preparedness, said, "Don't worry, Doc Joe. We're ready to go. I made sure of it."

I relaxed a bit, smiled and said, "I knew there was a reason I kept you around."

JoAnne retorted, "Well, somebody has to keep you in line." And we all laughed. It was a good way to break the tension that was in the room.

So once again, it was show time. I had just made a couple of opening remarks when I heard a shout from the back corner of the operating room, and I swiveled around to see who was speaking. It was one of the young medical students, who said that he couldn't hear me speaking over the buzz in the room. He politely asked everyone to quiet down so that all could hear me as I explained each step of the procedure.

I thanked him and said, "If there are others toward the back of the room who can't hear me, please raise your hand." Several hands shot up.

"Okay, our friend here is right. You all need to remain quiet, unless you have a question for me. And I'll try to speak as loudly and clearly as possible. I also realize that not everyone has a good view. So I'm going to ask those of you in the front to rotate to the back as we proceed with each step. That way all of you can have an opportunity to view part of the operation."

And so we began. First we needed to reclaim cartilage from the ribs to form the framework for the ear. Marks and measurements were checked and rechecked, and the chest incision made. Questions from observers began immediately, and a rapid-fire discussion ensued.

The procedure was tricky, because we had to remove the cartilage without rupturing the pleura (the membrane surrounding the lungs) and collapsing the lungs as we entered into the chest cavity. Our aim was to avoid the necessity of chest tubes, which would have prolonged the young lady's hospital stay.

I had thought this procedure through again and again for several days, and even though all was going as expected so far, tensions were high. There were already beads of perspiration on my forehead.

The procedure was going to require a different type of scalpel than the short-handled one that we used for so many of our facial procedures. "No worries," said JoAnne, handing me the new scalpel. As I reached out and took it, I did a neck roll to relax my own tension, and spoke nonchalantly to all those in the room to relax theirs.

The removal of the cartilage from the patient's chest went well without entrance into the pulmonary cavity. Next came the dissection and removal of the rib, which also went uneventfully. A very difficult phase of the operation was now over, and almost everyone seemed to take a deep breath at the same time.

I instructed a senior resident on closing the wounds. Meanwhile, JoAnne had moved to a separate table, on which she had placed the cartilage we'd removed from the patient. She also had the carving instruments and the form we had made from the young lady's normal ear, which we would copy. This was the part of the operation that was as much art as it was science.

While carving the ear framework, I continued to take questions from the students and residents. Each student was allowed to rotate to the table for several minutes to see what was happening. The cartilage carving and the assembly took about an hour and a half. By then the chest wound was closed and the dressing applied.

The anesthesiologist hyperinflated the young lady's lungs to full capacity, and no leaks were found. Everybody could now relax.

Then it was time for the next step. Many measurements had already been made, and marks placed with indelible ink on the right temple area, for the placement and alignment of the cartilage framework. This only took about thirty minutes.

A suction tube was placed at the same time, and then the patient was slowly awakened, having spent almost five hours under general anesthesia. She did well.

Although this was only the first of several procedures that would be required to fully construct the congenitally absent ear, the biggest hurdles had now been cleared. Everything had gone better than expected. Accompanied by applause from the room full of observers, I slowly departed from the O.R. Behind my mask I was wearing a big smile, my exhaustion quite forgotten. I felt better than I had in a long time.

Joseph Agris, M.D.

CHAPTER 39
For Want Of Petrol

One evening not long after our return from Puerto Cabezas, two of my male team members and I were spending the evening in a private home near Managua after having spent the day working at the hospital in the capital. Our hosts were kind enough to provide a room and meals for us. Theirs was one of the largest homes in the area, a typical Spanish style with light tan stucco walls and an orange tile roof. As was the case with so many of the large homes in the area, the entire property was surrounded by an eight-foot wall, the top of which was embedded with broken glass shards and razor wire. In addition to the high walls, most of these large private homes had one and sometimes two private security guards, often complemented by attack dogs patrolling the property, as I'd learned the hard way myself. The security precautions were perfectly understandable, of course, since Nicaragua was still for all practical purposes a country at war, with other unsavory elements of society all too willing to take advantage of that strife. Kidnappings, home robberies, and other criminal activities were quite common.

We returned from surgery at approximately 10:00 that night, just in time for dinner, as the usual dinner hour in Nicaragua was between 10:00 and 11:00 p.m. This gave us time to get a quick shower and put on a fresh change of clothes before joining our host family at the table.

The food was locally sourced, fresh, and typical of the region, which added to our enjoyment of the evening and the overall experience of being there. We had just sat down to eat when we heard the loud report of a shotgun. I thought to myself, *That can't be good.* Our host put his hand up and asked everyone to stay in their seats, whereupon he immediately got up, opened a drawer in the beautiful hand-carved mahogany china cabinet, and removed a pistol and a box of shells. I saw that there was a second weapon in the drawer, so I pushed my chair back, and stood up. Our eyes met for just a second, and our host nodded his head approvingly, so I reached in and took the second weapon from the drawer, since I didn't have my Glock on me at the time. He put his hand up again, motioning for the rest of the folks to stay in their seats as he and I went outside.

I followed my host as he carefully moved along the hedgerow, remaining mostly concealed. Then we heard someone groaning as if in agony, followed by screams of some expletives in Spanish.

Our host whispered, "I think the security guard has shot somebody who scaled the wall and came onto the property." He then called out to the security guard to let him know we were there, so he would not mistake us for intruders and turn his weapon on us.

The security guard said, "We have everything under control. A man has climbed over the wall, and I shot him, but he is still alive." The guard told us we could come forward. He said he saw at least two other intruders, but when he wounded the first man to come over the wall, the others disappeared and he could hear their footsteps as they fled.

I approached the wounded man cautiously. He had a pistol at his side, which I kicked away, out of his reach. The guard leaned over and frisked him, and pulled a long, thin dagger from the man's belt. He then turned him on his side and removed his wallet, which had his identification in it. I told the wounded man that I was a doctor, then reached down and ripped open his shirt.

He had received a belly wound from the shotgun and was bleeding, but there was no visibly active pumping vessel, as one would expect had a major vein, artery, or organ been hit.

I said to the security guard, "We are armed, and the situation appears to be under control. Please go to the house and get some towels and come right back."

Within a minute he had returned, and I applied the towels with pressure to the man's abdomen. Here is where it got even crazier.

I'd mentioned previously that during one of my discussions with President Violeta Chamorro, she had asked what I thought they needed at the hospitals. I told her that I did not see any ambulances. The people were poor and transportation was limited and difficult. An ambulance service was very much needed. It wasn't long before the ambulances I'd recommended were delivered. Every day I went to the hospital and there was a beautiful new, fully equipped ambulance. The driver was busy; he would wash and polish his vehicle almost daily, taking great pride in his work, and it would shine in the sunlight.

Now I was dealing with an intruder who had been shot and who needed to be transported to the hospital immediately. I had our host call the hospital to arrange the man's transport, and figured that the ambulance should arrive with sirens and lights flashing in five minutes or so. After ten minutes had passed with no sign of the ambulance, I was a little concerned. When twenty minutes had passed, and there was still no sign of the ambulance, I was livid. My patient was stable, but still in need of acute medical care. If he didn't get that care soon, his condition would likely deteriorate significantly.

My host called the hospital again and asked where the ambulance was. He was told it was at the hospital. He asked the obvious question: Why hadn't they sent the ambulance for the wounded man? The person taking the call couldn't answer that question. I said to my host, "Ask for the ambulance driver." The phone went silent for a few minutes, and then the driver was on the line.

My host asked the driver why he wasn't coming to pick up the wounded man, and he replied, "The ambulance is totally functional. It is fully equipped to handle the problem. I even have an assistant to come with me. But, we have one problem."

Growing impatient, my host blurted out, "And what is that problem?"

The ambulance driver stated, quite matter-of-factly, "We have no petrol."

"You mean there is no gasoline in the ambulance?"

The driver responded, "*Si, si*. No petrol. The government did not provide us with an allocation to purchase petrol, nor did they provide us with chips to present at the gas station in order to obtain petrol. So the ambulance sits, and I polish and I clean, and it sits."

There, but for a tank of gas…

I thought to myself, *That's government bureaucracy in a Third World country.* Then, out loud, I said, "The driver doesn't make enough money to fill the tank."

My host and I looked at each other in amazement, and he said, "Petrol is sometimes difficult to obtain, so I keep four or five cans, each holding five gallons, in the carport. Let's load several of the cans into the back of the SUV and I will drive to the hospital. I will fill up the ambulance and they can come back and pick this gentleman up. I am not going to let him into my SUV with all that blood."

I responded, "You shouldn't have to."

I helped load the gas cans into the SUV, and then my host left for the hospital, which was only a five- to seven-minute drive. Within fifteen minutes I could hear a siren, and a minute after that, I could see flashing lights as the security guard opened the gates for the ambulance to drive right onto the front lawn. I was still staying with the wounded man and applying pressure; his pulse had quickened, but that was not unexpected. He remained alert but was very uncomfortable.

The ambulance driver and his assistant pulled the gurney from the back and brought it alongside the patient, lifted him up, strapped him to the gurney, and then loaded him into the ambulance. After waiting another couple of minutes while I placed an intravenous line and hung a bag of I.V. fluid to help stabilize him, they were ready to leave for the hospital.

Just before leaving, the driver said that since this was a gunshot wound, he had already called the police, so they were coming to the hospital. He added that we also should expect them to come to the house for a statement. About thirty minutes later a policeman arrived with several men, including one who introduced himself as a detective. We gave the detective the intruder's two weapons and his wallet. He looked through the wallet and then turned to us with a big smile.

"I know who this man is. He is wanted for several robberies and several cases of assault with a weapon. We have been trying to apprehend him for several months. You have done the community and us a good service."

The security guard introduced himself and said, "There were two other men coming over the wall, but when I fired at this man, the others dropped down and fled."

Smiling even more broadly, the detective said, "Now that we have the leader of the group, I'm sure he'll be happy to provide us with the information on other members in the gang in return for better food, better jail accommodations, his medical care, and maybe even a reduction in his sentence. I don't see any problem getting the others now that we have the gang leader."

The detective turned to me and said, "I understand you are a physician and surgeon. What do you think was the extent of his wounds?"

"He took a shotgun wound to the abdomen at close range, so he probably has a lot of pellets in the small and maybe large bowel. This will require a surgical exploration of his abdomen and the intestines. There is also a possibility that a pellet entered the liver or spleen, but the amount of bleeding was minimal to moderate, so I don't think a major organ was struck. With intravenous fluid replacement, antibiotics, and good debridement of his wounds, he should survive it and recover fully."

The detective then shook hands with the security guard and again thanked him, repeating that the apprehension of this criminal was a good service, not only to the people he worked for, but to the entire community as well.

My host asked the detective if he would like to come in and finish dinner with us and have a drink. He politely declined, saying he had a lot of paperwork to fill out, and he wanted to question the man and see if he could get some information on the other members of the gang that had been terrorizing the area for the last few months.

I returned to the dining room, and we engaged the safeties on my host's weapons and placed them back in the drawer. The others of course wanted to know what was happening, and we recounted the scenario for them, especially the part about having a fully equipped ambulance, driver, and assistant, but no gasoline because the government had not provided for any. We agreed that if this was the case at this hospital, it probably was the same for all the hospitals throughout Nicaragua, and maybe even the two ambulance boats. I said I would contact the president's niece, Maria, in the morning and see if she could get us an urgent appointment so that we could discuss this glitch with Violeta.

I made contact with Maria the next day, and she called me back a short while later to inform me that we had an appointment with the president that evening. I told her that was perfect, as it would allow us time to take care of the children's surgeries at the hospital. I told her I would be ready by 5:00 p.m. to go to Managua with her. Maria and her driver showed up precisely at 5:00 p.m., and we made the trip in less than an hour, thanks to our lead-footed but safe driver.

When we drove up to the presidential palace, we were met by armed guards at the gates. They recognized Maria and me immediately, and we were admitted without delay. From there, we went directly up to the president's private office on the second floor. Violeta greeted us warmly, inviting us to please sit, motioning to the same lovely mahogany rocking chairs that we had sat in for the meeting about the Puerto Cabezas trip. We were offered iced tea, and she asked us some questions about the types of patients we were seeing, the surgeries we were performing, and the immunizations we were providing. She then asked how she could be of help, saying that Maria had told her that it was a rather urgent situation.

I told her that I was very pleased to see the beautiful ambulances that she had placed at each of the hospitals, and told her that the drivers seemed to consider the ambulances a treasure, to be kept so perfectly washed and polished that you could eat off the ambulances' surface. I told her that I had examined the inside of the ambulance in Chinandega, and found the supplies and equipment to be modern and up to date.

Violeta looked at me with puzzlement, then asked, "If the ambulances are what the hospitals need, and are being kept properly equipped and cared for, what then is the problem that brings you here?"

Anticipating her question, I said, "You've done so many wonderful things with the schools, with transportation, and now with the ambulances, but you have not allocated any gasoline for them!"

She covered her face with both hands as if ashamed, then separated her fingers and peeked out at me as an embarrassed child might do. As she removed her hands, she started to laugh. She said, "You're serious, aren't you? We have this beautiful new equipment to save lives and get people to the hospitals, but there is no gasoline!"

I responded, smiling in response to her gesture of innocence. "Madam President, that is the situation. I talked to an ambulance driver last night, and it seems there have been no funds made available for gasoline or maintenance. The driver told me that there are government-issued booklets with chits that are used to pay the gas station attendant when they fill up, and the station owner then turns the chits in to the government to be reimbursed. Unfortunately, none of the booklets of chits have been issued to the hospitals, so the fuel tanks remain empty, and the ambulances cannot be used."

She said to me, "Then the story I've heard is true; that a man was wounded – a gunshot wound, from what I've heard – and lay bleeding in the grass, but the ambulance couldn't get there because there was no gasoline."

Discussing gasoline and other matters with Madam President

"That is a true story. I was there. We had some five-gallon gas cans at the house, which we brought to the hospital, and filled up your ambulance. The driver and his assistant were then able to come and pick up the wounded man and return him to the hospital for treatment. It turned out that he was wanted for multiple counts of breaking and entering, as well as having been involved in several altercations involving lethal weapons. I didn't want him to die, but I didn't feel sorry for him either. He was a hardened criminal and because he has now been removed from the community, it is a safer place."

I then thanked Violeta for her time and her indulging us by taking care of this "monumental" problem, with which all other matters before her must surely pale in comparison. We all smirked at the obvious absurdity of my remark, and soon we broke out in laughter.

As we left, Violeta said, "Before your team leaves, I would like you to come to my home in the afternoon and be my guest for lunch."

I thanked her for the invitation and said, "I think that could be arranged."

We said our goodbyes, and returned to our car and driver who were waiting for us. We embarked upon the drive back to Chinandega, figuring that barring any unforeseen problems, we would reach the town early that evening. And thus would end yet another successful but exciting day in Nicaragua.

Joseph Agris, M.D.

CHAPTER 40
The Racing Bike

It was another Chinandega Sunday morning, a little after seven, and most of the town was not yet awake. No surgeries were scheduled for the day, but the team and I had made our rounds at the hospital earlier that morning to examine the children, change bandages, adjust medication dosages, and send home those who were doing well. The rounds completed, I decided to take one of my Sunday morning strolls.

At that time, there were only a few automobiles in Chinandega, none of which was in evidence at that early hour. But the three-wheeled chain-drive and bicycle-styled rickshaw taxis were lining up in the market area for the early customers who would soon come to purchase the food and other offerings being set out by the various shopkeepers and street vendors. I took a different route, away from the market, making a left turn towards the more industrial section of Chinandega.

As I crossed the street, I noticed a man sitting in a doorway, his head nodding up and dropping back onto his chest. He looked like a drunk who had found an available perch, dozed off, and slept there for the evening. He snored, lifted his head with closed eyes, and then leaned back against the wall in a rhythm unique to small-town drunkards.

I watched as a wagon, overloaded with heavy metal parts, rolled into the industrial area, struggling to maneuver through the narrow cobblestone streets on its high metal-rimmed wheels. My curiosity was piqued, so I followed the wagon for a while, leisurely ambling over the cobblestones, camera in hand, and photographing as I walked. This section of Chinandega was very different from some of the more affluent areas, in which multi-story homes that had tile roofs and were surrounded by high walls were common. In this area, all of the buildings were single story and built of wood, with their purely functional-looking fronts open to the street.

Standing in front of one shop, just outside the doorway, I could see heavy equipment inside, and men working, even on Sunday. Some were building or repairing the three-wheeled rickshaw-style taxis that filled the streets in the market area of every small town throughout Nicaragua. The men were all muscular and shirtless, wearing greasy stained overalls and leather aprons, and dripping with sweat even at this early hour. Some were barefoot, and a few wore leather sandals on their feet. I knew that they were like so many others I had seen in various small shops, just struggling to make their living in Chinandega's high humidity and unrelenting heat.

I continued on my solitary stroll further down the street, looking into these mini-factories/shops. At the end of the street, I took a left turn, and to my surprise, there were bicycles as far as I could see along both sides of the street. Along this part of the street, a vast array of bicycle fenders, chain drives, handlebars, and seats hung from wires spanning the front of the shops. A short, stocky woman startled me as she exited one of these shops. She obviously didn't know what to make of me as I stood there, staring at her in my long white lab coat, hospital greens, cowboy boots and Stetson hat. After a moment, she looked up at me and smiled sweetly.

She was a pretty woman, with soft brown eyes and broad shoulders. She wore a multi-colored pleated cotton skirt and a clean white short-sleeved fluffy blouse. Her hair was pulled back and braided. Atop her head sat a folded cap, and on top of this cap she balanced a large tray, on which sat several large colorful plastic bowls.

After staring at me for a couple of moments, she composed herself and asked, "May I help you? I am selling rice and hot beans this morning, with homemade tortillas. I made them all myself just this morning."

I asked her how much for the tortillas, and she responded, "Six córdobas for one, ten córdobas for two."

"I'll take two," I said, reaching into my pocket and handing her a well-wrinkled and stained ten-córdoba note. She removed the tray from her head and set it on the ground, then lifted the cover from the large plastic container in the center. Steam rose as she lifted the lid and removed two of the tortillas with a sheet of waxed paper and handed them to me. They were very hot to the touch. She covered the pot and replaced the tray on her head, then began walking to the next shop along the street to peddle her dishes to the workers inside.

Suddenly, she stopped, turned, and called out to me, "I thought I recognized you! You are our Doctor Angel. Thank you for what you have done for our children." I smiled and told her that it was my pleasure.

Miracles in Bedlam

At that moment, a giant of a man appeared from the adjacent establishment. He was at least six-foot-four, probably weighing in at 350 pounds, with a huge girth. He wore a clean white shirt unbuttoned at the neck, most likely because the size of his neck would never have permitted buttoning. His slacks were held up with a six-inch wide, well-worn leather belt with a huge hand-forged copper buckle. His eyes had a pleasant soft glow, and he seemed to be recording and analyzing everything.

He beckoned the lady with a wave of his hand. The two of them began talking rapidly, with the big man pointing to the different food items on her tray. As their conversation continued, the woman glanced over her shoulder at me several times. This clued me in to the fact that I was the subject of their conversation.

After a couple of minutes the man lifted his huge arm and waved for me to come forward, and he seated himself on a high three-legged stool next to a workbench that sat outside his establishment. He made no comment to me but again motioned for me to step forward. As I approached the shop I pointed to my camera, and his first words were, "*Si, si, photo por favor.*"

I saw that his salt-and-pepper hair was immaculately trimmed and slicked back, actually shining in the sunlight. He wiped away the beads of perspiration that coated his brow and motioned for me to sit on the other stool next to him. Looking at the tortillas I was holding, he said, "Eat, eat with me."

When I sat down he said, "You are the doctor who saved the life of and delivered the miracle baby, and who has helped so many other children in Chinandega. I read about you and the American team in *La Prensa*. We have all been following this story and the story about what you were able to accomplish in Puerto Cabezas."

I offered him one of my tortillas, and he accepted it, taking a bite that consumed half of the tortilla. I nibbled at mine. We still had not been introduced, so I asked him what his name was and he replied, "I am Orlando. I am the owner of this establishment. Everyone in this area makes or fixes bicycles, rickshaws, automobiles, and farm equipment."

At that moment, I caught a shadow coming across the table. We both looked up to see a young man with soft brown eyes that had a slight blue violet cast to them. The effect was almost mesmerizing. The young man was observing me very closely, clearly sizing me up. He was tall, muscular, and lean, probably weighing no more than 150 pounds. He had a hint of a mustache, and his mass of black hair was slicked back and as shiny as Orlando's. In fact he looked like a younger and much slimmer version of Orlando. I noticed that his fingers were long and thin, but grease-stained and callused from hard work. Though he had to have been only in his twenties, there was a no-nonsense look about him. He had a very determined set to his square chin, but his lips parted in a friendly smile as he put out his hand and introduced himself as Jose.

Though his mouth was full of rice and beans, Orlando spoke up proudly, saying, "This is my son. He will inherit this business. I have been working with him since he was a teenager, and he has become an excellent mechanic and can fix anything. When we finish eating, I have a surprise for you back in my shop, Doctor."

We talked a little more as we ate. Jose's English was quite good, and I commented on it. Orlando said, "I work hard. I save my money. I was able to send my son to the English school."

As soon we had finished our meal, Orlando stood up and with a wave of his hand, indicated that I should follow him. Entering his shop, I was amazed by the equipment that he had. It really was a small factory. It looked as though he could fix or manufacture any type of metal part. Orlando passed through the main portion of his shop, then abruptly turned and strode swiftly through a door in the rear of the shop that led to an inner room. I stood aside, but Jose laid his hand gently on my shoulder, indicating that I should enter the room too.

And there was Orlando, standing with outstretched arms, proclaiming, "My son's work. I helped him, of course. You have never seen anything like it. It's beautiful and it runs very well." I could see the pride showing in his eyes.

It only took me an instant to see what he was talking about, and once I saw it I could do nothing but stand there bedazzled as I looked upon a beautiful canary-yellow vintage motorbike.

Jose said, "It is more than one hundred years old, and we have been working on it a little at a time for several years. Finally it is finished. Would you like to try it?"

When I was able to speak, I said, "It's beautiful. My son Jacob rode motorcycles. He participated in what is called motocross racing in the United States. And I was an engineer prior to becoming a physician, and have a deep appreciation for what you have accomplished."

Jose began to explain the operation of the micro style racing bike to me. "A hundred years ago, the motorbikes did not have starters. You would mount the motorized bicycle and begin peddling. The electric current from the dry cell batteries would then excite the fields of the magneto, sending voltage to the coil and producing a high-voltage spark, which would ignite the gasoline in the cylinders. This is known as a B-train engine. I made some modifications to it, and it is more powerful than it was when originally produced."

Then Jose pointed to the handlebars, saying, "The throttle is in the grip on the right side, just like modern bikes." He handed me a leather cap with a chinstrap and a pair of goggles, saying, "You are familiar with motorcycles. It is Sunday, and there won't be too much traffic. I would like you to be my guest and take this 100-year-old racing micro cycle for a ride."

He pushed open one of the heavy wooden swinging doors and stepped outside. With one hand, Orlando easily lifted the cycle through the door to the street. Jose placed the cap on my head and snapped the strap closed under my chin, then put the goggles over the cap and indicated that I should adjust them.

Miracles in Bedlam

They could see that I was hesitant. Orlando pulled the goggles over my eyes and reached down and turned the valve to allow fuel to run from the gas tank to the carburetor. I handed my white lab coat and camera to Jose, took hold of the handlebars, and nudged the kickstand upward to the riding position against the rear fender. With Jose's help, I pushed the 130-pound bike onto the road in front of the shop. I swung one leg over the hard leather seat, which sat just above the rear wheel.

This bike was designed specifically for racing, and felt somewhat similar to a vintage English racer that I had once owned. The seat and handlebars were almost at the same level, requiring the rider to lean forward into the machine in a horizontal position, which would reduce wind buffeting and resistance when racing. I began to rapidly peddle the racing bike, and had gone about 15 to 20 feet when the engine suddenly popped to life with a high-pitched sound. I gripped the handlebars more tightly and gently rotated the throttle, whereupon the beautifully reworked antique bike moved forward smoothly and quickly. I found myself puttering down the cobblestone road at 20 or 25 miles an hour, but on the tiny bike, it felt like I was going much faster. And I had yet to open the throttle past the halfway point.

At the end of the road I turned left toward the center of town, where I was more familiar with the streets. I quickly became comfortable and twisted the throttle, driving faster, whipping around slower traffic and startled pedestrians. A big truck that was unloading farm produce into an adjacent shop blocked most of the road. No problem for me, as I bumped up onto the sidewalk, weaving between sacks and barrels of farm produce with only inches to spare. I re-entered the street at the corner, mistakenly veering into oncoming traffic, causing several donkeys to rear up and complain loudly, and angering their drivers. All I could think of was that I was lucky it was a Sunday morning, and that most people were either still asleep or had gone to church. I again gave the racing bike more throttle, which threw the drive into high gear, and the bike charged across the intersection and roared up the empty adjacent street.

If as I'd speculated any folks were still sleeping on this Sunday morning, the noise coming from the exhaust probably startled them awake. I continued for more than a half-mile at what felt like breakneck speed on the tiny bike, leaving the town's narrow streets and homes behind. Finally, I hit the brakes, skidding the rear tire and bringing the cycle to a quick stop. Smiling at the exhilaration of riding a motorbike again after many years, I turned the bike and headed back in the direction from which I had come. This time, however, I decided that I would ride more slowly and much more carefully.

Driving the hundred-year-old bike was a wonderful adventure. Jose and Orlando had done an excellent job in restoring it; it was a marvelous contrivance of steel, leather, and solid rubber tires. I again increased the speed, and the cycle screamed down the empty street. I was intoxicated by the ride and felt invincible, but I was entering a more populated area and slowed down, not only for my own safety but for that of the pedestrians and animals as well.

As I returned to the shop, Jose was waiting and shouted over the sound of the engine, "I trust you enjoyed your ride." I hit the kill button, silencing the engine, and assured him that it was a reminder of a long-forgotten rush. I thanked Jose profusely for the honor of letting me ride such a rare machine, but told him that I really needed to get back to the hospital and tend to my patients. I told him I hoped that we would have a chance to meet again before I returned to Houston, Texas.

Thanking Jose again, as well as his father, I returned the goggles and the racing cap, and replaced them with my lab coat and Stetson hat. With my camera over my shoulder, I strolled to the hospital, still filled with elation that the ride had sparked in me.

There was still some paperwork to do, and JoAnne directed me down the hall to a room that had no windows and poor lighting. An old desk and chair were situated in the corner, and a layer of dust seemed to cover everything. One wall was lined with several tall black metal file cabinets, all bearing the same dusty patina. Another wall was bare, save for a large, outdated calendar hanging from a nail. An imposing stack of patient charts sat on the desk, and I pulled one of the scarred wooden chairs away from the desk and sat down.

JoAnne was careful to keep things in order. She pulled one chart at a time from the stack and placed it in front of me. I flipped through the charts one by one, making notes and signing reports. There were patient records, anesthesia reports, and hand-written operative reports to be completed.

Copies were made using carbon paper, which I had not used in years, and which immediately smudged and stained my fingertips. The task went quickly, since the charts consisted of no more than one or two pages. They were very concise, containing only pertinent information, and none of the usual drivel such as legal liability waivers, permits, and the other obligatory non-patient care material that swelled the charts in U.S. hospitals. Patient charts in the States were often thirty, forty, or more pages thick, and most of the content had no medical value. But don't get me started on *that* again. With JoAnne's help, I completed these charts in 30 minutes and left them neatly stacked on the table.

Just as we were finishing, and I was looking forward to spending the rest of my Sunday at leisure, someone knocked on the door, startling JoAnne and me. I pushed my chair back, stood up, and opened the door. It was the hospital administrator. "What's on your mind?" I asked, trying to disguise my annoyance.

The administrator thrust forward his hand, shook my hand vigorously, and then proceeded to give me a big hug. After a few painfully long seconds, I managed to break loose from this unexpected greeting. Knowing how all administrators liked everything neat and tidy, I said to him, "We have completed all the charts and they are up to date."

"No problem. That can wait for another day. You and your team have done amazing things here and in Puerto Cabezas. It is on the radio. It is in the newspaper. The ABC-

TV news team will take it to the United States, and I'm sure it will go international. You and your team are very courageous. Before you leave, I want to throw a big fiesta this coming Friday to celebrate your accomplishments. I am making arrangements with a beautiful cantina overlooking the ocean at the Port of Corinto. There will be food, drink, and Mariachis. We will dance. I have arranged for cars to take us to the party."

I said, "That sounds like fun, but I am only one member of this team. Everyone participated, and everyone must be invited."

"*Si, si.*"

"When I say everyone, I mean all the doctors, all the nurses, all the ancillary medical help. Not just the Americans, but the local teams too. No one is to be left out. Those who clean the operating rooms. Those who wash and prepare the instruments. Those who clean and wash the sheets and operating room gowns are all to be invited. Like I said, no one is to be left out."

It was plain from the expression on his face that the administrator was not entirely comfortable with my stipulations. Clearly he had never associated or socialized with, much less partied with, hospital personnel other than the doctors. I could see in his face that he wasn't sure how to respond, so I immediately put on a broad smile and turned on the charm. "Everyone is invited. And I do mean everyone. And don't worry about cost. I will personally cover the expenses at the cantina."

An expression of relief came over his face, but there was still a trace of doubt in his eyes, so I added, "The hospital personnel have all worked long hours. They have put in overtime for which I know you are not paying them. This party in Corinto should be for them too, to say thank you to them and let them know that they are all part of the team. And not only should everyone be invited, they should be told to bring their spouses to enjoy the party as well."

The administrator agreed, though not exactly with enthusiasm. He wasn't going to have to foot the bill, but he didn't seem overly anxious to party with the rank-and-file workers. But I paid no attention to his discomfort, for I had other things on my mind. For now, I was satisfied that the fiesta in Corinto would be inclusive, but at that time I had no idea just how inclusive it would turn out to be.

Joseph Agris, M.D.

CHAPTER 41
Doc Matchmaker

The following week flew by, and it was Friday almost before I knew it. The team and I were looking forward to the celebration that would take place at the cantina in Corinto that evening. I was between surgical cases, and had just returned to the small office at the end of the damp, dimly lit hallway. My intent was to deal with the routine of going through the recent patients' charts and photographs. I had no sooner sat down at the desk than there was a knock at the door, and Kimberly walked in before I could respond. She said that the first project was to complete the visa request letters for two children so they could travel to Houston for their surgeries. From her long-time experience working with me, Kimberly knew I had a tendency to let things like this slip. I could handle the medical procedures and follow-ups with no problem, but paperwork was not my strong suit.

It was clear that Kimberly had something else on her mind as well, and it became even more obvious when she pulled up a chair beside the desk and focused on me. I didn't have to wait long to find out what the urgent matter was.

"Forgive me for asking, Doc," she said, "but have you called and checked on Michael and his scorpion sting? Everybody has been asking about him since you sent him home." Was there a slight tinge of accusation in her voice? I couldn't really tell. Maybe it was my imagination. Kimberly knew, better than just about anyone, why my decision to separate Michael and Marta had been necessary.

I forced a smile and placed both hands palm down flat on the desk. "That's a subject I was glad to leave in the past. And it's one that I had assumed was resolved for the time being." I reached down and handed Kimberly my outline for the two visa letters to go to the Embassy, as well as the letter to President Violeta Chamorro, thanking her for her support in this endeavor. Then I shifted around in the overstuffed chair, hanging my legs over one arm and staring out the window into the hospital courtyard. Without looking at her, I said, "Feel free to make any changes or suggestions you feel would be pertinent to the letters. You've done this before, and I trust you."

Kimberly replied curtly, "Yes, sir."

She abruptly rose from her chair to leave, but hesitated and stood facing the desk. "I don't mean to be pushy, but anything you could find out about Michael would be very much appreciated." I briefly wondered if Marta had sent her.

I swung around from the window and fixed my eyes upon her. She looked dead serious and I wanted to lighten the moment, so I gave her a silly little grin and said, "His leg wound was improving when he left. He is in good hands at the Medical Center."

At first, Kimberly said nothing. She walked to the door and opened it briskly, then turned suddenly, facing me, and said, "I think you need to call him directly and find out what is happening and how he is doing. The entire staff is waiting for an update and a report from you. I know you're still a little upset that he broke the rules, but common decency says you need to check on his condition and let the team know. He is still one of us, after all." She took a moment – just long enough to read the expression on my face – but she did not wait for an answer as she walked out of the room, pulling the door closed behind her.

I wanted to get back to my work, but Kimberly had set the tone and I couldn't just let it slide. I thought again about the passionate bond that had developed between Marta and Michael, wondering if I had been responsible for ending a relationship that could have actually gone somewhere. Although I had suggested to both Michael and Marta that their relationship could continue in the future, I wasn't at all certain that what they had shared was genuine and potentially lasting. I thought it might have been nothing more than a short-lived fling, a means of alleviating war-zone stress, nurtured by the forced closeness that exists in teams like this, and the raging hormones of the young. Similar things have happened to hundreds of thousands of couples throughout history. On the other hand, I hadn't given Michael and Marta's relationship any chance to blossom, because my primary concern was, of necessity, the well being of the team.

For her part, Marta had returned to work and performed admirably, and her spirits had seemed somewhat lifted after she and I had our talk. But whenever I looked at her, no matter what she happened to be doing at the time, I could see that her heart really wasn't in her work as it had been before. She went through the motions with the utmost professionalism, but her eyes revealed her sorrow. A nearly visible aura of sadness surrounded her, and I would have had to be completely insensate not to detect it.

But I had to force myself not to dwell on these matters, because the American medical team and I were here to help these children and adults who could not help themselves. We weren't here to play matchmaker.

After Kimberly left, I sat for several minutes with my head in my hands. Knowing her as well as I did after many years of working with her, I knew that the exchange we'd just had would not be the end of it. I really had no choice but to try to get Michael on the telephone, but I vowed to myself to keep my remarks short and to the point.

I pushed my chair back, grimacing at the scraping sound it made as it was scooted across the old tile floor. I stood up, retrieved my white coat from the wooden peg beside the door, and left the little records room for the hospital administrator's office. I knew that he had a telephone there, and I hoped it was working today, and that I would be able to place an international call with it. If that sounds a little quaint to you, bear in mind that this was before the existence of ubiquitous cell phones with reliable international networks. In those days, phone service was at best uncertain in remote spots such as this hospital in Chinandega.

As much as I was *not* looking forward to speaking with Michael, I was even less eager to have to discuss the matter with the hospital administrator. But I knew that during regular hours the administrator's office was never left vacant. I could only hope that the man had already gone to lunch, and that the only person I would have to deal with was his secretary, Violet, who might be marginally easier to handle.

Upon reaching the administrative office, I knocked softly and opened the door to the anteroom, and was relieved to see that only Violet was there, sitting behind her desk, typing. Violet stood when I walked in, and I could see she was wearing a home-made but nicely knit bright-yellow top with short sleeves, a full-length matching skirt, and yellow sandals with colorful little flowers across the top. For Nicaragua, she looked quite fashionable. She wished me a good afternoon and pointed to the chair next to her desk, saying, "I am sorry, but the administrator has gone to lunch."

"I am not here to see the administrator. I need to use the telephone to place a long distance call to the United States. I need to inquire about our injured nurse, Michael, who had the infected leg following a scorpion sting. The team is worried about him and would like a report." I spoke slowly, almost reluctantly, and was met only with silence.

Just before the silence became truly awkward, Violet said, "I see. Since the call is for medical purposes, I'm sure it will be all right for you to use the telephone."

She turned and opened the door to the administrator's office and walked me into the room, where she pointed to an old-fashioned black metal rotary phone, then excused herself, closing the door behind her. I picked up the phone and held it to my ear, and in a few seconds I heard a dial tone. I retrieved the list of team members with their emergency contact numbers from my wallet and slowly dialed the phone, hearing it go click, click, click with each turn of the dial. The first try was unsuccessful. I hung up and waited a couple of minutes, then picked the receiver up again and redialed.

This time I could hear the phone ring and was hopeful that someone was there. The telephone was answered on the third ring, and I heard Michael's voice, "Hello."

I said, "Hello, Michael. This is Agris, calling you from Nicaragua to see how you are feeling, and to find out how the leg is healing."

There was a fairly lengthy pause from his end. As I'd expected, my call came as a complete surprise to Michael. Finally he spoke. "Thank you so much for calling. The leg is almost back to normal, and I'm not limping any more. I even sleep through the night without pain. The doctors here said I could return to my nursing job at the hospital next week."

"I am glad to hear that. The members of the team were very concerned. I will inform everybody that you are doing well."

Just as I was getting ready to end the conversation, Michael suddenly blurted out, "I bought a ring."

Again there was silence, but this time it was my turn to be a bit confused and at a temporary loss for words. Michael must have realized that, and he continued, with the words coming rapid-fire. "I am in love with Marta and I bought an engagement ring. Since I haven't been working, I have been trying to borrow the money to return to Nicaragua... and propose."

I have to admit I was a little stunned. To myself I thought, *This young man is insane.* Then I thought of myself when I was younger, and the statement "love is blind" crossed my mind. But to Michael I said, "You really want to return to Nicaragua to see Marta?"

"I will find a way. That's all I think about."

I said, "Have you spoken to Marta?"

"Only once to tell her that my leg wound was improving and I was feeling much better."

"Have you talked of marriage with her?"

"I love her and she said she loves me."

"Michael, I don't want you to be disappointed if she refuses you."

"She won't! But even if she did say no, I could handle it. And I would understand, because we come from such different cultures and backgrounds."

I thought a moment and finally said, "I can see that one way or another, you need to get this out of your system. As a matter of fact, I think you should return to Nicaragua while we are all still here."

Michael, in a voice that was clearly pained, responded, "I would love nothing more, but I don't have the money for airfare."

Without hesitation, I responded, "Go to my office today, and tell the secretary to book you on the next flight to Nicaragua. I believe there is a Continental flight that arrives in Managua at around 4:20 p.m. I want you to tell my secretary to put the ticket on my American Express card, and if she has any questions, she can call me at the hospital administrator's office – she has the number – and she can speak with his secretary Violet for the confirmation. I will have our driver Julio, whom you have met, meet you at the Managua airport and drive you to Chinandega. It is important that you make that flight and arrive in Chinandega this afternoon."

By now I was smiling to myself, thinking, *Michael is merely a young fool and a sucker for a pretty face.* But on the other hand, I was now determined to help Michael and Marta decide whether they were in love or merely in lust. I felt that tonight's hospital party with music, dancing, and everyone in attendance would be a surprise for both Marta and Michael. If Michael was really serious about the proposal, the setting would be perfect.

I continued, "I want you to wear a suit on the airplane and be properly dressed. Also, throw some everyday clothes into a backpack. After we hang up, go directly to my office and have my secretary arrange the flight, then drive directly to the airport." There was no response, and for a moment I thought the line had gone dead. I tried again. "Hello, hello? Michael, are you still there?"

Finally, in a shocked voice, he said, "I'm leaving now."

"Good. Remember, put on a suit and jacket, clean shirt and nice shoes, and go to the office immediately. And then go directly to the airport."

"Thank you, Doctor. Thank you."

"The privilege is mine. Now GO!"

I heard the line click off, and I placed the heavy black metal earpiece back onto the receiver and left the administrator's office. On the way out, I stopped at Violet's desk and asked her, "Where can we reach Julio, the driver?"

"There was an emergency earlier today that required the patient be taken to the general hospital in Managua. Julio is there."

I said, "That will make it even easier. Do you have a way to reach him?"

Violet replied, "He should be arriving shortly at the General Hospital's emergency room, and I can leave a message for him and ask him to call us back."

"Tell Julio to be at the Managua airport to pick up Nurse Michael on the 4:20 p.m. Continental flight. Tell him to bring Michael directly to the Don Callejas home in Chinandega. He is not to stop anywhere else, and is not to discuss this with anyone."

Violet, who had been eating her lunch, stopped in mid-bite with an expression of utter surprise on her face. She asked, "Nurse Michael is returning to Nicaragua?"

"Yes, and you are not to tell anyone. I want this to be a surprise for the medical team."

Violet said, "We have to tell Marta. She was very worried about him and I know she wants to see him."

"Absolutely not! This is supposed to be a surprise, and it will not be a surprise unless you keep this secret. I don't want Marta or any members of the team to know about his arrival until he appears at the fiesta in Corinto."

"I understand. I can keep a secret." She crossed herself as she spoke.

"Call the General Hospital immediately and have them set this up with Julio."

"Did I mention Julio was driving the hospital ambulance? He will have to pick Nurse Michael up at the airport in the ambulance."

I said, "Good! With an ambulance he should find it easier to drive right in to the airport grounds. If he puts the ambulance lights and siren on they should be able to get from Managua to Chinandega in half the time. So... tell Julio to drive like he has an emergency!"

A big smile washed across Violet's face. She stood up from her desk and excused herself to go to the administrator's office and make the necessary phone calls.

I returned to the operating room, where they were ready to start the next series of surgical procedures, in particular another hand case with webbed fingers. All of the fingers were webbed like a duck's foot. The resident doctor from León said he had read about this procedure and asked if he could make the markings.

While he was doing that I took a couple of steps to the adjacent table, where the local doctor who had been working with me for several weeks was preparing to do a simple unilateral cleft lip. He went through the markings with me; I made one adjustment and told him to begin the operation.

I stepped back to the other operating table and looked at the markings the resident had made on the little patient's hand. I made some measurements and told the resident we would also need skin grafts from the child's upper thigh. I explained that while we were working on the hand, the nurses needed to wash and put towels around the upper thigh in preparation for the skin graft.

With the child's fingers now separated and the skin flaps interdigitated, the skin grafts were being applied. This required only simple sutures that the residents were very capable of doing, and I excused myself from the room.

I briskly walked down the dimly lit hallway to the doctor's lounge. After a quick change of clothes, I walked to the machine shop where I had met Jose and his father the previous Sunday. I couldn't get my mind off of that canary yellow 100-year-old motorbike. I wanted to use it tonight to take Michael from Chinandega to the fiesta at Corinto; I figured it would be quite a spectacular entrance.

It only took me a few minutes to walk the four blocks into the industrial area of Chinandega and locate Orlando and Jose's shop. The yellow motorbike was parked outside. As I entered the shop, I saw Orlando working at a lathe, and just beyond him, I saw Jose, busily huddled over an engine block and covered in grease.

I didn't want to startle Orlando while he was working on the lathe, and patiently waited just inside the shop until he looked up. He raised the face shield and said, "Doctor, what a nice surprise!"

Time being short – I needed to get back to the hospital as quickly as possible – I said to Orlando, "I need a big favor. I need to borrow the racing bike tonight for a fiesta. I would also like to invite you, your son, and members of your family to come to Corinto and join the fiesta."

Jose immediately looked up from the engine block he was working on, and turning to his father, he said, "I really want to go. Can we?"

Orlando slowly removed the face shield and turned to me. "*Gracias*, we will be there tonight. The bike is gassed up and ready to go. You have already demonstrated your ability on it. Take it with you now and we will meet you in Corinto tonight."

Jose rushed over, kicked up the metal stand and steadied the bike while I mounted it. He then gave it a push onto the dirt road and it immediately roared to life. Within minutes I was back at the hospital. I took delight in the surprised looks I got from the front gate guard, as well as several other people who were on the sidewalk. I dismounted and walked the cycle through the hospital's main gate and behind the high protective walls, knowing that the yellow motorbike would be safe here until I was ready to use it this evening. My only big concern now was whether or not the hopeful groom would get here in time to make the grand entrance with me.

CHAPTER 42
Racing To Corinto

I entered the hospital in a dead run, going directly to the doctor's lounge, where I washed, changed, and returned to the operating room for the remainder of the afternoon. I was hoping against hope that the plane would be on time and that Julio would have no trouble locating Michael and bringing him to Chinandega. There was no way I could monitor the progress in real time, so all I could do was hope for the best. I hoped I could count on Julio to do his part. I thought to myself that Michael would get a kick out of the ambulance ride with the lights and sirens going. Who wouldn't?

One other puzzle piece remained. I had to make sure that Marta attended the fiesta. These days she didn't seem to be in much of a mood to socialize or celebrate, and I was afraid she might volunteer to stay behind tonight with the skeleton crew at the hospital while the rest of us partied.

When surgery ended, the team gathered in the doctors' lounge to review the day's procedures, and then we went to the children's ward for late afternoon rounds. Marta was in attendance, and I made it a point to take her aside and extend my personal invitation to the fiesta in Corinto.

Much to my relief she replied, "I bought a new dress just for tonight. And I hope you will find it attractive and will dance with me." I smiled and said that I would save a dance for her.

Now, if only Michael got on his flight, and if only the flight would be on time... details, details, details! I was surprised all over again by the emotional stake I now had in making sure Michael and Marta had every possible chance to solidify their relationship.

Our group went from bed to bed, talking to the parents, changing dressings, checking the intravenous lines, and dispensing medications as needed. Everyone was clearly excited about tonight's fiesta, and they all seemed to move more efficiently and quickly, probably because they all wanted to have time to shower and dress for the evening.

Apart from my matchmaking project, I was also very interested in studying the interaction at the party. This would be the first time that the hospital's administrative people and the local doctors would be mingling with the other hospital personnel at a dinner party and dance. Since these two groups normally did not socialize, I figured that if nothing else, this party would be a fascinating – at least fascinating to me – social experiment.

* * * * *

I needn't have worried about Julio, who was no stranger to the airport and its personnel. Being in the ambulance, he was able to get the guards to open the front gates and allow him to park directly in front of the main entrance, as he later reported to me. The Continental flight arrived a few minutes late and Julio was beginning to feel a little anxious, but once it arrived and everyone had deplaned, he quickly spotted Michael with his backpack over one shoulder. Julio told me that Michael had a big smile on his face and almost a skip in his walk. His first thought upon seeing Michael was, *To look at him, you'd never know that he had recently come close to losing a leg.*

Julio left the ambulance and took the few steps to the front of the terminal, where he greeted Michael with a handshake and directed him to the ambulance. I would have liked to have seen the expression on Michael's face when he was told that they would be returning to Chinandega in an ambulance.

With Michael safely belted into the passenger seat, Julio started up the ambulance, turned on the flashing lights, and hit the siren. Pedestrians scattered as he slowly rolled forward through the gates of the airport, turning right onto the main street. Traffic was usually heavy at this time of the day in Managua, but with lights flashing and siren wailing, he moved quickly out of Managua and north towards Chinandega.

* * * * *

Barrett, Dixon and I walked through town to the Callejas home, where we were all still staying. The other nurses were taken by car to the homes where they were guests. Upon arriving at the Callejas home, I saw that Marvin Zindler, Lori, and Bob were on the veranda with iced tea in their hands, already dressed for tonight's occasion.

Don Roberto and Doña Etta greeted us, and told us to hurry and get ready. Everyone was in an exuberant mood.

I asked Mr. Dixon to join me in my room for a quick word, and his facial expression immediately changed to one of worry. I put my arm around his shoulder and whispered in his ear, "It's something good, Jose, I promise. It's a surprise."

I told him that Michael was returning on the late afternoon flight and that Julio was in Managua with the ambulance and would be driving him back to Chinandega. He would be coming directly here to the Callejas home. I added that at this point, I didn't want anyone else to know that Michael was going to join us at the fiesta this evening.

"And you and Barrett will be going with the ABC-TV team in SUVs from here," I said. "But I won't be riding with you. I will be on that yellow motorbike – the one I have parked at the hospital. Michael will be with me."

I could see by Dixon's expression that he was absolutely flabbergasted by what I had just said. Finally he said, "Well, it's your party. I guess I have nothing more to say."

I said, "This is not just about Michael's surprise return to Nicaragua, or about him going to the fiesta; I'm also really quite anxious to see Marta's response when she sees Michael tonight. She has no clue he is coming."

Dixon just stood there looking at me quizzically. I said, a little cryptically, "For better or for worse, that is the way it is, and I hope the surprise is a happy one for everybody."

Apparently not catching the meaning of "for better or for worse," Dixon nodded, then patted me on the shoulder and said, "Good luck!"

By the time I had showered, shaved, and dressed for the evening, the first car had already left with the ABC-TV team and some members of the Callejas family. Dixon and Barrett were just getting ready to leave with Roberto, and I asked them to give me a ride back to the hospital so I could get the motorbike. I was getting worried because Michael had not yet arrived. Then I heard the siren of an ambulance coming closer and closer.

Without thinking, I burst out, "That's Nurse Michael and Julio." Dixon looked at me in surprise, and I realized that I had violated my own code of secrecy.

Barrett said, "No, that's an ambulance siren."

"Michael is arriving in an ambulance from Managua and Julio is driving."

Barrett still looked confused, and I said, "Discuss it with Mr. Dixon on your way to Corinto. Get going now!"

Less than a minute later I opened the door of the Callejas home just as the ambulance was parking in front. A small crowd had gathered. Julio and Michael stepped out of the ambulance and shook hands with everybody. Clearly Michael's arrival in Nicaragua was not going to be a surprise for everybody, but Marta was the main one who needed to be kept in the dark for the time being. So I swore everyone to secrecy.

Julio looked at me with a worried expression on his face, as if to say, "I hope this all works out the way you planned." I just grinned.

I took Michael's backpack from him and threw it through the door, then told Roberto to lock up and take the others on to Corinto in his car, but to drop Michael and me off at the hospital first.

Everyone seemed thoroughly confused as we piled into Roberto's car and headed for the children's hospital. Once we got there, Michael and I jumped out, waving to the rest as they turned around and headed off towards Corinto.

I waved to the guard at the front of the hospital, and he slid the big steel bar across the gate and admitted us. Then I grabbed Michael by his sleeve and pulled him through the entrance and into the courtyard, where he stood transfixed, staring at the canary yellow motorbike.

I donned a leather helmet and goggles, wishing I'd thought to get a helmet for Michael too. Well, I would just have to drive extra carefully and hope for the best. As I swung my leg over the hard leather seat, I pointed to the carrier rack sitting over the gas tank behind me. That was what passed as a passenger seat. Michael dutifully climbed aboard, looking a little doubtful.

I then pedaled the cycle through the front gate, bounced down the curb onto the cobblestone street, and began to pedal a little faster. I reached down, rotating the valve that allowed the gasoline to flow from the tank to the carburetor. As I pedaled faster, the engine came to life and the exhaust pipe emitted a loud staccato popping sound that startled the pedestrians into jumping out of the way. I gradually twisted the throttle, and the bike's front wheel lifted off the pavement for a second as it lurched forward. At that point, Michael seemed to be taking our little jaunt much more seriously, dramatically tightening his grip around my waist.

Dusk had fallen, and it was quickly growing dark. The few streetlights, if you could even call them that, had come on just in time for us to see an open construction ditch, unmarked, at the end of the road. I barely had time to dodge the ditch, but I did manage to do so. I continued racing the cycle along the main street, then took a left at the street adjacent to the old library. Bounding down the road, I gripped the handlebars even tighter because of the vibration from the cobblestones.

I don't think Michael was used to being on a motorcycle, much less at this speed, and with my driving antics. I was pretty sure that bouncing over the cobblestones made Michael's leg wound ache, but to his credit, he ignored the pain and soldiered on. Then again, I don't think I had really left the poor guy much choice.

Continuing south toward the beach, I approached the corner where Iglesia Guadalupe was situated. There was a farm wagon loaded with produce blocking the intersection; it was slowly being pulled by two small mules. Fortunately the sidewalk that encircled the church was wide and empty of pedestrians as I brought the cycle onto the pedestrian walkway, swung a sharp left, and twisted the throttle, producing a thunderous roar from the exhaust pipe.

The startled mules reared up on their hind legs, and the wagon lurched suddenly to its side before righting itself again. I took a quick glance over my shoulder and saw that the driver was shaking his fist and screaming at me, but I could not hear him over the roar of the cycle. I probably could have gone back to see what he was trying to tell me, but I thought better of it.

Michael gripped me even tighter and pulled himself in closer to keep from being thrown to the pavement as we made another sharp left turn. Not wanting to remove either hand from the handlebars, I poked Michael with my elbow to get his attention. I shouted at him to reach under my arm and squeeze the bulb on the handlebar, sounding the big horn mounted next to me on the cycle.

The squawking of the horn did its job, sending the pedestrians hurriedly from the street to the safety of the narrow sidewalk. I wondered what they thought of this brightly colored contraption and its driver, decked out in a leather helmet and huge goggles and racing down the center of the street, with a wide-eyed passenger clinging to him for dear life. There were nine more blocks of cobblestone streets, and I honestly think that Michael was having misgivings about what he'd gotten himself into when he mounted the racing bike with me. In retrospect, I have to admit that his apparent misgivings caused my opinion of his judgment to improve significantly.

Actually, as Michael later told me, he was thinking to himself, *He really is the Crazy Texan.* At one point he leaned in close and yelled into my ear, "Have you tested the brakes on this mechanical marvel?"

I shouted back, "Not great, the only brakes are on the rear wheel!"

Thank goodness the cobblestone ended and blacktop appeared as we spun into the rotunda that took us south onto Route 24 to Corinto. We passed a large Texaco gas station, an open market, and a food mart, as well as the usual three-wheeled rickshaw taxis, donkey carts, and one bus. These were far more obstacles than I wanted to deal with, but fortunately the deep roar of the cycle and the squawking of the horn forewarned the pedestrians, most of whom fled from the intersection. Others tempted fate, standing motionless – even catatonic – until the very last moment, whereupon they would snap out of their stunned state and run away from the yellow menace that was bearing down on them. It is probably not to my credit that I was so thoroughly amused by this little game, but in all honesty, I was having a ball.

My attention was now totally fixated on the rapidly approaching traffic circle. To avoid obstacles on the west side of the circle and keep from being hit myself, I had to quickly and almost violently weave back and forth, alternating between throttle and brakes as if driving through a constantly-shifting maze. A third of the way around the circle, I exited on to the route that would take us south to Corinto. At this point, Michael was not the only one who had butterflies in his stomach.

Joseph Agris, M.D.

CHAPTER 43
Everyone Loves A Party

I pulled hard on the handlebars and brought the cycle back to vertical as I threaded my way between two oncoming vehicles and a wagon. Michael and I were now leaving the southernmost edge of the city of Chinandega, and thankfully, the heavy late afternoon and early evening traffic had begun to thin out. The few pedestrians, wagons, and automobiles became sparse as we sped out of the city.

The fact that the road was now smooth blacktop, and much wider than the narrow cobblestone streets in Chinandega, not only made for a much more comfortable ride, but also for a considerably safer one. The wider road allowed me to maneuver around any objects that might suddenly appear.

I rolled on the throttle a little more, and we flew along the smooth straightaway. The faster the bike went, the more stable it was. Being on a smooth, wide road with little traffic, I indulged the urge to go into true Crazy Texan mode, so I twisted the throttle all the way to its stop, and soon we were moving along at more than 80 miles per hour. The racing cycle roared down the open road like a maddened rhino, and I have to admit that I was grinning wildly, intoxicated by the speed and the swirling clouds of dust kicking up in our wake. I am not so certain that Michael shared my sense of exhilaration, judging from the death grip he had on me. At one point, Michael tapped me sharply on the shoulder and pointed ahead. We were rapidly approaching a fork in the road, with two signs. One read "Paso Caballos," with an arrow pointing to the right, and the other read, "Corinto," with an arrow pointing to the left.

I braked hard and veered left, causing the back tire to slide as we exited at the turn. Midway into the turn, I twisted the throttle to full, turning the skid into a power slide as we accelerated rapidly out of the turn. As we barreled down the straightaway, telephone poles were streaking past in a blur, and to be honest, I was having fantasies of being a member of the brotherhood of world-famous motorcycle racers, like the legendary Giacomo Agostini. I imagined the crowds cheering, *AY-Gree, Ay-Gree* (as opposed to Agostini's *AH-go, AH-go*) as we thundered past. Then, I noticed that the wind slapping our faces now bore the aroma of salty ocean air. We were coming closer to our destination.

The stretch of road suddenly became rutted and rough, torn up by the heavy eighteen-wheelers carrying containers and other loads inland from the port in Corinto. Michael's death grip intensified to the point that it felt like a vice on my shoulders. Now, I might be that Crazy Texan from time to time, but I'm not stupid. I geared down and quickly reduced our speed, which inspired Michael to gradually relax his grip. It was only then that I realized how painful that grip had been. At this more leisurely pace, we could both enjoy the strikingly beautiful sights and delightfully refreshing smells of the palm trees and thick green foliage that lined the sides of the road as we motored ever closer to the beach. Fortunately, at this time of evening, the main road through town was almost deserted, with no container trucks or heavy equipment transports. As a matter of fact, we passed only two parked automobiles and a few donkey-drawn wagons that were hitched to posts along the side of the road.

Several boys were walking up from the beach, one carrying fishing poles and another with a basket on his head, which I assumed was filled with the boys' catch. They turned and gawked, speechless as the yellow racing machine roared past them, and both Michael and I smiled and waved at them. *AY-Gree! AY-Gree!*

We were now driving right down the center of the road through Corinto, careful to avoid the sand that had collected to either side, not wanting to kick up a dust cloud or lose control in the slippery sand. A small hand-painted and well-worn sign appeared before us, bearing the words *Playa* (beach) and underneath that, *Cantina*, with a red arrow pointing to the right. I slowed into the turn and then twisted the throttle, increasing our speed and the scream of the exhaust as the cycle zoomed quickly towards our final destination. Thunder was roaring from the exhaust pipe.

The evening air had turned cooler now that the sun had dropped behind the high volcanic peaks, and a comfortable breeze was coming off the ocean. We had no problem finding the cantina, as the road leading to it was lined with a row of colored lights. The parking area was filled with many cars, and the cantina itself was a vast building with a screened-in veranda facing the ocean.

Michael later told me that an overwhelming wave of anxiety, bordering on terror, swept over him as we approached the cantina. But then, he said, that terror, along with a good part of his self-restraint, had begun to evaporate when he heard the music playing as we rolled into the parking lot.

I pulled the cycle to the side under a palm tree, stopped, and told Michael he could get off. Then I killed the engine, leaned the cycle against a palm tree, and climbed off, removing my big goggles and the brown leather helmet and hanging them over the handlebars. I was pretty sure that the bike, helmet, and goggles would be quite safe.

Michael and I brushed the dust and sand from our clothes and entered the cantina. The party was taking place in a large room at the center of the cantina, where folding tables and chairs had been arranged in a square for our group. Beyond the square, dozens more folding chairs had been placed in haphazard rows. The American team was seated with the hospital administrator and his assistant. As we maneuvered around the tables toward the already-crowded dance floor, Michael's head was moving rapidly from right to left, his eyes panning each section of the room. I knew what – or more accurately, whom – he was looking for, but she was nowhere to be seen. He looked a little downcast, but I whispered, "Don't worry. I am pretty sure she's going to be here, if she's not here already."

I spotted her first, dancing with Jose Dixon. Her back was to us, but Dixon had seen us enter. I gave him a wave of my hand, and shook my head, motioning for him to keep her positioned with her back to us. He did so until we were only a few feet away. Then at my cue, he twirled Marta, stopping her directly in front of Michael.

The look on her face as she found herself gazing directly into Michael's eyes is something I will remember forever. Their eyes met and managed to have a lifetime's worth of conversation before either of them spoke a word. Michael stood there as if in shock, but you could see the excitement building rapidly within him. Marta grew pale, and her hands flew up to her face. She bit her lower lip, looking as if she was lost and did not know what to say. As Marta stood there, drinking in the vision of Michael's face, joyful tears welled up in her eyes, and though Michael was turned away from me, I am certain his response was the same.

He reached out and took both of her hands, pulling her in close, until they met in a tender embrace. Then, standing right there in the middle of the dance floor, Michael kissed her, at once tenderly and passionately. She suddenly realized where she was and gasped when he released her, gently withdrawing from his embrace and looking slightly embarrassed, as people began to gather around them.

Meanwhile I had quietly and quickly slipped away to bring the Mariachi players forward. They now formed a half circle around Michael and Marta. I slipped through the crowd, and when I reached Michael I patted him gently on the shoulder. Michael looked at me for a moment and I nodded, not saying a word, then I retreated to allow them their special moment.

Michael knelt down on one knee, reached nervously into his pocket, and pulled out the ring. He held it up to her and said, "I love you, Marta. Will you marry me?"

As the Mariachi band played, the small crowd that had gathered around the couple began to applaud and cheer. Michael continued to hold the ring up as Marta looked down into his sensitive features and glowing smile, joyful tears welling up in her eyes. It took her a while to find the words to respond, but when she did the words poured out in a rush.

"Michael, it's all so fantastic. I am in love with you. I cannot explain why it happened so suddenly, but it did. And yes, I will marry you!"

As he put the ring on her finger, she looked down into his face and beheld the love that so filled him. Her embarrassment vanished instantly as she leaned forward, placed her hands on either side of his head, pulled him up, and kissed him on the lips.

Marta was literally trembling as Michael led her to a seat at the closest table. By then, almost everyone in the cantina had gathered around the newly betrothed couple, and to a person, they were completely enthralled by this unexpected event.

Marta turned to Michael with a pleading look in her eyes. "Can we please move away?"

Michael chuckled softly, then replied, "I could never refuse a request from a beautiful lady."

As they walked out onto the veranda in the moonlight, the Mariachi band returned to the stage and continued playing. Some of the guests returned to their tables, and others began to dance.

And me? I was beaming. I looked out across the room and my smile grew even wider when I saw that the hospital administrators and the doctors were intermingling with the other hospital personnel, both at the tables and on the dance floor. Everyone loves a good party, especially if it includes a love story with a happy ending.

I decided then and there that each of our mission trips would end with a similar party to thank *all* of those who participated in caring for the children. It was the beginning of a tradition that we have carried forward all over the world for nearly three decades as the Agris-Zindler Children's Foundation and the People Helping People organizations have conducted their many mission trips in more than forty different countries.

The fiesta in Corinto continued until 2:00 a.m., when the Mariachi players finally said good night and left the stage. The event was a resounding success, not only as a party with good food, good drinks, and good music, but also as a means of bringing all levels of hospital personnel together. Not to mention that it brought Michael and Marta together at last. In retrospect, that scorpion sting was probably the best thing that could have happened to Michael.

And falling in love with Nicaragua is one of the best things that has ever happened to me. Love doesn't always win, but it triumphs often enough to keep me believing, and to keep me inspired to return again and again to the beautiful country that captured my heart so many years ago.

Joseph Agris, M.D.

EPILOGUE
Building Bridges

My love affair with Nicaragua. which goes back decades, has only grown stronger with time. One of the advantages of returning year after year to the same towns and villages throughout Nicaragua was the opportunity to perform staged surgical procedures as well as revisions, because turning good results into exceptional ones requires that many plastic and reconstructive surgeries be staged, typically at six-month to one-year intervals. This is particularly true for reconstructive procedures for severely burned patients, as well as the correction of congenital anomalies such as reconstructing or creating an ear, or separating multiple fingers to correct a webbed fingers deformity.

It doesn't end there. Patients you have treated as infants and pre-teens have grown up and are now in their twenties and thirties. You are afforded the overwhelming gratification of seeing them grow up, prosper, and have families of their own in the very close-knit structures of their small towns and villages. This provides an opportunity to follow the results of your surgical procedures for twenty or even thirty years. This type of follow-up means a lot to the surgeon, as it offers opportunities for self-education, wherein the surgeon is able to continually improve his or her skills. Such long-term observation of the results of a surgeon's work helps to ensure better surgical results in future cases. The work becomes a living legacy, generation to generation, for the doctors and the other members of the medical teams that return each year.

Recently I returned to Chinandega for my yearly visit to see children and adult patients, and also to visit with the patients we had treated more than two decades ago. The most memorable visit was with a young woman named Monica Escundero Abaunca.

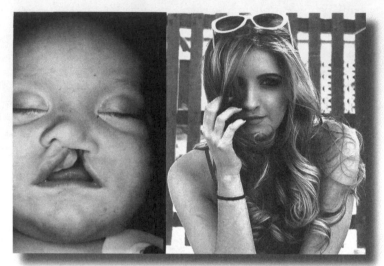

More than twenty years ago I had repaired this young lady's unilateral left cleft lip, and on a return visit I had fixed her cleft of the hard palate and the soft palate with a muscle repair in a single operation. The lips scar is almost invisible, and she demonstrated that with a little makeup, you could not see it at all.

The muscle repair and cleft palate repair had made it possible for her to speak in a normal tone. This changed her entire life, and she went on to the English school. She is fluent not only in Spanish but also in English, and she speaks the latter with only a barely noticeable accent.

It's almost unheard of to have a twenty-year followup on a surgical procedure. I was very proud of her and of my result. But then the surprise came; I could hardly believe what I was hearing. All I could think of was holding this young lady as an infant twenty years ago, when she had such a significant defect in her lip, hard palate, and soft palate that she had difficulty eating.

She blurted out, "I am a candidate for Miss Nicaragua." I got choked up, and had tears in my eyes. This just supports what I have always said: these operations are more than just surgical procedures. *They are life changing.*

And as I have also said many times, it is never just for the patient. The attitudes of the immediate family, the distant family, neighbors and friends, and the entire community change toward our patients with the repair of these congenital defects, or the repairs of burns and injuries that we have dealt with every day for decades in Nicaragua and throughout the world.

Then another beautiful woman entered the room.

Miracles in Bedlam

Alejandre Corea was born without a right ear. As you know if you read her story earlier in this book, it wasn't possible to do her surgery in the primitive facilities in Chinandega. We were fortunate enough to gain entrance into the University Hospital in León to undertake this complicated ear reconstruction surgery.

The surgery was successful, and Alejandre, who also attended the English school and is fluent in English as well as Spanish, grew up to be a beautiful, outgoing, and productive member of Nicaraguan society. She is working for her family's corporation as a business manager. I could not have asked for more.

And these are only a couple of examples of more than 12,000 children and young adults whom the medical team has operated on over the past couple of decades.

The dividends it pays in young lives are immeasurable – not to mention the good-will towards, and support for, the United States that we create in Nicaragua and the other countries in which we have worked. The people we help are always saying, "An American doctor did this for me, my family, my country – and they did not accept any money."

* * * * *

Though President Violeta Chamorro brought Nicaragua out of lengthy civil war and laid the groundwork for a stable economy, it was Enrique José Bolaños' administration (January 2002-January 2007) that brought new and improved roads, transportation, communications, and improvement of the quality of life for the residents of places such as Puerto Corinto, and an overall higher economic standard for everyone. Nearly two decades after their first visit, Marvin Zindler and the ABC-TV team returned to Nicaragua with our medical team. Naturally, the TV team wanted to interview President Bolaños, but they also wanted to take yet another opportunity to show the outside world the surgical procedures that the medical team was performing for the children. The overriding purpose of the program they wanted to present was to show the progress that had taken place in Nicaragua in the two decades since the end of the Contra-Sandinista war, and to increase awareness of the young and vibrant democracy that was taking shape in Central America under the leadership of President Bolaños.

I mentioned this trip in passing earlier in this book, and I noted that it happened around the time of my mother's 85th birthday. I really cannot do justice to my mother's legacy here, but I hope it's evident how much I admired her. She was strong, vibrant, and very active, well into her senior years. She could dance the night away, and bounce out of bed the next morning, ready to do it all again. Mom and her husband Leonard Rokaw, whom we all called Len, had traveled throughout Europe, but they had never been to Central America, or any other Third World country for that matter. I wanted to give them the experience of seeing the places I had come to love, and I contacted my good friend, President Bolaños, and secured an invitation for them to visit Nicaragua.

But these are stories for another book. In this book, I've only recounted a few of my experiences in Nicaragua that took place on earlier visits. My diaries are full of stories and random notes I was inspired to jot down, and my photo albums are filled with hundreds of pictures, and I look forward to sharing more of them with you in the future.

For now, my small hope is that I have adequately expressed why I am so in love with Nicaragua and its people. I hope you've enjoyed this journey, but as has been the case with my previous books, I also hope that a larger message has come through.

I believe that the history and future of Nicaragua and indeed all of Central America are intertwined with that of the United States, and in some ways it is an even more intimate involvement than that we have with our closer Southern neighbor, Mexico. For decades and for better or worse, the U.S. has intervened (and interfered) in the military, political, and economic affairs of several Central American countries, including Nicaragua. For that reason I feel that we have a special responsibility to the people into whose history we have insinuated ourselves.

No, I'm not suggesting that everyone should jump on a plane and head down to Nicaragua or El Salvador on a mission of mercy. That type of undertaking isn't for everyone. What I am suggesting is logistically far easier than a medical mission trip, yet it is something that continues to elude so many of us. I think that as individuals, everyone needs to make more of an effort to open his or her mind in order to learn about other people and cultures. And an even more difficult but proportionately more rewarding task is for every American to make an effort to open his or her heart and look upon these "others" with compassion, rather than viewing them as threats.

As the great American author Mark Twain wisely wrote, "Travel is fatal to prejudice, bigotry, and narrow-mindedness, and many of our people need it sorely on these accounts. Broad, wholesome, charitable views of men and things cannot be acquired by vegetating in one little corner of the earth all one's lifetime."

For those who cannot physically travel to faraway places as Mr. Twain seemed to be suggesting, it is still possible to make the journey from insularity to open-mindedness, simply by studying other cultures and people with an eye to learning about them, rather than criticizing them. You don't have to get on a plane; you only have to open a book, visit a web site, or – better yet – make an effort to get to know people in your own community who are "different" from you. Visit their markets, eat at their restaurants, listen to their music, attend their festivals. Open your mind and your heart to new experiences, and you may be very pleasantly surprised.

The U.S. has some work to do before it is truly a "good neighbor," as we once proclaimed ourselves to be in our relations with Latin American countries. We need to develop empathy and appreciation for the struggles of the people in these countries. We must develop an awareness of the different cultures in individual countries, instead of just lumping all brown people together as "Mexicans" (or some derogatory equivalent) and viewing them as lesser human beings.

And we need to finally create a sane and merciful immigration policy that will protect the integrity of the United States, while recognizing the value of the contributions of people from all of the Americas, and the rest of the world as well.

It is this open-mindedness and willingness to "build bridges, not walls" that, in my opinion, will truly make America great again – or greater than it already is. I love my country and I love it deeply, but I also recognize that we are all on this planet together. And the very least that we in the United States can do is to develop rapport and a sense of common interest and mutual respect with the people who share the American continent with us – not just our neighbors to the North, but *all* of our neighbors to the South as well.

In the end, we're all just people, and it has never been more important for each of us to be aware of this simple fact, and act accordingly.

- "Doc Joe" Agris, Houston, May 2017

Joseph Agris, M.D.

PHOTOGRAPHS
Why We Do What We Do

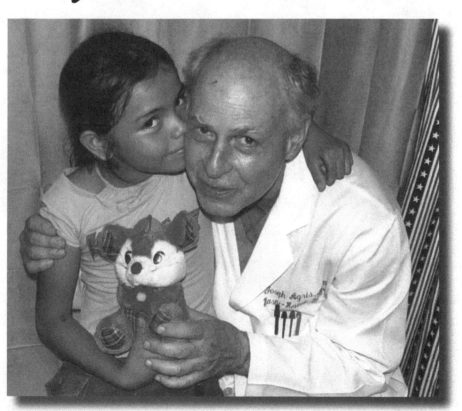

I've often been asked why we would leave our comfortable lives to go to the poorest and most inhospitable places on earth, leaving families, patients, jobs, and earnings behind. I think that by looking at these pictures, you will get an inkling as to what we get in return. Sure, we are thanked profusely by our patients, even those who aren't old enough to speak. And to their parents, we seem like miracle workers. And yes, I'll admit, the appreciation our patients and their families express are precious to us.

The real "payoff," however, means so much more to all of us than any expression of thanks. And it's a payoff we rarely get to see; the children who were previously doomed to be shunned by friends and hidden away by their parents are able to go on and live normal, happy lives, without feeling the dread that surrounds a child who looks different or deformed, or bears the disfiguring scars of a birth defect or injury. Even if we never see these children and young people again, just knowing that we played a part in giving them the opportunity of a life unmarked by cruel fate is enough to keep us going back again and again, and seeking new places where with such little effort, we can make a real, positive difference. What greater gift could we possibly receive?

Happy faces, these on children from the Miskito Coast, make it all worthwhile!

And now, I have a confession of sorts that I have to make. The purpose of including photographs of some of our patients is not to impress you with our skills. Most of us are pretty well convinced of those, anyway. My real motivation for writing these books and sharing the pictures is to let you know that by supporting our Children's Foundation, you too can play an important and significant role in bringing real change to the lives of people who cannot comprehend the advantages we have. I want you to see the faces of our patients, both before and after the procedures we perform, and to imagine how you would feel if it was your child who was saved from the cruelties that so many of these children around the world suffer.

Please forgive me if this feels like I'm trying to lay a guilt trip on you. I won't apologize, but I will ask you, *Is it working?* If it is, and you feel guided to make a tax-deductible gift to support the work we do around the world, I hope you will accept my heartfelt thanks in lieu of an apology. You will also be the beneficiary of thanks that you will never hear, save for the knowledge that you've made life infinitely better for people who deserve a far better shake than they've gotten so far.

Immediately following this section, you'll find information on how you can help to support missions like these. We hope that you'll feel inspired to donate as much as you can afford – and that you'll get out your checkbook and credit card now, before you forget, and before the memory of the good you can do is overshadowed by the details that so quickly fill our lives.

A beaming surgical support staff, with Mr. Dixon holding the "Miracle Baby."

On behalf of myself, our volunteer staff,
and most of all, our patients and their families,
thank you, and God Bless.

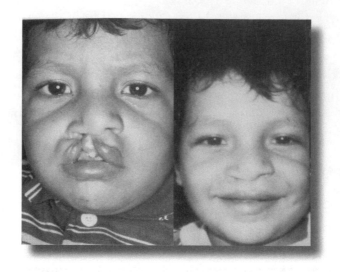

*Before and after Dr. Agris' repair
of a little boy's cleft lip.*

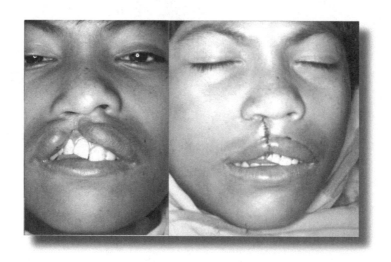

*Before and after the successful correction
of a cleft lip defect.
Completed under only local anesthetic.*

*This infant had a double cleft lip, which we repaired
in a single operation. His mom was very pleased.*

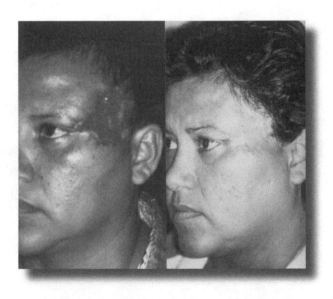

*This woman required a large skin graft.
We were all very pleased with the results.*

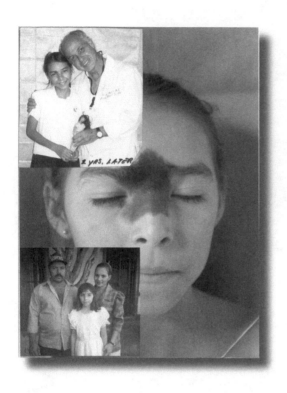

A young woman with a hairy nevus,
a pre-cancerous congenital defect,
corrected with a skin graft.
Shown here pre and post-operative.

The same young woman in the above
photograph, a couple of years later.
Lovely, isn't she?
Beyond being a surgical correction, procedures
like this restore the child's chances for a normal
family and social life and education. Without
the procedure, she could expect to be shunned
for the rest of her life.

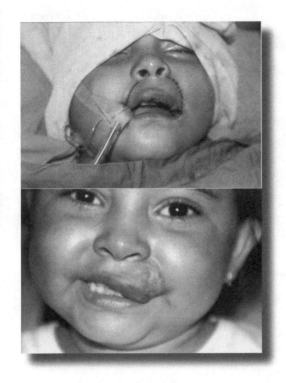

Successful correction of a blood vessel tumor of the face and lips, immediately post-op.

Surgical Nurse Assistant Barrett Phillips, holding another satisfied "customer."

Pre and post-op pictures of an infant who came into the clinic with a severe cleft lip deformity, corrected surgically by Dr. Agris.

A very happy mother holding her child, whose cleft lip has been corrected, and who will never have to hide her smile.

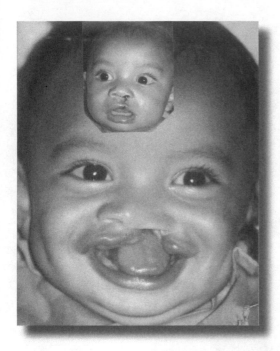

*One of more than 10,000 little patients,
this child's post-operative results were as good
as we could ever hope for.*

*A happy patient who will live her life
free from the scorn and shunning
that comes with looking "different."
This is truly why we are here, and why we will
return again and again.*

The Crew

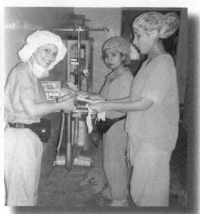

Laurel Ann Agris (left) joins her Dad and the team.

Marvin Zindler with Bob Dows and Lori Reingold of ABC–TV 13, Houston

Marvin Zindler with the O. R. crew

JoAnne and Jose Dixon

Miracles in Bedlam

Photographer Jamie Zamora, of ABC - TV 13 Houston

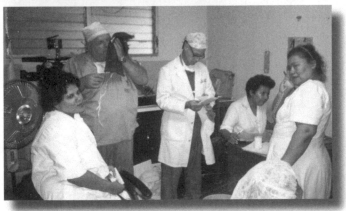

Dr. Agris in clinic

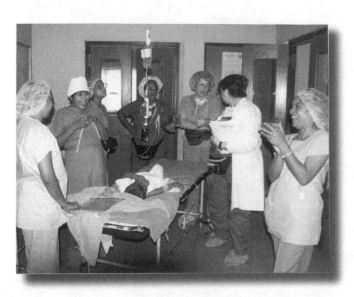

Joseph Agris, M.D.

Simple Lives In The Shadow Of War

*Russian and Cuban military equipment supplied to Sandinistas.
Reporting by ABC–TV 13 was the first publicly documented evidence of
Russian and Cuban involvement in the Contra-Sandinista
civil war in Nicaragua.*

Miracles in Bedlam

Even in the shadow of a brutal war that is all they have ever known,
children can find a reason to laugh.
And even in the grips of crushing poverty, their parents find the will to endure.
Perhaps we "sophisticates" could actually learn from these simple people.
I know I have.

Who's Who

Dr. Agris,
*standing in front of
the Presidential Palace
in Managua*

*Dr. Agris
and
President Violeta Chamorro
(1990-1997)*

*Mr. Marvin Zindler and Dr. Agris
with President Enrique Bolaños
(January 2002-January 2007)*

*Dr. Agris with President Arnoldo Alemán
(January 1997-January 2002*

*President Daniel Ortega interviewed by ABC–13 television crew
during a meeting*

Unwavering Support

These are some of the people who make our medical missions possible, through financial, logistic, or material support, and some who have graciously opened their homes to our team members. Our missions could not function without every one of them.

ABC - 13 President and General Manager Henry Florsheim and his wife Doe, with Marvin Zindler and Dr. Agris

*Dr. Agris
with ABC–13 Houston
news anchors
Melanie Lawson & Dave Ward.
Thje people at ABC–13 are
longtime chroniclers
and supporters
of our medical mission trips.*

ABC–TV 13 Producer Lori Reingold, with our hosts in Chinandega,
Etta and Roberto Callejas
and Marvin Zindler

We owe a great debt of gratitude to the people of Nicaragua who saw to
our needs for housing, assistance, and the many delicious meals we were
served. This was on the second floor porch at the sawmill, across the street
from the Red Cross compound in Puerto Cabezas.

Maria Haydee Callejas de Holmann and her husband Hugo,
COO and Editor of the La Prensa newspaper,
supporters of the medical teams from day one.

Robertito Callejas and his father Roberto,
with Roberto's wife Etta,
supporters of the medical teams for 35 years.

*A more recent picture of artist Roberto Callejas,
with his wife Etta (seated), and Terry Agris,
at his home/art studio in Chinandega.*

*Children's Foundation Director Beverly Winter
meets with President Enrique Bolaños
at his home in Nicaragua.*

What You Can Do To Make a Difference

Every two minutes a child is born with a birth defect. Cleft palates, disfiguring birthmarks, and other defects are "silent catastrophes" that can ravage any child. Even if the condition does not threaten a child's health and is "merely" cosmetic, it can be psychologically and emotionally devastating. These children need special attention, yet a heartbreaking number of them fall between the cracks of the system.

The Children's Foundation, a non-profit 501(c)(3) organization founded in 1981 by Joseph Agris, M.D., and the late Marvin Zindler, exists to help these forgotten children. With your help, we have been able to deliver badly needed care to children in some of the poorest areas on the planet, including Central America, the Middle East, the former Soviet bloc, China, and many other places. We have also helped many children and their families in the United States.

The Children's Foundation and its sister organizations, Smiles Gone Wild and People Helping People, are dedicated to identifying the problems, bringing about solutions, and mobilizing resources for the implementation of needed care and support services. This encompasses medical care, surgery, medications, and prostheses, as well as family support. And, while these clinical applications are certainly needed, research leading to cure or prevention is also paramount. We owe to children the best that we can give. Every child has a right to necessary medical care. But not all children are born equal. The world is full of desperately poor children whose families can scarcely afford food and shelter, say nothing of medical care. However, though medical care is often costly, it is an affordable cost... if we all give something.

Give a child a chance, by giving your tax-deductible gift to the Children's Foundation & Smiles Forever today. Send your check or money order, made payable to THE CHILDREN'S FUND, to:

The Children's Foundation
P.O. Box 271501
Houston, Texas 77277-1501

Please include your name, address and daytime phone number.

We also accept Visa, MasterCard or American Express.

Please call **(832) 288-2185** to give credit card information, to obtain information about matching funds for employers, or to find out how you can volunteer of your time and services to help "Doc Joe and his kids." Or you can email Doc Joe at DocJoeAgris@gmail.com.

And remember... a portion of the profits from the sale of *Miracles in Bedlam* will be donated to the Children's Foundation and its sister charities.

"The kids" thank you!

About The Author

Doc Joe poses with the "angel on his shoulder"

Besides being one of Houston's premier cosmetic, plastic, and reconstructive surgeons for many years, with a bustling practice in the world-famous Texas Medical Center, Dr. Joe Agris is an activist and philanthropist, especially when it comes to children's health problems and education issues. More recently he has also become more involved with fighting the effects of the horrible abuses to which women in countries such as Pakistan and Afghanistan are subjected. He has helped repair and restore the faces and bodies of many victims who have suffered the devastating results of acid burning and kerosene burning. At the same time, he has continued his commitment to the children of Nicaragua, as well as other countries in Central America and the rest of the world.

Years ago, Doc Joe and the late Marvin Zindler formed The Agris-Zindler Children's Foundation to deliver needed medical care to kids all over the globe. A true Renaissance man, well read in the arts and sciences, Doc Joe is a world traveler and an accomplished photographer who has exhibited his spectacular photos on several occasions.

When he's not off on a medical mission to some remote corner of the planet, Doc Joe is in Houston, Texas, tending to his practice, enjoying time with his lovely wife Terry and their menagerie of animals on their ranch at "Eden," planning the next project or mission, and working on his next book.

If you enjoyed Miracles In Bedlam...
Check out these other books by Joseph Agris!

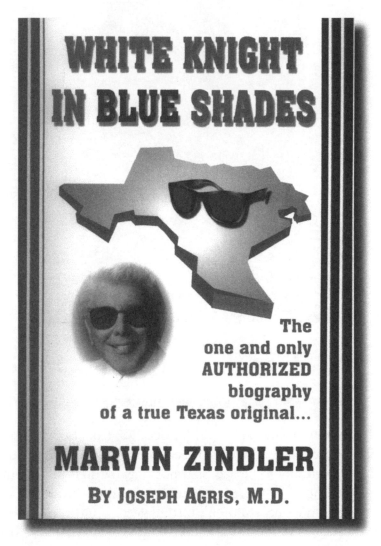

Marvin Zindler was a true Texas legend. He was best known as the colorful consumer advocate at KTRK–TV13 in Houston, Texas, and for playing a major part in shutting down the brothel that was the subject of the hit Broadway play and movie, *The Best Little Whorehouse In Texas*. But he was so much more than that – an advocate for the underdog, philanthropist, detective, and lawman. And to Doc Joe Agris, he was the best friend who could always be counted upon, but was never predictable. Doc Joe was the obvious – indeed, *only* –choice to write Marvin's biography. *White Knight In Blue Shades* is a true labor of love.

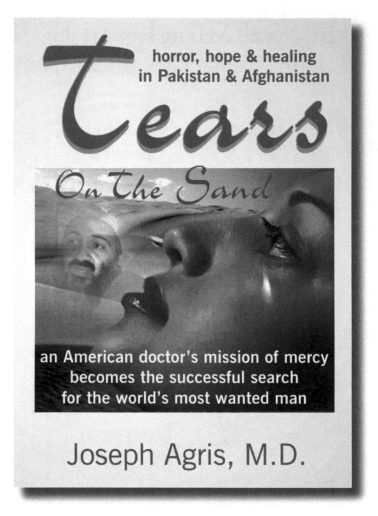

Doctor Agris has been traveling the world for decades, from South America to Russia and the Middle East, offering surgical correction for children's birth defects, thereby giving them the opportunity to be accepted not only by their peers, but also by their families. But something has changed in recent years in the Middle East, and he has found himself treating not only children's birth defects, but egregious wounds suffered by women who were the victims of attempted "honor killings." He has also treated many adults and children who have been caught in the periphery of civil wars, tribal conflicts, and other violent skirmishes. On the medical missions described in *Tears On The Sand*, he describes his work with badly wounded women as well as his encounters with Al Qaeda and ISIS fighters, treating their wounds and demonstrating to them the best of America. Travel with a man who has earned the trust and respect of people throughout Pakistan and Afghanistan, from humble herders and merchants to the most vicious fighters in the modern world, and who emerges alive and relatively unscathed from places where even the mighty military sometimes fears to go.

Doc Joe writes, "This is actually my third book, but it had lain idle for awhile as I focused upon the struggles of the people of Nicaragua. In *Mission Divided*, my focus returns to the Middle East, particularly Pakistan, where I have gone many times over the past few decades, treating those born with birth defects, as well as those who have fallen victim to the brutal, eternal wars – not to mention the women who are valued less than livestock and often treated much worse for even the most minor breach of Sharia Law. *Mission Divided* is a novelized version of some of my all-too-real adventures.

"But it's not just an adventure story. The outcomes of the struggles taking place in Pakistan and the surrounding areas are yet to be determined. All indications, at least to those who have observed the reality beyond the 'news' reports, point to outcomes that are as unthinkable to most Americans as they are inevitable to most Middle Easterners. I feel that it is our duty as freedom loving Americans to learn of and understand what these people face, lest we end up facing the same here at home."